EXPRESSION
of
HONOR

GEORGE RICHARDSON & RAMONA VALLEE

EXPRESSION

of

HONOR

ARPress

ILLUMINATING IDEAS,
EMPOWERING VOICES

ARPress
45 Dan Road Suite 5

Canton, MA 02021
Hotline: 1(888) 821-0229
Fax: 1(508) 545-7580

Ordering Information:
Quantity sales. Special discounts are available on quantity purchases by corporations,associations, and others. For details, contact the publisher at the address above.

Printed in the United States of America.

ISBN-13:   Softcover   979-8-89330-964-5
             eBook   979-8-89330-965-2

Library of Congress Control Number: 2024902510

CONTENTS

Dedication iii

Special Thanks: v

Chapter 1 1

Chapter 2 31

Chapter 3 49

Chapter 4 66

Chapter 5 81

Chapter 6 94

Chapter 7 101

Chapter 8 114

Chapter 9 149

    Part 1 149

    Part 2 156

    Part 3 176

Chapter 10 196

    Part 1 196

    Part 2 206

Chapter 11 229

Chapter 12 236

Chapter 13 248

    Part 1 248

    Part 2 264

    Part 3 282

    Part 4 292

Chapter 14.. 304

Chapter 15.. 321

Chapter 16.. 339

Chapter 17.. 349

Chapter 18.. 367

Chapter 19.. 377

Chapter 20.. 383

Chapter 21.. 396

Chapter 22.. 405

Chapter 23.. 427

Epilogue.. 434

DEDICATION

This book is dedicated in the memory of my grandfather
Homer N. Richardson.

Special Thanks:

My son Marc and my daughter-in-love Nicole. I could not have done this without them.

FOREWORD FROM GEORGE RICHARDSON

This book, "Expression of Honor", is entirely fictional as to the characters. Places of battle and theater of operations are real.

The 26th Kansas Cavalry is a fictional number. However, the various units of the Kansas volunteer cavalry played a decisive part in the Rebellion.

The source of information was from word of mouth from my beloved grandfather, Homer N. Richardson, who told the past glories of the cavalry. His father was a member of the Indiana Cavalry and saw service in the south. Also, the many states historical archives and pictures were helpful. Monuments and battlefields and military parks were a useful source of information.

My wife helped me type the book and caught any grammatical errors and corrected them. My story is about a cavalry commander, his troops, his decisions, and his military work to be done; the humorous and serious.

- Signed George Richardson

FOREWORD FROM RAMONA VALLEE

I have finally completed the rewrite of my father, George Richardson's book. I have promised to do this for him on his deathbed. My father was enthralled by the stories his grandfather Homer Richardson had told him as a child. Homer had been a drummer boy in the Civil War with his father James Bailey Richardson. With the help of my mother Eleanor Richardson, he wrote the first novel. He tried to get it published which did not pan out at the time.

I rewrote it over a large span of time and filled out the main characters with a fuller history. I tidied up the grammar also. In Chapter Three concerning Fort Donelson there is a shoutout about some Richardson Ancestors, Alexander Richardson was the father of Ed and James Richardson who were brothers. James was the father of Homer, and Homer was the father of William, who was the father of George. Ed had his forearm amputated and Alexander gave a patriotic speech for the Union.

I want to thank my parents for producing this novel under stressful conditions. They had three small demanding children. They have accomplished their task, and now I have fulfilled my promised revision. I hope the readers enjoy it.

CHAPTER 1
Introduction to Frank Winslow

Lieutenant Colonel Frank Winslow mopped his brow with a limp red handkerchief then stuffed it in his pocket. He absent-mindedly laced his fingers behind his head as he sprawled up against a willow tree trunk escaping the sun's glare.

"How long is this blistering heat going to dog us?" He asked.

Next to him sat a young recruit, his face beaded with sweat, "Well sir, I reckon that it bein' mid-September, that this hot spell cain't last much longer," He responded.

The year was 1861 and the unseasonably hot and dry month of September was burdensome after a long, hot and dry summer. So dry, the low water level of the Mississippi River hampered the delivery of army supplies. Two thoughts were giving Lieutenant Colonel Winslow concern: the ongoing heat, and homesickness for Topeka, Kansas. Quickly he had enlisted into the Union Forces. So quickly that the lag time of the sultry afternoon was helpful in adjusting to his new reality as a lieutenant colonel in the Union Army. Presently, being in Cairo, Illinois, under the command of General Grant, wasn't all bad.

Frank Winslow was a man's man, six-foot-tall, all one hundred eighty pounds in hard muscle. He had wavy auburn hair which framed a handsome face, clear cut and true. His smile flashed pearly white teeth and revealed a dimple in each cheek. His piercing brown eyes seemed enigmatic and hard to read. Winslow was a prosperous lawyer in Topeka, Kansas, when the Civil War broke. Deeply patriotic, he was exuberant to join the Union Army. His talent for delegating tasks allowed him to tie up loose ends in Kansas, yet keep his law office open, for registering land claims was ongoing. The law office was left in the capable hands of Widow Hardy. As far as Winslow was concerned, the Civil War had begun years earlier in Bloody Kansas. Now that it was officially declared, it was time to settle hash and be done with it.

Frank said, "What's your name son?"

The boy, just a young sprout of twenty, looked at Winslow and said, "Jest call me Ezra, that's what my folks named me...my full name is Ezra Peabody."

"Well, Ezra, let's go for a stroll cause I'm in no mind to be idle. I reckon we'll have orders from General Grant by and by." Frank said as he rose from the ground. Ezra stood up also. Meandering along the banks of the Mississippi brought memories flooding back for Winslow, while Ezra stopped to skip rocks...

Frank Winslow was born in the fall of 1828 on a farm near Covington, Indiana. His parents were farmers. He was second of four children. First born was Lemuel who was eleven years older than Frank. Following up the rear was his two sisters, Eliza and Sara.

Farm work was hard for most women. Not being of robust health, it was particularly hard on Frank's mother. After her first born, Lemuel, Martha had several miscarriages and a still born boy she named Jack after Frank's father. A small cemetery was situated in the northeast corner of their farm. It was off by itself on the crest of a hill. Jack was buried there with his other miscarried siblings. The common grave was well tended. A wood cross marked it. Often there were wildflowers lain on the grave, season permitting.

Martha and her husband Jack were hard workers. What Martha did not have in strength she made up with drive and spunk. Lemuel picked up on their work ethic and the modest farm did well with crops of hay, wheat, beans, an apple orchard, cows and chickens. Frank's earliest memories entailed being out on a blanket while Jack, Martha, and Lemuel cut hay. As the years passed Frank joined in farm work too. A couple of years passed, and Martha gave birth to Eliza.

When Frank was eight years old events forever etched themselves into his memory. Martha was due to have her fourth full term baby. The whole family stayed close to home as she went into labor. His mother gave birth to a beautiful baby girl that she named Sara. Martha was feeble and stayed in bed one week then two. Each day that passed Martha became even weaker. One evening after supper which Lemuel had prepared, Martha asked her family to gather around her bed.

Martha's thin body was propped up with extra pillows. Jack brought little Sara to rest in her arms. "Remember, Lemuel, Frank, Eliza," she gazed fondly at the baby Sara, "and Sara how much I love you." Her children's tears began to fall.

Silence as she mustered up the last dredges of strength to continue. "Sara needs a wet nurse. I know Mrs. Abigail Hartman just birthed a baby boy three months back. Lemuel, I need you to ask Mrs. Hartman if she would be willing to wet nurse our dear Sara."

Jack's worn; leathery face crumpled. His shoulders shuddered as a deep sob climbed to his throat. He tried to suppress it. Lemuel put a comforting hand on his father's shoulder. At nineteen he was a full head taller than his father.

Martha beckoned quietly, "Jack, come here." Jack came closer and clutched the frail hand she offered him. She smiled wanly. "We worked side by side through the good and the bad. I want to thank you for being such a steadfast husband and good father. God must have a greater need of me than this life does. I am sorry to leave you and the children, but I must trust in His divine will. I will be praying for you if God allows…" with that she breathed her last.

It was calamitous times. Lemuel bundled up Sara that dark rainy night. Frank hitched up the buggy and put the cradle and Sara's belongings in it. Lemuel and Frank put Sara between them as they drove over to the Hartman's. Lemuel and Frank knocked at their door. Pa had stayed home to tend to Martha's body and comfort Eliza. Mrs. Hartman came to the door. As she opened it her eyes widened with surprise and alarm. Hurriedly, she bid them enter. The three guests were dripping wet. Sara was crying.

Lemuel said dejectedly, "Mrs. Hartman, my Ma just passed away two hours ago from fever. Before she passed, she remembered that you just had a baby boy a few months ago."

"I am so sorry for the loss of your dear mother!" Mrs. Hartman put a comforting arm around both boys. She felt Lemuel's shoulders quaking and Frank's shivering.

"Ma's last request was would you be obliging to wet nurse little Sara?" Lemuel's voice broke with grief.

When Mrs. Hartman had first heard Sara's cries, her milk had let down and dampened her bodice and dripped on the floor. "Children, God has sent you here for good reason. My breasts have ample milk and at this very moment I need Sara to suckle." With that said she motioned for them to sit by the fire to warm themselves. She took Sara from Lemuel.

She sat in a chair aimed away from them. She lifted a rigid, vein corded breast from her bodice Sara latched onto the nipple choking a bit on the gushing milk until she had mastered the flow. Tentatively, the boys ventured over to see. Sara's small face was beaded with sweat as she labored for the milk. Little Sara suckled the breast in happy fulfillment and looked up to her benefactress in sweet wonderment. Mrs. Hartman's heart melted.

Frank asked Mrs. Hartman, "Is this the milk of human kindness?"

Lemuel, embarrassed, interjected, "It makes perfect sense, Frank, Mrs. Hartman is a kind human, and she has milk."

Mrs. Hartman looked up smiling. "I have extra swaddling and my baby, Jack, will be happy to have company."

Lemuel and Frank exchanged significant glances. That was their deceased brother's name! Faintly, a low coo emanated from a cradle from the far side of the fireplace. Mrs. Hartman handed Sara to Lemuel and went to the cradle to gather up Jack. He was a handsome baby, a suggestion of a smile played over his drowsy face.

Mrs. Hartman said, "I'll ask my husband Seth to make a cradle for Sara."

Lemuel cleared his throat, "No need, Mrs. Hartman. Pa made one that all of us used. It's out in the buggy. We'll have no use for it…now."

"Thanks for the cradle." Mrs. Hartman smiled. She observed how Jack was reaching out toward Sara.

Frank said boldly, "Mrs. Hartman, where is Seth, your husband? We need to ask his permission too."

Mrs. Hartman said approvingly, "Why certainly, Frank. I'll go rouse him from his bed and have you ask." Mrs. Hartman handed Jack to Frank and retrieved Sara from Lemuel. She headed into the bedroom.

Jack was a quiet, happy baby and entertained his guests with gentle gestures and a sweet countenance. Seth emerged first, cradling Sara in his arms, his brown hair askew. Mrs. Hartman approached the rear. Both were smiling.

Frank cleared his throat, "Mr. Hartman is it alright with you if Mrs. Hartman nurses Sara?

Without missing a beat Seth said, "It is an honor that we can be of help to Sara and your family." Lemuel and Frank breathed an audible sigh of relief.

"Remember, Sara's your sister. Hope to have you and your family visit by and by." Seth said reassuringly. Sara was left in the loving home of the Hartman's.

Thereafter, every Sunday the two families would gather at the Baptist Church and the Winslow's would sit close to the Hartman's. Abigail would have them over for Sunday dinner and they all would enjoy watching Jack and Sara play together. It was apparent that the Hartman's loved Sara as their own. On those occasions when the Winslow's and Hartman's were together Eliza seemed the happiest. She would gaze longingly at the Hartman's family. Eliza's deep yearning for the motherly attention that Abigail lavished on the little ones, spilled over to Eliza.

On one such occasion, Abigail said, "I want to tell you folks that I am in the family way again." Everybody smiled with happiness.

Abigail got up from the dinner table and motioned Jack Senior to accompany her out to the porch. He joined her. As he came to her, she said, "Jack, I wanted to ask you privately, if it would be acceptable to you if I asked Eliza to stay with me and help with the two toddlers and the baby that is coming?"

Jack Senior had seen Eliza's eyes brighten at the announcement of the baby-to-be. He knew she was lonely for motherly attention. "Abigail, let's go ask Eliza." They went inside.

In slow, measured words Jack Senior asked, "Eliza would you feel like helping out Mrs. Hartman with her children and the next to be born, starting right now?"

Eliza leapt for joy. Excitedly she shrieked, "I'm so happy to help out! Thank you! Thank you! Thank You!" Every one of the Hartman's and Winslow's had a smile on their faces. A sad but contented smile played over Jack Senior's countenance.

Jack Senior never remarried. There was no need. Martha had always been his true love. Eliza's motherless state had been resolved. There was comfort in knowing that Eliza was in good care. A couple of years passed as the two families continued the Sunday get-togethers. In that time Lemuel found a nice young woman at church. Her name was Phoebe. In short order, Lemuel married Phoebe. Jack Senior reasoned that young Frank had a good set of new parents in Lemuel and Phoebe. The last hold was freed from him. He turned the farm over to the newlyweds and stayed on the farm as a helping hand. He even built a smaller cabin adjacent to the family cemetery near Martha and their deceased children. Jack Senior's heart was always with Martha.

Frank moved into the cabin with his Pa. He felt the most at ease there. Yet the unspoken sadness was heavy in the atmosphere. Frank liked the hard farm work. Every day he gave all his energy to chores so that when he was done for the day, he would eat supper with his Pa and fall into an exhausted sleep. Thus, he side-stepped the mournful atmosphere. In less than a year his father had joined his mother in the cemetery. His Pa had simply pined away for her.

Frank now felt a sense of disorder. His parents were dead, his sisters were being raised by another family, his brother had married Phoebe and taken over the farm, and they had become parents. Frank was living alone in the cabin his Pa had built. Disorder became angst. He felt he no longer fit in. He became wild in his behavior not knowing then that he was trying to cope with so many upheavals.

It was now 1842 and Frank was fourteen. He was a capable young adolescent who had been into his share of mischief. He had become resourceful and wise by sharpening his wits and innovative by living off the land on extended hunting trips. Although Lemuel was only eleven years older than Frank, he had become a foster father to him.

One spring day Frank said to Lemuel, "Lemuel, I need to leave here and get on with my life…see the world". Lemuel listened, nodding his head in an approving manner.

Frank continued, "If you can spare me Jubal and a week's worth of grub then I'll be on my way come morning."

Lemuel took in the scene down to the breeze that parted Frank's auburn hair. After a pregnant moment he clutched his brother in a bear hug. "I'll be writing you so keep me posted to your whereabouts."

Frank gave his brother a friendly punch in the arm. He hopped on Jubal and rode over to the Hartman's. He said his goodbyes and gave hugs to all. That evening Phoebe made a splendid going away feast for Frank. Next morning, early, he saddled up Jubal, packed up his food and supplies and headed west.

Jubal was a dark mottled gelding, high spirited, with great endurance. For about three weeks Frank roamed in a southwesterly direction. He didn't hurry because he didn't want to miss a thing. He savored the moment because it smacked of potential adventure, around the corner, behind a tree, or on a high slope. All of his senses were sharply honed in anticipation. He tried to steer clear of people and towns for sensible reasons since he was still green as an adolescent. These people were strangers and could do him harm. Also, he was of an independent nature. At times it was lonesome but as he adjusted, he enjoyed the solitude and being alone with his thoughts, musings, and problem-solving skills. At the same time, he was finding out his strengths and talents.

Before daybreak was a favorite time for him. His days fell into a comforting routine, starting a fire, preparing coffee, and frying up hoe cake (corn bread without leaven) in a skillet. Also, finding a likely campsite for the night restored and renewed him for his continued adventure. Some days he would take time to snare a rabbit or spear a fish. It would reaffirm the joy of doing for self. He was his own man.

Before Frank left, Lemuel gave Frank, Ma's Bible and some writing paper. He put it in a leather case in a saddlebag carried by Jubal. Of an evening, Frank would take out the Bible, open it at random and read a little paragraph. Other times he would simply take the Bible out and caress it, remembering how his mother cherished it.

He had stretched his food supply an extra couple of weeks by adding fish and rabbit to the menu. After so long avoiding people, Frank had taken on a skittishness for human society. He surprised himself for even entertaining the thought. Fear was behind it and fear would not best him. At daybreak, the next day he scouted around and found a place where two roads converged into a junction. He hunkered down in a cluster of trees up on a knoll overlooking the spot. There would be an occasional buggy, wagon or horses headed west. By late afternoon, these same wagons and horses would head east laden with supplies.

Early the next day, Frank made himself breakfast from the last of the cornbread and coffee. Then he positioned himself in his hiding place. Jubal was beside him, well concealed in the brush. People went by that were a little questionable; first, a group three of men, outnumbered, then a lone man, enigma? Next approached a wagon going west with an older man and woman. They looked trustworthy.

Frank hopped on Jubal and quickly rode down to the couple. "Hallo, folks." He said as he tipped his hat to them. "I'm a traveler and was wondering what town lies up ahead?"

"Tarnation, boy! You gave us a start!" The old man with grizzled whiskers and missing teeth sputtered in surprise. His female companion had taken off her bonnet to fan her flustered face revealing salt and pepper hair twisted into a tight bun.

"Sorry, folks, I'm traveling alone. I was sizing up people from my vantage point and you seemed like the most friendly of the lot so I took a chance to speak with you." Frank said apologetically.

The old man composed himself and said in a quieter tone, "That's alright. I'd probably do the same if I were in your place." He paused and smiled and said, "What's your name youngster?'

"Frank Winslow."

"Well, up ahead is Chester, Illinois, which is situated on the Mississippi River. Across the river is Missouri. Chester has a well-stocked general store. Cargo boats regularly bring supplies. It even has fine sewing needles from France. Why don't you follow us in? My name is Zekiel and my wife's name is Edna. We're the Smythes."

Frank grinned and nodded his head in agreement and followed the Smythes to Chester. It was a beautiful mid-May morning. They traveled through gently rolling hills with clumps of wooded areas and a glimpse of the Mississippi on occasion. They arrived about noon. The main street was wide with muddy ruts which made for a bumpy ride for the Smythes. With ease Jubal discerned potholes and ruts and kept at an even trot.

Frank hitched up Jubal to a post and the Smythes parked their wagon nearby. Frank had a few coins from last year's harvest of apples that he had sold at the general store in Covington, Indiana. The Smythes knew the clerk and chatted with him as they paid for coffee, flour, cornmeal, salt, calico cloth, and other sundries. Frank had enough money to purchase small amounts of coffee, corn meal, and salt.

After helping Zekiel load up supplies on their wagon, Zekiel said casually, "Frank, why don't you follow us home for a hot meal and a good visit?"

Frank grinned, "I'd be mighty obliging to do so. Thanks for the invite."

They all pulled up at the Smythe's homestead about dusk. Edna had a beef stew simmering on a partially banked fire. The aroma was tantalizing. Frank was quick in offering to bring in more wood. Zekiel cut some greens from the garden for Edna to steam. Edna sliced some bread and put it and fresh churned butter on the table. Finally, they all sat down at the table. Zekiel said grace.

"Tell us about yourself, Frank," Edna requested. So, Frank filled them in on the present state of his family. He mentioned that both parents were dead and how his sisters were being raised by some good neighbors. He also mentioned that his married brother had inherited the farm.

Zekiel observed, "You must have felt like the odd man out."

Frank answered, "In a way, yes. I have no grudges against God or man. That's just how life unfolded. I am a pretty contented individual. I do get into some predicaments probably due to my curiosity. One example of that is my buddy and I found a barrel of black powder that had washed up on the shore of the Wabash River. We were at loose ends, so we made a fire, put a hole in the top, inserted some dry twigs as a fuse, lit it, shoved the barrel back in the river. It blew the barrel to smithereens, killed a bunch of fish, and parts of the barrel made holes in my neighbor's smoke house. We spread the word that there were fish to fry on the shore to all we knew. So, nothing went to waste.

Frank asked them, "Why don't you tell me about you folks?"

"Whoa boy, that's a lot of jaw flapping!" Zekiel smiled good naturedly. "We're originally from Lewisburg, Pennsylvania. We heard of cheap land in Illinois. So, we headed out here. We had five, half grown children when we moved here, four boys and the youngest, a girl. All the boys moved to Kansas. Our daughter, Ruby, stayed here and married. She has six children and teaches school. Edna and I have been living in this home for twenty years."

Time escaped them. Frank noticed that it was late. He said reluctantly, "Guess I'll head off. It was sure nice to enjoy a meal with you. It had been a mighty long time since I sat down to a meal with people."

Edna said decisively, "We'll hear of no such thing at this late hour! You bed down here tonight. We have a spare room with a comfortable bed."

Frank grinned and said, "Who am I to argue with the lady of the house?" they all laughed then settled in for the night.

The aroma of coffee drifted to his nostrils as a welcome to the new day. Rousing himself, Frank dressed, combed his hair, and entered the kitchen where cornmeal mush, ham, dried apples and fried eggs were spread on the table.

Edna smiled full of purpose and greeted him. "Good morning, Frank. Hope you have an appetite."

Zekiel stepped in the kitchen with a load of firewood. "Edna, when does a fourteen-year-old not have an appetite?" He smiled from memories of his children.

They all laughed and sat down to a hearty breakfast. After breakfast Zekiel put on a more serious expression. He cleared his throat and poured himself another cup of coffee. "You know, Frank, if you aren't in an all-fired hurry, you'd be welcome to stay as a helper on the farm. We can pay you in the fall, at harvest." He looked at Frank in askance, steeling himself for his response.

Frank smiled. His dimples framed his straight white teeth and he said, "I'm beholden to you and appreciate your offer. I'll take you up on it. I'm pretty strong and can do anything that a full-grown man can do."

With that they all laughed. Frank was now in their employ. To make it official, Frank and Zekiel shook hands. Edna and Zekiel were richly rewarded for hiring Frank. Not only was Frank a hard worker, but he also enjoyed entertaining them with stories and showing them horse tricks that he had taught Jubal. Some of the horse tricks he and Jubal could do were impressive. Frank mounted the horse from the barn roof while Jubal trotted in a circle in the barnyard near him. Once mounted, Frank stood up on Jubal's back as he continued in the circle. Then Frank would do a head stand on Jubal then hang off one side of Jubal then the other. Jubal could do a canter in dance-like steps then rear up on his back legs and tread air with his front legs. On the command of 'hide'. Jubal would hide behind the barn or in a grove of nearby trees. Frank would signal him with a whistle and Jubal would come running like a pet dog.

With relish, Frank embraced the busy spring and summer seasons that involved plowing, milking, cutting hay, collecting eggs, picking apples and many other tasks. At the finish of the fall's harvest Zekiel said to Frank, "Frank, I hope you stay with us another year. Edna and I can't tell you how much joy you brought us, let alone that bumper crop of apples and a plentiful harvest."

Frank grinned his happy grin and said, "I've enjoyed it too. I'd be pleased to stay."

Over the months that Frank had stayed with the Smythes, he became acquainted with their daughter, Ruby and her family. Ruby was married to Herbert Collins. Herb was a jack-of-all-trades and professions. He was a farmer, well digger, lawyer, and minister. The Smythes, Frank, Ruby, and her children would gather at the west Frankfort Baptist church where Herb would preach. Although Herb's sermons were impromptu, the simple eloquence and fervor kept the parishioners attentive. For the Smythes and Frank, after church was a time to go visit Ruby, Herb, and the children. Ruby was an excellent cook and would prepare a fine meal right after church. While the meal was in the works, Frank would entertain the Collins children with horse tricks, storytelling, and physical games of prowess.

Ruby and Herb took him under their wing, also. One Sunday in November Frank was at the Collins home in a quiet mood perusing one of Herb's law books. Herb had invited him to stay longer. Zekiel and Edna went home to tend to evening chores.

Herb said, "Frank, I want you to come with me to the barn."

It was about thirty yards to the barn. It held hay for the livestock. A few chickens had nestled in the loft. All the children were in the house doing chores for Ruby. Upon entering the barn Herb let out a low whistle that sounded like a whip-poor-will. The hay undulated then separated in the far corner of the barn floor. A black man, tall and well-muscled, emerged. He smiled uncertainly.

Herb said apologetically, "Sorry, Able, for your long wait in the hay."

Able said, "Is fahn wid me, suh. Fust time ah bin warm in many nights."

Frank's eyes widened in wonderment. He studied Able.

Frank ventured, "Where in tarnation did you come from?"

"Ah come from Alabam." Able said looking at his feet.

Herb looked over at Frank. "It's a natural thing to want to ask questions, but the less you know about Able, the better it is for the both of you."

Herb hesitated before he continued, "Frank, the reason I had you meet Able is because I need help to get Able further North. The basic reason is that my absence would be quickly noticed. As for you, you could say you went hunting. Do you think you could assist me in this endeavor?"

Able's eyes widened as he assessed young Frank's capabilities. Frank felt the frightened eyes upon him, so he straightened to his full height and presumed a confident pose. After a long pause, affording Frank an opportunity to further scrutinize the raw slash marks and healed scars on Able's arms, he said, "I'd enjoy a trip north. I feel a touch of cabin fever coming on."

Herb smiled, "Because of the Fugitive Slave Act of 1793, we need to get Able further north away from the slave catchers."

Herb continued, "In that very same year of 1793, besides the Fugitive Slave Act's passage into law, Eli Whitney invented the cotton gin which speeded the processing of cotton by removing the seeds from the fibers. That encouraged more cotton production, then more slaves were needed. So, between 1794 and 1804, the South's cotton crops multiplied to eight times the previous production. The South's perceived need, or I should say greed for slaves was more firmly entrenched."

Around midnight Frank and Able left on horseback headed North. One horse had been provided for Able. Frank would ride Jubal. Of course, the horses were black and dark brown to blend in with the night. The plan was to follow the Mississippi River until they reached the outskirts of Quincy. Frank and Able did not take any chances; they lit no fires. Herb had given them, dried apples, hoe cakes, beef jerky and a jug of water. They were now five hours into the journey, and it was a few hours before daybreak. They had stopped to eat.

As they were eating their grub, Frank couldn't help but ask, "Able, how old are you?"

"Ah's about thirty-four," He looked at Frank directly in the eyes.

"Do you have family, wife and children?" Frank asked.

There was a hesitation. Able looked down to compose himself. "No mo', ma massah sol' ma woman, ma two sons, and ma lil' girl… Split us up like so much cord wood. Ah was born on that plantation…grew up there. Same massah knew us, yet harmed us in the worse way."

Frank grasped the portent of the pain and anguish in Able's words. The atmosphere was laden with emotion. Lamely, Frank asked, "What did you do about it?'

"Nothin." Able's eyes clamped closed with tears streaming. "Ah did nothin' but runned away, mah fust chance." His shoulders shook with emotion.

Frank said, "You did right by coming north. One slave alone can't do much for justice…but up North where it's freer… there's always opportunity."

Able assessed him with new eyes. They were now filled with a glimmer of hope and deepening trust. After two night's travel they were near their destination. They camped in a cluster of trees just outside the town of Quincy. Around ten at night when the streets were deserted, Frank went to the livery stable on the edge of town. He had been told by Herb that the owner's name was Kevin O'Donnell. Frank knocked on the door of the livery stable.

A man opened the door. "Howdy. What can I do for you, son?" The man said in a sleepy voice.

"Are you the proprietor, Kevin McDonnell?" Frank asked. The man nodded.

"I have two horses to trade. They are fleet of foot but short in stature." Frank said in a measured voice. It was a coded sentence for the right person.

O'Donnell came to full attention. He said, "I have a two-year-old gelding and a black mare to trade." It was the correct response.

Frank said, "That will do."

O'Donnell followed Frank to camp in silence. He was a little more talkative once there. He shook hands with Frank and Able then said,

"We are doing God's will. I am much heartened through this work that there are so many brothers and sisters in Christ who help out."

He kindly patted Able on the back and smiled. "We are going to Winona, Wisconsin, where someone will take you all the way to Canada."

Frank gave Able a pat on the back and firm handshake. Then he said to them both, "Godspeed."

Frank mounted Jubal and led the extra horse back to the Collins home.

Frank left Quincy elated that he had been of help. He ruminated on what the slave owner had done to Able and his family. It struck Frank to the core. He tried to imagine the pain of never seeing a brother, sister or parent again; not knowing their whereabouts, and not being capable to write them. Slaves were forbidden to learn to write and they couldn't practice their religion. It was plain evil. On his way back, not more than a day's ride, he spotted a deer. He killed it with one shot. He partially dressed it and secured it to the extra horse. His hunting trip was completed. The trip was not told to anyone.

With the success of the trip, Herb took Frank into his full confidence. He would have Frank escort many more fugitive slaves North on several different routes to be less predictable. He would also have Frank read certain cases in his law books. Then Herb would debate Frank relentlessly, both honing their skills like knives against flint. Frank discovered he had a passion for the law.

Five years had passed. Frank had become very fond of Zekiel, Edna, and the Collins family. The Smythes farm had become very prosperous. The first born of the Collin's children had learned how to help both their parents and grandparents with farm chores. Frank felt it was the perfect time to move on and set up a legal practice further west where there was a scarcity of good lawyers.

One morning over a cup of coffee, Frank said, "Zekiel, I have sure enjoyed working for you and Herb but right now I feel that I am a full-grown man and must be about my future. I was thinking of moving to Kansas and was wondering if you could write me a letter of introduction? Herb wrote me one a couple of days ago."

Zekiel's jaw loosened for a moment. His countenance then managed a big smile. "You are right. Time waits for no man."

Edna poured Frank another cup of coffee and said, "I'll miss you Frank. If you want to go to Kansas my four boys are there: Daniel, Paul, Zeb, and Drake. They and their families are living around Kansas City. They can direct you on what to do or where to go for your law practice."

"Thanks, Edna!" Frank beamed.

At nineteen, Frank reflected on where he had been and where he was going. He was in the full bloom of manhood with high hopes and plans for the future. As a parting gift Herb had given him some treasured law books. Zekiel and Edna had given him a rifle and pistol as a parting gift. It was the right time. Frank headed off to Kansas on his faithful horse, Jubal.

Zekiel and Edna's son, Daniel, had been most obliging to introduce Frank to Kansas City. Frank soon discovered that there were already too many lawyers competing among themselves for legal disputes and land claims. Frank, being young and curious, decided that it was a little too crowded in Kansas City. He continued to head west. He stopped in Lawrence. It was a friendly little village of Free Soilers. It was hardly more than a trading post, not enough people for a thriving legal practice. He continued on his way and ended up in Topeka.

With the money Frank had saved from working on the Smythes farm, he had a storefront office built. Proudly, he hung out his shingle "FRANK WINSLOW—LAWYER". Being the only lawyer in Topeka at the time, he had good business due to all the settlers coming into the area. Among the newly arrived was a surveyor by profession, Rodney Black, who soon was a business associate in a short span of time. The Federal Government was slow in providing section maps of land surveys which were necessary before land titles could be located and registered. With the help of Rodney Black, and his prior work with the Federal Government, Frank was able to facilitate land ownership, at least, unofficially, until the government sanctioned his fair and meticulous pre-survey work with the eventual arrival of the section maps. It was spring and business was brisk. Frank's reputation grew as a fair and honest lawyer. Mired down in paperwork, Frank put a HELP WANTED sign in his office window. He now had been a lawyer for more than two years. At twenty-one he felt like he was drowning in paperwork. He sat at his desk and stared at huge stacks of land claims.

A square built woman entered his office. She appeared to be about forty, with a crown of dark brown braids on top of her head. She was wearing spectacles. "Good morning, Mr. Winslow. I noticed your HELP WANTED sign in the window. If you are still needing help I am interested." She spoke pleasantly, in a low register.

Frank said, "You have the advantage, what's your name?"

"Sorry," she said. "It's Mrs. Myrtle Hardy."

"It's a pleasure. So, what are your qualifications?" He felt a bit nonplused. She was his elder and he wanted to be respectful.

Mrs. Hardy collected her thoughts. "I can read, write, cipher, and am good with people. I used to work in a mercantile store back east in Ohio. My husband wanted to improve our lot in life, so we headed west to acquire some land. We found us a nice piece northwest of here on the Soldier River. Last spring, he was gored by our bull. He died quick."

Frank said, "I am sorry for your loss."

"Thank you." said Mrs. Hardy becoming pensive. "I had to sell off everything to pay debts. I couldn't run a farm without my husband.

I need a job in the present moment. Otherwise, I have just enough money left to go back east."

Respectfully, Frank said, "Well, Widow Hardy you are hired. I am neck deep in paperwork. If you can organize this," here Frank motioned at the tall piles of paper. "into some meaningful order, I'll pay you five dollars a week, plus ten to start for tackling these mountains of claims." A pleased look spanned the square features of Widow Hardy's face. She cleared her throat and scanned the paperwork with a practiced eye. "Mr. Winslow, I will have this organized in three days."

Frank asked, "When can you start?"

Widow Hardy said, "Why, now if you like."

Frank grinned, "Have at it!"

Widow Hardy was good to her word. The paper piles were nicely stacked into different categories, then cross-referenced, alphabetized, indexed and catalogued. At her request, Frank had some large cabinets made to hold the records, deeds, wills, contracts, and claims. Since all these papers were valuable, again, at her suggestion an already existing backroom was reinforced with thicker walls and iron bars in the one window. Frank also purchased a safe for any monies receivable. Widow Hardy was a wise and knowledgeable woman. Frank trusted her and gave her the keys to the backroom and safe. He also bought her a pistol to keep in the front desk drawer. Widow Hardy came to his employ in 1850. A deep bond of affection grew between them. It filled an empty place in both their hearts. For him, she filled the place of a mother. For her, it filled the place of a son. She would often have him over for a meal.

The years melted one into the other. Being an unsettled territory, Kansas had seen more than its share of violence. Pro-slave settlers would establish farms. The Free Soilers who were anti-slavery were also establishing farms. Border ruffians would foment hostilities until the opposing factions would attack each other in guerilla skirmishes.

In 1854 the Federal Government passed the Kansas-Nebraska Act thereby repealing the Missouri Compromise which then left it up to the individual settlers to decide whether to own slaves or not. This was divisive. Frank thought that it was putting the stamp of approval on anarchy. After that, a frenzy of immigration was being fueled by the New England Emigrant Aid Company whose purpose was to send anti-slavery settlers.

Competing pro-slavery immigration was being encouraged by the southern states. In the first territorial elections of November 1854, pro-slavery forces won with the aid of sympathizers from Missouri who crossed the border to stuff ballot boxes and to threaten legal voters.

Kansans, who were against slavery, refused to accept the new pro-slavery government. It culminated in the activist anti-slavery forces to write their own constitution. Frank played an integral part in drawing up that constitution in Topeka. State officers elected under the constitution were recognized only by the Free State Party.

These were tough years for Frank. The acrimony between the pro-slavers and anti-slavers played out in burned crops, burned towns and murders. A festering wound of hatred culminated in the Massacre at Potawatami and the burning of Lawrence.

In 1857 a convention dominated by pro-slavery forces supported by the national government met in Lecompton. They drew up another state constitution which legalized slavery. After this last legal wrangle, Frank said sadly to Widow Hardy one day at the law office, "Widow Hardy, with Kansas brawling over slavery for such a long time, I feel my life is on hold. We are living on quaky ground. I can't get on with my personal life. It's plain balderdash."

"Well, Frank, I feel the same way as you," said Widow Hardy. They both were silent for a while as they pondered the sad state of Kansas.

Widow Hardy broke the silence. "By chance, I made an apple pie this morning. It might take our minds off this Kansas turmoil." With that she went back to the records room and brought back a still warm apple pie. As soon as Frank was within nostril range of the heavenly aroma, he began to salivate. Soon they were enjoying a hot cup of coffee and warm apple pie.

Frank's spirits lifted, "That's the best apple pie I ever ate this side of the Mississippi River!" Widow Hardy beamed with pleasure.

Frank was not alone in his sympathies for a free Kansas. In 1859 he again helped in writing a state constitution at Wyandotte prohibiting slavery. It was not accepted by the U.S. Congress until 1861, the very year Kansas officially became a free state and after the secession of the southern states.

Frank was deep into his memories when the high-pitched voice of Ezra brought him back to the present. Observing Lt. Colonel's reflective mood, Ezra noisily cleared his throat and said, "I am a mite lonesome, kind a wish I had a girlfriend what was thinking' bout me up here in Illinois. The red hair and freckles jest slows me up something awful."

Emerging from his musings, Lt. Colonel Winslow burst out with a hearty laugh, "I am thirty-three and still single! But right now, I'm glad I haven't a sweetheart to worry about. If I come out of this war alive and have my health, I aim to find a pretty woman, and settle down."

"Ezra, I feel for the past many years that I have already been at war with the South, in Kansas. Year in year out, since I arrived in Topeka in 1847, southern sympathizers stuffing ballot boxes and threatening legal voters, all in order to make Kansas a slave state. We have battlefields already, Potawatami, and Lawrence among them. I am sick and tired of being sick and tired. So, I am ready to whelp it out once and for all."

Ezra said, "Yup. We have unfinished business. I am plain weary of how Kansas is...border ruffians from Missouri shot my Pa dead in Kickapoo. After that Ma and I moved close to Topeka. This war is made to order. I have faith in Old Honest Abe."

Winslow said, "Sorry to hear of your loss, Ezra." He paused in silence for a moment. "We do have hope in President Lincoln. When he took the oath of office to uphold and defend, he stood by it."

Winslow continued, "Governor Pickens of South Carolina spoke from the balcony of the Charleston Hotel after southerners forced the surrender of Major Anderson at Fort Sumpter. Governor Pickens then thanked God that the struggle had begun and pledged himself and his hearers to die before they would submit… So, there are raging passions on both sides."

The two men stood in their dusty tracks. In the distance they could hear the bugler call softly for assembly, then louder. It came from headquarters in Cairo, Illinois. They began to walk in that direction.

General Ulysses S. Grant came to the balcony of the brick house appropriated for Union Headquarters. He was average height with unevenly set eyes. A dogged look of determination defined every line of his face.

Grant said in a loud voice, "It is good to see such a large group of loyal men here to fight the Rebellion. What the future holds no one knows. Whether by plan or surprise, we will train and be ready! We already know that God is on our side, but we have to roll up our sleeves and dig in and He will give us the increase. No one knows how long the war will last. We will put the South in a vice, crushing it through blockading of goods. Using what goods they do have to fuel our army. We will not relent until we have won the peace."

An approving shout arose from the gathered soldiers. Grant ordered all officers from lieutenant colonels through Generals to meet in the lower part of the building. The rest were dismissed. Once the high-ranking officers had gathered, General Grant addressed the officers, "The word idle and soldier don't belong together. I want all of you to organize training drills, scouting operations, and foraging units."

Grant circulated among the officers and came upon General Vale and Lt. Colonel Winslow. He told them, "I want you and your men up one hour before daybreak on the ridge north of town. Be battle ready. That's all you need to know for now."

Under Lt. Colonel Frank Winslow's command was around six hundred men. Twelve companies with about fifty men in each. Winslow had a bugler, a major, a surgeon, an assistant surgeon, one quartermaster, one saddler, and one chaplain. This composed his headquarters staff. Each company had a captain in command, sometimes a first lieutenant. They held elections and elected one for each company, second lieutenants also. Each company had two second lieutenants and four to six sergeants and as many corporals. The remaining thirty or so men were privates.

Frank Winslow was given his command in Topeka, Kansas. A consensus of citizens chose him. Factors weighing in his favor were his profession as a lawyer, attributes in leadership, delegating of tasks, and just his plain likeability, and honesty.

Frank Winslow had his men ready one hour before daybreak on the ridge north of town. They waited for orders. General Vale rode up to Winslow and said, "You and your men are going to do some hard riding into Missouri. The objective is cohesiveness, simply put, make movements seem like second nature." Vale moved to the next unit to give orders. Some were ordered to go off in other directions.

Down below the crest of the hill the Mississippi River lapped weakly on the shore. The water was low due to sparse rain and there were sandbars and shallows. Easily, Winslow's men crossed into Missouri. They rode deeper into the state.

It was about midmorning when Winslow announced, "We are going to divide into three groups. Captain Tobias will head the first group, Captain Bell will head the third group. I will head the middle group. I will have the bugler with me. Tobias, you and your men will go in a northwesterly direction. Bell, your group will head in a southwesterly direction. My group will head due west. We will ride in our respective directions for one hour. We begin to converge starting in the second hour. That means that at that point Tobias heads southwest, Bell heads northwest. I will continue due west until we reunite. If at any time you need extra help, have someone from that group whistle three sharp bursts. Since I have the bugler, if need be, I will have him blow three blasts. Otherwise, we will regroup in two hours when the bugler will blow the signal. Captains, check your watches for starting time. Let's go now!"

They headed off in their separate directions. The terrain was mostly flat with clusters of trees and scrub brush clumped around dry creek beds and stagnant ponds. About an hour into the operation, Winslow's group came across some rebels camped in a gully. Winslow's men whipped out their guns and sabers and swept through camp. The Yanks did a good job of scattering the rebels. A few of Winslow's men dismounted and gathered up all unclaimed pistols and rifles.

They rode on leaving the rebels stunned and in disarray. Upon departing some of the rebels got a few bullets flying. One bullet zinged right through Ezra's hat, knocking it off his head. They slowed and reunited with Tobias and Bell.

Winslow announced to all, "Men be at ease we are going to break for lunch."

Over coffee and hardtack Winslow said to Tobias and Bell, I almost lost my bugler. It must not have been his day to die." Afterward, they rode back to camp.

That night, in the headquarters tent, Winslow spoke with Captain Tobias. "Captain Tobias, this is just the beginning. I feel that we have such a long way to go. All these young fellows under my command... I look at their young faces and know some will never return home. I have to get a grip, but it keeps gnawing at my gut." Frank was still thinking about the bullet that shot off Ezra's cap.

"Come, come, Winslow. I think I have what you need right now, a good stiff drink. When it hits your stomach, you will relax." Tobias, a stocky man, lumbered over to his worn carpet bag and produced a bottle of whiskey and two small glasses. He poured each half full. He gave a glass to Winslow. Downing the spirits in one fell swoop made them gasp momentarily.

Cocking his head as his mind latched onto an errant memory, Winslow confessed softly, "I'm just pining for the familiar."

Captain Tobias eyes twinkled knowingly under bushy gray brows and a wry smile. He was a man about forty-five with unkempt gray hair that was a stranger to a comb. His demeanor had a calming effect on Winslow. A reflective tone came into Tobias' voice, "I'm a married man, got me three kids. It's a bit lonely for them and my dear wife. I know why I'm here. It is personal. I have to defend hearth and home. A man's got to do what he's got to do to preserve that. That thought always brings me back to my fighting sense, my resolve." The two men settled down to routine conversation which drifted into the technical side of war.

Along with Captain Tobias, others of the immediate staff joined them in the headquarters tent. Among them, Ezra Peabody and Doc Parker and a few others who had come with Winslow from Kansas.

Doc Parker asked, "How's the family doing back in Indiana?"

Winslow answered, "They are doing alright. It sounds like my two sisters' husbands and my nephew have joined up. I received a letter yesterday. I'll go ahead and read it to you folks." All were interested for any news.

Winslow read the following letter:

Covington, Indiana

Sept. 20th, 1861

Dear Frank,

I take pen in hand and will devote some time to you. We are all in good health. Phoebe and the children are out picking apples. Phoebe has all the navy beans picked and dried. We have put them in a wooden barrel. As you may surmise it takes a great deal of food for ten of us to live. The butter has been churned for the week. I believe it is five pounds worth. I killed two hogs yesterday. The two oldest girls are rendering lard, some of the meat goes to the smoke house, the pork back will be brined for salt pork. We use everything but the squeal.

I'm down at the store writing. People are all out working, mostly women. Some of the women are haying, cutting and stacking the hay in the barns. That is mighty hard work. Some of the more clever women, including your sisters', Sara and Eliza, are hauling the hay near the barns and stacking it, then putting rails up to keep the cattle off till winter. Sara and Eliza work well as a team, especially since their husbands joined the Union Army. Their children are helpful too.

I gather that there are more soldiers than equipment from other folks receiving letters from loved ones in the army. We have a few local men who are members in the Knights of the Golden Circle around here. Most of these men are harmless but in southern Indiana they have more potential to do damage. They hold their meetings in secret but talk openly, 'leave the South alone.' It is plain flat out sedition. You may run across some of these people that spy for the South.

In August, my son, Lemuel Junior, put up hay for our delivery horse and my own buggy horse. I purchased a horse for Junior. He'll need one. He's going to join up. Like you suggested, I bought a dark brown horse for him. He is twenty-two and a man and must do as he sees fit. Write when you can.

Your brother,
Lemuel

It was good for all of them to hear of thoughts from home. It seemed to anchor the listeners in a peaceful moment. They all called it a day and retired to their respective tents.

The tent was a modest one, shared by Winslow and Major Lester and Doc Parker. A lantern on a hardtack box provided light. Wool blankets and cots completed the Spartan furnishings. They extinguished the lantern, and all were soon in a deep sleep.

Frank awoke bleary eyed, roused by the sound of reveille. His eyes focused on his tent mate, Major Lester, as he jumped out of bed like a coiled snake. Approaching the age of thirty-eight, Major Lester stood a bit less than six feet tall, his muscles flaccid from years behind a desk as a banker. Thinning brown hair, a down-turned mouth, and a prominent hooked nose made him appear hawkish. Accentuating his raptor-like appearance was his intense stare and abrupt movements. He dressed faultlessly bordering on pompous; every button was buttoned, every crease pressed, all leather polished to a high sheen. He was fond of gold braid and sported more than some others of his rank. Thus far, Frank was trying to be unbiased. It was becoming difficult. Major Lester grated on his nerves.

Haughtily, Lester would swagger upon the scene, saber clanking, relishing every military ceremony and contriving more occasions of fanfare to flaunt his finery. In civilian life he had obtained his position of banker through a socially advantageous marriage. One of these advantages was that his wife's uncle was a brigadier general back east where Lester also hailed. The general had the sagacity to send Lester far away to the Western Campaign under General Grant.

Officially, Major Lester's duties were requisitions and logistics. This entailed keeping track of army supplies, food, weapons, clothing, equipment, and medical supplies. Most of his energies were poured into his appearance seemingly with the minimum left over for his tasks. All he proved capable of was a fair to middling job performance.

"Lt. Colonel Winslow, I would like the soldiers to shine up more, instead of just on Saturdays and Sundays." Lester said emphatically, mustering a belligerent glare.

Frank was sitting on his cot enjoying the aromatic vapor from his morning cup of coffee. He usually savored a peaceful moment at dawn to collect his thoughts. They were collected. "Major Lester, as long as I am in command, I won't brow beat my men. If he is wearing the blue and smiles at us, that will suffice. But if he doesn't smile, it won't be long before he has a pistol drawn, cocked and fired at us. We must not prioritize the dress parade. The fancy dress parade and officers detached from the common soldier is Napoleon's doings. Napoleon did not want any privates or fighting men near him. He treated them in a debasing manner. The average soldier is your lifeline, don't make him your enemy."

Frank continued, "I have six hundred men under me, and I will talk to any one of them. They can bring their problems to me. The top command in our outfit can't be bothered by the common soldier, but I make it my business to be bothered. Those young men have enough to concern themselves, least of all a dress parade."

Major Lester responded with exasperation, "I disagree with you! I insist in neatness and a clean looking dress parade. I feel that I have some rank and I insist the soldiers submit to my orders. Some are born leaders and I am one of them."

Winslow slammed his coffee cup on the hardtack box. He rose to his full height and thrust his body past Lester. He showed him his back because his anger was becoming too obvious. He did not look back as he spoke, "Major Lester, if you keep those ideas you will travel down an empty road. It doesn't pay to be severe with the men. There is a much greater power to guide us. Under Him there is no rank or discrimination. Those who exalt themselves will be humbled."

Lester realized he was treading on thin ice. To placate Winslow without changing an iota of ideology, he said in a subdued voice, "Maybe you are right. After all, rank is something that could be gone tomorrow." With those words, Major Lester's eyes burned holes into Winslow's back.

CHAPTER 2
Introduction of Juliette Bellechasse

It was a beautiful June morning in 1861, Paris, France. Juliette made her way through the streets carrying a parcel wrapped in brown paper and twine. In a familiar, yet elated manner, she greeted the shop keepers as they opened for business with a cheerful 'bonjour'. Hurriedly, she made her way to Le Mouton Noir, her parent's restaurant, which was situated in a working-class neighborhood. She entered the threshold of the drab but respectable establishment. Excitedly she exclaimed, "Ma mere the dress Madame Bernard altered for me fits parfaitement!" Juliette glowed with gratitude as her mother emerged from the kitchen.

Michelle Bellechasse smiled sweetly at her daughter and said, "That dress was wasting away in the trunk. I am happy you can wear it."

"I must show you how it looks on me!" Juliette gushed. She sprinted upstairs to her room with the parcel. Minutes later she reappeared before her mother wearing the newly altered dress.

Long, shiny, loose black curls cascaded down her back. Her light complexion was flushed pale rose. Uncannily her large peridot eyes matched the pale green satin dress. Juliette assumed a pose, elongating her svelte, five-foot three-inch frame to its maximum height. Her mother smiled approvingly.

At that moment, her husband entered the restaurant with parcels of meat from the butcher. Antoine Bellechasse's mouth was thin, but a wreath of smile lines appeared on his cheeks and at the corners of his eyes as he beheld his beautifully bedecked daughter. A shock of white hair poked from under his cap. He was left speechless by Juliette's ethereal beauty.

Looking expectantly at her father, Juliette queried, "Mon pere, qu'est-ce que vous pensez de cette robe?"

"Magnifique!" He said admiringly.

"Now I will be presentable for the General Reception at the Hotel de Ville!" She glowed at the prospect. Rare were the opportunities for the working class to hob nob with people of the higher classes, or even international businessmen. Many countries would be represented.

Both parents doted on Juliette and remembered as if it was yesterday when Curé Sevigny brought the little girl to the childless couple. At the time, Curé Sevigny was a desperate priest. The mother of the child had been a prostitute and had come to the priest once she realized that she was pregnant. She wanted to make a confession. Not wanting to bear a child into such shameful circumstances, once she had been forgiven by the priest, she made a firm purpose of amendment and became a seamstress under the brief tutelage of the nuns from nearby convent. For more than two years she made a valiant attempt at being a seamstress, but after Juliette was born her health took a turn for the worse. Consumption was draining her of good health and preventing her from sewing. Several customers had not paid her for work she had already completed, which didn't help. On a visit to pick up some mended items, Curé Sevigny knocked on the apartment door. He waited. Not hearing anything, he said, "Teresa, are you there?"

He heard a muffled "Entrez."

Tentatively, he opened the door and came upon the bleak scene of the bedridden mother and the sad child. Teresa's face was ashen under her light brown complexion. Tight wavy hair framed her face. A hopeful smile flickered across her full lips. "Curé Sevigny, you are the answer to my prayers. Please take little Juliette and find her a good home. I know I will not be here much longer."

The Curé sensed the truth of her words. He always carried items for the last rites. Solemnly, he put his stole on said the simple prayers and gave her a small fragment of the Eucharist, food for the journey home. Serene peace and joy entered her expression as she breathed her last.

Forlorn little Juliette, who had withdrawn to the corner of the room sensed a change in her mother. Juliette, only two years old, seemed to know the gravity of the moment. She emerged from the corner, climbed upon the bed next to her mother. Nuzzling her small face into the niche of her mother's neck, she urgently said, "Ma mere, je t'aime." She repeated the phrase, expectantly awaiting a response. She lifted her mother's lifeless arm and draped it around her. Instinctively she shut her eyes tightly and burrowed closer as if for protection.

Curé Sevigny viewed the eloquent scene which touched him to the core. Patiently, he waited a long while as Juliette clung to her dead mother. Then gently he patted Juliette's tiny shoulder, and stooping close to her ear he said, "Maintenant ta mere est avec les anges."

The Bellechasses were the priest's dim hope. They were the only childless couple in his parish young enough to raise a small child. It was a dark, rainy April night in 1842 Paris. The priest knocked on the door of the restaurant hoping someone would answer. Juliette was strangely quiet in his arms. She was such a thin little girl; he hardly felt his burden.

Presently, there was a man's voice behind the door gruffly asking, "Who is it?"

Impatient from the cold wet night, the Curé responded, "It is I, the priest!"

Immediately the door swung open to dim candlelight. Damp and chilled, the priest and his human bundle wrapped in his cloak, entered the restaurant. Michelle came from the kitchen to greet him.

"Bon soir, Curé Sevigny. What brings you out so late this evening?" Her gaze fell on Juliette as she peeked out from the priest's cloak.

"I have come, Monsieur et Madame Bellechasse, to throw myself and my charge on your mercy and ask if you could take in little Juliette to raise as your own," he blurted out. The priest was not one to mince words.

Dumbfounded, Michelle and Antoine pulled out chairs and sat simultaneously. It was a lot to absorb. After what seemed like an eternity, Antoine gestured for the priest to sit. Michelle went to the kitchen and made the priest a hot chocolate and brought bread and some warm milk for the toddler. The scene went forward in silence. The familiar ritual of serving food was a comfort to Michelle.

As she watched little Juliette gobble up the bread and drink the milk, Michelle's heart melted. Michelle began to weep uncontrollably as her husband, Antoine and Curé Sevigny observed her in wide eyed wonderment. Michelle surrendered completely to her tears as she sat at the table with her head down in her arms. So many years had passed in her marriage where she secretly yearned for a child, then felt guilty. She would bury that thought because her husband was such a kind and good man that she didn't want to distress him that she was unhappy. Primordial sobs rocked her as if a dam had broken. A fluttering caress touched Michelle's arm. She looked up to see Juliette's small fingers stroke Michelle's arm. In amazement she perceived Juliette's green eyes flooded with tears of empathy. She picked up Juliette and embraced her.

She looked at her husband and pleaded, "Dear Antoine, please let us adopt this child!"

Taken by the child's gesture, Antoine said firmly, "Certainment!"

Michelle then showered Juliette with tearful kisses. Juliette embraced her with all her might.

Curé Sevigny silently prayed in thanksgiving. Before he left the new family, he said, "God thanks you and I thank you." He left with a joyful heart.

Monsieur and Madame Bellechasse welcomed the raising of Juliette. When she was six years old, she attended the parish school and excelled in all subjects. One of the nuns who could speak English, found that Juliette, after completing her assignments, was bored. To entertain her, the nun taught her English. Juliette became insatiable in learning the English language. She sharpened her skills to perfection. She practiced on anyone who would cooperate, mainly her parents and their family friend, Madame Bernard. She was Juliette's piano teacher and a seamstress by trade.

A vivid memory of her natural mother would be triggered by the scent of lavender in the market, or the tight waves in a coiffure worn by a passerby, or even a full lipped smile of a patron in the restaurant. Curiosity and intelligence go hand in hand. When she asked about her mother, the Bellechasses were honest and open. They told her how she had arrived in their care. Curé Sevigny had a close friendship with the Bellechasses and was given permission to tell Juliette of her natural mother's story. The right time fell on Juliette's twelfth birthday.

Curé Sevigny arrived early on a sunny Saturday morning in May at Le Mouton Noir. Juliette greeted him with hot café au lait and pastry. "Juliette, your parents have hired a calèche and soon we will all go for a ride to the cemetery where Teresa Sidamo is buried, your birth mother."

Juliette excitedly went to the kitchen garden in the alley way and picked a bouquet of lilies of the valley and tied them together with a blue ribbon. Later in the calèche, Curé Sevigny told the family as much as he knew of Juliette's mother.

"Juliette, Teresa Sidamo was an immigrant to France coming from Algeria. She had been born to a French diplomat and a mulatto slave. Teresa grew up as a slave alongside her mother. Around the age of fifteen she attracted a minor official at the embassy who took her as a concubine. He was an older gentleman and after his service to France in Algeria, he took Teresa to Marseilles, France."

"Soon after, that gentleman died. Not knowing anyone, she found herself in Paris with very little money. So, she fell into prostitution. When she became pregnant with you, she couldn't bear to raise you in that sinful environment. She came to me for confession and became Catholic. She had amended her life. With the help of the nuns at a local convent she learned to sew and mend. Gradually her health declined, and she died of consumption. She was a good woman who wanted the best for her child." Curé Sevigny concluded reflectively."

Mentally, Juliette, digested the information. Hesitating, she then asked, "And my birth father, did my mother ever say who he was?"

Pausing and looking down to collect his thoughts, the priest looked up and said, "It was one of her clients…one who she saw exclusively for less than a year prior to your conception. All I know was that he was a minor bureaucrat here in Paris. She didn't reveal who he was."

By the time the calèche arrived at the cemetery, it was noon, and they were on the outskirts of Paris at the pauper's burial grounds. The meadow larks were singing, and a gentle breeze weaved through the newly greened branches. They all gathered around the burial site. Curé Sevigny lead them in prayer, citing Psalm 129, De Profundis and an Our Father. He ended with, "May the soul of Teresa Sidamo rest in peace."

All of these things about her natural mother, Juliette stored. She felt somehow it should be kept private. The Bellechasses were grateful for her discernment and peacefully accepted her silence on the subject.

The years went by, and at the age of fourteen, Juliette felt she had learned all that could be taught at the parish school. Besides, her parents were aging, and they could use an extra pair of hands to help in the restaurant full time. She enthusiastically embraced her role as restauranteur. In the course of a typical day, local humanity would pass through the restaurant in a somewhat structured way. First, the students, delivery people, seamstresses, dyers, and cleaners would eat their grand repas about two or three in the afternoon. It usually consisted of soup and bread. A more opulent meal was served starting about six in the evening for the lawyers, minor government officials, shop keepers, bank clerks that had closed their business for the day.

At Le Mouton Noir, lamb, mutton, beef, pork, and chicken were staples. Along with the main courses of meat, Juliette took extra care to shop before the restaurant opened for fresh vegetables and fruit that were in season. She would help make cakes and tarts rather than spend extra money to buy the already made pastries at the bakery. With such enthusiasm fueled into the restaurant's quality of food, she did have to outsource for fresh baked bread because she didn't have the time to bake bread. Very shrewd for her age, she bargained with the local bakery for a discounted price for the bread and achieved a mutually beneficial agreement; the bakery provided a large volume of bread and the restaurant received it at a discounted price.

Meticulous in providing an inviting atmosphere for dining, the tables were always clean with fresh flowers when available. Juliette had a stage presence which was symbiotic with her beauty.

Toward the end of the evening, she would sing in a clear and earthy voice. As time progressed, she would add gestures and antics and act out songs. Her performances could be amusing and comic. Once in a while, poignant and touching. She noticed that the regulars preferred the lighter spirited songs. Her performances were much welcomed by the weary patrons after a long day's work. Word of mouth spread about

Le Mouton Noir and patronage increased. People would patiently wait in line for the good food and cheerful entertainment.

Restaurant work was hard and long. After the last patrons would leave, Juliette would scrub the floors on her hands and knees, help her mother start the next day's soup stock, and marinade meat for stews. So, life went for Juliette until the age of twenty. Frustration was growing in her heart. The men she was exposed to in the restaurant, were taciturn, jaded, and uninspired by how they perceived life's circumstances. Over the years she had observed many of the male patrons. They mostly fell into two desolate groups; perpetual students, absinthe drinkers, self-proclaimed Bohemians, these were the youth. They all had a similar mindset and behavior. They were idle, vain, self-absorbed, and without goals. They ate earlier in the afternoon. For the more established male citizens, it was almost bleaker. The minor government officials, bank clerks, and shop keepers had arrived and weren't going further. The dismal lives of the patrons of Le Mouton Noir spoke of a larger, heavier weight on France.

Louis Napoleon III, who came into power in December 1851, by a nonviolent coup d'etat, was astute in seeding the path to political power with alliances to advance his claim to rule France. Once in power it was a benevolent dictatorship that was felt in all social classes.

One of the regular customers, who ate his grand repas each evening looked forward to the hearty meal and the friendly ambiance of the respectable little restaurant. An older man, he lived a single life and had lodgings in the neighborhood. Joseph Gastineau was in his late forties, short, potbellied, with ample salt and pepper hair waved back over his ears. His steel rimmed glasses glinted in the candlelight as he perused the newspaper, 'La Presse". Only gossip, trivia, and serial stories were allowed to be published by the government, a poor substitute for true news. Also, the song of national pride, La Marseillaise, had been banned in 1852 by Napoleon III.

Frustration with men in general and now with France's present governance had culminated in disillusionment and concern for her parent's wellbeing. Juliette, young and vibrant, had great loyalty to her parents. Even tempered and kind throughout her formative years, they had been her main source of joy. She had dreamed of a better life for her parents and herself. Her hopes were now dashed by her perception of men of marriageable age and the present ruling government of France.

Joseph Gastineau had begun to patronize the restaurant when Juliette was ten years of age. He had observed Juliette grow into a lovely young woman. She had cooked for him, served him, and entertained him. With the Bellechasses in the friendly background, it had fulfilled his needs for family. On this particular evening Juliette sat down at his table and sighed deeply, "Monsieur Gastineau, I feel so trapped in Paris. There doesn't seem to be a future for me or my parents." A pensive lull ensued.

She continued, "The government just raised taxes on our restaurant so Napoleon the Third can wage war on Mexico. I heard that from another patron."

Resignedly, Mr. Gastineau nodded his head in agreement. He said quietly, "It's so true, tax the middle class again and again, the work horse of France, and soon it's like trying to get blood out of a turnip."

"Monsieur Gastineau, our restaurant was just getting by before and life went on with meeting our taxes and paying our bills, but this newly imposed tax makes it almost impossible. We have fallen into a rut." Juliette said glumly.

Joseph Gastineau ponders her words in deep thought. "Juliette, there will be a General Reception at the Hotel de Ville next month in the middle of June. Perhaps there might be some sort of opportunity for you there." He took out his government issued invitation.

"I don't care for large parties. Please accept the invitation. You can make better use of it." He smiled kindly as he presented it to Juliette.

Juliette was so delighted; she leaped to her feet and gave Monsieur Gastineau a kiss on the cheek and danced around the table. She sang lightheartedly, "Merci beaucoup, mille fois!" and repeated this chant several times with great joy. Monsieur Gastineau flushed pink with gratification for having changed Juliette's dark mood to one of such happiness.

Her parents were quite pleased to know that she had received the invitation to the reception. The next morning, her mother went in the attic in search of her hope chest. Inside it she found the green dress she had worn on her honeymoon years before. It was lovely but a bit too large for Juliette. It needed to be altered and embellished by their friend, Madame Bernard.

To impart the current fashion of the day, Madame Bernard added leg of mutton sleeves and extra cream-colored satin panels to the skirt to add flounce. Crucial to its draping was a whole bone undergarment given to her by Madam Bernard that gave it dramatic billow and volume and emphasized Juliette's small waist.

The day of the General Reception arrived. Juliette had taken great lengths to improve her appearance. Her jet-black hair was skeined back into a glossy chignon with coils of corkscrew curls cascading down her left shoulder. As the bright, late morning sun streamed through her bedroom window, it reflected off her coiffure revealing cobalt blue highlights. The recently altered and augmented green dress enhanced all of her feminine lines. She scented herself with lavender and sported pearl earrings, a gift from her mother. Only using a scant amount of lip rouge, she accentuated her full heart shaped mouth.

Every night for a week, prior to the event, Juliette coated her work-worn hands in lanolin and wore cotton gloves to bed. There were a few callouses, and rough cuticles subdued to new softness in this manner. It was early afternoon by the time she felt she was prepared. Her parents were happily impressed by her polished appearance. They hugged her as she departed on her mission.

The hired calèche drove her to the Hotel de Ville. Upon arrival she disembarked in a swirl of satin and purpose. The doorman was agog by her beauty. It hardly registered when he received the invitation from her. His eyes were locked on her. Other men in the reception area had a similar reaction. She misread it and thought that maybe her petticoat was showing. She shook her dress to make sure that all was in order.

It was then that her gaze came across a tall young man with steel gray eyes who was staring at her. He had spotted her when she first entered the reception area. His eyes had not wandered from her presence. Their gazes locked when their eyes met. They gravitated toward one another.

He came close to her and said, "Bonjour, Mademoiselle." He firmly shook her hand.

"Bonjour, Monsieur. Comment allez-vous? Je m'appelle Juliette Bellechasse."

A little flustered, he responded, "Excusez, je ne parle pas bien en Français."

"You speak English! Wonderful!" Juliette exclaimed. "I enjoy speaking English!"

His face brightened. "I do understand enough that I caught your name, Juliette Bellechasse. My name is James Lambert. I am very pleased to meet you. I come from the state of Mississippi. I am here on business. I've already sold half my cotton for a good price." A slow smile revealed even white teeth and gave warmth to his steel gray eyes. He was not quite six feet in height. He was slim and fit. All of his sandy blond hair was cut short combed neatly in place with a precise side part.

A young waiter came to offer them a cup of punch from a tray. There was a puddle of liquid on the tray so when he handed James the wet cup it dripped on his highly polished boots. James paled. His eyes darkened to shades of gun metal. Under his breath he tensely murmured, "If I were back home, you'd be horse whipped for less."

Juliette couldn't make out what he said. She only noticed a momentary hardness in his face. It was lost on the waiter also. A bit puzzled, she asked, "What did you say, James?"

"Don't bother your pretty little head about it." He said gruffly as he bent over and wiped the punch off his boots.

Juliette dismissed it. They enjoyed their punch together. All the pomp of the General Reception dimmed for they only had eyes for each other.

"James, I would so like you to meet my parents. Would you like to?" Juliette asked, her black eyebrows arched like raven's wings.

"I would be delighted to meet them. The sooner the better." He replied. His southern drawl sweetened every syllable. Mesmerized by the honeyed tones of his courtly speech, Juliette happily asked, "How about now, James? The reception is so boring now that I have met you."

Eagerly, they left the reception and hired a carriage to take them to Le Mouton Noir. Time had escaped them as they watched the last trace of sun settle into the horizon on their way. When they arrived at the restaurant only her parents were there cleaning up after a busy day.

Juliette had taken James by the hand as they entered. "Ma mère et Mon pere, attention!" She spoke excitedly in English, "I would like you to make the acquaintance of James Lambert."

In unison her parents said, "We are happy to meet you."

"I am very happy to meet the parents of the most beautiful Juliette." James responded as he shook both parent's hands.

The Bellechasses were quite impressed by his elegant manners.

Michelle asked, "'ave you eaten? We 'ave much food eef you are 'ungry."

Both Juliette and James realized that they were very hungry since they had not eaten at the reception. So, her parents soon served them a hearty meal of beef Bourginoine, bread, and red wine. They only had eyes for each other. They ate and talked into the night. James spoke of the beauty of the South, the balls and garden parties. Juliette told him of the beauty of Paris, the Louvre, Notre Dame, and the Seine at sunset. Finally, James reluctantly left for his lodging but eagerly requested to see her again.

So much had happened to Juliette on every level of her being that she felt herself floating on a huge invisible wave that carried her upstairs and somehow maneuvered into bed for what remained of the night. She embarked on a dream world of ocean waves tossing her about on a small raft while James appeared at the helm of a sleek cutter that created a turbulent wake. She frantically waved at him to rescue her. He and the boat continued away from her then disappeared. She woke up remembering her dream. It puzzled her. Then she dismissed it.

James Lambert had his guard down. He was hypnotized by Juliette's beauty and the romance of Paris. The next two weeks went by in a whirlwind of carriage rides, sightseeing, fine dining. It was an adventure for both of them.

On one of these outings James said, "My dear Juliette, let's go look for some new dresses to expand your meager wardrobe."

Juliette bristled because James used the word 'meager'. It was true. She bit her lip, recovered her composure and then enjoyed the moment. After several days of shopping, Juliette and James mutually agreed upon seven beautiful dresses, shoes, and accessories. Actually, some of the dresses were a little too revealing with the low cut back and the décolletage exposing too much neck and shoulders, but James opinion prevailed over hers. Juliette was very touched by his generosity and told him sincerely, "How very sweet of you to buy me all these things. Thank you so much."

Solicitously, James loaded up the carriage with the purchases of the day. He helped her up and into the carriage seat and then sat close to her. He pulled her close and said, "There is a better way to thank me than with words," as he embraced her tightly and began to kiss her on the mouth then the neck.

"James!" Juliette gasped. "Please stop! I am not a toy or a woman of the night! You are frightening me!"

"I am sorry, Juliette. I succumbed to my emotions of the moment." He talked in a flat voice that held no inflection.

James had completed the business of selling his cotton that he had brought from Mississippi. It was time to return home with his purchases of weapons and other supplies. Sadly, they both knew he had to leave soon. James did share some general facts about the conflict between the North and the South in his country.

"Juliette, the North is not happy with the bounty of the South. Those Northerners want to stick their noses right down to the detail of how we run our business." James spoke in disgruntlement.

Juliette intrigued by the disclosure said, "Is it like our leader, Napoleon the Third who sticks his nose in our very newspapers and taxes us for a pointless war in Mexico, No?"

Nodding in agreement, James responded, "Exactly. It comes down to plain old dictatorship."

That struck a chord with Juliette. "It does make perfect sense to protect yourself from government meddling." What James artfully did not mention was that slavery was the human machine that kept the South's business viable.

Deftly, on Juliette's part. She allowed James to believe that the Bellechasses were her blood parents. It was too much to explain that she was born out-of-wedlock to an immigrant who was a slave, concubine, prostitute, and seamstress.

On their last evening together, they had a leisurely ride in a calèche to Versailles for a dinner at a renowned eatery. Eager to wear one of the new, more modest dresses, Juliette chose a cream-colored satin dress. The pale satin contrasted well with blue-black hair and set off her pale green eyes like jewels. The meal was sumptuous. Afterwards, James enchanted with her visage, allowed the driver to slowly explore the boulevards, gardens, and byways. James savored the evening reluctant to leave the moment. He asked the driver to pull over in a public garden. They disembarked for a pleasant walk. They came upon a park bench facing a lovely fountain surrounded with white and red roses.

"Come, Juliette. Let us sit here. The moonlight is so beautiful, shining on the fountain and flowers." James said sweetly. Solemnly, he knelt on one knee beside her as she sat on the bench. He took her hand. "Would you do me the honor of becoming my wife? It would have to be after the conflict. Those damn Yankees bit off more than they can chew."

"James! I'd be so happy to be your wife!" Juliette exclaimed.

James reached in his pocket and produced a small box and opened it. A small teardrop-shaped diamond dangled on a delicate gold chain necklace. It sparkled in the moonlight showing its many facets.

"Oh, how beautiful!" she gushed. James put the necklace on Juliette's neck and closed the clasp.

They got up and walked around the fountain. He stopped and pulled her to his lips and kissed her repeatedly. "Juliette, you are so beautiful. I have never laid eyes on such remarkable beauty in a human creature."

It made Juliette uncomfortable to be praised for her appearance. "Looks are fleeting, dear James. Will the years change your interest in me?"

"Never! How can you ask such a question?!" James cleared his throat uncomfortably.

Juliette led the conversation away from his last comment. "Oh James, it seems like I waited for this moment for most of my life. Now it seems so sudden. You have talked about the North and South fighting. Where could our romance fit in?"

"I assure you; the war will be short-lived, and we can have a life together soon." James responded.

Lambert continued to gaze into Juliette's eyes. His own sharp gray eyes reflected back to him. Longingly, his eyes followed the curve of her lips then urgently he kissed her in a passionate embrace. Juliette broke the embrace, her face wildly flushed, eyes wide. "I have never been kissed like that."

"That kiss is only the prelude to what our marriage holds in store for us. It seals our devotion for one another. He picked a white rose, removed the thorns and put it behind her ear.

Later that evening they arrived back at Le Mouton Noir. The Bellechasses were ecstatic for the young couple's plans. James wanted to make certain that the Bellechasses were aware of his honorable intentions.

"Mr. Bellechasse, I am leaving with you $3,500 for your safekeeping. Please take care of the money for Juliette which will help provide passage for her in late September on a ship called the Tambeau. I am scheduled to leave tomorrow by train to Le Havre where the day after I catch a boat to Mobile, Alabama. I hope to see Juliette eventually at Fair View, my parent's plantation as a guest until the war is over." James concluded. Juliette's parents were speechless with the life-changing deluge of information.

The next morning arrived. It was James's last day in Paris. He and the Bellechasses went to the Paris train station. He purchased a train ticket for Le Havre. While on the platform James took Juliette's hand and placed a sealed envelope in her palm.

"This is important. Read it later." James said.

Juliette was in tears while they stood on the platform waiting for James' train to board passengers. Gusts of wind blew Juliette's tears like raindrops from her face. James put his arms around Juliette and their lips met in a parting kiss.

"Good-by, James." That was all Juliette could utter because she was fraught with emotion.

The train was ready for boarding. James dashed into his compartment which faced the platform. He opened the window and waved again. A cold wind chilled her to the bone as the train moved away. He disappeared from view.

She looked at the envelope that James had placed in her hand. She opened it. There was a short note from James with a ship schedule. The note reads as follows: Dear Juliette, I have handwritten the date and location of the ship you are to take to Mobile, Alabama. The ship is the Tambeau. It is not on the regular published ship lines. It is an independent. I know the captain from other connections. His name is Captain Armand Belmont. He is capable, shrewd and trustworthy for his type of work. You need to be in Le Havre by the first week of October. Fondly, James.

Juliette realized that most of July was gone. She had barely two months to arrange things for her big trip. A big trip that would change her life forever.

CHAPTER 3

Fort Donelson

Winslow and his men were in the middle of battle at Fort Donelson. It was February 16, 1862.

Fighting dismounted, Winslow and his men executed a flanking operation. The Union gunboats aided the army in the attack. Winslow and Ezra were right up front with their company of soldiers. Still raw recruits, they were slightly out of step but held their line.

The company had scaled the top of a hill. "There are Rebs over there!" Ezra shouted.

"Blow charge!" Commanded Winslow.

Eager for a fight, Ezra blew charge for all he was worth. So loud was the sound of the bugle, it echoed all around, clear and hard. The Rebs heard it too but the echo obscured the origin of the sound. The six hundred men under Winslow were a sight to behold, all held their lines. Many unarmed were marching next to a soldier with a pistol. For any soldier who was killed or wounded, the next man picked up the weapon and continued the action. Some men even had old flintlocks, family heirlooms. Before each battle, the men had melted lead to make bullets.

The conditions were miserable even for mid-February. A light drizzle began to fall and added to the already swollen Cumberland River. Troops and equipment had been slowed by the muddy, rutted

Tennessee roads, too muddy for horses. Confederate Fort Donelson had the advantage of being on high ground. Union Flag Officer, Andrew Foote, had collaborated with General Grant in the battle. Foote had moved his iron clad navy gunboats into a strategic position as support for the ground troops. The Rebel troops were facing away from Winslow's men distracted by other Yankee bullets. Adding to the noise were the iron clads shooting directly at Fort Donelson. Winslow's men advanced on the unaware Rebs. Winslow's men were approaching the backs of the Rebs at a right angle, now closing into an acute angle.

"Fire!" Winslow commanded as he advanced swinging his saber. Those rebels heard Winslow too late. By the time the Rebs did an about face, it was a fatal hesitation. The spray of Yankee bullets decimated the Rebel ranks. Relentlessly, the next wave of Yanks fired on the Rebels having telling affects. Winslow had lost several men, also. Ten days earlier at Fort Henry, the battle there had been a rout for the Yankees. In just over an hour the rebels had surrendered. Grant's terms were met which was unconditional surrender. With that recent victory behind them, it now added to the morale of Winslow's men.

The gunboats on the river were taking the brunt of the shells. A brigadier general appeared and joined the fight signaling Winslow and his men to follow. They followed the Confederates to the earthworks. What ensued was a surrender parlay with top Confederate generals and Union generals.

In the midst of the tentative surrender some aggressive Confederate soldiers noticed an opening in the Union lines. The Rebs quickly encroached on the weak spot but were denied entry by the even quicker reaction of the Yanks. Winslow had his men step lively and close the line like a cork in a bottle. The Confederates surrendered Fort Donelson in short order.

The scene of the carnage and destruction surpassed the ability of a man's senses to comprehend. The acrid smoke of gun powder mingled with the drizzle. There was a strong scent of fresh spilt blood. Grimly, Winslow surveyed the scene: dead soldiers, broken equipment, and debris.

As he was assessing the damage in the battlefield, he checked the outcome of his men and other Union soldiers nearby. The more common injuries were shots to the arms and shoulders. Winslow and Ezra came upon a man hit in the left forearm and was lying in the field.

"Hey soldier." Winslow greeted him softly. "What's your name?"

"Ed Richardson." He said weakly.

Winslow summoned the assistant surgeon, James Fox. The doctor began to work on Ed by putting a tourniquet just below the elbow. The tools of surgery were basic and crude. The doctor produced a saw and a bottle of whiskey. "Here soldier, take a long pull on the whiskey bottle. Where are you from? "

Ed winced from the whiskey. "I'm from the twelfth Illinois Infantry."

Dr. Fox waited a couple of minutes for the whiskey to take effect. "Bite on this piece of wood. I have to cut the forearm off. It's just too mangled." The doctor amputated right on the battlefield. Dr. Fox was solid and strong. He muscled the saw through flesh and bone swiftly as well as mentally forging through the screams of agony. In no time he had the stump neatly wrapped in bandages. The whole process took less than ten minutes.

Winslow turned away from the grizzly scene. He felt queasy and bone tired. He finished the head count and status of his men. Winslow and his command were intact that is to say all companies and officers were within bugle call. The wounded and dead had been gathered off the field and were duly accounted.

Wearily, Winslow mounted a flat-topped boulder. "Men, I am proud of you on this day. You have stayed well in rank and worked together. I am proud of the 26th Kansas Cavalry though we fought dismounted, we did well. We have won the battle at Fort Donelson. Presently, the terms of surrender are being negotiated. We have aided the wounded and they will be given shelter. That comes down to us able-bodied men. I don't know how able my body is any more. It's mighty stiff from sleeping out in the cold and wet last night." The men laughed at the truth for they also spent the night outdoors.

"Tonight, it will be the lap of luxury, a hot meal, a warm cot, in a tent." Winslow said emphatically with a big smile showing his dimples.

Winslow hopped down from the boulder. The men whose average age was barely twenty-one worked hard getting a field hospital in shape. There was a shortage of female nurses, so the lot fell to the invalid corps. These were men who had been injured in prior action, who had recuperated from amputations and other injuries but were no longer able to soldier.

A rather aged man, his face lined and haggard, was driving a two-horse ambulance. His passenger was Ed Richardson who just had his forearm amputated. There were tears in the old man's eyes. The drizzle had plastered his white hair to his head and his uniform was coated in mud.

"Why are you so upset, Dad?" One of the boys was heard to say.

The tears started to roll freely down the old man's face. In a tortured voice he said, "I would gladly have died for my son, Ed. But it was he who got hit." His eyes rested on Ed who was leaning forward resting his head on his knees.

The men all felt sorry for the old man and Ed. One soldier spoke for the rest. "We'll help you take your boy to the hospital and have someone watch over him, Dad." Many soldiers stepped forward and expedited the old man's son to the safety of the hospital shelter.

Pvt. Tompkins said, "Please tell us about yourself and your boy." The soldiers and old man were just outside the canvas field hospital.

The old man responded, "I am from Indiana. My boy, Ed and I live close to State Line City. We joined the army there and were put in the Twelfth Illinois Infantry. I have four grown sons, Ed is in company C. Aleck is in the Twenty-Second Ohio Infantry, Henry is in company D, Fifty-Seventh Indiana Infantry, and James is in the Sixth Indiana Cavalry.

Some of the soldiers built a fire and made coffee while the other soldiers unhitched the horses for the old man and tied them to a nearby tree. They settled around the fire placing the old man on a log with a blanket over his shoulders.

"I haven't heard from the other three boys since I joined up," He said sadly. "My name is Alexander Richardson. I entered the army for pure patriotism to serve the Union cause. A house divided cannot stand. I'm just an old man but as long as I pull breath, and this war is being fought, I will help, even if it's digging ditches. When I'm used up as God so choses, then I will rest in peace."

After those words from the old man, there was a solemn galvanizing silence for all who heard him. The spirit and passion of his speech captivated them. It was getting late and all the soldiers said good night to the old man and went their respective ways. Alexander tended his horses, and the men went back to the Twenty-Sixth Kansas Cavalry camp. The campfires were dying. The men were hard pressed to find more wood. Some took their sabers and chopped some small limbs off the trees.

"What a day!" Pvt. Tompkins said to Pvt. Jones as he hacked off some more tree limbs to feed the fire. "So many Union forces came to fight the battle that a horse can't wag his tail sideways. It is that crowded."

"That's good for the morale Tompkins. We have more dog in the fight. Anyway, we won't be here too much longer. I hear from the bugler that soon we'll be going to Mississippi and we might get the job of foraging. Lieutenant Colonel Winslow must have talked someone into that one, a Philadelphia lawyer without Philadelphia, ha, ha! Winslow is okay. He is right there in the thick of it. Remember today how we were after Johnny Reb and were doing alright too, and Winslow was shoulder to shoulder with us?"

"I won't ever forget it." Said Pvt. Tompkins solemnly.

The top officers had the surrender terms worked out. The captured equipment amounted to more than fifteen thousand rifles, many cannons, tents, and other non-weaponry equipment. Early the next morning the rifles were passed out to the burgeoning army.

The next morning the sky was clear, and the sun shown. Winslow came out of headquarters and mounted his horse and jogtrotted to his camp. He dismounted and told Ezra to call assembly. The men gathered.

"I have just come from headquarters. It is official. General Vale says we are to be a foraging party." Winslow spoke with purpose. "Men, I know we couldn't utilize our horses in battle yesterday because of the muddy conditions. Today is a better day, especially in the grassy meadows where we are to go to next. In our recent past together, we have not explored the potential of the horse to its fullest capacity in battle. We have used the horse as merely transportation. Of course, the muck and mud in our engagement here at Fort Donelson did not lend itself to the use of the horse. But when conditions are right, the horse has speed, and that speed will get us in and out of a situation quickly. Not only is he quick in battle, mounted on his back, your perspective is greatly increased. This is an overwhelming advantage over the average foot soldier. He is a weapon also, because you can mow the enemy down, trample them if need be. There are snipers who say men on horseback make a mighty fine target, but if we practice, we'll gain speed, maneuverability, and confidence. With full confidence in your horse and yourself, the snipers will be hard pressed to put a bead on you.

"In my youth I had a horse called Jubal. I trained him to do all sorts of tricks. He of course, has gone to greener pastures. So now I have brought Ben, my present horse, from Kansas. I will show you that there is even more you can train your horse to do. Watch fellas." Winslow mounted his horse and rode a ring around his men. He then stood up on the horse's back keeping perfect balance as he went around the men again. He then took a sitting position then slid off the saddle to the left with one foot in the stirrup on that side and his hand on the saddle's pommel so that he was out of view to the men as he rode around again going clockwise.

He dismounted. "Men, I hope that inspires you to go beyond field exercises with the horse which we are about to undertake. So now saddle up, mount up in full weaponry."

"I never seen any trick riding like that! I heard tell of it in the circus. Winslow kept that under his hat for quite a spell." Pvt. Jones marveled. The Twenty-Sixth Kansas Cavalry saddled up their horses. The men were mostly armed with rifles and sabers.

Winslow said, "It is time to practice! Mount up and follow me in rows ten abreast. Major Lester, follow up the rear.

They moved two to three miles from camp to a meadow. "Alright men, this is a fairly level spot to train." Winslow said. There were some trees and underbrush, but the men could see each other.

"Here is the lay out, men. There will be four hundred men in one row, in front of bugler Peabody, Major Lester, Lieutenant Vogel and myself. There will be two hundred men in one row behind us officers."

The men moved into formation. Winslow rode up and down the two lines of men and addressed them again. "I see twelve men who don't have sabers and I want to know why!" Captain Tobias spoke up. "Sir, we are in short supply."

"Duly noted, Captain." Winslow remarked.

Winslow eyed his men carefully. "Lieutenant Vogel, as of now you are in charge of munitions. Sergeant Morrison and Sergeant Larson will assist Lieutenant Vogel to stand guard over the munitions. We won't go into battle with excess lead and powder. Some of you men have your horses weighed down so that they would lag behind in a fight or retreat. Now give surplus munitions to the designated officers."

The men then handed Sergeant Morrison the excess powder and lead. They piled the surplus of lead and powder on a piece of canvass tenting. As the last man filed past the first sergeant, Winslow yelled. "Blow Charge, bugler!"

The men thought the real thing had come. Winslow held his saber high and said, "Charge!" Ezra and Major Lester were on his right side.

They all took off in a westerly direction away from the sun. Nearly six hundred men on horseback at full gallop was the sound of thunder. They galloped for a three mile stretch dodging trees, bushes, and finally a fence and entered in a clearing finally pulling their horses to a walk. On the far edge of the clearing was a farmhouse. A woman and her two children were out by the washtubs hanging wet clothing on a wooden fence. The men dismounted at the farmhouse covering Winslow with their rifles for any tricks.

Winslow went to the woman doing the washing. "Do you have any guns in the house, Ma'am?"

"I have a pistol my husband left me." She trembled in fear.

There was a first time for everything. This was Winslow's first in requisitioning arms from civilians. Winslow cleared his throat. "Ma'am, the Union army needs it for the war. I will give you a receipt for the pistol and you can redeem the receipt for Union money. Please go fetch the gun. Pvt. Angenlak, please accompany her."

When Pvt. Angenlak and the lady returned with the pistol, Winslow wrote a receipt for her. "That receipt is worth more than the pistol. Where is your husband?"

"He is around Nashville last I heard. He is in the Confederate Army." Her voice quaked.

Winslow smiled. "Just on the wrong side of the war. These are hard times. I sympathize with you and give you my word as a union soldier that we shall not distress you further or harm you or your children in any way."

This happened in the days before the army properly evaluated the opposing army's strength, unit numbers, regimental numbers, other similar details, and standardized reimbursements for different types of requisitioned weapons.

"Good day Ma'am." Winslow said as he mounted his horse. He made Ben bow to the lady and trotted back to the men.

Ezra, cued by a hand signal from Winslow, blew charge again with Winslow pointing his saber east. The men galloped back to the munitions pile. Under his breath Winslow said to himself, "A group of horses can get in better step than the men. Oh well we are cavalry; marching is for infantry. We are a work in progress."

As they were nearing the munitions, Winslow yelled, "Blow retreat!"

Ezra was dumbfounded but did as commanded. Ezra blew retreat twice so all could hear. The men stopped their horses and then turned them around a little slowly, but no one tripped his horse, observed Winslow. All got underway, not in step but in line.

"Blow charge!" Winslow shouted. Ezra complied. All the men started moving west and did so for five minutes.

"Retreat!" Winslow shouted and Ezra blew retreat. They soon arrived back at the munitions.

"Dismount and pick up your individual munitions." Ordered Winslow. "Men who don't have a pistol, will draw straws for the pistol I just requisitioned."

"Men, eventually I want all of you to have a pistol. I notice that many of you don't care to own one, even if given the opportunity. I must emphasize that it is for your protection. Most of you might not have holsters but you can put the pistol in an outside coat pocket or shove it into your belt. With our rifles in a common stack at night, that rifle isn't as handy as a pistol on your person. Now here is an example, say we are all sleeping at night and the guard dozed off too. The Rebs slip into camp to ambush us. Unarmed, all you can do is to yell a warning and scramble for the rifles, if they are still there. But if you had a pistol at the ready you could do two things at once, call the alarm and shoot. You must remember as a foraging party, we will be more on our own and must be more self-sufficient. Let's use our Yankee ingenuity. It's up to each one of us to stay alive to fight another day and end the Rebellion."

Winslow continued, "Since we are short of sabers, have they been ordered from the government?" He stared at Sgt. Morrison.

Sgt. Morrison responded. "Sir, all I know is the sergeant in charge of requisitions ran out of sabers. His hands are tied if he doesn't get the okay from his superior to order more."

"I understand the situation." Winslow stated flatly as he made a mental note to talk to Major Lester.

Winslow redirected his attention to the men. "How many of you men have carbines? To a man, all held up carbines. Some of the carbines had been rifles. Some of the men had cut off the barrels to standard length carbines. The cutting tools were left in the Fort Donelson workshop. "Most of you men know that carbines are the middle ground between a pistol and a rifle. The advantage of a carbine over a pistol is accuracy because you use your shoulder to anchor the stock while shooting. Also, there is less recoil as in a pistol. On a moving horse a carbine is best, pistols are good for surprise attacks, and rifles are great for long range shooting if you are infantry or a sniper."

"Blankets?"

Everyone had blankets. The soldiers all held up their blankets. They were not regulation, but they would do.

"Water canteens"?

All held up canteens but four men. Those men held up earthen ware jugs.

"Those are pretty cumbersome to tote with you. They'd serve better as a vase for flowers." Winslow joked. All the men easily laughed.

"Men you did well today in drills out in the field. We will continue to do drills in lag time. Since I witnessed what quick learners you are, I've decided we will go out on a scouting mission to the west of here. Depending on what we find, it could end up being foraging duty. Load up cap and balls, we may need them."

A mighty yip and yell went up from the men. Because they were already armed and with extra ammunition from the morning drill, they simply mounted their horses and followed Winslow in a slow cantor crossing brooks and going through thickets. They rode two hours west and came upon a well-maintained plantation. The grounds were a verdant green with cattle grazing in the adjacent meadow. The barnyard noise was a mix of oinks, honks, and clucks. The plantation was on the top of a knoll with magnolia trees surrounding it. A rectangular white fence surrounded the house, trees and lawn. There was a tall hedge that ran the entire perimeter of the interior side of the fence. It was picturesque.

On the outside of the fence at a quarter mile distance from the house and one hundred yards from the separately fenced barnyard, Winslow said, "Men, if this turns out more than we can handle, take back to camp. The bugler will blow retreat if need be. We will now check out the barnyard with a small search party." He motioned for Sgt. Morrison, Pvt. Angenlak, Pvt. Jones, Pvt. Peabody, Pvt. Tompkins, and Major Lester to accompany him.

They made it easily over the fence and into the barnyard which was empty of human activity. The quiet of the day seemed strangely brooding when out of the stillness was distinctly heard the sound of a mockingbird. With Winslow in the lead the men all followed his actions as he sidled up against the front of the barn approaching the barn door. They came upon four slaves who were cleaning the barn floor of manure.

Winslow covered them with his pistol. "Don't say a word." Barked Winslow.

The oldest of the four was an ancient, grizzled man who answered in a surprised high-pitched voice. "We ain't goin' to say a word atoll!" The others nodded in vigorous agreement.

"Who is at home in the big house?" Asked Winslow.

"Why Missy Jean Buford and her two little gals, General." Said the slave.

"Any gray coats around?" Continued Winslow.

"Ah ain't seed a one atoll. They's mighty scarce and dat's funny, cause this place used to have a lot ob dem too."

"How long ago?"

"Bout two months ago, General."

"I'm not a general. I'm a lieutenant Colonel." Winslow continued. "Just the lady and the two girls, eh? Does she have any guns?"

The old slave answered. "Yes, General, she has two dueling pistols, cause I done seed them."

Winslow, satisfied, said, "Well then, carry on with your task unless you'd like to work as cooks in the Union army."

The old slave responded, "No thanks, General, we all don't think we want to cook for you blue debbels. Den too, we don't like does bullets flyin' round. It's too noisy. We likes it peaceful."

"Indeed! Pvt. Jones and Pvt. Tompkins stay here until alerted otherwise."

The remainder of the search party left the barn and returned to the other soldiers on the outside fence. Winslow said, "Men, I will divide you into three groups. My group will be on the inside yard in order to gain entry to the back door of the house. The two other groups will flank the right and left, outside fence and quietly approach the house."

Winslow signaled for the men to dismount. Quietly, he divides his men into thirds. There was a wide gap in the hedge where they had dismounted so he motioned for a third of his men as well as his officers and himself, to go inside the fence. The remaining two groups of men spread out on both sides of the outside fence advancing toward the house close to the inside border hedge which hid them from view.

Winslow's group easily made it past the wash woman doing laundry in the wash house undetected. They slipped in the back door which opened to the hallway of the big house. It was not luxurious but large and comfortable. Pistols drawn and cocked, sabers held in hand to keep from banging, they continued. The sitting room was vacant with a fire ablaze to keep the winter chill at bay. The small crystal chandelier sparkled from the firelight. Except for a newspaper carelessly folded on a needlepoint stool, all was in its proper place.

A new daguerreotype of a man in Confederate military uniform, with what appeared to be his wife and two girls was the subject of the picture. The family picture seemed peaceful except that the military attire belied its very nature with the unspoken word of 'war'.

Quietly, they slipped out of the sitting room and into the dining room. There sat the lady of the house, intent upon writing a letter at a desk. The men with pistol drawn, covered the lady. "Be quiet lady!" Major Lester commanded.

"Oh!" She gasped as she whipped around to get a better look. She then gave a startled cry but muffled it with her hand as her eyes gazed upward then to the floor.

"You are thinking of your children, I see." Observed Winslow. "Sgt. Morrison, Pvt. Angenlak, go collect the two girls upstairs." Morrison and Angenlak headed upstairs.

"Pvt. Peabody, go outside and give the signal." Winslow commanded.

"Yes sir!" The bugler responded and left the house.

As Winslow and Lester heard the retreating footsteps, it fell silent. Suddenly, there were many footsteps outside the dining room window. Much to the incredulous displeasure of the lady, soldiers could be seen surrounding the house.

"A whole army!" The woman wailed. "And Cabot said no Yankee would get into Tennessee."

"So, your man's name is Cabot Buford and he's a general. Where is he?" Winslow asked.

The woman brushed soft blonde curls from her face and answered defiantly, "He is in New Madrid, Missouri, defending the cause."

"Do you have any arms in the place, Mrs. Buford?" Winslow asked flatly.

"No."

"Major Lester, take a few men from outside and search the house." Lester left the room collected some soldiers and began to search the premises.

Winslow smiled consolingly. "Mrs. Buford, you must be frightened."

After a moment to mull over his comment, she hesitatingly shared, "Yes, I am too scared to move. I am afraid for my children's welfare."

Winslow smiled again taking in her appearance. She was easy on the eyes, too easy. It had been a long time since he had seen such a pretty woman and with admirable maternal instincts. He bowed taking off his hat. "Mrs. Buford, no harm will come to you or your children. All we need are the guns."

"Yes, I have two dueling pistols, the only ones in the house."

"I suppose they are loaded for bear, in this case, a Yankee lieutenant colonel." He smiled wryly.

Major Lester reappeared, "Lieutenant Colonel, I've searched all the rooms but here. So far, no guns."

Winslow said to the woman, "You just point to where the guns are located, and we'll do the rest."

She pointed to the sideboard and Major Lester retrieved them from the top drawer.

Mrs. Buford watched as Major Lester opened the walnut case revealing vintage dueling pistols. She said wistfully, "Those are heirloom dueling pistols from my father who bought them in New Orleans. After he passed away, I inherited them. They've never been used since I have owned them."

Winslow stepped outside to reassure the men everything was going smoothly. He announced, "The lady has surrendered the pistols. Men search the premises for more goods. Come back when done."

Winslow went back into the house as the two little girls came down the winding stairs with Pvt. Angenlak and Sgt. Morrison behind them. The oldest girl was maybe eight years old asked, "Mommy, is this General Lee's army?"

"No, it isn't." Mrs. Buford said as she stood up then moved to place herself between Winslow and her daughters.

Winslow was pleasantly surprised by the closer proximity of Mrs. Buford. Reassuringly, he said, "We won't be here much longer, ma'am."

Mrs. Buford responded, "Thank you for that small kindness."

The little girls were tugging at their mother's dress. The oldest said, "I heard daddy say he was in General Lee's army. Then who are these soldiers, mommy?"

Winslow said, "We are in General Grant's army."

"Those dumb Yankees!" The girls shouted in unison.

Winslow was momentarily lost in Mrs. Buford's sky-blue eyes. Suddenly He got a hold of himself realizing much had to be accomplished. "I will give you a receipt for the goods received. We need beef cattle to make broth for invalids in hospital and also tobacco the men might find for chewing." He gave her the receipt and she tore it up.

"Suite yourself." Winslow said. "We will leave you enough stock for you to get by on."

Mrs. Buford's eyes followed Winslow as he and his officers left. Sadness traced itself on her face.

On compulsion, Winslow slipped back in, bowed at the waist, and kissed her hand. He stood up to his full height and said, "No matter what the circumstances that happened here today, it has been a pleasure doing business with you." Then he disappeared.

Mrs. Buford couldn't help but smile.

Both of Winslow and Mrs. Buford's behaviors were not lost on Major Lester as he jealously watched from outside the dining room window. He said to himself, "What a rake."

CHAPTER 4
Juliette's Sojourn to America

Six months had passed. The War Between the States was in full motion for Lieutenant James Lambert. He was in a fast-moving cavalry brigade. He was a busy man, busy making his boasts come true. It was a rude awakening for him that the Union troops were sticking together and slugging it out. Already, Fort Henry and Fort Donelson had fallen to "Unconditional Surrender Grant." At the moment, all the Confederate troops had abandoned Nashville, Lambert among them. The order to retreat did not set well in Lambert's mind.

Lambert was in a mess. He hadn't figured on the fortunes of war turning against him in such a way. His training at military school seemed like only play acting now that he was actively engaged in the war. He had seen his comrades fall in grisly detail. The news from the front was not good. New Orleans was about to fall to the Union. The ports up northwest had already fallen. But now a new concern, the North had a naval blockade all around the South's port of entry.

To get his mind off the current condition of the South, Lambert opened a dated letter that had been forwarded to him by his parents to his present location. The letter was about four months old.

Dear James,

Wednesday, October 2nd, 1861

Hello my dearest. I hope this letter arrives safely. I am posting it just before boarding the Tambeau. My parents had the good fortune to retire to the country to run a small inn. I don't have time or space in the letter to give details. Their future is settled in happy circumstances. Madame Simone Bernard is accompanying me as a chaperone. She is a dear and trusted friend and a great seamstress. I hope that you receive this letter so that you know that I am on my way. I must be patient but can hardly wait to see you.

Love,
Juliette

That letter was dated October 2nd. James wondered aloud, "Four months have passed. Where are you now, Juliette?"

It was a beautiful, early October day when Juliette and Madame Bernard boarded the Tambeau. There was a midmorning bustle of activity in the port city of La Havre. Men were loading ships with cargo for their respective destinations. Walking up the gangplank, Juliette and Madame Bernard were greeted by Captain Armand Belmont.

The women were oblivious to the Tambeau's cargo which consisted of gunpowder, weapons, cloth, and miscellaneous. All was much needed by the Confederate Army. The Tambeau was a narrow width schooner. She was 380 feet long, 20 feet wide, and had four masts. She was built for speed; sleek, fast, and silent. The ship was kept clean by an efficient crew. Nature kept the sails clean and white by rain and sun. The Tambeau had begun its journey west. It slid out of port and was in open water within the hour. The cool salt air blew in from the ocean through their cabin porthole invigorating Juliette with renewed energy after a long journey to La Havre. Juliette and Madame Bernard shared a cabin. There were two other passengers according to Captain Belmont, the rest were crew members.

Captain Armand Belmont was a clever and watchful seaman. He had to be, to remain alive and do his trading. These were dangerous times to be sailing the Atlantic Ocean. Before the United States was officially engaged in the Civil War, he had legally transported goods. He did have to dodge icebergs from time to time. When in iceberg waters he slept in the day and was on watch at night. Now he navigated the Southern Atlantic Ocean. He kept his routine because he no longer watched for icebergs, but Union gunships which were out looking for blockade runners like himself. The Tambeau had left port at noon. He was officially on alert.

After settling into their cabin that they would share, Juliette and Madame Bernard said a prayer to Saint Christopher for a safe journey. Madame Bernard was tired and then laid down for a nap. A heightened sense of excitement and the thought of adventure brought Juliette out on deck to watch the rapidly diminishing shoreline. She shifted her gaze to the open Atlantic and the gently rolling waves. She reviewed all that had transpired since James departure that late July day. It was so much in such little time.

After James had left, there was sadness yet hope. Hope for her future in America. She had many things to take care of before she would even consider leaving her aging parents. Two days after James had left, Monsieur Gastineau came in for his regular evening repast. Full of angst for her parents, Juliette sat down with him after he had eaten.

"Monsieur Gastineau, you are a good friend and have helped me so much. I have had the good fortune to meet a young man from America via the invitation to the Hotel De Ville that you gave me. I can't thank you enough for the invitation." She spoke pensively.

"My dear Juliette, you are most welcome, but you seem so preoccupied, not your bouncy, happy self." Gastineau observed.

"You are right," said Juliette. "I am concerned about my parents. I cannot leave them in their present circumstances of running a busy restaurant. My parents are older. I know they are past the age to travel long distances, let alone, to a country at war. Yet I am engaged to be married. It is such a dilemma! It hurts my head to think about it.

Monsieur Gastineau was silent for a while, gazing at Juliette's troubled face. "You know Juliette, life can be very strange. Sometimes our troubles or dilemmas can be turned into opportunities."

"How can that possibly be?" Juliette asked incredulously.

"I also have a dilemma. First, I must explain a bit about myself.

I was raised in a small village just outside of Rouen. My parents owned a small inn. My mother passed away several years ago. Recently my father passed away. I am an only child, so I inherited the inn. I was thinking of selling it because I wouldn't know how to run an inn, though I would much rather be outside of Paris breathing the country air. My dilemma is that I need trustworthy people to help me run the inn, otherwise, I am stuck here in Paris. If you follow me, there is a solution to both of our problems. Your parents could help me run the small inn and have a much-lightened workload. They could help me learn more about running the inn from their experience."

"Oh, Monsieur Gastineau! So, you would be willing to hire my parents to help run the inn?" She asked excitedly.

"Certainly! But here we are discussing them without seeing whether they agree or not." Gastineau smiled.

"You have a point." Juliette agreed. "At this very moment we will ask them." Juliette bolted from her chair, went to her parents and asked them to come to Monsieur Gastineau's table.

Michelle and Antoine sat down tentatively sensing something was in the air. It was at the same table where Michelle and Antoine first met Juliette. "Monsieur and Madame Bellechasse, I have a proposition to offer you. Not too long ago I inherited my father's inn in a small village

69

just outside of Rouen. I don't know the first thing about running a small inn. You are the only people I'd ever consider asking this, would you consider helping me run this inn? If you would, I could retire to the country with you and do the accounts or whatever else needs to be done." Gastineau finished waiting for their response.

Juliette spoke, "My dear parents. I love you both so much. I have more than enough money for my trip so I will give you half to help you move, if you chose to go. I pray that you do, because the country is ideal for both of you now that you are getting older. So much has happened in such a short period of time. I haven't had an opportunity to talk to you, but I know a voyage to America is difficult. I can't ask you to come with me. I would feel so guilty if anything happened to you."

Some tears trickled down Michelle's cheeks. A beautiful smile came to her face at the same time. "I love you too, Juliette, and I know Antoine does." Antoine nodded, his head downcast.

"We have been so blessed to have you and raise you as our own. You are a gift from heaven. Just as a beautiful butterfly lights on a flower then goes to the next flower so you too must go to spread the joy of life." Michelle wiped her eyes with her apron. "I am so proud to have you as a daughter. Yes, it is hard for you to leave us, but that is part of life. We must live our lives the best we can."

Michelle continued, "What do you think Antoine? A move to the country might be good for us."

Antoine looked up. "I have never shared my dream with you, Michelle. I have always wanted to live in the country. I am sad that dear Juliette must move so far away, but she must live her life as she sees fit. Who knows the future? Maybe she will come see us later on when things are more settled. In the meantime, it would be fun to go fishing and have goats to make cheese. Since Juliette wants to give us half the money, we can buy goats with some of it." Antoine smiled.

Monsieur Gastineau said, "I am so happy that you have decided to join me in the country!" He shrewdly added, "Juliette, I think I can help you in one additional way. Let me exchange the entire amount of your paper money into gold coinage. With the unsettled condition of America, it is most wise to have gold instead of paper money."

Juliette agreed, "Why of course, Monsieur Gastineau, you work for the government and are so wise in these matters. Thank you for the advice. I will get the money to you, tout de suite."

Juliette got up from the table and put herself between her parents and hugged them both with her eyes shut tight. "What did I do to deserve such wonderful parents?"

Then Juliette ran over to Monsieur Gastineau and gave him a big hug. "There are no words to tell you how thankful I am for what you have done, Monsieur Gastineau! You are a saint!" He blushed contentedly as she danced for joy.

The days went by in an amazing blur. Providence seemed to lift its lovely head at every turn. Madame Bernard was thrilled to be asked to chaperone Juliette to America. She was a widow without children and Juliette was like her child. Monsieur Gastineau retired from his government job and left one month later so he could move at the same time as the Bellechasses. Juliette was able to see the inn. It was quaint and lovely. There was a river nearby and a barn on the inn property which already housed two cows, two goats, and numerous chickens.

Besides missing her parents and Monsieur Gastineau, Juliette would miss Cure' Sevigny and his wonderful Sunday sermons. A few days before her departure from Paris, the Bellechasses went to mass at St. Francois d'Assisi Church where he pastored.

Father Sevigny began, "Today is the feast of the Archangels: Gabriel, Raphael, and Michael. These are the work horses of God as messenger, power source, and defender for all that is good. These angels, among many who are without name, are myriad. They are humble and doers of God's will. These archangels are the pillars of heaven, for through their humility is their strength. They do whatever God wants, when He wants, as He wants, and as long as He wants."

He continued, "Dear friends, the archangels are noble examples on how to embrace life and all the challenges and situations God allows us to encounter. If, with our free will, we seek always to do good, God will help us. If we are angry in whatever situation befalls us, and choose to do what is not good, to speed its resolution, that situation or similar circumstance will reoccur until you embrace the true path of goodness.

Father Sevigny smiled. "I know this to be true in my own life. I didn't want to be a priest in my youth, but God would put me in certain situations that would occur again and again until I finally discerned His will. I embraced it and became a priest. Now that I have surrendered to His will, I am content and more fulfilled in my life. I finally answered His call."

Looking out at the congregation, his gaze fell on Juliette. "God is a relentless and patient teacher until we learn the lesson. Our minds cannot fathom His omnipotence aided by His celestial assistants, the archangels."

After mass, her parents said their goodbyes to Cure' Sevigny. They walked back to Le Mouton Noire which had been purchased by the owners of the neighboring bakery. They would spend the night in their old rooms due to the new owner's kindness, then leave in the morning for the inn. Juliette lingered to speak with Cure' Sevigny.

"Father Sevigny, I will miss you so. Thank you for all that you've done for me in my life. There are no words of appreciation that would be adequate for all that you've done for me throughout the years." Juliette's eyes welled up with tears of gratitude.

"My dear Juliette, I only do, by God's grace what He wants." He smiled wryly as it echoed his sermon.

Changing the subject, Father Sevigny said, "I am thankful you wished to talk to me. It reminded me of something I must give you. I have a package for you in the parish office." Both of them went to the parish office. Father Sevigny motioned for her to sit. He went to a dusty cupboard and produced a package wrapped in brown paper.

"On the night your mother, Teresa Sidamo, died, I found this package in the corner of her garret apartment. It was addressed to you, to be opened on your twenty-first birthday. Since you are leaving France, it is my last opportunity to give it to you. I would advise you to open it in calmer circumstances. Perhaps when you have time during the journey at sea." Father Sevigny said.

"Thank you so much!" Juliette was touched that her dying birth mother had the kind forethought to prepare a package for her. She gave Father Sevigny a lingering hug. She then picked up her package and left.

The next day Michelle, Antoine, Juliette, and Madame Bernard took the train north. They would stop at Rouen and say goodbye to Michelle and Antoine. Then they would continue to La Havre.

Juliette's inward gaze came back to the vision of the gray undulating waves of the Atlantic then shifted to a gentleman clearing his throat noisily. "That salt air is very healthy for a person," said the balding stocky man in his fifties.

Juliette was in good spirits. "I agree. It is also refreshing."

"I should introduce myself since we will be on this schooner for a month or more. My name is Clayton Armstrong. What's your name Missy?"

"I am Juliette Bellechasse. Enchanted to meet you." She offered her hand.

Mr. Armstrong firmly shook it. "Glad to meet you. Now I have someone to chat with besides my business partner."

Juliette smiled at Mr. Armstrong and noticed his neatly trimmed beard and tidy appearance. At the same time, he noticed how young and beautiful she was as her black tresses flowed in the breeze. "So, Juliette, what brings you on a sojourn to America during this time of war?" Armstrong was direct.

"It is love. I am engaged to James Lambert." She smiled sweetly.

"Don't mean to discourage you but it seems that this war is in dead earnest and if your fiancé' is between the ages of sixteen to sixty, he is in battle somewhere."

"Yes, I feared that, but knew it in my heart. I will just wait for him at his parent's plantation." She sighed resignedly.

"Your show of patience is only outmatched by your charms."

Blushing at the flowery compliment only enhanced her beauty. She said, "You sing apple too well."

At that moment another man in his fifties came on deck. He said, "There you are, Armstrong, up to no good, I see."

"Paxton, my good man, are you settled in then?" Armstrong, flustered, switched subjects.

"I'm as settled as I'll ever be on this moving target!" Paxton exclaimed

"Target?" Juliette asked. "We are a target out in this big ocean? Whose target?"

Both men looked incredulous at one another, then at Juliette. "Why Missy, those Yankees are out on the high seas to stop any supplies that might get to the South. Didn't you know that the Tambeau is a blockade runner? That means we have to outrun the Yanks, sink, or be captured."

Armstrong further ventured. "What was your fiancé thinking putting you in a potentially dangerous situation?"

"Incroyable! "Juliette gasped, clutching her throat. "I thought the war was over in America on dry land!"

Laughing until they bent over slapping the railing triggered by her surprised naivety, the men went into a crescendo of whistles, wheezes and snorts. Finally, they pulled out their handkerchiefs to wipe away the tears of merriment at her expense.

Juliette stared at them her mouth agape by the startling news.

Paxton was the first to recover. "Now don't you worry your pretty little head about this. We are on a fast schooner with an excellent captain. Belmont is a wily fox. I've been a passenger of his before. He is a skillful seaman. He has kinfolk in New Orleans."

Juliette regained her composure. "I am so much in love that nothing matters. Just getting to my destination and finally into the arms of James, is all that matters to me."

Mr. Paxton said, "My dear, you are indeed in love. I hope you will reach your lover's arms safe and sound." His mustache quivered with emotion.

"Mr. Paxton, thank you for your kind sentiments." Juliette warmed to Paxton. "You know, you must have been very handsome in your day. You have the clearest blue eyes and the cutest little mustache. I like to watch it wiggle when you speak."

Paxton, completely befuddled, reddened noticeably. "Ah, thank you, Miss?"

"I am Juliette Bellechasse, Mr. Paxton."

"You can call me Beamus."

"Delighted to meet you Beamus."

Armstrong glowered since the focus had shifted away from him.

Juliette said, "It seems I have so much to learn about America, especially plantations, since I might be living in one soon."

Armstrong cut in. "Well Missy, I can expound on plantations over dinner. That should be served in one hour. We all might as well rest up for a spell."

"C'est une bonne idea." Juliette said then walked toward her cabin. The men headed toward their cabin.

Juliette arrived at her cabin and changed from her gray wool traveling clothes to a petal pink satin dress with a high, cream lace collar and cream lace cuffs that covered her wrists. The collar emphasized her slender neck. The huge skirt flowed and rippled over the hoop skirt beneath. Madame Bernard had shown Juliette how to manipulate it so as to sit discreetly. Juliette had become adept at managing the hoop skirt. In fact, her agility and grace entwined with the physics choreographed into a graceful dance that was a delight to observe.

Madame Bernard awoke from her nap. She watched Juliette flounce about in pink satin. "Juliette, I am so happy your dress fits you so well."

"You should be happy. All the dresses you made or altered fit perfectly. I'm so happy to have you as a doubly talented lady in sewing and chaperoning." Juliette sat on Madame Bernard's bed and gave her a hug.

"I don't know how wonderful a chaperone I am. I was sleeping on the job just now."

"I did go on deck and had an interesting visit with our travelling companions." Juliette cryptically volunteered. She didn't want to make Madame Bernard anxious about the Tambeau being a target.

"Really? And what was the topic?" asked Madame Bernard as she rose to her five feet of height. She was pleasantly plump with her henna hair swept into an up do. She wore a nicely tailored Kelly-green wool dress. She was an attractive woman in her mid-forties.

"Oh, that it would take a month or more to reach our destination." Juliette was looking in a hand mirror trying to redirect an unruly curl, not making eye contact.

"A month or more, we can do it. Just take it one day at a time," Madame Bernard set her jaw in determination as her periwinkle eyes sparkled with excitement.

"That's the spirit!" Juliette smiled.

Madame Bernard rifled through Juliette's trunk and found an ostrich fan dyed pink. "When I worked for the theater making costumes, I also made props and accessories. A fan is both a prop and an accessory. As a prop, it can hide and reveal your face as required. It is a useful accessory to add drama to fashion and to actually cool your face or keep bugs from your person." Her face revealed a wise smile. "A tip, my dear, do not reveal too much about yourself. Draw the other person out in conversation. Be a listener. It is a worthwhile art to be mastered. You have the capability."

With that, they went to dinner. The ship had a small dining room. The entire ship was constructed of oak which creaked and groaned with the wind and ocean waves. They were the last to enter the dining room. The others at table were Mr. Armstrong, Mr. Paxton, and Captain Belmont. The men stood politely as the women entered. Captain Belmont motioned them to their seats.

Captain Belmont said to all, "Please sit down." He was spare with light brown hair, in his fifties, His bronzed, leathery face formed a smile revealing even white teeth. He said, "Bienvenue, Madame et Mademoiselle."

Juliette and Madame Bernard flanked the Captain, while Paxton and Armstrong were at the other end of the table facing each other. Armstrong was next to Juliette and Paxton was beside Madame Bernard.

One of the crew entered from the galley kitchen and poured wine for all. Captain Belmont said, "I would like all of you to know that this voyage ideally will take four to five weeks. It could last a bit longer if we encounter Union ships. It is my third voyage since the war started and there are more ships on the lookout for us blockade runners than when the war started. During the past three voyages I was only shot at one time. The cannon ball completely missed the Tambeau."

At this, Madame Bernard lifted her eyebrows, and her lips became a thin line. She gave a significant glance to Juliette.

The look did not escape Captain Belmont. He continued, "To reassure you, I have a top-notch crew that I completely trust. There is always one of us up in the crow's nest checking for enemy ships day and night."

Mr. Armstrong cleared his throat, importantly. Thank you, Captain Belmont. Miss Juliette, would you introduce us to your lovely travelling companion?"

"Certainly. I am pleased to introduce to you, my dear friend and chaperone, Madame Bernard." Juliette then spoke in French to Madame Bernard to explain who all the men were. Madame Bernard could speak tolerable English because of Juliette's inclusive need to practice English with her, but she appreciated Juliette's gesture. Madame Bernard nodded politely and said, "Enchantez to all of you."

Armstrong harrumphed noisily as he leaned in toward Juliette. "Permit me to describe our gorgeous plantations in response to the curiosity you voiced on deck earlier."

Juliette smiled as a signal to continue.

"Most plantations have colonial architecture. That is pillars out on the veranda or all across the front portico. A lantern is usually suspended over the front entrance. Most of the lanterns are imported from Europe. The large front door opens, and a staircase greets you to the right. The hallway is to the left. The floors are hardwood, sometimes teak, but mostly polished oak. A banquet or party hall is usually further right, sometimes it is left or even upstairs. The banquet hall usually has twelve chandeliers, depending on the cotton crop." Armstrong smiled knowingly.

He continued, "The doorknobs are hammered silver. The kitchen is in a separate building apart from the main house. Otherwise, it would be too hot for the owners. The slaves do the cooking. The slaves also make clothes from the fine cloth imported from Europe."

When Juliette heard the word 'slave', she picked up her pink ostrich feather fan, opened it and brought it up to her face to hide. A sickening knot was forming in her stomach. She gained enough composure to smile weakly and ask, "What do you mean by slaves? Is a slave someone who is a paid servant?"

"Miss Juliette! We don't pay slaves. We buy them, then own them lock, stock and barrel. Once they are ours, we do whatever we want with them. Whether it is to do house chores, sew, cook, wet nurse, or pick cotton. Plus, there are many other things they do which I won't bore you with the details." Armstrong slyly added.

Behind her fluttering fan, Juliette's face became ashen. "How do people obtain these slaves?"

"Years ago, we would buy them from slave ships. The government put the lid on that in 1804. We still would get some slave ships from Africa, but it was risky since it was illegal. It was easier to just breed them and sell the whelps or we can use them as extra labor."

Juliette became very quiet. She was reeling from the shock of Armstrong's nonchalant description of human beings as commodities.

Armstrong assumed the silence was encouragement for continuing. "Some of these niggers have it better than us. They drive their masters around in carriages imported from Europe. Why Miss Juliette, that is what this war is about. We are trying to preserve our culture and these northern scoundrels are stepping on our toes." Armstrong said with a loud emphasis.

Juliette felt nauseous. She scanned the dinner guests faces, finally resting on Madame Bernard. Madame Bernard spoke with her eyes repeatedly glancing at the door. Juliette stood up and grabbed her stomach and said, "Please excuse me. I am a bit seasick. I think I will go to my cabin and rest. Please stay, Madame Bernard. Enjoy the dinner." Madame remained for dinner.

Once in her cabin, Juliette laid down and reviewed the two shocking revelations of the day: the Tambeau was a target for Yankee gun boats, and slavery was the main reason the South was at war. Juliette's mind whirled in circles seeking a rationale of why she was so surprised, deceived, fooled. She was seeing James in a new light. The pit of her stomach contracted into pain. It wasn't seasickness. It was revulsion.

CHAPTER 5
A Spy is captured

Lieutenant Colonel Frank Winslow was sitting in his tent headquarters with Major Lester, Reverend Blake, Captains Tobias, and Bell. The March weather was still chilly and made them relish their hot cup of morning coffee.

Captain Tobias said, "Slow and steady we are making progress. The Rebs abandoned New Madrid, Missouri. That left it open for the union to take Island Number Ten."

"It's good for the men's moral, anyhow." Bell added.

Outside the tent the officers heard muffled voices. They became louder. The flap of the tent opened. "Corporal McGinnis reporting, Sir. We caught a fellow sneaking through our lines. He might be a spy. One of the men saw him making his way around camp and Private Strands ran out and grabbed him."

Winslow made his way to the tent opening. He surmised that fifteen of his soldiers had this unfortunate person well-collared. "Have you searched him?"

"No." The men said in unison.

"Search him." Winslow commanded.

The poor fellow was stripped bare in the chill of March 1862. It was brief. McGinnis said, "We found a letter on him, Lt. Colonel."

Winslow moved closer to the captured man. "I'll question him. Where are you from?"

"Alabama."

"Where are you going?"

"Rock Island, Illinois."

"Why?"

"I'm going to see my aunt in Rock Island. My parents are both dead and the work in the south has played out. I worked all around the Gulf and inland selling paintings. There are no sales for paintings now." The man appeared wan and thin from many missed meals.

The men gave the letter found on the unfortunate man to Winslow. It was dated April of 1861. It was frayed and worn. The general contents were for the nephew to come home and get out of trouble. The name of the man was Loyd Malland.

"Well, now that you know what side you want to be on, we will take care of you. Sgt. Morrison you have another recruit to put on roll call!" Winslow said loudly to make sure Morrison heard him.

The young man's face seemed more content. Winslow extended his hand, "Private Loyd Malland, welcome to the Union Army."

He was put in Company L. The men were all sympathetic to the emaciated young Malland. In an unspoken consensus, they led him to the mess tent. Sergeant Morrison went in and came out with a dry mud ball.

"Here is some chicken baked in mud." Said Sergeant Morrison. "You look half starved. Crack it open and start eating!"

At Sgt. Morrison's invitation Pvt. Malland sat on his haunches and broke open the mud ball and devoured the whole chicken, saving the bones. Morrison was fascinated by Malland's starved condition. His fellow soldiers, including the sergeant, had not missed a meal. They all had been eating as a force of habit. And now, along comes a fellow and shows them the art of eating. The back and wings were usually discarded, but Malland patiently finessed every morsel of flesh from the tiny bones. What he couldn't retrieve with his fingers and teeth, he sucked off the bones.

About ten solders watched Malland, fascinated by his meticulous cleaning of the bones. After he had finished with the chicken back, all the men examined it, admiringly. One said, "Nary a speck of flesh." The other men nodded in solemn affirmation.

Meanwhile, some of the other soldiers found a coat and pants, but no cap. Pvt. Malland would have to go around hatless for a spell. The men went with him to pick out a horse. He picked out one that was unruly. The men cornered the chosen bay horse in the make-shift corral while Malland saddled and mounted him. The horse jumped around briskly but Malland stayed in the saddle.

Sgt. Morrison said to Malland, "You'll do Billy, otherwise you'll be a foot soldier. Ride around camp and get used to that horse."

Pvt. Malland waved his hand and off he went around camp. He was greatly enjoying himself. As he rode through the nearby woods, he saw cattle and pigs in a corral. "No wonder the Union Army eats so good!" He exclaimed.

The horse had calmed down considerably. Malland was an excellent horseman. The horse picked up on the confident rider. Both horse and man united in purpose and action. He was on the outside perimeter of camp, so he turned his horse down a lane lined with trees. Also, brush grew alongside the fences on both sides of the lane. Malland decided to go back to camp. He pulled gently on the reins and noticed a black splotch on the reddish-brown bay's neck. "Darkstar will be your name." He patted the horse affectionately on the neck.

Suddenly, a horse and its rider came out of nowhere. They were going at breakneck speed and bearing down on Malland. He put up his hand to signal the man to stop.

"Out of my way!" Yelled the stranger gruffly.

Pvt. Malland let him pass. The horseman's behavior seemed suspicious, so he got alongside of the stranger and rode with him, forcefully guiding him with Darkstar. The camp was to the left of the two horsemen and Pvt. Malland kept to the right of the galloping stranger. The unknown horseman was headed straight to the Union Camp. Too late, the stranger realized his grave predicament. Malland yelled, "Stop this man!"

Corporal Keller of Company C had a derringer confiscated from Ft. Donelson. He drew it from his pocket since he was in closest proximity to the stranger and fired it into the air. It frightened the stranger's horse enough to throw the rider to the ground. The men seized the stranger and held him.

"I wonder if it's another recruit." One of the men said.

"He sure was in a hurry to join our army." It was one of the many good-natured remarks to be heard.

"We'll hold this fellow here till the key man investigates." Said another.

Second Lt. Johnson said, "Detain him men. I will get the Lt. Colonel."

"Yes sir." Said the men in unison.

Johnson went into Winslow's tent and said, "Colonel, we have another man like this morning, only this time he is on horseback."

"I'll be right out Lieutenant." Getting up from his cot, Winslow went to the tent flap and surveyed the scene. The man in question was detained about fifty yards from Winslow. Winslow walked over to the man and said, "Search him."

In a few moments Sgt. Morrison said, "I found some papers in his hat. Here." He handed the papers to Winslow.

There were four narrow slips of paper that had been hidden in the inside hat band. The papers were small but contained a wealth of information; General Adams's command, 3,200 men infantry, General Vale, 1,250 men infantry, General Sexton 500 men and 24 cannons artillery, General Briles, 3,350 men infantry.

Winslow said, "I did see General Sexton two days ago when he was riding by and I did count twenty-four cannons in all."

Winslow demanded, "What's your name?" Intransigent, the stranger coldly stared at him giving no response.

Winslow said to Sgt. Dillon, "Go get General Vale." Vale was the unit's superior officer. Vale was three miles away at Colonel Melton's Camp.

Sgt. Dillon had his horse saddled up and was off like a streak. Not long after, he and General Vale were back.

"General Vale, we have caught a spy. He won't divulge his name. He isn't an ordinary spy, either. He has four outfit numbers totaling 8,300 men in all. Even the number of cannons are listed." Winslow stated flatly.

"I see you have some alert men in your outfit." Said General Vale.

Sgt. Morrison said, "It was a brand-new recruit, Pvt. Malland. He was trying out a horse around camp and suddenly came back at breakneck speed, forcing the spy into camp and yelled for us to stop him."

General Vale was examining the papers. "He sure has our figures correct, down to the last man, not counting stragglers."

"I wonder how he lists our stragglers. We don't even know ourselves what the effective strength is to the last man." Said General Vale almost smiling.

"How do you list stragglers?" General Vale pointedly asked the spy

The sergeant let the spy have his clothes back minus the information. "I count them in the camp that's how."

"What's your name?" Asked General Vale.

"I don't care to give it to a Yankee dog!" The spy barked.

"Come, come, now. Maybe I could get you off the fire. How many men does the Confederates have in the Trans-Mississippi region?" General Vale asked.

"I'll NEVER tell you!" Sputtered the spy.

"You look like an educated man. You talk like one. I could spare your life for information. We have so little, just general estimates. For example, one southern cavalry leader is near here one day, then the next day he is fifty miles distance. I couldn't do that, let alone, get the 1200-man unit fifty miles distant." Explained General Vale.

"He's just a better man than you!" Hissed the spy.

A resigned sigh escaped from General Vale. "As far as I am concerned, you just had your trial. But military justice prevails."

Meanwhile, Pvt. Malland, after hitching his horse had come closer to the unfolding of General Vale interrogating the spy. He was quietly standing there listening when several of the soldiers including Pvt. Angenlak, moved closer and patted him on the back in appreciation of getting the spy forced into camp.

In a deep voice, which seemed to come from somewhere else, "It's not on the size of the army that victory rests, but on the strength that comes from heaven."

The men looked around and realized Malland had spoken.

"Sorry, General. I was thinking aloud." Pvt. Malland apologized.

General Vale gave Malland a wry smile of acknowledgement. He turned back to the spy. "Three general officers will sit in on your trial in front of Lt. Colonel Winslow's tent in one hour. Colonel, get the message to Generals Adams and Briles."

Winslow sent Sgt. Dillon to the generals. Within the hour the trial commenced. The men gathered around the tent and were cautioned by the captain of Company C to remain silent while the trial proceeded. The spy stood his ground, cool, calm, and collected.

"We are now in session. The duly authorized officers in this military command will try the case now." Ordered General Vale.

"I give myself in the name of the Confederate States of America."

"I caution you to spare yourself and help our side." Advised General Vale. The spy stared at General Vale as though he were turning a few things over in his mind.

General Vale's tired blue eyes roamed upward; a full head of ash blond hair feathered out beneath his hat. His figure was gaunt, and his face was lined with the anxieties of war, too many lines for being only forty.

"No! Never!" The spy shouted.

Winslow commanded, "Call Sgt. Morrison."

Sgt. Morrison stepped up. "Here sir."

"Sgt. Morrison, did you take these papers from the stranger's hat?" Asked General Vale.

"Yes sir."

"Did you read it, sergeant?"

"Yes sir. I read the papers which indicated several generals and strength of numbers were listed on them: General Vale, General Sexton, and General Briles. I noticed in particular our own outfit's strength is on paper. It's sort of funny to me. That means we are beginning to get on the enemy's nerves."

General Vale continued with the next witness. "Pvt. Angenlak, did you see the said papers and numbers on them?"

"Why yes sir." Said Pvt. Angenlak.

"That is all Pvt. Angenlak."

General Vale ran his hands over his eyes as if to ease the strain of his thoughts. "All the witnesses have been heard. Have you anything to say stranger?" The stranger shook his head.

"I don't' know your name but you have been treated in a military manner. You have been offered safety by divulging the Confederate's strength. You refused. By your actions you have condemned yourself. I pronounce you to be shot at sunup tomorrow by firing squad."

There was a hushed silence after General Vale pronounced execution. Most of the soldiers lowered their eyes. The impact of the trial seemed to impress the men of the deadly consequences of the spy's choice. Implicit with the sentence was that some of the soldiers were required to be on the firing squad. It had a sobering effect on all present.

The spy had information on 8,300 men and the harm he could do to them was appraised in a new light. It was clear by the spy withholding his name, he would go down on the glory list for the cause of the

South. His appointment would never be made, but by his absence the Confederates would know he had been caught. The sobering effect of the trial cast a subduing pall on the camp. It made it clear to a man it was not a romp in the woods. It was life, death, victory, or defeat.

The prisoner was placed in a guarded tent by Sgt. Morrison. The Sgt. asked, "Would you care to see Reverend Blake?"

"Well, Yes I do." He said. "That's about all there is left."

The guard called the Corporal of the Guard. He in turn called Sergeant of the Guard, and the officer of the day, Lt. Glasser. Glasser went to Winslow and asked if the spy could have Reverend Blake visit.

"Yes" said Winslow. "I'm sure Reverend Blake would like to spend time with him."

When notified, Reverend Blake consented and went promptly to the tent of the prisoner. "Hello, I am Reverend Blake from Topeka, Kansas. I am a Baptist minister. What's your name and home state?"

"I can't give my name, but I am from Louisiana. I used to go to church when I was a boy." The spy said mechanically. His skin was pale next to his dark brown hair and his eyes were black as obsidian; all light seemed reflected, not absorbed by his pupils.

"I see you come from a church going family," Black observed. "I ride with the boys in every skirmish and if a bullet finds me, I am ready. I do love life but if earthly time ends, then eternal time begins. If I do God's will and ask daily for forgiveness, then every day is my best last day. It can only be my best last day if I always forget, forgive and love."

"I am ready too, but I have a purpose and a cause." Responded the spy.

"We all have a purpose and a cause. You will know if it is a good cause by the inner peace that comes from it. If it is a cause that comes from power and greed, there is no inner peace. God loves us and is merciful.

Even if your last thought is sorrow for your sins and you simply think, Jesus, please forgive me. You will be in paradise, in His loving arms."

"Would you like to pray with me, stranger?" Invited Reverend Blake.

"No, no… I don't care for that." Responded the spy in an uncertain voice.

"I see. I will leave you now. It's late. We will be up early, you and I."

Reverend Blake left the prisoner's tent and went back to Winslow's tent. All were under great strain. Major Lester, Captain Bell, and Captain Tobias. Captain Bell was the Provost Marshall at this time. He has been on the Syracuse, New York, Police Department and had asked Winslow for the Provost Marshall Job. Winslow had readily agreed since he had been trained in police work. A Provost Marshall is one who is officer over the guards and the officer of the day. He also guards the camp. He has the responsibility of prisoners who have been penalized for infraction of rules, their custody, and for detaining prisoners of war. In other words, the Provost Marshall is the Chief of Police in an army camp.

"How am I to pick the firing squad, Colonel?" Asked Captain Bell. "This is getting rough. I never had to execute anyone on the police force in Syracuse.

Winslow's auburn waves were rumpled as though he had been running his hands through his hair many times. He was distressed because coldly killing a man bothered him to the core…unless neck and neck battle. "Why don't you draw straws: twelve companies, twelve straws. The shortest straw means that company is on the firing squad."

"I never would have ventured that I would have to deal with a spy let alone, have him executed." Said Winslow.

Winslow appeared weary and haggard as he said, "Let's turn in men."

They all said good night and Captain Bell and fellow officers went to their respective tents.

The next morning many men were up before dawn. Low hills edged the eastern sky where clouds shrouded the hilltops, cloaking the sun behind them. It seemed as if the clouds were delaying the sun's appearance. A deception to the eye but not time. The bugler owned a pocket watch and blew the reveille at precisely 5:30 then all were up.

Soon the men had the campfires going. They fixed sow belly and beans with hardtack and coffee. One of the soldiers, Pvt. Angenlak, had a ham tied up in a tree. Feeling the condemned man needed a fine last meal, he cooked the small ham over an open spit doing a fine job. Pvt. Angenlak went to the prisoner's tent with the spy's last meal' roasted ham, hardtack and coffee.

The prisoner nodded to Pvt. Angenlak as he accepted the meal. He noted absently, as he sipped the last of his coffee, the hills smudged with scrub against a heavily clouded sky. The sharp silhouette of the black hills cut into the gray clouds like the knuckles of a clenched fist. Suddenly, the sun broke through, skimming the clouds with rose and mauve splashes of light.

Some of the men had salvaged some boards from the river and had fashioned a coffin. A team and wagon had been secured by some scrounging. The team of horses was from the Union Army, the wagon, Confederate. The boards for the coffin were of unknown origin, but Union workmanship.

It was now 6:30. The time had slipped by too fast for the Provost Marshall. The prisoner had eaten and was joined by Reverend Blake. All of the twelve companies had drawn straws. Company L had drawn the shortest straw and thus was selected for the job of execution. Pvt. Malland, who was recruited the morning before, helped to catch the spy, was put in Company L, was now part of the firing squad. The Generals were all at the place of execution, a bare tree up on the flat top of a hill. Provost Marshall Bell brought the prisoner to the tree and blindfolded him. Dr. Parker stood by at the ready.

The spy was wearing a brown suit, not on the conservative side, more like a dandy. His head was tilted upward, as his heavy brown hair shifted in the breeze. His face was waxen as though death were already present. He bit his lower lip and swallowed hard.

Reverend Blake was with the stranger to the last. Reverend Blake began to pray the Lord's Prayer. The prisoner's voice joined in at, "forgive us our trespasses as we forgive those who trespass against us." They ended it together.

True to military form, Captain Bell read the execution, "You have been found guilty by duly constituted officers of spying for the enemy. Have you anything to say before the execution?"

"I die nobly for the cause I believe in. By my absence they will know I have met a superior military force. That is all."

"Ready! Aim! Fire!" Shouted Lt. Deerfield who was in command of the rifle detail. The rifles barked and the prisoner crumpled into a heap.

Dr. Parker walked over to the body and checked his pulse. He softly said, "He is finished."

The men retrieved the coffin from the wagon and laid the deceased in it. They nailed down the lid with boards that had been prearranged, nailed and sawed to size. Some men had shovels and started digging the ground near the tree where the execution took place. More men helped with the task than was needed. It took their minds off the scene of death. With ropes they gently lowered the coffin into the grave.

The men gathered as Reverend Blake said a final prayer for the deceased, "The just and unjust die the same. Lord have mercy on this poor departed soul." All the men bowed their heads in a moment of silence.

Malland who was dazed by the landslide of events heard Winslow say to no one in particular. "Seems so pointless for the stranger to choose death… And for what? To Champion the vile, dehumanizing institution of slavery? Pride darkens reason and intellect." He shook his head.

Soon the sun was up above the hills. The clouds had disappeared. The tree under which the stranger was buried waved its budding branches in a southwesterly breeze, holding the promise of spring.

CHAPTER 6
Juliette's Package

Juliette's nausea had subsided. Her mind whirled down convoluted paths desperate to assimilate what had transpired on the voyage so far. She thought by stating the shocking facts aloud they would diminish into a more mundane, manageable appearance. She said to herself in her most blasé tone, "We are targets of Yankee gunships because we are aboard a blockade runner. The South went to war to defend slavery. James Lambert went to war to defend slavery. I am his fiancé."

She still felt queasy. Try as she would with many repetitions, it still was shocking. Her composure was slowly returning. Still, she couldn't go back to dinner and face everyone. She began to tidy her trunk to get her mind off her worries. Juliette came upon the package from her birth mother that Father Sevigny had kept for her for so many years.

She caressed the package, which was wrapped so lovingly, with perfect creases and tight twine ending in a bow on top. She visualized her mother taking painstaking, yet loving steps, to complete one of the last tasks for her daughter before she died. She encompassed it with her arms and laid her head on it. She felt her deceased mother's love with all her human senses, the crackle of paper, the dusty smell, and the tension of the twine.

She opened it slowly, savoring the anticipation of discovery. The first item she laid eyes on was a bold colored dress with black, red, and yellow stripes. It was simply sewn with a round neckline, no sleeves, and loosely gathered at the waist. The dress was wrapped around a daguerreotype of a beautiful, dark skinned woman. The woman in the photo was about eighteen years of age. Her hair was skeined back from her face. There was a cluster of three white roses behind one ear. She had beautiful bone structure and full lips. Incongruous to her features, were how pale her irises were in the black and white picture. On the back was written, Teresa Sidamo, 1840.

Underneath the photograph was what appeared to be a letter addressed to Juliette. She opened it and began to read:

Dearest Juliette,

April 9th, 1842

The saddest and happiest day of my life was the day you were born. Sad, because you had been born to a poor woman who had been a slave, concubine, prostitute, and finally a seamstress. Happy, because the good Lord had blessed me with the miracle of life; you my dear Juliette. If you are reading this letter you must be twenty-one and I am with sweet Jesus.

If I had not known Father Sevigny, I would have been a prostitute until the end. The hand of God directed me to the local Catholic Church where Father Sevigny helped me redirect my life. He helped me to receive training as a seamstress at a nearby convent.

Most children would like to know about their relatives, siblings, aunts, uncles, and grandparents. I think you would like to know also. Of course, I am your closest relative, your mother. I was born in 1822 in a coastal area of Algeria. Unofficially, there had been French people living there for decades. My mother's name was Daheera, your grandma. She was a slave and concubine to a Monsieur Alain du lac.

He was your grandpa. Your grandma, Daheera was not pure black. Her mother's name was Kitha. Kitha, your great-grandma was pure black. She was sold by her own parents who were Abyssinian and lived in the

Sudan region. They sold Kitha as tribute to another black tribe. That tribe sold Kitha to Arab slave traders. For a while, Kitha, your great-grandma, worked in a prominent Arab household in Algiers. You might know that this was the time of Napoleon. He had a large army with many soldiers who went to different countries such as Algeria. He would establish colonies of French people. It encouraged more to migrate to Algeria. The Arab owners offered Kitha to a French businessman as a gift. I do not know who your great-grandpa was. All I know is that he was a businessman. Kitha worked in his home and had my mother Daheera. I remember my mother and grandmother as kind, gentle and loving women.

I was born to Daheera and Alain du Lac in February of 1822. Later, when I was older, I was told by my mother that she kept her pregnancy secret as long as she could. She explained it was to safeguard my birth. She was successful till the sixth month. Then it was certain that she could keep me.

I was raised in more fortunate circumstances than most slaves. I was taught to read and write in French. In 1830 the French officially established an embassy in Algiers. I was also given as a gift to the embassy, unofficially, for performing menial work there. By the time I was fifteen, an older embassy employee in the diplomatic service had a growing interest in me. I eventually became his property and mistress. He retired to Marseilles, France, and took me with him. His family found out. They put pressure on him to quit the relationship. He died suddenly. Anyway, with the little money and the few clothes I had, I moved to Paris. What was I to do? I didn't have a good opinion of myself, so fell into prostitution. It is an awful life, to be with many strangers. I felt I had a reprieve for a while; a minor government official wanted an exclusive relationship with me. So, the parade of nameless men ended. When I became pregnant by him, I could see I was repeating my mother and grandma's history. They had no choice. They were slaves. I was no longer a slave. I wanted a better life for you.

I no longer wanted to be a prostitute. I began to go to the local Catholic Church. Cure' Sevigny gave a particular homily that first Sunday. It stressed that Jesus loves the worst sinner. We only need to repent and turn from sin *and we will be in His full graces. I went to confession and God forgave me through Cure' Sevigny. The priest helped me to receive sewing classes at a convent. I moved close to the nuns without telling your father that I was pregnant with you. He would have been a huge temptation to continue as a prostitute. So now I have turned a new page, washed in an ocean of Jesus merciful blood. He has allowed me to see the birth of my beautiful Juliette and to have her with me a little while.*

Your father is Joseph Gastineau. He is a good, intelligent, and kindhearted. He just didn't know Jesus. Anyway, if you are reading this letter, that is a miracle in itself. If you can forgive me, that is another miracle. Please pray for me and ask my guardian angel to watch over you. Please pray for me that I can be in the beatific vision of God. That would be the third miracle.

If God allows it, I will be praying for you.

Love and prayers always.
Your mother,
Teresa

"Mince alors!" Juliette exclaimed aloud. "Monsieur Gastineau is my father!"

Instead of distracting Juliette from her present burden, the letter added to the weight. Weariness seemed to collect from the whole day's events and with the final impact of the letter's contents, Juliette surrendered herself to unconsciousness. She fell into a deep sleep. So deep, that at a certain point she was dreaming of being chased by shadowy figures and was nearing a cliff. She was desperate to awake. In her dream, she fell to the ground and the darkened figures piled rocks on her, holding her bound in the unconscious state. She struggled and struggled to no avail. It was a frightening sensation of total helplessness. She yielded to dark oblivion thinking to herself, if I can't escape, I give up.

She awoke to a cold gray light entering the cabin through the porthole. Madame Bernard was fully dressed in a brown wool dress and a linen collar. She held a tray of hot tea and biscuits. "Juliette, you must have been so tired last night that when I came to the cabin, you had fallen asleep fully clothed. How do you feel?"

Juliette sat up in bed feeling a bit groggy. "I do feel better than last night." She reached for a cup of the hot strong tea. Madame Bernard said, "I'll go see if I can get you a slice of meat from the galley."

Juliette seemed blissfully blank in thoughts as she enjoyed her tea and biscuits. Her gaze traveled about the cabin seeking reassurance in familiar surroundings. Her glance stumbled on her birth mother's picture. All of her fears came surging into her brain.

Alone, she quietly spoke to herself as a comfort. "Certainment, there are many things to be alarmed about, but my father," She happily lingered on the word 'father' with the recent revelation that Joseph Gastineau was her birth father. "My father, Joseph Gastineau, said that problems can be a blessing in disguise. My mother, Teresa says I can ask her guardian angel for help. And the last mass that Cure' Sevigny celebrated, his sermon was about the archangels and guardian angels. I can ask for their help too. There is a reason for this set of dilemmas. I am to learn something special." She reveled in the fact that she now knew who her birth father was and that she was genuinely fond of him.

Returning to her thoughts, she said a prayer, "Dear Jesus, with your help, let me embrace the day. Bless all who I hold dear and those I don't. Guide me in what I say and do. Help me deal with all the things I've learned since yesterday. Please let my mother be in your heavenly embrace. In Jesus name, amen."

Juliette bounced out of bed and took off her dress and hung it carefully. Surprisingly, there were few wrinkles. She refreshed herself by pouring a little water from a pitcher into a wash basin. She splashed her face and arms. She dried off with a towel. Selecting a more practical dress of red wool with a black and red wool shawl, she quickly donned it. With a comb she parted her hair in the middle and skeined it back into a chignon at the nape.

There was a polite rap at the cabin door. "It's me."

Juliette recognized Madame Bernard's voice. "Entrez."

Once in the cabin Madame Bernard inspected Juliette's appearance. "Your attempt to look severe did not succeed."

Undaunted, Juliette smiled and said, "So be it."

Madame Bernard proffered a plump piece of ham. "It is all the galley could give me since it is three o'clock in the afternoon."

"Goodness! I must have slept more than sixteen hours!"

Juliette picked up the daguerreotype of her mother and showed it to Madame Bernard. "I have to hide this picture, dress and letter." She allowed Madame Bernard to read it. Madame Bernard wiped a few tears from her eyes.

"I have the exact place for it." She showed Juliette the false bottom of her trunk. She opened the hidden compartment and placed the picture letter and dress in the trunk. She closed it and put her clothing over it.

"Well, Juliette, this voyage is turning into quite an adventure. I learned from Captain Belmont that we are a target for the Yankees in the open sea because we bring supplies to the South. And now of course, we both found out that the South's main reason for the war is to maintain slavery. Since your fiancé is on the side of the South, that is what he is defending. Then, after I brought you tea and meat, you allowed me to read your birth mother's letter and you found out Monsieur Gastineau is your birth father. Mon Dieu!! Now we both have learned a great deal in very little time. No wonder you slept so long. You were overwhelmed." Madame Bernard was also trying to get a grip.

"What can we do? The captain won't turn the boat around. That door is closed. So, we must meet the challenges laid before us." Madame Bernard was thinking aloud.

"I fully agree with you." Juliette responded. "I like your idea of being a listener and not divulging too much information. Using the fan as a prop to conceal my face was a life saver last night when I had to leave."

"You were a natural with that fan! Ah, the theatre! Therein lies a wealth of tools of the trade which can be applied to real life. If needs be, we can utilize these tools in defensive and offensive modes. What are us women to do? We can't shoot our way out of these dilemmas."

"Now we must embrace one challenge at a time so that would be to get through this voyage and stay on the good side of everyone. Be model passengers. Loose lips sink ships, literally." Continued Madame Bernard.

"Agreed. We are a team. We can do it. One day at a time." Juliette said.

CHAPTER 7
Hospital Visit

April of 1862 seemed to slip in unobserved. Winslow's camp had moved again just outside of La Grange, Tennessee, near Wolf River. The tents had been pitched in a haphazard manner. After inspection, General Vale had suggested that Winslow have his men line up the tents in an orderly manner. Winslow divided the tents into four quadrants. Each quadrant had fifty tents with three men to a tent. He decided to put the officer's tent in the northwest quadrant, nearest the river. After the last battle at Fort Donelson, all the letters had been written and sent to families whose loved ones had been killed in battle. The wounded from his command were hospitalized in La Grange.

The early morning chill of April was on the wane as Winslow rubbed the nose of his present favorite horse, Ben. He unhitched the horse from a post in front of the officer's tent. Major Lester emerged from the tent flap in full parade dress.

"Major Lester, you are in charge while I go visit our wounded soldiers in La Grange. In my absence find out why there is a shortage of sabers since one of your duties is requisitions. When I return, give me a full report." Winslow said as he mounted his horse effortlessly.

"Yes sir." Lester responded in a terse voice.

The sun felt warm and welcoming on his broad shoulders as his horse carried him to town. It began to cloud up in the northwest sky.

He arrived in La Grange proper about forty minutes later. The town consisted of a tavern, blacksmith, a few homes behind the businesses and a church. The church had been converted to an army hospital. He dismounted his horse and tied him to a tree and went inside. The former church no longer had pews. They had been replaced with straw mattresses. At least fifty men were convalescing.

Winslow recognized four soldiers from his company. All eyes were on him, some trying to salute him in their feeble way. "At ease men."

Winslow's clean-shaven face was wreathed in a big smile emphasizing his dimples. His dark eyes glowed with affection for his men. He was like sunshine after a storm. He continued in a booming voice, "In a hospital no one is burdened with military courtesy."

"Where are you from?" He asked a soldier to his left.

"I am from Madison, Wisconsin, and am in the Wisconsin Infantry."

"May you get well soon, soldier."

He went on to all the other men and greeted them with encouraging words. Lastly, he came upon his own men and greeted them, "Pvt. Saderly, Pvt. Smith, Pvt. Taylor, and Corporal Lamb, how are you doing today, men?"

Corporal Lamb raised up on his elbow and said, "Fine. When can we get out of here?"

"How many of you can walk?" Winslow asked, as he smiled.

Only Pvt. Saderly managed to totter to his feet for a few seconds. A deep flesh wound in his thigh was his infirmity. It wasn't only pain from the injury site, but general weakness from loss of blood. Private Smith and Taylor had the flu. Lamb had a broken toe from a supply wagon running over it. It was impossible for Lamb to walk.

"When you men can make it back to camp on your own power, we are southwest of here by Wolf River."

A comely young woman appeared in the doorway. Her merry blue eyes couldn't resist sending a come-hither gaze to Winslow's dark amber eyes. She was attired in nurse's garb, a long white starched apron over a pale blue dress. The nurse was plump and fair with honey blond hair plaited in a tight braid and bundled into a net to keep it out of the way. Her voice belied her brazen gaze as she said in a timid voice, "Is there anything I can help you with?" She then crimsoned as though afraid of her own voice.

Flirtation had lifted Winslow's spirits. Lightheartedly, he said, "Perhaps a kiss from maiden fair would lighten the load of earthly care." He looked askance at all the men who watched him expectantly.

Her white hands flew up to her sweet young mouth as she was at a loss for words but completely under the spell of Winslow. He moved closer, pulled her hands from her mouth, and then soundly kissed her.

"There, I have done my best! If this does not do the trick, we will just have to wait until the war is finished." Said Winslow with a dimpled grin and a sly wink to the men.

The nurse stammered, "Well sir, I hardly know what to say...except, when will you come again?"

All the men laughed. Winslow gave no answer, just a self-satisfied smile as he nodded to the men and disappeared through the door. All the men shouted goodbye and smiled because they enjoyed the performance as much as Winslow.

It had taken the greater part of the day for the hospital visit. He made it back to camp by three in the afternoon. He was in good spirits, still revelling in the soldiers' happy reaction to his theatrical antics. As Winslow entered camp, he noticed that the soldiers had made quick work of organizing the tents. The four quadrants of tents were easily distinguished with a wide-open center and concise avenues, going south to north and east to west. The avenues crossed in the center of the quadrants. Everyone had his rifle oiled and saber polished. There were still some men lacking sabers. He noticed the bridles were all oiled as well. The men must be getting ready for rainy weather. In the past, he had noticed after each battle, a rainstorm had followed. It's as if the rain were tears from heaven lamenting the casualties on the battleground.

Winslow found Major Lester in the officer's tent. "Major Lester. What is the present status of the sabers?"

"Lieutenant Colonel Winslow, I checked with the men and there are about fourteen men who do not have sabers. I have just written up an order for them and sent it to general headquarters."

"Good work, Major." Winslow said.

Evening came. The sun flickered weakly into the grayness, then was extinguished prematurely by a low-lying cloud. The bugler blew taps, and the soldiers saluted the flag.

The officers gathered in Winslow's tent and talked shop. He said, "You have been doing fine on training Captain Bell and Tobias, especially, getting it across to our soldiers to watch for hand signals."

"It sure solved the problem of communicating through the noisy artillery." Tobias said.

"Even the soldiers contributed by suggesting an extra signal to designate specifically, the exact company involved in the action by holding up certain fingers. Currently, the right-hand thumb correlates with company 'A', the index finger with company 'B', and so on up to company 'E'. On the left hand, starting with the thumb to the last finger, are companies 'F' to 'J'. The last companies were designated by right hand fist with thumb out for 'L' and raised index knuckle is 'M'. The left fist same way; the thumb is 'N', and the raised knuckle is 'O'. That accounts for all twelve companies." Added Captain Bell.

Winslow beamed, approving of his officers' team effort. Nodding, he said, "Those artillery boys are a noisy bunch for so small a unit. They sure use up the horses. They unhitch them and let them run. We always get called on to supply them with more horses. So far, we have had enough to do this. If we can't manage to supply enough, we will let main headquarters know. They might have more horses for those men."

Winslow yawned and stretched his long muscular arms to each side and asked. "What news from the outside?"

"The navy has the ports of the south blockaded. They're closing in on New Orleans waiting for the right time to attack." Said Major Lester.

Reverend Blake added, "It's a strange situation. We have more control of the South with the blockade yet fifty miles north of here the rebels have control of the Mississippi."

"Reverend Blake, Grant is letting the Rebs control it for now because it isn't a priority. They'll be out of there faster than a dogged fox when we'll need it."

For the next few days, the camp fell into a quiet routine. The Tennessee peach blossoms emitted a soothing fragrance. Then on Sunday, April 6th, 1862, the peaceful respite ended. Confederate General Johnston attacked Union troops at Shiloh, about thirty miles from Winslow's camp. It was a desperate move by the South. General Johnston felt he must attack before Union General Buell accumulated more troops.

A messenger soldier galloped into camp mid-morning. He alighted from his horse and said to Lieutenant Colonel Winslow, "Sir! You and your soldiers are needed at Shiloh as soon as possible." He gave the tattered paper written by General Grant. Winslow glanced at it and gave it back. The messenger mounted his steed and left for the next camp.

As the messenger was leaving, Winslow shouted after him, "Tell General Vale that we have mobilized and that our cavalry is headed to Shiloh." Within the hour his six hundred men were saddled up with weapons oiled and at the ready.

Winslow announced to his men, "We will ride four abreast. When we arrive at the scene, it will then be determined what maneuver or maneuvers to use once apprised of the situation. We will jog trot the horses so as not to wear them out, it being nearly thirty miles away."

With that, they took off in a clatter of clanking metal and thudding horse hooves. The miles melted away. Approximately ten miles toward their destination they were suddenly deep into enemy position being lambasted from all sides by bullets.

Consternation momentarily set in. Winslow signaled to the men to make a semi-circle facing outward. There was a hill behind them that helped as a barrier to their rear. Winslow set his jaw in deadly determination. Wave after wave of Rebs came at them. A high-ranking Reb general came at Winslow with a saber. A quick dismount from his horse saved him. Winslow read puzzlement in the attacking officer's eyes. Winslow surmised that it was because his men were holding their ground. But for how long?

Winslow knew his men were outnumbered. Silently, desperately he prayed for help. He signaled the bugler to blow charge, a last futile act. The Confederate General was surprised to hear charge blown for such a small number of men who were surrounded.

Suddenly, out of the bushes on the ridge of the enemy side of the line came about thirty men on horseback, whooping and hollering. Sure enough, they were wearing Union blue. Fearing that there were more men coming, the Reb general had his bugler blow retreat.

The survivors of the encounter were traumatized by the ambush nature the Confederates. As the dust was settling on the aftermath of the battle scene, the thirty-three men that had come from out of nowhere, dismounted and saluted Winslow.

A lean, lanky, fresh faced youth dismounted and approached Winslow. "Pvt. Willie Barlow reporting for duty." Most of the thirty-three were still adolescents.

Winslow, himself, was hit by a wave of emotion which he shook off and regained his composure. He did a headcount of the youthful group responsible for saving most of his troops. "Willie, where did you and the rest of your men come from?"

"I was left for dead on the battlefield weeks ago. My company had to retreat. Luckily, I had only been knocked unconscious from the fall off my horse. When I came to, I knew my company was long gone and that I had twisted my ankle in the fall, so I had to find a hiding place while I healed up. I realized that I was deep behind enemy lines. I would scavenge at night for food and weapons and also slowly move north. My fellow soldiers each ended up separated in similar circumstances. Somehow, by God's providence most likely the thirty-three of us found each other over a period of weeks. "

Willie continued, "It was our good fortune to stumble upon some fine Reb horses picketed just far enough from their camp to be procured unobserved. We kept an eye on those particular Rebs from a safe distance. We followed them here to this battle."

Winslow looked more closely at the rag tag bunch. Young as they were, there was a toughness about them that shone through the hard lines etched in their faces. "Willie Barlow, it's truly a pleasure to lay eyes on you and your companions."

Suddenly General Grant came over the ridge and barked, "Men, you are needed at Shiloh follow me!"

There was no time for talk. All who could, mounted their steed and followed Grant to Shiloh.

It was June sixth. A gentle early June breeze ruffled the flaps of the tent where Ezra Peabody was sleeping. At four in the morning, as part of the duties of the Corporal of the Guard, Milo Sisk, harrumphed at the tent opening. "Ezra, time to get up!Daylight is nigh!"

Not being dull edged, Ezra responded, "Thanks Milo, and good morning!" Ezra's easy-going nature made him a friend to most soldiers.

With ample time to prepare for revelry, Ezra dressed and joined Milo for an early cup of coffee. "How'd your watch go?"

"Quiet except for some snoring." Milo smiled. "I went over to where the horses are picketed on my rounds. They would whinny and neigh begging for affection. I'd stop and give their heads a rub as I passed. As a saddler, it keeps them mellow and open to approach. Also, time seems to pass quicker when busy."

It was time to blow revelry, so Ezra made his way to the center of camp and then blew the bugle with energy and pride. The men all got up and started making breakfast. Soon fires were ablaze, and the mingled pleasant aromas of coffee and ham rose in the camp. Their breakfast consisted of the best Tennessee ham and stored potatoes from some plantation's root cellars combined in a cooking pot over a fire made the best slumgullion stew. Served with coffee and hardtack, completed the hearty meal.

Lately, Lt. Col. Winslow had used wagons on his foraging parties. The main group on horseback would find the food and word would be sent back to wagon drivers to come to that location to retrieve potatoes, turnips, beets or whatever produce was found.

They had all finished their breakfast when word flashed through camp that a great river battle was about to take place on the Mississippi River. The men were excited that the North had finally put together a fleet.

Pvt. Smith said, "The South had the Mississippi under control since the beginning of the war."

Ezra said to Winslow, "The boys would like to see the river battle Colonel."

"I know how the men feel, Ezra. We can't possibly leave camp to watch the naval engagement without breaking the rules. We must always be at-the-ready for the enemy. But we could use the rules in a forthright foraging operation, and I reckon the best route to our objective is right along the Mississippi River." Winslow smiled a slow expectant smile.

"I get it Colonel!" Ezra exclaimed.

"Blow assembly, Ezra."

The men had gathered around Colonel Winslow. "Men today we are going west on a foraging party. We will leave the wagons behind. Mount your horse's men, and we'll be off."

The men went to their horses which were scattered about the camp. Whenever the opportunity arose in a foraging operation, the men would upgrade to fresher horses and give their old horses to the artillery who were a needy lot. They all made formation. Although it was a clear June day, the men's faces ranged from sullen to grumpy. It was also Friday, a day to stay around camp and catch up on chores. Even soldiers at war fell into routines. Usually, foraging was done earlier in the week. They started out on the command to 'advance' and soon were in a gallop. As they went westward, they veered north.

The expressions of the men had gone from dour to delight. Word had traveled fast through the ranks as to the purpose of the foraging party. As they were clopping along, Winslow noticed that everyone was in their proper position. The main line of four hundred were in front and were backed by the rear line of two hundred. The same position they had engaged the enemy at Shiloh.

The recent battle of Shiloh entered his mind. After the Confederates had ambushed Winslow and his men, Willie Barlow showed up with thirty-three stragglers and redeemed them from certain death, then from nowhere appeared General Grant commanding them to follow him to Shiloh. Still shocked by the ambush, they mechanically followed his orders. During the battle of Shiloh, the carnage was so bloody, the field where they fought was covered with mangled bodies. So thick were the dead, some lay on top of the other. A foot couldn't find a patch of dirt to stand on in that field. Dead eyes staring at the sky or entire faces blown off made Winslow shudder. There was no decisive win for the North. They won at great costs. He mentally scrambled back to the present moment.

His men were still in proper position. Winslow wished pictures could capture his command in action. They rode for ten miles which found them north of Memphis. Spirits lifted to exuberance upon sighting the Yankee gun boat's black smoke on the distant horizon. The Confederate gun boats were south of the Yankees in front of Memphis. The townspeople were on the bluff beside Memphis proper near the Mississippi River.

The men could see the crowd, but Lt. Col. Winslow restrained the men from interfering with the civilian populace. Cheering wildly, they threw their blue soldier hats into the air as a welcome to the Yankee gun boats which were in plain view now. They were the only soldiers along the river at eleven in the morning. It was a pretty sight, paddle wheelers reinforced with iron plate. They were twin stacked vessels built in rectangular shapes, sturdy and secure. They could be used as rams also. The Confederate gunboats were also ironclads with ramming capabilities.

Ezra rode his horse up to Winslow's horse as they both observed the ironclads positioning themselves for the impending battle. Winslow became aware of him and said, "Ezra, it's a beautiful day for a river battle of the ironclads."

"The best part is being on the outside of the action for a change." Ezra hesitated, then continued, "I am one lucky soldier to have you as commander. I've wanted to tell you that many times, but you have so many more important things on your mind than to be bothered with a plain old compliment."

Winslow smiled kindly, "Ezra some day you are going to find a good woman and she will have to be a good woman to be deserving of such a true fellow."

"Wished I could have a way with the womenfolk such as you. I heard how you flirted with Mrs. Buford and fancy kissed the nurse. Had I kissed one of them, I would have myself one sore face."

"Ezra, if I could meet a woman who would slap me for a kiss, then I could get interested. I like to fight for what I get."

Ezra smiled broadly, exposing his slightly bucked front teeth. "I know what you mean, sir. But with me it's different, I am far from handsome and am getting older."

"What? You are barely into your twenties. Look at me, Ezra, I am thirty-four and still unhitched. But of course, Bloody Kansas and the Rebellion have hamstrung that aspiration. On top of that, my hair is getting gray."

"Bloody Kansas, now the Rebellion, it does take a toll. I feel much older, too."

"What I really want is a woman with whom I can share in happiness, some privations, and a few pleasures. I would want a wife to come to me in love and virtue. I would gratefully embrace her. God willing, we would be blessed with children. She has to be out there. Where is she, is the question?"

Ezra looked at Winslow quizzically. "Ain't you a mite bit fussy, sir? But, I guess, since it is until death do you part, might as well make it a tall order."

Winslow's auburn hair fluttered in the morning sunshine revealing a few gray hairs at his temples. His face was slightly somber and pale and then his eyes crinkled at the corners as a wry smile appeared. "A tall order indeed! I might as well shoot for the stars then there are better odds God would hear me. So, I will make it an even taller order: I would like to have her slim with a complexion like cream, dark curls, and nice teeth, and pretty inside and out. How's that for tall Ezra?"

Ezra looked a Winslow with a bright smile. "Tall, for sure. So tall you have shot past the moon."

The thunder of cannons drew their attention to the river. The river battle had commenced. A Union ironclad rammed into a Confederate ironclad and she sank in a few minutes. Shortly afterward, another Confederate ironclad rammed that Union ironclad in her paddle wheel which put her partly out of commission. Another Union ship was following the disabled ironclad, while two Confederate boats were approaching in opposite directions toward the damaged Union ship. The shrewd captain was able at the last minute, to suddenly reverse his ship out of their oncoming paths at the last second. It was too late for the two Confederate ironclads. They rammed each other disabling both of their own ships. One beached itself on the Arkansas shore. The other had its boiler pierced by a shell and sank. Most of the Confederate crew escaped and swam for nearby shore. The battle was a morale builder for Winslow's men many of whom had brothers or acquaintances on the Union ironclads. It was like rooting for the home team.

As the battle on the river became more intense, the men went from boisterous to solemn. Winslow's men witnessed some casualties on both sides. At least, he thought, it was a change of scenery and his men weren't in the thick of it as his thoughts again went back to the gruesome sights of Shiloh. A more pleasant thought floated into his mind, a beautiful silhouette of a slender woman. Was it battle fatigue? He wasn't even actively trying to distract himself. He dismissed his musings and looked to his men for distraction.

There was heavy foliage along the river where the men had instinctively sought cover. The men had dismounted and the tall grass hid horse and man well. Prudence was becoming ingrained as the Rebs could be anywhere and they seemed to rely on sniper and ambush attacks. Winslow's men continued to watch the naval battle and it went clearly in favor of the North, more by chance than pure brute force. The South was equal to the North in naval prowess but out gunned. Winslow ordered his men to mount. The cavalry troop then headed back to camp. Since the river battle had been a decisive victory for the North, now the majority of the river was in their control.

Once in camp, Winslow announced to the men, "Men, since our foraging expedition was unproductive that doesn't mean that the day went to waste. We did have the good luck to come upon a river battle that gained more control over the Mississippi. Since the cooks went with us today, we will allow them a little extra time to fix supper. Along with supper, I have a barrel of cold storage apples to add to the meal and to help celebrate the conquest of the ironclads." At that moment, Winslow felt very close to all his men. They weren't just soldiers; they were his friends.

The sun wavered crimson on the horizon. The gloaming of the day into the evening twilight was like the changing of the guard. The last waves of heat lifted the myriad fragrance of wildflowers intoxicating perfume around the camp.

CHAPTER 8

The next several weeks aboard the Tambeau went smoothly. Becoming a good listener had been the best advice Mme. Bernard had given Juliette. With Mme. Bernard's expertise in costume and props, and along with her sage advice about disguising Juliette's raw emotions behind a smoke screen of practiced facial expressions, and the faithful standby, the fan, Juliette became a woman of masterly subterfuge.

The voyage continued in an orderly routine. Juliette would awake at the break of dawn. After an hour of prayer and meditation, she would wash in cold water, dress herself, and go out on deck. She would walk around the perimeter of the deck many times before breakfast.

By then Mme. Bernard would join her on deck and walk a few turns with her. They both would then go to the galley and have breakfast with Mr. Armstrong and Mr. Paxton. Breakfast usually consisted of strong hot tea, sea biscuits which were a flat, unleavened crisp bread, salted meat, either pork or beef, and apples.

Mr. Armstrong would expound on a subject as long as there were ears to listen. After remaining with Juliette for several of these tortuous lectures, Mme. Bernard would quietly excuse herself. She was often mending, sewing, or embroidering. Juliette had given her the gold coins from Monsieur Gastineau's exchange of James Lambert's paper money for the gold coins at a reliable French bank. Intermittently, Mme.

Bernard would use the time to sew the coins in various garments for safe keeping, since she didn't have much time to do so before the voyage.

At first, Juliette felt abandoned by Mme. Bernard, but as she meditated on it, she realized it was a gift. Somehow, she knew she was being afforded valuable training in nimbly maneuvering the conversation as well as hiding boredom, shock and astonishment. Feigning interest, excitement and pleasure were the most challenging. As a finale' to a particularly long diatribe, she would yawn or hide behind a fan. One hour of listening to Mr. Armstrong was quite taxing. With the first socially acceptable opportunity, Juliette would excuse herself and then join Mme. Bernard in the cabin. Mr. Paxton would stay in the background observing it all. Was he onto the charade? If so, he was too much the gentleman to say a word.

The lunch menu was the same as breakfast. Afterward, they would go to their cabin for a nap. Supper was served at 7:00 P.M. It was the only hot meal of the day and usually consisted of a stew or soup made with root vegetables such as carrots, potatoes, and onions. Accompanying the meal was wine and treacle for dessert. Once a week the crew and passengers were given a lemon to consume, in their tea or however they wished to eat it. It was to help prevent scurvy. A few hours after the evening meal all the passengers retired to their respective cabins.

One morning after breakfast, four weeks into the voyage, Juliette, Mr. Armstrong, and Mr. Paxton were out on deck as usual. Mr. Armstrong braced himself against the chilly wind and turned his gaze on Juliette. "Well, Missy, we are more than halfway to America, way past the point of no return. I can hardly wait to eat some fresh greens and fresh meat." Juliette smiled in agreement. Simultaneously they all looked westward for the sweet promise of land.

Captain Belmont was at the helm scanning the horizon for a different reason. He was looking for Yankee gunboats with his spy glass. Up to now there had been no encounters. Suddenly, on the northwest horizon, his spy glass stumbled on a dark speck. As it moved closer, he distinguished that it was a Yankee steamboat which was also a gunboat. "Full sail!" He yelled to the crew. In less than a minute all sails were unfurled into the cloud darkened sky.

Captain Belmont had turned the helm over to the first mate, so that he could keep a better eye on the Yankees. "First mate steer the boat southwesterly."

"Aye sir!" The first mate responded with precision and speed. Just as the sails billowed with the full brunt of the wind, a cannon ball tore through the main sail, just missing the foremast timber.

One of the crew scrambled up the rope ladder and threw a square of canvass over the tear. Rain began to fall, and with the help of the wind, the canvass square adhered to the torn sail. The sailor stabbed several holes through both layers of fabric along the perimeter of the square and then wove a thin rope in and out till fully encompassing the tear, and then tied the two ends together to secure the patch. On completion of the mend, a strong gust of wind filled all the sails and assisted in evading the gunboat.

The wind propelled the schooner toward the southwest away from the Yankees. The Yankees were in pursuit for a short time, but the strong winds and rain aided the Tambeau in outdistancing the cumbersome steamer.

Juliette felt frozen to the railing by the shear gravity of the attack. Recovering slightly, Juliette said, "Mr. Armstrong, where is our ship headed now?"

"Most likely, Cuba. That's a fairly safe haven for the blockade runners." He answered.

Five days later the Tambeau made landfall. The weary crew and passengers disembarked in Havana, Cuba. It was a bittersweet encounter with the good earth. Happy to be on firm land, yet all knew it was only a brief respite until the last dangerous leg of their journey was completed.

Still, the diversions of Havana lifted Juliette and Mme. Bernard into happy moods. They enjoyed themselves despite the present circumstances. They ate in local restaurants and enjoyed the fresh food and friendly people.

Captain Belmont went to a local bar that he had frequented on other voyages. He found an old sailor who was a regular at the bar and knowledgeable about the current scuttlebutt on the Yankee gunboats. The old sailor told him that Mobile was open on the southern coast of the United States.

A week had passed. The Tambeau's sail was properly repaired. Supplies had been purchased for the return trip to France. The schooner took off in late afternoon. Over the evening meal Mr. Armstrong was showing signs of worry. It was noticeably quiet on the Tambeau. He asked Captain Belmont, "What time of day will we be arriving in Mobile?"

"Tomorrow evening." Belmont responded.

Captain Belmont addressed all passengers over the meal. "I cannot risk lingering in Mobile. As quickly as possible my crew will unload your supplies and then leave. We should arrive tomorrow in the dark of night which will aid us in avoiding the gunboats. As soon as we unload, the Tambeau leaves for France."

"Mr. Armstrong, you are from this area and most of the goods are yours. Since we must make haste, where can we quickly unload?"

"Once inside Mobile Bay, I will direct you to my warehouse. All should go without a hitch. I have the keys to the warehouse on my person."

The time to leave the ship arrived. It was dark and overcast. Silently, they approached the harbor. The moon broke through the clouds and momentarily lit the way. Then, with stealthy efficiency, after docking the ship, the crew moved the supplies from the ship to Mr. Armstrong's warehouse. The four passengers disembarked. The crew also placed all their baggage in the warehouse as well. As silent as a shadow, the Tambeau cast off to sea. With no words exchanged both crew and passengers waved farewell. The Tambeau disappeared into darkness.

Armstrong harrumphed as he realized out loud, "At this hour we must walk to the hotel."

Juliette and Mme. Bernard had each packed a small bag for just such a contingency. All were happy and relieved for a safe landing. It felt good to walk a few blocks to the hotel. The hotel clerk was dozing at the front desk but woke up when he heard the door slam. The two men took a ground floor room, and the ladies were given a room upstairs. They all retired to their chambers. Clean sheets, fresh water in a pitcher, and the warm glow from an oil lamp welcomed them. All slept soundly for the first time in two weeks.

BANG! BANG! Someone hammered on the women's door. "It's me, Clayton Armstrong. You ladies meet Beamus and me in the lobby in one hour. I'll take you gals to breakfast."

"Merci, Monsieur Armstrong. I am famished!" Juliette said exuberantly.

Juliette and Mme. Bernard met the men in the lobby, and they all went to Armstrong's favorite restaurant for breakfast. They walked about a half mile north along the shore. As they neared the restaurant, delicious aromas wafted toward them. Odors of fresh brewed coffee and onions and pork chops frying tantalized their appetites even more.

Armstrong strutted with confidence inspired by being on familiar territory. At the entrance to the restaurant, Armstrong pulled the door open for the others and said, "Welcome to the Black Eyed Pea. Sidney has been running this place for nigh on to ten years. We had the good smells and next the good eats."

Upon entering, Armstrong spotted a cheerful blond woman in her mid-forties. "Hello Tessy, is Sidney here?"

Tessy's face rounded into a pleasant smile. "Why it's Mr. Armstrong! You've been gone a spell. Sidney isn't here now. He left a week ago Tuesday, to go fight the Yanks up north. He left me in charge to run this place the best I can."

"You must be doing a good job because the aromas coming out of this place are heav-en-ly!"

Tessy smiled, "Follow me I have your favorite table in the back."

When they were all settled, everyone ordered the same: fried pork chops, black eyed peas, collard greens, coffee and paw paws. By their silence and sharp appetites, there was a consensus that the food was delicious.

Beamus Paxton was thoroughly enjoying his pleasant surroundings and the delicious food. "Clayton Armstrong, you are a gracious host. If there is anything I can do to help you out, please let me know."

"Think nothing of it. In fact, come to my plantation and rest a bit before embarking on your journey to New Orleans." Clayton rumbled with self-importance. "I have the wagons and slaves to transport your French imports home with you."

For that kind gesture, I will be forever grateful and will happily give you recompense for your inconvenience."

"Think nothing, absolutely nothing, of it! You'd do the same for me Paxton." Expounded Armstrong unctuously. Tessy came to clear the table.

"Tessy, do you have a fellow to send word to my plantation, that I have arrived with guests and am in need of transportation for ourselves and our baggage?" Armstrong asked.

"Most fellows are at war right now, but my daughter, Corintha, is good on a horse and knows how to get to your place." Tessy said.

Corintha, a slender wisp of a girl of the age of thirteen, emerged from the kitchen with a smile on her face, as her blond curls spilled over her shoulders. She had overheard and seemed enthralled at the idea of a horse ride.

Frowning, Armstrong said, "She'll have to do. I'll write a note to send with her and take it to my wife lickity-split." He gave Corintha a hard look.

Tessy said, "Corintha, fetch Mr. Armstrong paper, quill and ink." Corintha did so. Armstrong quickly wrote a note and handed it to the girl. She was off in a flash.

While they waited for transportation they strolled back to the hotel and gathered their things. Armstrong paid the hotel clerk for everyone. Then they all walked back to the warehouse.

Armstrong announced. "I sent word to bring us a large wagon to haul our luggage and a carriage for the four of us.

Later, Juliette watched the wagon and carriage pull up in front of the warehouse. A wave of sadness washed over her as she perceived the dejection and hopelessness expressed in the downcast eyes and slumped posture of the two drivers. Their heads drooped submissively. One tall, the other short, both jumped out of their respective vehicles. With hats in hand and heads bowed even further, they stood silently before Armstrong waiting for orders.

Armstrong bellowed, "What kind of livery are you wearing? That's plain shabby!"

The short one stuttered, "Sorry, suh. We's jus wear wha's gibben us, Massah Armstrong."

"Don't you back talk, you no account nigger! Now both of you get hopping and load up the baggage!"

Juliette felt like someone had pierced her heart with a knife. Armstrong's words were too strong and cruel. She knew Armstrong dare not know her true feelings. With a quick presence of mind, she looked down the wharf and saw some sea gulls gathering in a cluster in the water. "Monsieur Armstrong, what kind of fish do gulls catch here?" She tried to make her eyes blank.

Distracted for a moment, Armstrong noticed her wide-eyed innocent gaze and responded, "Why, Missy, there's a bunch of fish in there, but around these parts gulls like red snapper mostly."

"Hmm, if red snapper is tasty to the birds, it must be tasty for people too."

Armstrong laughed, "You are right as rain. It's very tasty for those who like fish."

Now that she had his attention off the slaves, she felt relieved and continued asking questions to prolong the dialogue. Coaxing Armstrong along with nodding her head in feigned interest and locking her gaze with his in rapped attention. By the time the wagon was full of their trunks and valises, Armstrong was deep into expounding on varieties of fish. He was cut short by one of the slaves who cleared his throat to let the travelers know all was ready.

Mellowed by her interest, Armstrong helped Juliette and Mme. Bernard into the carriage making sure that he sat across from Juliette.

Paxton said, "Well, I thank God that we have made it safely thus far."

"Monsieur Paxton, I feel exactly the same way." Responded Juliette with a beautiful smile. It did not escape Juliette that a flash of jealousy slipped over Armstrong's face for a second, then disappeared. What lingered was a lecherous stare that ground into Juliette's eyes. Shifting her gaze, she watched the passing scenery, instead. As they pulled up to the plantation it was a beautiful scene. Spanish moss hung from the cypress trees in tattered shreds along the lane leading to a beautiful white mansion.

A large boned woman emerged from the front door. Dark hair parted in the middle and swept into a bun made up her severe hair style. "Hello, Clayton." She said as she walked down the porch steps to greet Armstrong.

After descending from the carriage, Armstrong gave the woman a short hug and said, "Greetings Vera Lee." He then turned and helped Juliette and Mme. Bernard out of the carriage.

"As you read in my note, we have company. I want you to meet Juliette Bellechasse, Mme. Bernard, and of course, you know Beamus Paxton. All of you might guess by now, this is my wife, Vera Lee."

Mme Bernard and Juliette curtsied to Mrs. Armstrong and said in unison, "Enchantez, Madame Armstrong."

Mrs. Armstrong acknowledged them by saying, "Welcome to Veil Wood."

There was a thin young black boy, maybe ten years old, standing expectantly at the double doors to the mansion. Mrs. Armstrong motioned for him to come forward. "Rufus, show the guests to their rooms. Lunch will be at one in the afternoon. If you are hungry or need anything before, just ring the bell in your room and it will summon Rufus to your quarters."

"You are such a gracious hostess, Mme. Armstrong. Thank you for your kindness."

"I'm an old hand at having guests especially when Clayton is at home." Purposely, Mrs. Armstrong locked arms with Mr. Armstrong while at the same time glared at Juliette as though protecting an expensive knick-knack from breakage.

After being shown to the beautifully appointed guest room, and all their trunks had been hauled up by the two slaves who had chauffeured them to Veil Wood, the two women settled in by unpacking a few of the most needed items.

Once done, Mme. Bernard said to Juliette, it did not escape me how cold, yet jealous Mme. Armstrong was."

Juliette agreed. "It was as obvious as a block of ice."

Both were silent as they puzzled over their situation and all its implications. "It will be very difficult to stay here for more than a few days." Juliette said. "Just for now, let's go forward with what needs to be done. We can mull over any ideas or solutions as we do tasks."

The guest room they occupied was large, beautiful and opulent. A Persian rug covered a portion of the gleaming dark wood floor. There was a sitting area with a chaise lounge and a wing back chair facing a table with a beautiful porcelain gilded oil lamp. Other chairs and ottomans were upholstered in dark red damask. The theme of red damask was continued on the large mahogany four post bed in a coverlet and the drapes framing the French doors to the private balcony. Even a chamber pot was made elegant and private with a foldable red damask screen. The pot was under a customized chair that had an opening for guests to relieve themselves plus toilet paper on a small table next to it.

Both women opened their trunks to air. Juliette opened the French doors and transferred most of her clothing to the balcony to air. Mme. Bernard did the same. It was a beautiful sunny morning in late November.

Rufus came back with a basket of paw paws and some dried peaches. He said, "Ladies, if you needs anythin' else jus' pull the cord by the door and it rings a bell downstairs for us servants to come."

Juliette asked, "Rufus, is it possible for Mme. Bernard and I, to have a bath?"

"Yes Ma'am. The cook house is da usual place for that. Cuz the water pump is close to the stove to heat the water."

"How soon would the bath be ready?"

"'Bout an hour's time."

"Magnifique!"

While the bath was being prepared, they packed small valises with their clean clothes and towels and had another cotton sack with soiled clothes. Soon Rufus knocked at the door. "The water is ready. Follow me, please."

They gathered their things and followed him downstairs to the main floor, passing the parlor they noticed a gleaming grand piano, then out the door, down the path to cook house. When Rufus opened the cookhouse door the women were pleasantly surprised by two metal tubs full of warm water. Rufus showed them how to bar the door and pull the shades before leaving them. Juliette had brought two bars of lavender soap which she shared with Mme. Bernard.

Both ladies undressed quickly and gave an audible sigh of contentment as they submerged themselves into the soothing warm water. Each washed her hair and body and lingered a while after rinsing. After drying themselves and dressing, they used the warm bath water to wash some clothing. There still was some warm water in the stove's holding tank, so they put a large, empty tub under the spigot and rinsed and rung out their laundry then put it back in the cotton sack.

Tentatively, they opened the door. Rufus was waiting for them. He led them back to their room. Happily, they draped their freshly laundered clothes in the warm sunshine on the balcony. Each braided the other's hair. Both felt exhausted and laid down for a nap. They fell into a deep sleep.

A knock at the door awakened them. It was Rufus. "Mistus Armstrong wants to know if you be joining 'em for dinner. It's now five and dinner is at seven."

Both women looked at the other for a moment's hesitation. Juliette was tempted to stay in her room to avoid Armstrong's unwanted interest. Mme. Bernard lifted an expectant eyebrow. "Certainly! Mme. Bernard and I will be there."

"Yes'm!" Rufus responded happily.

Juliette heard Rufus descend the stairs. She turned to Mme. Bernard and said, "Mr. Armstrong has become too interested in me. What should I do? Where would we go? I am sickened to know that James lives this lifestyle. I abhor slavery. I couldn't endure marrying into that darkness."

Mme. Bernard sat up on the side of the bed and stared at the floor for a long time as Juliette patiently waited. Finally, she lifted her head and looked at Juliette with aplomb. "We can only concern ourselves with the present moment. Do not concern yourself with the James dilemma. Today our challenge is the Armstrong's. So, as far as I have discerned, you have two choices. You can choose to be meek or bold. I believe you can do best at being bold."

"In what way should I be bold, slap him in the face?"

"In a way, yes. Remember at Le Mouton Noir, you'd sing, you'd flirt. You played the coquette, yet you remained in control. I don't think you are aware how attractive you are to the opposite sex. This attractiveness is a gift from God. It can be used for good or evil. It is another tool or prop. On the ship you used the fan to hide your face. Now it is time to reveal your face and the rest of you. Given the predicament we are in, we must pull out all the stops. I include myself in this equation. I am thankful that you took piano lessons from me. Remember that medley of songs that you sang last spring at Le Mouton Noir?"

"Why, yes! The customers gave me a standing ovation! That is brilliant, Mme. Bernard! I will put on my boldest gown and give my best performance ever! I know they have a piano. I saw it when we went for a bath." Juliette was excited by the plan.

With renewed purpose they selected a red satin gown which matched a red feathered fan and ostrich plume for her hair. At exactly five minutes past seven. They descended the stairs. Mme. Bernard wore a periwinkle blue gown that matched her eyes and lead the way a dozen steps in advance. Just enough in advance to alert the dinner guests. Juliette floated down in a red cloud of satin and feathers. Her green eyes sparkled. Blue highlights glinted from her jet-black hair under the light of the chandelier. She had styled her hair in a heap of curls while some curls trailed over her left shoulder with the red ostrich feather pinned behind her left ear.

"Good evening to my kind hosts and Monsieur Paxton." Juliette said

Both Mr. Armstrong and Mr. Paxton were mesmerized by Juliette's transformation. Their mouths were agape, and their eyes were glued to Juliette.

Mr. Paxton recovered first. "What a lovely vision you are, Juliette!"

"You are too kind Monsieur Paxton!" Juliette said demurely.

"Why, yes, you are as pretty as a picture! Mr. Armstrong exclaimed. He furtively glanced at his wife whose eyes narrowed and mouth grimaced downward in a fixed frown. She spoke no greeting. Mrs. Armstrong remained silent then smiled coldly.

The first course was shrimp gumbo soup, then the main course fried chicken and steamed collard greens with corn fritters. Desert was peach pie and chicory coffee. The silence weighed heavy over the table.

"It was all so delicious. I was intrigued by the little round balls that were with the chicken. What are they made from, Mrs. Armstrong?" Juliette asked innocently.

"Why those round balls, as you call them, are made from corn meal batter and deep fried. We call them corn fritters." Mrs. Armstrong replied condescendingly.

Throughout the entire meal, Mr. Armstrong silently smoldered with lecherous glances at Juliette. Sporadically, his wife caught him glancing at Juliette. She glared at him, knowingly.

After dinner Mr. Armstrong said, "let us retire to the parlor."

The dining room doors opened into a large room with a divan, beautifully upholstered chairs, a white Italian marble fireplace and a grand piano. At the sight of the piano both Juliette and Mme. Bernard smiled.

Juliette announced, "I am so happy that you have a piano! Mme. Bernard and I would like to entertain you with some songs."

Although it had been a while since the two women had done anything musical together, it was as if they tapped into their mutual history of piano lessons and popular French music. After singing the entire medley, the small audience coaxed them to do more. The ladies continued with even more extemporaneous American music.

"Excuse me if I don't know the exact lyrics for the next few songs. If I can't remember I will hum the melody maybe you can sing the lyrics for me. In France, we heard about the popular songs of Stephen Foster. So, I will begin with 'Oh Susannah'." Juliette clears her throat and signals to Mme. Bernard.

Mme. Bernard was superb on the piano. Juliette gave a stellar performance. She danced and mimed her way through the songs with animated gestures and facial expressions. Her listeners were enthused. When it came to the chorus, Juliette cupped her ear and leaned forward with her other hand on her hip and mimicked listening to the audience. They chimed in with a vigorous rendition of the chorus on each of Juliette's cues. They joined in for Swanee River and Old Folks at Home. Juliette enjoyed the men's participation. Mrs. Armstrong didn't sing but in an unguarded moment, smiled.

The evening melted away. All were fascinated and somewhat surprised by Juliette's performance, even Mrs. Armstrong. The house slaves were peaking around the door frame with big smiles also.

After the performance was finished, Mme. Bernard and Juliette curtsied deeply and bowed their heads. The men stood up and clapped vigorously. Mrs. Armstrong reluctantly followed suite.

Juliette stood up with a flourish and said, "Voila! Thank you. I am happy you have enjoyed the music. I have sung for my supper. Now I am sleepy and will retire for the evening."

"Just a cotton pickin' minute, Missy." Armstrong said. "Before you leave, I have some sheet music that you could learn and maybe you could sing for us again?" He handed it to her.

"I do love learning new music. I will take it with me to my chambers and try to learn those songs. Thank you." Both ladies retreated to their room. As Juliette arrived at the landing, she glanced back at Armstrong who seemed frozen at the first step with a baleful stare directed at her.

Once in the room Mme. Bernard said, "See what power you have Juliette? You had their rapt attention."

Juliette responded, "Yes, but is it a power I have control of? Or did I open Pandora's Box?" Mme. Bernard gave her an uneasy smile because her thoughts were similar to Juliette's.

"I will lock the door and put a chair up against it." Mme. Bernard volunteered.

Early the next morning, they awoke and packed all their baggage and trunks to be ready for anything. Both Juliette and Mme. Bernard went down to the dining room for breakfast. Mr. Paxton was seated at the dining room table when the two ladies entered.

"Bonjour, Monsieur Paxton. How are you today?" Warbled Juliette pleasantly.

Paxton got quickly to his feet to greet the ladies with a pleasant smile and responded, "Very well. I am still bedazzled by your heavenly performance yesterday evening."

"You are too sweet." Juliette smiled back at him.

They were seated by Rufus. Mr. and Mrs. Armstrong were absent. A young lithe black woman appeared with a pot of hot corn meal mush, molasses, cream, and a platter of fried bacon and ham. All the items were on a large tray that she carried on her head, bracketed by her up-reached arms. She brought the tray down gracefully to the table and unloaded the food.

"All of you folks can eat. Da Armstrong's are late risers, so its da usual case to eat wit out dem." The young woman bowed and said, "Ma name is Phinney. If you all need somethin', ring the bell on the table. A'l be fetchin' the coffee now." Phinney was dressed in an empire style calico dress of green hues. Her head was wrapped in the same fabric. She was attractive in the style of dress and the way she deported herself. She left the room.

The three said grace and began to eat. Not losing a moment, Juliette urgently asked, "Mr. Paxton, when are you leaving for New Orleans?"

"I was going to leave today, but after you two ladies retired for the evening, Clayton asked me a favor. How could I refuse? He wants me to deliver some supplies to Montgomery. So now I must leave today for Montgomery instead."

"Certainment." Juliette said quietly, crestfallen. "Then would you return here before going to New Orleans?"

"Yes, I would collect my imports from the warehouse and load them on Clayton's wagons, then head to New Orleans." Mr. Paxton added, "The trip to Montgomery might take two to three weeks before I would see you lovely ladies again."

Disheartened even further by the news of Beamus' long absence, Juliette was silent for a while. Then she added, "Upon your return, could you take us with you? Mme. Bernard and I would love to visit with you for a while." Juliette added thoughtfully, "I will be writing my fiancé's parents at Fair View to see how James is doing. I want to do that before I travel there."

"Oh, I would be delighted to have such talented traveling companions!" Paxton's mustache quivered with joy.

With new purpose Paxton said, "Well, I must get going. Hopefully, it won't be any longer than two weeks."

"I will miss you and your wiggly mustache, Mr. Paxton. May I call you Beamus?" Juliette smiled flirtatiously as she twirled one side of his mustache with her tapered fingers.

The Armstrong's entered upon the tender scene. Peevishly, Armstrong glared at Paxton and Juliette. "I see someone likes mustaches."

Paxton a bit flushed said, "Juliette seems to like mine and I am flattered to know that such a beautiful woman can find something attractive in a balding middle-aged man," It was meant to placate Armstrong. Instead, it added to Armstrong's foul mood.

"Balding and middle aged is right. And what goes right along with it is foolishness, which is the sum total of a buffoon!"

There was dead silence after Armstrong's emotional outburst. It even surprised Armstrong. His wife witnessed how enflamed her husband was, and her suppressed anger was now revealed in her face. Her eyes burned into her husband's.

Armstrong changed tactics. "Paxton, I see you have finished with breakfast. All the supplies are loaded on two wagons and await you, Montgomery bound."

Paxton relieved for his dismissal said, "I already have my bags packed and loaded. So, I will say good-by and hopefully will return in two weeks.

They walked Beamus to the wagons. Armstrong, pleased that Paxton was leaving said in a patronizing voice, "Have a good journey and keep the supplies safe."

Juliette waved, "I'll be praying for your safe return, Mr. Paxton"

He smiled and said, "Thanks." Then he shook the reins of the six horses which were pulling both wagons. The rear wagon was attached to the lead wagon Paxton was driving. He rattled away from view.

Juliette's heart sank. Mr. Paxton would have been a means of escape from Mr. Armstrong.

Suddenly Armstrong had locked arms with Juliette and was leading her back to the house. "Come, join us for breakfast."

"Thank you. We have already eaten, and now I feel tired. I need to rest. Please excuse me." She said truthfully. "Thank you for being such wonderful hosts and for being so understanding for my need to rest." With that she disengaged her elbow from his and joined Mme. Bernard who walked upstairs with her.

Miffed at being out manipulated, Armstrong shouted to them, "We can't have you gals languish in that room too long. I know, I'll send Phinney up to give you backrubs by and by."

Juliette turned and smiled weakly, then disappeared into the room. "Mme. Bernard, what are we to do? Mr. Armstrong has sent Mr. Paxton away. He was our means of escape. Now we are trapped like birds in a cage!"

"Now, now, Juliette, Armstrong does have some wrong ideas, but he is married, and his wife is not a fool. We will keep her as informed as possible to his every move. That will put a fly in the ointment." She said reassuringly.

Juliette sighed, "Truthfully, I am exhausted after this morning's events. Let's take a nap." They both laid down on the bed and were soon asleep.

Later, a soft knocking came from the door. "Miss Juliette, it's Phinney. I'z suppose to give you a backrub, iffin' you wants one."

Juliette and Mme. Bernard roused themselves. "Come in Phinney I'd love a backrub." Juliette said.

Phinney opened the door and glided into the room. She was carrying some bottles and towels on a tray. "Please take off you dress and slip so I can rub your back." Juliette complied. Phinney gave Juliette the first massage she ever had. With experienced fingers Phinney massaged away tension and muscle knots in her neck and shoulders. Afterward, Juliette felt relaxed and invigorated.

"That felt very good. Mme. Bernard, you would enjoy it too." Juliette encouraged. Mme. Bernard nodded in agreement.

"Phinney, could you give Mme. Bernard a backrub also?"

"Sure can."

Mme. Bernard had a similar positive experience. She asked Phinney, "Where did you learn such skill in massage?"

"I learnt from my mammy. It jus' come down from the No Where to the Here."

It was then Juliette noticed Phinney's left hand. Half of her little finger was missing. Juliette asked, "Phinney, what happened to your finger?"

Phinney was silent for a while, studying her missing finger as a forgotten feature of her left hand, then calculating how much truth these women from France could handle. She felt that they were up to it.

"When ah was 'leven ah didn't live here. Ah come from Georgia. The people that owned me put me up for sale. Ah didn't want to leave ma fambly; my mammy, paw, and three sisters. But they sent me off to the black slave market in chains. We had to walk there. We walked and walked all day with the slave driver crackin' his whip on our backs and legs. Finally, we had to rest for the night. We was in the woods. While everyone was sleepin', I fount a sharp-edged rock next to me and a flat one was under me. So, I put my finger on the flat rock and wit all my might came down wit the sharp rock and cut off my little finger at the second joint in one blow."

"Mon Dieu! Why ever would you mutilate yourself?" Juliette asked horrified.

"Cuz then ohm damaged goods. If ah be damaged, ah won't fetch a good price and maybe not be bought." She looked sadly at the floor. "Ah was tryin' to stay wit my fambly."

Both women understood why Phinney chose such a desperate measure. She loved her family and did the only thing she could think to do when eleven years old.

"Didn't work so good. Ah was solt anyway for a cheaper price to da Armstrong's. Ah been here nigh on to nine years." Phinney said resignedly.

From the telling of her dire history something made her grab at her middle. The two ladies helped her sit down. "For a long time, ah worked in the fields pickin' cotton. After a while ah was caring for the newborn slaves in da nursery and the older chilins up to four years old. Ah cooked for them made good soups and stews from the garden ah grew. Dose chilins grew healthy and strong. Then the cook at the big house up and died. So, the masta learned ah was a good cook. He brought two other cooks from the nursery and me to the big house just' afore he went to France. The good part is we eats better than before, mo' meat an a bit of cheese. The bad part is ah has to sleep wit Mr. Armstrong many a time."

Juliette and Mme. Bernard were stunned again. Mme. Bernard, being older and from a theatrical background was slightly less impacted by the last revelation. She asked, "Phinney, is Mrs. Armstrong aware of the situation?"

Phinney looked them both in the eye. "Mistus Armstrong knows 'bout it, heps it to happen, and mus' like it, cuzzin she won' haf to oblige."

"Diabolique! From the pit of Hell!" Juliette whispered to Mme. Bernard.

Feeling the compassionate attention of Juliette and Mme. Bernard, Phinney further divulged, "Now ahm wit chil'. Ah don' want dis poor innocent babe born into the misery of slavery." Phinney's shoulders shuddered in abject despair as she protectively embraced her womb.

Juliette and Mme. Bernard were brought to tears… too much, too grim, too sad. Both ladies moved to the chaise lounge where Phinney sat with tears rolling down her face. They sat on each side of her and gave her a hug.

Finally, Juliette said, "When we are broken and helpless, we must pray to God for help."

All three went to their knees and joined hands. Juliette gave voice to the prayer in her heart. "Dear God, please help us. I implore all the angels, saints, and souls in purgatory, especially St. Polycarp, St. Augustine, St. Rita, and my dear mother, Teresa Sidamo, to pray to Mother Mary to plead the blood of Jesus over every living soul on this plantation. We plead protection for Phinney and her babe in the womb. Please baffle the Armstrong's and whoever holds evil intentions here from perpetrating those actions. In Jesus name, bind up the demons that obsess, oppress, or possess anyone in this place. Bind them up thrust them into Hell. Continually wash them in your precious blood. Let the scales fall from their eyes, may they repent and join your flock, Jesus. Please let the Armstrong's be open to your grace and uncover the good. We thank you for hearing us. We consecrate ourselves to the Immaculate Heart of Mary, the Most Sacred Heart of Jesus, all in union with St. Joseph, Mary's Most Chaste Spouse. In Jesus name, Amen."

Having prayed, gave the three women peace.

Juliette said, "God is on our side. I will trust in Him."

Both ladies gave Phinney a hug as she squared her shoulders took her tray of lotions and towels and left the room.

Mme. Bernard and Juliette prayed intermittently throughout the rest of the morning. They dawdled in their room as lunch came and went. About two in the afternoon, they emerged to go for a stroll. They walked up the wide lane that led from the house to the main road.

Silently, they walked pondering their strange predicament when from behind them they heard horse hooves pounding. It was Mr. Armstrong on a large mahogany horse. Clumsily, he dismounted and said, "There you are ladies! Now that you have rested and had a backrub, you ladies should be up for a tour of my plantation."

Memphis fell the 7th of June 1862. No bombardment of the city was necessary. The Confederate army slipped out of the city at night.

The Confederate Commander promised he would be back. Several days had passed since the river battle near Memphis and its subsequent surrender. Yet Winslow's men would still talk about the dramatic event in more detail.

One soldier said, "Commodore Davis sure could move his vessel!"

"Yep, all he had to do was pull out of the way, and the two attacking Reb boats damaged each other. His fleet hardly needed to lift a finger." Another soldier added.

A rider hurriedly galloped into camp. He was from General Vale's headquarters. He entered Lt. Colonel's office. Winslow was sipping a midday cup of coffee. The Union courier said, "Colonel, sir! You and your men are to head south today!" He then unrolled a scroll of papers and read, "You will proceed east to the Tennessee River and then south in the most direct route." Then he handed a more detailed order to Winslow.

The rider departed as quickly as he had arrived. Winslow went outside his office tent and caught sight of Ezra grooming his horse. "Ezra, blow assembly!"

When the men had gathered, Winslow announced, "Men we are moving south again."

A mighty yip and hurrah went up. Winslow felt that his company of men was like a small cog in the big wheel of the North's military machine. Seemingly insignificant, yet so necessary to turn the wheel to move forward in the Great Cause.

"Men, get your gear ready in a half hour. Assemble here again at that time."

One soldier asked, "Sir, what are we going to do with all the tents, equipment and bedding?"

"General Vale is a good detail man by his written orders I received from the courier. Before we head south, we will relay our tents and such, over to the waiting riverboats on the Tennessee River and float it down to a designated point. All horsemen, cavalry, and wagon masters will go by land. The cooks will follow in their wagons, so we won't miss a meal." Winslow smiled at the plump soldier who had asked the question.

Winslow looked at him in particular and added, "So help them, men."

"Yes, Sir!" said the plump soldier who apparently had a vested interest in the cook's welfare.

"Does everyone have plenty of ammunition?"

"Yes Sir!" They all shouted.

"I also received word that we will not only forage for ourselves, but we will also be foraging for several other companies under General Buell. Same objectives: cattle, poultry, cloth, wagons, and any usable articles or provisions."

The men were in good spirits. Morale seemed high in general for the entire army. Solid indications were the many new units that kept pouring into the area around Shiloh from the different states under elected officers. There was an eagerness in the male citizenry to enlist in the Great Cause. Some more recalcitrant governors concerned about public opinion, allowed regular army officers to take charge of the eager enlistees.

The 26th Kansas Cavalry moved into Mississippi. The camp was ideally situated, not far from the Tennessee River. It was also close to the Alabama and Tennessee state lines. Winslow's men staked out a remote forested area near the northeast corner of the Mississippi wilderness. Their orders for relocation originated from a staging area around Shiloh. The ripple effect of the new recruits swelled the army rolls. Winslow's ranks burgeoned as the many new soldiers were sent his way. Their new location was ideal with nearby cold spring water, a plateaued knoll for the tents which was strategic for observing the enemy, and it was well camouflaged with trees and brush. They settled in like second generation fleas on a dog's back.

Everything went well in the new Mississippi camp as Winslow and his men took a greater interest in foraging because there were many more soldiers to feed. General Vale and Colonel Melton oversaw the other unit designated for foraging operations. Their prescribed area was in a different section so there was no overlap. The army had to eat, and now. It was a priority. The army had little means of preserving meat, so all the livestock were driven on foot behind the army.

A few days after settling into the new encampment, Lt. Col. Winslow headed out on a foraging mission with his more seasoned soldiers. He took a more southeasterly direction. After traveling about fifteen miles, he came upon a secluded plantation. It was of dark gray brick construction. The buildings were rather new. The Greek colonnades were of white marble, all eight of them. The shutters were all white with the crowning glory of a red slate roof. The barns were well-maintained.

Winslow gave his men a command to spread out around the plantation. "Men, you see the front lane to the house? Major Lester, Captain Tobias, and I, will go investigate and disarm. Bugler, dismount and keep your eyes on me. At the first shot, blow charge."

"Sergeants, take your men to positions indicated." Winslow pointed to the four corners of the exterior of the house. "Bugler will sound orders as instructed. Listen for the bugle call."

"Yes, Sir," said the officers as they put their spurs into their mounts and headed for their assigned positions.

Lt. Col. Winslow, Major Lester, and Captain Tobias went down the outside lane, the bushes covering their advance. The objective was to secure the house unobserved and obtain potential firearms within.

A loyal slave gave a yell to alarm the household. The slave happened to see a few blue coats in front of the house but did not see Winslow, Lester, and Tobias on their approach outside the bushes. A white male came out of the front door and shot a pistol at the blue coats. Ezra blew charge.

The six hundred cavalry made a charge for all they were worth. Winslow and his select group were overtaken by the cavalry within a few feet of the front door. The man who had shot the pistol was visibly frightened. He put his hands up in surrender. All three hundred and five slaves followed suit as well as an older white man that had been out in the fields.

The man on the front veranda had dropped the pistol when he had put his hands up in the air. He said with a quaking voice, "G-Good morning, General," as he looked to Winslow.

"Pleasantries to you, Sir." Nodded Winslow. Looking back at his men, he asked, "Men, are any of you hurt?" A silent pause affirmed no death or injury.

Winslow asked the young man on the veranda, "What's your name?"

"Terrell Bouldergreve."

"Well, Terrell Bouldergreve, do you know what you did when you fired that pistol?"

"You set off a cavalry charge." Winslow smiled. "With your pistol shot, the house and grounds have been taken. We advanced on your signal."

Winslow had been in the Union Army more than a year. Gray hair had become visible at his temples, and furrows had chiseled deeper into his brow. "Who is the older white man in the field?"

"That is my father-in-law."

"How many guns do you have Bouldergreve?"

"Just the one I have here." He nodded to the pistol he had dropped.

Winslow gave a tedious sigh. "Bring the women and children here." Some soldiers entered the house for that purpose. Soon there appeared two little girls and their mother behind them. They entered the circle of which Winslow was the center and the cavalry surrounded them.

Winslow smiled down at the little girls. They must have been five and eight years old. He kneeled to their level and took each one into the crooks of his arms. "I would like to have two such pretty daughters. Maybe someday I will. I like your soft, dark curls. You both look like angels." The girls giggled and closed their eyes as they were very shy, but they liked the handsome officer who was so kind to them.

"Does Daddy have any more guns for me?"

"Yes, Daddy has a trunk full of guns upstairs."

Winslow got up on his feet and grinned at Bouldergreve as he said, "We won't have to track all over your house, now, Bouldergreve."

Bouldergreve edged closer to his wife who wasn't pretty but striking. Her hair was deep chestnut and was swept loosely into a bun. Her face was quite pale which contrasted dramatically with her dark brown eyes. Her husband, Terrell, looked bland with watery blue eyes and blond hair. Incongruous, was his heavy ruddy features to his flaccid physique. It was as if Bouldergreve sought a strong barrier of protection between Winslow and himself. Mrs. Bouldergreve was that barrier.

Winslow studied Bouldergreve a long time. "Why aren't you in the Confederate Army?" As Winslow observed Bouldergreve's furtive behavior, he grew contemptuous.

"I am sitting it out! The danged Secessionists won't protect my property."

"Would you fight for the North?"

"No, I wouldn't." Bouldergreve answered.

"Do you have a Confederate uniform?"

"No."

Suddenly, the youngest daughter looked very happy as the thought occurred to her, "Daddy has a uniform like yours, General, only it's gray."

All the soldiers roared with laughter at the sweet incrimination of the little girl's revelation. Winslow joined in with a hearty laugh.

"Why don't you have your uniform on?" Winslow asked. "I could have you charged as a spy, here and now—you know that?"

Bouldergreve took a step forward, his face unusually flushed, mostly from embarrassment. "I'm disgusted with the way the war is run so I came home to sit it out."

"You can still join the North and I will overlook some of the incidents."

"No, never..." Hesitated Bouldergreve. "The Southern people would take revenge on me."

"Well, go and get your uniform on. You are now a prisoner of war." Winslow grimly concluded.

Major Lester cast a look of disdain at Winslow as he said under his breath, "Winslow's too easy for my tastes."

Winslow said, "Men! Gather the guns from the trunk upstairs. Then bring them here."

The men followed orders. They brought the trunk of guns to Winslow. There were twenty-five firearms in all. There were French,

English, and Spanish pistols. The men drew lots for the weapons. All the new weapons found homes in a holster or belt.

"Men, Terrell Bouldergreve is a prisoner of war. We will take him with us to camp." Said Winslow.

"Also, round up the cattle, horses, mules, and other livestock. Fill your canteens with water. Post a guard at the well while doing so." Shouted Winslow over the din the men were making as they went their various was in order to execute his orders.

"Come along Officer Bouldergreve," said Winslow. "You look like a Brigadier General. I'll see how far wrong I am." Winslow motioned for him to go into the house. A sumptuous interior greeted them. Highly polished mahogany floors, carved oak doors, and gleaming copper doorknobs sparkled in the late afternoon sunlight that came from a large parlor window.

Some of the soldiers helped Bouldergreve's father-in-law onto the veranda and seated him in a chair. All of the present events were too much for him. He had tears running down his cheeks. His granddaughters rushed to his side to comfort him.

Winslow, Bouldergreve, Lester, and Tobias were mounting the stairs and passed a gilt candelabra on the rounded staircase landing. There was also a window beside it which viewed a brook in the distance. First room on the right was the little girls' room. Next, to the left was a guest room. Then the third on the right apparently, was Mrs. Bouldergreve's. There was another guest room and finally, Mr. Bouldergreve's.

"Lester and Tobias, stand guard here. I will go in with Officer Bouldergreve while he changes into his uniform. I still say he is a Brigadier General. Tobias, what's your guess?

"Same as you, Sir"

"Lester, what's your guess?" Winslow was trying to lighten the gravity of Bouldergreve's cowardice and bereft family by focusing on the diversion of a guessing game.

"Captain, I'll say, Sir."

Bouldergreve and Winslow vanished into the bedroom, the door slightly ajar. It was an opulent room, housing an intricately carved mahogany dresser and four poster bed. The room had three windows that faced north overlooking the wooded lane that approached the house. The walls were curved with light green floral themed paper that extended to the high ceiling ending flush with the crown molding. In one corner there was a white marble fireplace. On the floor before it was a brown horsehide.

"Nice rug, Bouldergreve." Winslow commented.

It was my wife's favorite riding horse. She loves horses."

Bouldergreve opened the closet door. Inside were many suits and one uniform. Winslow had been sitting on the bed and now got up and examined the collar tabs. Removing the uniform from the rack, he then handed it to Bouldergreve. In a loud voice Winslow states, "Lester wins. Bouldergreve is a captain."

Lester overheard and smirked silently with self-satisfaction on winning the wager over Winslow.

"Yes, I made captain in a blanket order from Tennessee out of the statehouse." Bouldergreve said ruefully. "I would be a higher rank than captain but for one thing, I didn't polish any apples around Nashville."

"Nashville has fallen or is in the state of being occupied," said Winslow.

"I expected as much." Visibly reluctant to go forward and put on his gray captain's uniform, Bouldergreve asked, "Where are you from?"

"I am from Topeka, Kansas, and most of my unit is too. Many men will claim states where they were raised. I figure with all the sacrifices I have made in my personal life for Bloody Kansas, I am a Kansan." Winslow's voice gained in fervor.

"Where were you raised, Colonel?" asked Bouldergreve.

"Near Covington, Indiana, doubt you've heard of it."

"Is that near State Line City, the railroad interchange?"

asked Bouldergreve.

"Yes, you know that place?"

"I went through there one time, maybe ten years ago. I was seeing the country. Busy place."

"Small world," philosophized Winslow. Sensing the motive for Bouldergreve's questions and wanting to satisfy his curiosity, Winslow asked, "I don't want to be too personal, but I noticed you and your wife have separate rooms, why?"

Bouldergreve crimsoned and said, "There is a war on. A pregnant wife or a small baby are too vulnerable."

Winslow smiled sheepishly. "Sorry, I was too personal."

Winslow changed the subject. "Where is your sword?"

"On the closet shelf."

Winslow confiscated it since Bouldergreve was a prisoner of war and had now dressed in his uniform. Winslow and Bouldergreve left the room. Tobias and Lester followed. At the foot of the stairs stood Mrs. Bouldergreve with her daughters who were nervously playing with their dolls.

"What are you going to do with my husband?"

"Now that he has his uniform on, he is prisoner of war." answered Winslow.

Mrs. Bouldergreve began to cry as she brought a handkerchief to her eyes. Both girls wrapped themselves in the generous folds of their mother's skirt, peering out at Winslow. With eyes that had suffered betrayal.

"Mama what are we going to do?" the girls asked.

Mrs. Bouldergreve regained her composure. "Dear Blanche and Susan, we will pray for this horrible war to end soon so your father will be back soon. We will keep a lamp lit at the window for him to see upon his return."

It was all he could do not to look into the sad eyes of the children. "Captain Bouldergreve fired a shot at my men. He could have been shot as a sniper." Winslow said in a hollow tone.

Mrs. Bouldergreve ran to her husband and embraced him around the neck. His children hugged his legs. His wife kissed him with real feeling. A shadow crossed Captain Bouldergreve's face as he said, "Your love for me will keep me out of danger, don't forget that."

"I'll never forget," responded his wife gravely. All soldiers present were visibly moved.

Winslow was flummoxed, "Come, come, it isn't as bad as all that. It's 1862. I daresay, in a year all hostilities will be over, and your husband will be free."

Mrs. Bouldergreve looked sternly at Winslow as she said, "I believe you love capturing people and taking them away from their families. You can't possibly be a family man because you have no feelings!"

Blanche and Susan were tugging at their father's pant legs and frantically repeating, "Don't go, Daddy please!" It brought tears to Bouldergreve's eyes.

The eloquent scene touched everyone. Reluctantly, duty prevailed, and the soldiers escorted Captain Bouldergreve to one of his own steeds. He waved to his wife.

As the men disappeared, Mrs. Bouldergreve, who had watched from the front window went to retrieve a lighted lamp and placed it in the window.

While the sad scene of the Bouldergreve's was taking place, the other soldiers in the same company had rounded up the horses and stock. The young slaves that wanted to join the Union Army were induced to do so. Twenty young men in all, joined. They rode on the extra horses. Thirty horses had no riders. The wagons held the poultry, geese, and ducks. When all were leaving, Captain Bouldergreve rode next to Lt. Col. Winslow, Major Lester, and Captain Tobias.

"Well Colonel, I am fortunate to be alive. A hot-headed commander would have shot me," acknowledged Bouldergreve.

"It's a good thing you didn't hit any of my men in the thicket or I would have been forced to execute you as a sniper. The men thought you were firing at me while I was making my way down the lane. You didn't even see the three of us, did you?"

"No."

The conversation was carried on in low tones. Commander and prisoner were ignored as the soldiers paid practical attention to the livestock, horses, and former slaves who had joined their ranks.

They arrived back at camp to the welcoming aroma of the evening meal. The cook had made kettles of beans with bacon and pots of stewed chicken.

Colonel Boyd Melton was in Winslow's tent reading the Memphis Newspaper, which was fifteen days old, but news was news.

"Hello, Colonel Melton. Did you get anything on foraging operations, today?"

"Not much." Melton answered as he looked up from the paper. "Just a few scrub cows and a wagon load of chickens."

Winslow said, "We did slightly better. Plus, I have one prisoner of war, meet Captain Terrell Bouldergreve, C.S.A."

"Good evening, Captain Bouldergreve." Melton said.

"Good evening," said Bouldergreve in a subdued voice.

The men outside their tent were busy eating. The cook brought in five portions for the officers and prisoner: Bouldergreve, Lester, Tobias, Melton, and Winslow. All ate heartily.

"Bouldergreve," said Winslow between mouthfuls, "likely you'll be headed north tomorrow."

Bouldergreve put down his fork and asked, "Where will they send me?"

"Rock Island or Chicago, Illinois."

Bouldergreve had a worried expression. His shoulders slumped in despair.

Winslow sensed his mood, "We'll send word to your family. Go ahead and eat."

After they had eaten Winslow called for the Captain of the Guard and said, "Here is a prisoner of war, Captain Terrell Bouldergreve. Take him to the guard house." A cabin in the woods was used for this purpose.

Winslow sat down on his cot. Wearily, he ran both his hands through his hair. Bracing his elbows on his knees with his hands supporting his head, he looked downward and muttered, "I feel like a dog for doing this, he seems like a good family man."

Lester was sitting on his cot nearby. "I personally would have shot him for a sniper. He did shoot first."

"That is heartless considering he killed nobody." Responded Winslow.

"War is war. This is not a picnic. We are here to fight and get it over with so we too can go home to our wives and children. But we put our lives on the line in sacrifice for The Cause." Snapped Lester.

Tobias agreed, "War is hell for all. At some moments even worse. Today is finished. There were no casualties. Nothing further can be accomplished."

Winslow was more at peace with his treatment of Bouldergreve after hearing what Lester would have done. His mind turned to the tender scene of the Bouldergreve's separation. In his heart he yearned for a faithful and loving wife like Mrs. Bouldergreve. And children, many children as he drifted off to sleep.

CHAPTER 9

Part 1
Rebel Raid

All was peaceful in camp until a little after four in the morning. A bugle call in the distance could be faintly heard by the Sergeant-of-the-Guard in his guard hut and it was not a Union bugle call. Moments later he heard a sound like dull thunder that increased to a loud roar. He determined that it was Confederate Cavalry headed toward the camp. The sergeant stepped outside his hut and shot his pistol into the air. It made a loud report and everyone close to the guard heard it. By now there were Confederate Cavalry riding through camp screaming like Indians. The bluecoats barely had time to scramble pell-mell into the trees for protection. From Winslow's persistent reminders, most men had pistols on their persons and were ready for close quarter fighting. The Confederates, with the darkness and the thick stands of trees, failed to scatter the Union horses. Some tents were crushed in the foray.

Lt. Col Winslow found himself behind a tree, coatless, hatless, and his bugler nowhere nearby. Without his bugler, Winslow's ability to communicate orders in the semi-darkness was nonexistent. Feeling vulnerable as thoughts rifled through his mind such as his men effectively had no leader, no commands could be made, and no order executed. If the Rebels decided to stop and take Union prisoners, it would be a rout. Fortunately, the Rebels had been met with such a hot reception of pistol-packing Yankees that they had hurried through camp as though wildly enchanted, pressing their steeds into a furious gallop. The Rebels headed back in the direction they had come. As the sun rose, the Rebels became perfect targets for the Yankees who were well concealed in the trees and brush. It seemed surreal how quickly the Rebels had attacked camp, and how quickly they had disappeared.

"Men, assess damages, then report to me." Winslow said reeling from the Rebel's surprise-attack. Trying to regain his focus, he began to walk the perimeter of the camp.

He came upon his bugler, Ezra Peabody, who was sitting on a log rubbing his shoulder. He saw Winslow and said, "I'm sorry, Sir, that I didn't make it to your side for orders. I tried to get to you, but the stampede of horses was too thick to forge through. I bounced off a galloping horse and banged up my shoulder."

"It's alright, Ezra. The Rebs are gone. As far as I have walked through camp, there are no casualties. Have Doc give you some horse liniment to rub on your shoulder." Winslow said.

Winslow continued his walk. Several soldiers reported to him on his walk. Angenlak spoke to Winslow. "Sir, I have checked the whole camp. My observations are that there are a few trampled tents, no casualties, two of our men were knocked out but have returned to consciousness. The men have caught four Rebs, a sergeant and three privates."

"Good work Angenlak." Winslow responded.

The camp was falling into the morning breakfast routine. Still not feeling inner calm, Winslow continued to walk. His vulnerability at the beginning of the surprise attack haunted him. It opened the door to the many horrors he had experienced since the war officially began. Each battle, skirmish, ambush, execution and now the recent surprise attack seemed to make it harder for him to find peace. He glanced about and found Reverend Blake nearby brewing a pot of coffee on a campfire.

"Come, Colonel Winslow. Join me in a cup of coffee. The morning is still young, and I hanker for our morning brew." They both moved closer to the blazing campfire and its inviting warmth. Winslow reached over and lifted the scorched pot from the metal grate, then poured two tin cups full of the amber brews. Silently, they sipped the hot coffee comforted by the other's presence. By now, the morning was bright and still which contrasted with the short, noisy attack that happened a brief time ago.

Winslow broke the silence and said to Blake, "I never gave it a thought until now about camping in the thick of the woods, but it sure saved our necks."

Reverend Blake smiled. "I had to dash about twenty feet from my tent to a tree, and there were two other fellows already there. I never let on that it was me in the dark, a commanding officer, seeking shelter behind a tree."

"No one killed in this skirmish. A few fellows were knocked cold. A Confederate sergeant was knocked from his horse and captured along with three privates." Said Winslow.

"Sometimes our Maker smiles down on us in a big way." Said Blake.

Winslow finished his coffee, feeling calmer, he continued his walk through camp with Reverend Blake. He noticed that the disruption from the Reb raid had stalled the men's routine. Some were finally putting on their uniforms.

They came upon the Sergeant-of-the-Guards. "Where is the Confederate Captain Bouldergreve?" Asked Winslow as he noticed the cabin door ajar where Bouldergreve had lodged.

"I discovered him gone just as you walked over here. I'll send some men after him." Said the sergeant. Some raw recruits were standing nearby, tender in years, ranging in age from sixteen to eighteen.

Winslow spotted the young soldiers and said to the sergeant. "These men will do." He turned to the young men and said to them, "Go find that Rebel captain. Don't shoot him unless he is balky."

"Yes Sir! They eagerly responded.

After the young men departed, Reverend Blake, who had observed the scene, said to Winslow, "I get it. You sent greenhorns to recapture Bouldergreve. They are less likely to succeed."

Winslow responded, "I have done my duty detailing a search party."

Winslow motioned to Blake to continue with him on his walk. He still wasn't himself since the surprise attack. An emotional numbness seemed to be settling in his brain. His mind was desperately trying to escape feelings of vulnerability. Winslow noticed the dark, gloomy shadows cast by the trees and foliage. The stillness of the woods for mid-morning was a somber reminder of how quickly it could change. The gloom seemed more oppressive as they walked deeper into the trees. Winslow was acutely aware of the stark countenance of war. Now more than ever, he fervently hoped that he would live through the horrific ordeal the war had become for him. His heart ached for the warmth of a home and a family of his own. He had seen glimpses of good homes when both of his parents were alive and well. Also, when Zekiel and Edna Smythe welcomed him as a teenager.

He observed that families are the building blocks of humanity. Everyone has or had a family they were from, and most people started families. Then he remembered Able, a black man that he had helped to escape to the north to be free from slavery. When he had asked Able if he had a family, Able had shed bitter tears of being betrayed because his slave owner had sold off his family as so much cord wood. It brought Winslow's mind back to a renewed resolve to see the war through to the end so that families could flourish, unbroken. Winslow and Blake returned to camp.

The men in camp were cheerful. Horseplay and laughter were heard. It seemed like a holiday frolic. One fellow held up his crushed canteen. It had been trampled by the galloping horses in the surprise attack. "Now ain't that purty?" Said the gleeful private. He went on, "That rebel horse had a mighty big foot!" All the men laughed along with him.

The search party had only been gone a couple of hours. They marched into camp with Bouldergreve in front of them. The party of five went to the commander's tent to report their prisoner. Reverend Blake and Captain Tobias were with Winslow.

"Here is the rebel captain, Sir."

"Good work, good work." Said Winslow with obvious surprise. "Take him to the guard hut."

"Will do, Sir."

After the group had gone, Winslow said ruefully, "I was sure wrong on my guess about those youngsters! I now think it would have been better to have sent older married men after the escaped prisoner. They would have felt sorry for him and not have been so successful."

Blake chuckled, "It just dawned on me that the youngest had mentioned to me the other day, that he was a trapper, and could find a trail anywhere."

Tobias laughed, Live and learn."

Winslow just shook his head and smiled.

An hour later General Vale and Colonel Melton came into camp. They surveyed the broken tree limbs and the scuttled tents that Winslow's soldiers were trying to salvage. Vale said, "Looks like a windstorm hit your camp, Winslow."

"Yep, some Rebel outfit found our camp. I sense they are disgruntled for being called to retreat from Memphis." Winslow added with a glance to the Colonel, "We sure saved your hide Melton. The attackers got a taste of pistol bullets and high-tailed it back to their camp instead of continuing in the same direction. Otherwise, you'd be next."

"Yes, you sure did save our hides." Melton agreed.

The Rebs like skirmishes, surprise attacks, and raids, small scale stuff. I hear tell of many camps that have had to deal with this, so be prepared at all hours."

General Vale added, "You were quick witted by camping in the woods. It gave you plenty of cover."

Winslow said, "Take cover where you can. Find it from now on, in a grove of trees, plantation buildings, whatever." He changed the subject as the Sergeant-of-the-Guard appeared. "We have an assortment of prisoners, one captain, one sergeant, and three privates. Bring them here." He addressed the Sergeant of the Guard.

The guard hut was quite a distance, so the guard jogged over to the make-shift prison to retrieve the captives. Soon he reappeared, out of breath with the captives, and with the youngsters from the search party who were guarding the rear. "Here they are, Sir."

"That's all sergeant."

The Confederate Captain Bouldergreve looked sullen and the four others looked relieved and happy. No doubt, if turned loose they would fight like wildcats again, all except Bouldergreve.

General Vale said, "I will take these prisoners back with me escorted by the Sergeant-of-the-Guard and those four extra soldiers."

"Very well." Winslow said knowing his attempt to allow freedom to Bouldergreve had gone awry. Now the prisoners would be taken to Memphis with General Vale. They departed.

It was getting very dark. The woods looked haunted and lonely. A chill went down Winslow's spine. He felt abandoned and homesick. Soon Ezra was blowing taps. Quietly, Winslow slipped under his blanket. He locked his massive hands under his head and closed his eyes. He had a dream girl and soon she appeared in his mind. There she was with dark cascading curls, brilliant eyes, and gracious smile. Then she suddenly disappeared like a wild bird.

"Wait for me, wait for me." Said Winslow in a half whisper. Soon he was sound asleep.

Part 2
Tour of Veil Wood, November 1861

"Why Monsieur Armstrong! You startled us! Certainly, we'd enjoy a tour of your plantation but first let me return to my chambers for a parasol." Juliette smiled at him.

"Why of course!" Armstrong beamed, feeling things were going his way. He dismounted and walked his horse alongside the ladies.

When they arrived at the portico Mrs. Armstrong stood in the frame of the door. "What's wrong Clayton? You took off on that horse like a house afire."

He sheepishly glanced at his wife, gained a moment, then said, "Scamp needed to run."

Juliette took it in but acted oblivious to Mrs. Armstrong's dour mood. "Why Mrs. Armstrong, your husband wants to take Mme. Bernard and I on a tour of the plantation. Will you join us? I am sure there are highlights of this place that could only be told from a woman's perspective."

Mrs. Armstrong's frown evened out into a flat line as she considered Juliette's complimentary invitation. "I've lived here all my married life. It doesn't interest me. You ladies go ahead." A long pause followed. "Enjoy yourselves."

With that, Juliette and Mme. Bernard went upstairs. While in their chambers Mme. Bernard said, "Besides a parasol, bring a fan and wear sensible shoes. We need a lot of props today." Quickly, they collected the items, put on the sensible shoes, then headed downstairs to a waiting Mr. Armstrong.

The carriage was ready and manned by the short plump slave who had picked them up in Mobile. Once the ladies were seated in the carriage, Armstrong said, "Let's go, Chitlin'. We will begin the tour on the road that circles the house."

"Yas, Massah," Chitlin said loudly to make certain Armstrong heard him.

Mme. Bernard and Juliette sat on one side of the carriage and Armstrong on the other side, directly across from Juliette. He was staring at Juliette again. His eyes bored into her like chisels. Juliette opened her parasol low over her head, cocking it at an angle that hid most of her head. Also, she opened her fan and covered her lower face. Only her eyes were exposed. Conveniently, she turned her gaze to the passing scene.

Disgruntled, Armstrong cleared his throat. "This is the main cook house where most all our meals are prepared. We are fortunate to have three good cooks. Each has some special recipes." It was the whitewashed building where the women had bathed and laundered their clothes.

"There is the kitchen garden which has played out except for root vegetables and some herbs." Continued Armstrong.

Within a stone's throw was another building. "This is the smoke house. In the fall we usually slaughter a dozen or so pigs and smoke hams, bacon, and what not. We also make salt pork. Built on the smoke house is an extra kitchen so if we have many guests over for a gala event, a ball, or a political meeting, there is plenty of stoves to cook up vittles.

In the next building we render lard from pig fat. It is used in making soap, and in cooking and baking."

"The house slaves like the innards so they make chitterlings out of the intestines. So, everything is used except the air in their lungs," laughed Armstrong.

They came upon a row of twelve whitewashed cabins with two cabins at a distance from the others. The two were slightly more resplendent than the others with whitewashed picket fences and curtains in the windows. "Those two houses with the fences are for the overseers. The rest of the cabins are the house slave's quarters. Those slaves keep the main house and grounds running smoothly plus the barn animals. Their job titles are cooks, laundresses, maids, butlers, house boys, carriage drivers, gardeners, livestock tenders, barn keep, and smithy."

Juliette thinking that was the end of the tour, said, "It is like a little village, tidy and clean. Thank you for the tour. I can walk back to the house." She stood up in the motionless carriage about to get out.

"Whoa! Sit down Missy. We're not done with the tour." Armstrong commanded. "We have the cotton fields yet to see."

Juliette sank back into her seat. The carriage continued down the narrow dirt road. Eventually, they came to the cotton fields. There were some slaves picking cotton and putting it in long bags they dragged behind them. Other slaves were hoeing. Women, men, and adolescents worked together. Upon closer observation, Juliette noticed some slaves had raw wounds or healed scars on their backs and legs. They wore scant rags for clothing.

Armstrong bellowed proudly, "We have had a bountiful cotton crop this year!" He added, "Cotton can be harvested as early as October and as late as December."

The distant silhouette of a man on horseback caught their eyes as the carriage rounded the corner of the next field. The man on horseback rode toward them. He was short, stocky and well-muscled. "Mr. Armstrong, greetings." Sweat dripped from his face. His smile revealed large spaces between his teeth. Narrowing his eyes through the sun's bright glare, he appeared calculating as he studied the two women in the carriage.

Armstrong puffed up like a bullfrog, "How's it going today, O'Leary?"

"Not too bad. I did have to whip the bare haunches of a nigger wench who wouldn't come to the fields to work." O'Leary proudly showed him the whip still wet with blood. Grasping the tail of the whip, he slid his hand down the cord and purposely smeared the fresh blood on his trousers all the time watching Juliette.

"Let me guess, was it Callie?" Armstrong ventured.

"Yep. She said she wasn't feeling well so I was obligated to make that true!" O'Leary chortled as spittle shot through the spaces in his teeth.

After O'Leary's comment, Juliette was in turmoil. Anger, frustration, and revulsion played a tug of war in her mind and body. She retreated further behind her parasol and fan. Mme. Bernard was feeling similar emotions. Under both their voluminous skirts she secretly nudged Juliette's thigh.

"Oh-h-h-h..." Mme. Bernard uttered as she swooned and slumped limply on Juliette's shoulder. "Monsieur Armstrong! Take us back to the house! Mme. Bernard has fainted!"

Disappointedly, Armstrong complied. He nodded to Chitlin and they headed back to the main house. By the time the carriage had come to the front portico, Mme. Bernard was coming out of her faint. "Mmm, Oh." She moaned as she touched her forehead with the back of her hand."

"Chitlin, carry Mme. Bernard up to her room." Armstrong commanded.

"Thank you." Juliette said to Armstrong as she hurried up the stairs after Chitlin and his burden. Chitlin gently placed Mme. Bernard on the bed, bowed and left the room.

Juliette whispered after him, "Thank you," then she shut the door.

When Juliette turned around, Mme. Bernard was alert and staring at the ceiling. "Are you alright Mme. Bernard?" Juliette asked tentatively.

"Mais oui! I am fine physically. Mentally, I am a mess."

"You are my sister in empathy, Mme. Bernard!" exclaimed Juliette then sat on the bed and gave Mme. Bernard a hug. She burrowed her face into Mme. Bernard's shoulder seeking escape. "I cannot stand to be in this awful place! What are we to do?" Juliette implored.

"Today is Saturday." Mme. Bernard stated flatly. "Tomorrow is Sunday and our day of worship. Pack a small bag. God willing, we are going to Mobile today for confession. We have much to confess since we haven't stepped into a church for two months. Of course, the next day is Sunday mass, a holy day of obligation."

They both packed a small bag and went down to the parlor. Mrs. Armstrong was there looking out the window. Mme. Bernard said to her, "Good afternoon, Mme. Armstrong. Juliette and I need to go to town. As Catholics, we need to go to confession and also attend mass. We've packed a small bag and will leave the rest here. We'd greatly appreciate a carriage ride to Mobile."

Mrs. Armstrong was still looking out the window. She then turned to them and said, "Clouds are gathering. It could rain. I'll have Chitlin drive the covered carriage for you." An almost imperceptible smile curled the corners of her mouth.

Within minutes they were in the covered carriage on the way down Veil Wood's private lane to the main road. It began to rain. Just as they were about to turn onto the main road, an angry Armstrong on horseback, galloped up to them. "Where in tarnation are you women going?" He asked angrily. "Stop the carriage, Chitlin!" Chitlin did as he was told. The carriage came to a standstill.

Mme. Bernard said, "Monsieur Armstrong, we are going to town to practice our Catholic faith. Time and distance requires us to spend two days in town. We will be back Monday afternoon." Then she reached out and touched his hand gently. "We've entrusted the rest of our things to you for safekeeping until we return."

For once Armstrong was speechless. It was the first time he had heard Mme. Bernard talk with purpose and with more than a few words of agreement or a head nod. "All right then, see you Monday." He added uncertainly. He waved, then trotted Scamp back to Veil Wood.

Just to be on the safe side, Juliette spoke in French. "Mme. Bernard, I thank you for your quick thinking and choice words. It's a miracle we escaped that place for a while."

"Remember, we prayed for the good of the Armstrong's. I acted in faith. Through God's grace both were compliant to our request. Mme. Armstrong furnished a carriage and driver. Monsieur Armstrong was confused and let us go."

"We have a few days reprieve." Juliette sighed.

"Dear Juliette, you never know what each day will bring." Mme. Bernard affectionately patted Juliette on the knee.

The steady patter of rain subsided as they neared the outskirts of Mobile. Chitlin slowed the horses and apologetically said, "S'cuse me ladies but ah don' know where wez a'goin. Do you ladies knows where is de Cat'lic church?"

Both women looked at each other, the Mme. Bernard said, "Stop at the hotel on the wharf, please."

Chitlin drove the carriage to the hotel. Both women debarked and went into the lobby and asked the clerk the location of the Catholic Church. He gave them directions to the only Catholic Church in Mobile, Saint Mary's. With that, they were soon parked in front of Saint Mary's Catholic Church. Chitlin's ignorance of the location of anything to do with churches or religion was part of a widely held practice in the South subjected to most slaves by their owners. They were not even allowed to worship. Reduction of outside influences kept slavery more intact.

"Please wait here, Chitlin." Juliette said.

Both ladies went into the unpretentious building. Built of stone and mortar, it faced the bay with a gray stoic, presence, as if unperturbed by the goings-on of man. In the foyer of the church was the baptismal fount. As they entered the church proper, they saw solid oak pews that faced the altar where a plaster crucified Jesus hung on a wooden cross. To the far right was the confessional.

There were a few people in the back pews, kneeling or sitting. Juliette went up to a middle-aged lady nearest the back of the church. "Excuse me. Could you tell me where I could find a priest?"

The lady answered, "Why, he is in the confessional taking confessions from the people."

Juliette thanked her then went to Chitlin. "Chitlin, you can go home. Please remember how to get here so you can pick us up Monday afternoon. "Yes'm." Chitlin nodded to Juliette. He turned to the horses and said, "Giddy-up" and was gone.

Both Juliette and Mm. Bernard waited their turn to receive the sacrament of reconciliation. Juliette went before Mme. Bernard. Once inside the confessional, Juliette began, "Forgive me Father for I have sinned. I have missed mass for more than two months. I have withheld the truth about myself from my fiancé. I have heard and seen firsthand, the wicked treatment of slaves, yet have done nothing to help them. Isn't it a sin of omission not to help those in such terrible distress?" With that she broke down and wept with deep sobs, her shoulders shaking with emotion.

A calm gentle deep voice drifted through the confessional grill. "Empty your heart of all that troubles you."

Juliette took a deep breath and regained her composure. "Where I am staying, a woman slave says she is going to have a baby sired by the slave owner. And the slave owner's wife silently gives permission for him to continue to molest her. The woman slave doesn't want her baby to be born into slavery…To make it even more sad, my chaperone and I had a tour of the plantation and one of the overseers told the owner, in my presence, that he had whipped a young girl slave and gloated about it with sadistic relish as he wiped her fresh blood from the whip onto his trousers. I am sick at heart from all this. I dread going back because I feel the plantation owner has evil designs on me. I must, because all our things, mine, and my chaperone's, are still there. There, I am finished."

The priest spoke. "I want to read some of Psalms 103 to you: The Lord secures justice and the rights of the oppressed. Merciful and gracious is the Lord, slow to anger and abounding in kindness. Not according to our sins does he deal with us, nor does he requite us according to our crimes. For as the heavens are high above the earth, so surpassing in kindness toward those who fear him. As far as the east is from the west, so far has he put our transgressions from us. Now say the act of contrition"

"My God, I am sorry for my sins with all my heart. In choosing to do wrong and failing to do good I have sinned against You whom I should love above all things. I firmly intend to do penance, to sin no more, and to avoid whatever leads me to sin. Our Savior Jesus Christ suffered and died for us. In His name, my God, Have mercy. Amen."

"In the name of the Father, Son, and Holy Spirit, I absolve you of your sins. For a penance say a rosary of the Sorrowful Mysteries. If you are able, please wait for me to finish with the other confessions. I think we should talk further."

"Thank you, Father. I would like that."

Juliette exited the confessional and went to a pew, kneeled and said the rosary. Mme. Bernard joined her after her confession and did the same. When there were no more people, the priest emerged from the confessional. He was quite tall, stooped, with a thick wavy, salt and pepper hair. He was in his late forties. They were the only remaining people in the church.

"Thank you for waiting. I am Father Clancy. Please come with me to the rectory. It also doubles as a parish office."

It was an old stone house within five minutes walking distance from the church.

Father Clancy knocked on the door. A short plump woman in her sixties opened the door. Father Clancy said, "Hello, Aunt Irene." Turning to his guests he continued, "This is my aunt, Irene Clancy, who recently joined me from Dublin, Ireland, to help with the orphanage we have just started, due mainly to the war. She is a great help and a very good cook. Aunt Irene, I would like to introduce you to----"

"Juliette Bellechasse, and my dear friend and chaperone, Mme. Simone Bernard. "Juliette answered. They all shook hands.

Irene exclaimed, "I'm so happy to meet you both! I hope you can stay for dinner. I've made a beef stew and Irish soda bread and there is plenty of it. We also have three more permanent guests whom I'd like you to meet. Nathaniel, Elizabeth and Veronica! Come meet some nice ladies!" Irene had turned her head to direct her voice toward the rear recesses of the rectory.

Three children came running to greet them. They all resembled one another, fair complexions, with a light sprinkle of freckles and abundant chestnut brown hair. "Hello!" they said in unison.

Irene added more plates and utensils to the table, with a big pot of steaming stew at the center. The scene reminded Juliette of Le Mouton Noir. Father Clancy said grace. The children had good appetites and politely ate their meal in silence.

Keeping the conversation general, Father Clancy asked Juliette,

"What part of France are you originally from?"

Juliette answered, "Both Mme. Bernard and I are from Paris. We left early October on a schooner." She didn't want to add that it was a blockade runner and was attacked by the Yankees.

Juliette asked, "What brings you to Mobile, Father Clancy, and how long have you been here?"

"I've been here all of two years. I came at the request of Father Shanahan. I was here three months with him and then I replaced him as the priest for St. Mary's. Father Shanahan had to go back to Ireland because his mother was up in years and he was her only child. It was just enough time to introduce me to the members of parish and become acquainted with them and their needs. It made for a smoother transition."

Juliette asked, "What are their needs?"

"The main need now is to build an orphanage. These three children are without parents because their mother died in childbirth as well as the baby. The father had gone to war just before that, so the children have no one to care for them. Their neighbors brought the children to me. There are other children being cared for by some parishioners."

"Children, it is time for bed." Irene said.

"I would be so happy to tuck them in. I'd love to tell them a story and hear their prayers if they would let me." Mme. Bernard cast an open gaze to Nathaniel.

Nathaniel noticed her look and said, "I like your accent. It's all curly cued. It would be fun to hear you tell a story."

"What a nice thing to say!" Mme. Bernard smiled.

Irene said, "Children, go get ready for bed and then come and fetch Mme. Bernard for a story and prayers."

"Yeah!" they gleefully shouted as they hurried to comply. Shortly afterward, the children returned for Mme. Bernard.

Juliette was helping with the dishes and kitchen clean up. It felt good to be busy in a kitchen again.

Irene remarked, "You certainly know your way around a kitchen."

"Why, yes. I used to help my parents run a restaurant. I love cooking and just being busy." Juliette smiled with pleasure.

When they were done in the kitchen and Mme. Bernard had tucked the children in bed, they all gathered in the parlor with Father Clancy who was busy at his desk. He turned from his paperwork. "Juliette and Mme. Bernard, whatever is said here will go no further. I speak for Aunt Irene, also. With four good heads on our shoulders, sharing ideas, and trusting in the Lord, we will, by His grace, come up with something. If you do not want to share the details, we can simply pray."

"I do want to share. I trust you both and when I can talk about it with someone I trust, I feel it is much more manageable." Juliette responded with Mme. Bernard's complicit agreement through her silence.

"Then we will begin with a prayer, to ask God's grace in your situation." Said Father Clancy. He said a short prayer.

The evening seemed to evaporate. A relaxed and comfortable ambience afforded those present an opportunity for productive discussion of Juliette and Mme. Bernard's predicament. Ultimately, it was decided to do exactly as they had told Mr. Armstrong. They would return to Veil Wood, Monday afternoon but then they would collect their things and stay at the rectory and help Irene. Father Clancy would accompany them as an added protection. There they would wait at St. Mary's until Mr. Paxton came back from Montgomery.

"Well, hopefully everyone can sleep soundly tonight." Father Clancy said in a positive tone.

Irene showed them the guest room. It was Spartan yet perfect. Perfect, because it was on sacred ground. Mme. Bernard was exhausted and went immediately to sleep. It had been a long day with all the events packed into it: Paxton's unplanned departure, Phinney's predicament, the plantation tour, and finally, escape to St. Mary's.

There was a writing desk in the room with quill, ink, and paper. Juliette felt compelled to write James Lambert's parents a letter.

Saturday, November 30th, 1861

Dear Mr. and Mrs. Lambert,

Greetings. I hope this letter finds you well and in good spirits. I wanted to tell you I finally arrived in Mobile, safe and sound. I am so looking forward to meeting dear James's parents. Please let me know when you would be able to receive me. Presently, I am staying at St. Mary's Church in Mobile. Please write me at this address. In the meantime, you are in my prayers. Please greet James for me if possible.

Respectfully,
Juliette Bellechasse

With that, Juliette went to bed and slept soundly. She awakened early feeling at peace in the quiet surroundings. Breakfast was simple and good, hot corn meal mush with molasses and cream. Mass was a t ten o'clock. There were many in the church, so many, some stood in the isles.

Father Clancy's homily seemed appropriate for all that had happened.

"Weeping may endure for a night, but joy cometh in the morning. No matter what we face in life, when we realize God is with us every step of the way, then our burden is light. Each burden that we carry, we carry for Him. There is a greater goodness that is derived from it by entrusting it to Jesus. Trust is the receptacle that holds His graces for us. The more we trust, the more that receptacle can hold even more abundant graces. Likewise, if we trust little, then little grace is given. If you have a difficult time to trust in Jesus, then pray. Here is a short prayer, easy to remember: Jesus, I trust in you! Please increase, my faith, hope, love, and trust even more through your grace. Amen"

After church and a simple lunch, they all sat in the parlor enjoying a cup of peppermint tea. The peppermint had been grown in the rectory garden. Nathaniel said to the adults and siblings, "let's go for a walk. I'd like to show you something."

The whole group of four adults and two children agreed by following Nathaniel outside. Running ahead of them, he motioned them to stop. They were three hundred feet to the rear of the rectory. Nathaniel pointed out several stakes in the ground that dotted the ground. He then rejoined the group. "That is where Father Clancy staked out the future building for the orphanage." Nathaniel shared breathlessly.

"I am happy to see how enthusiastic you are about it." Juliette marveled.

"I can hardly wait 'cause I have some buddies that could play games or go swimming with me. Right now, there is no room, and they are temporarily at some parishioners. So, it's kind of boring." Elizabeth and Veronica looked at Nathaniel sullenly.

Diplomatically he added, "Of course, my sisters would enjoy other girls to play with, too."

Father Clancy smiled at Nathaniel. "Why wait, Nathaniel? Starting Monday, you can have the church shovel and begin to dig a trench following the stakes. I'll tie string to the stakes so that you can align the trench more closely to the staked out rectangle foundation. Plus, on our walk we'll stop at the Wimpells and Norberts to see if Steve and Jeff can help you." He was referring to the other two foster boys.

"Great! I'll run ahead to the Wimpells and tell Steve. I'll wait for you there."

On the walk, they met the Wimpells, Norberts, Steve, and Jeff. Enthusiasm was contagious. Among them, a plan of work formulated. The three boys would each have shovels. They would start digging after breakfast. Veronica and Elizabeth would haul the dirt in an old wheelbarrow to a nearby ravine to dump it. The building project put everyone in a happy mood which carried them through the day. Dinnertime had arrived and Irene had cooked another delicious meal of ham and yams.

"Can I tuck you children in tonight?" Juliette asked pretending to pout by having her lower lip protrude.

"Nathaniel, thinking Juliette's mood was serious, responded, "By all means, we'd enjoy it." Veronica and Elizabeth nodded in agreement.

Mme. Bernard pretended jealousy. "Why children, where's your loyalty? Didn't you enjoy my story last night?"

Not to be caught without a solution, Nathaniel put a practical twist to the situation. "Both of you can tuck us in! I'm sure both of you have interesting stories to tell us."

Mme. Bernard and Juliette both broke out laughing. Juliette said, "Nathaniel, what an extraordinary boy you are! You are the perfect diplomat."

Nathaniel turned red. "You ladies were joshing me! He collected himself. "We'd still love to hear stories from both you ladies."

Father Clancy said, "Since it's the start of Advent, how about something along that theme?"

"Certainment!" The ladies exclaimed in unison.

After all three children were each tucked into their cots, Mme. Bernard went first by dramatically adding facial expressions and suspense in the telling of a beautiful story of the Archangel Gabriel announcing to Mary that she would have a son and that she was to name him Jesus.

It was Juliette's turn. "Let's hear your prayers." In unison they said a Hail Mary.

"Now I will sing you to sleep. She sang What Child is This?Soon they were fast asleep with smiles on their little faces.

Next morning all went to the seven o'clock mass. Then they had breakfast. Soon the children were gathered with their tools and digging in earnest on the foundation for the orphanage. Once they had settled into the work, Juliette went to the post office to mail the letter to the Lamberts. She was dreading going back to Veil Wood.

Upon her return to the rectory, Father Clancy picked up on her mood. Mme. Bernard was feeling the same way. Not long after he had them helping Irene make apple pies. Lunch came and went. Soon it was two o'clock in the afternoon and Chitlin had showed up with the carriage.

"I will accompany you ladies on your return trip to Veil Wood to lend moral support and say a rosary." Father Clancy told the women as he saw Chitlin and the carriage parked at the front gate of the church.

They walked to the front of the church where Chitlin was waiting and got into the carriage. When all passengers were settled, Chitlin had the horses head back to Veil Wood. Father Clancy led them in the Joyful Mysteries of the rosary. Chitlin intently listened.

When they arrived at Veil Wood it seemed like a different place. The front portico had been decorated in red and blue bunting and three Confederate flags hung from the upper balcony. The tall skinny carriage driver was dressed in purple livery in the style of the 1780's sporting a white wig which had a ponytail.

Not only was the somber plantation transformed with festive decorations, but a change also seemed to have occurred with Mrs. Armstrong. She startled Juliette by flourishing down the front stairs with a welcome smile on her face. She wore an off-the-shoulder neckline with billowing sleeves and voluminous skirt all in dark green satin, with a diamond broach at her bosom. As she approached the carriage she said, "Good afternoon, ladies and Father. I am so happy that you have arrived." Her smile revealed even white teeth and softened her face.

For a moment, all in the carriage were speechless. It was such a change in Mrs. Armstrong's demeanor and appearance that Juliette thought it might be another woman. She regained her composure and her roleplaying skills and said, "Why, Mrs. Armstrong, how lovely you are this afternoon and dazzling in your beautiful gown."

"Why, thank you!" Mrs. Armstrong blushed but regained her composure. "We are happy to have you back and as you all can see; we have prepared to celebrate with a much-honored guest. Our most esteemed guest is the President of the Confederate States, Jefferson Davis, and his entourage. At this moment, Clayton is meeting President Davis at the train. Also, my dear brother Terrell Bouldergreve has just arrived." At this point, Mrs.Armstrong turns to glance up the stairs she had descended and motions to a tall blond man to join her. He is dressed in a Confederate captain uniform. He sees her invitation and swaggers down the stairs.

"Why I do declare, you must be Juliette, of whom my sister has heartily praised, looking as fresh as an evening breeze."

The syrupy compliment floated over to Juliette. They all had descended from the carriage. The whole atmosphere pleaded exaggeration. So, Juliette curtsied deeply and bowed her head with her fan in front of her face. Then raising herself to her full height and fluttering her black eyelashes, she responded, "How kind of you, Monsieur Bouldergreve." He took her hand and bowed over it. She was shocked by the soft flabbiness of his palm.

He then greeted Mme. Bernard. "Mme. Bernard, it's a pleasure to make your acquaintance." She curtsied graciously, also.

Father Clancy walked up to him and shook hands. Greetings Terrell Bouldergreve. I am Father Clancy from St. Mary's in Mobile."

"Hello Father! My grandparents, God rest their souls, were Papists." Bouldergreve said. "Their faith didn't seem to rub off on my father, myself, or my children. Presently, you would consider them heathens." He laughed derisively.

Father Clancy responded, "I'd say they've only lost their way. The situation can always be remedied with good religious instruction."

"Why fix what's not broke? They are doing fine presently. Thank you very much." Bouldergreve added condescendingly.

Father Clancy knew when lines had been drawn. He retreated behind his smile in silence.

"Well, now that introductions have been made, come, you all, into the ballroom and see how I had it decorated." Mrs. Armstrong led them into the ballroom where more bunting and Confederate flags graced the walls. There was a bowl of punch on a table with crystal glasses. A stage had been hastily built and arranged flush with the wall under the bunting with two Confederate flags at each end of the stage. The grand piano was at one side of the stage.

Mrs. Armstrong took Juliette and Mme. Bernard aside. In an imploring tone she said, "It is providential that you arrived when you did. Would you be so kind as to entertain our guests this evening with singing and dancing?"

Juliette smiled at her request. "Certainly. May I ask how long your guests will be here?"

"At least three days for President Davis and two weeks for my brother. The rest will leave this evening."

"Wonderful! Mme. Bernard and I will go up to our room and prepare for the entertainment and then come back down to perform." Mrs. Armstrong looked relieved.

She walked over to Father Clancy and said quietly, "I think I will be safe and can handle the present situation for three days, maybe more. Since there are many house guests, it distracts certain people from idle pursuits."

Father Clancy said, "I think God is aiding you. Be of courage, prudence, and wise actions"

After saying farewell to all, Chitlin drove Father Clancy home.

Upstairs, in their room, Juliette and Mme. Bernard brainstormed about their next performance. They browsed over the sheet music that Clayton Armstrong had given Juliette after her last performance. They were simple, catchy tunes. Juliette chose a pale cream-colored satin dress that followed the lines of her figure that flared into a wide skirt for ease of movement, and also had been shortened by Mme. Bernard to reveal her feet in order for the audience to see the dance steps. Juliette decided to go barefoot for more ease in dancing. She had her familiar fan with cream colored ostrich plumes. Mme. Bernard chose a dark coffee colored crepe dress.

A commotion occurred about seven in the evening at the front entrance. They went to the front balcony and could see that President Davis, his entourage, and Clayton Armstrong had arrived.

They practiced a dry run of their newly arranged medley of songs accompanied by some dances, and mimes to go with certain lyrics. About eight in the evening, they came down the stairs in dramatic procession. Juliette was wrapped in a bright red satin cape. Her blue-black hair flowed freely down her back. As in the last night of entertainment, Mme. Bernard came down first to alert the audience of the impending performance. Several of the guests loitering at the foot of the stairs caught a glimpse of Juliette's ethereal beauty. A wave of hushed expectation spread throughout the guests and into the ballroom

Juliette had climbed the steps to the stage. Mme. Bernard stood next to the piano with a fully lit candelabra on top of the piano as well as two chandeliers illuminating the stage. The audience remained in expectant silence. Seizing the moment of quiet, Juliette announced, "I am so happy to be here tonight. Mrs. Armstrong has asked us to attempt to entertain you with our small talents. I should introduce ourselves. I am Juliette Bellechasse, and the lady accompanying me on the piano is my dear friend and chaperone, Mme. Simone Bernard. Hopefully, we will amuse you or at least bring a smile to your face." Mme. Bernard had seated herself at the piano and began with a rousing rendition of the Yellow Rose of Texas. Juliette tossed away her red satin cape and sang and danced through the song. The audience clapped vigorously for more. Juliette continued and was enjoying herself. They weren't the only ones watching. O'Leary was hidden in the bushes by the side of the house spying through the window. He had an excellent view of Juliette on stage. He nursed a half full bottle of whiskey and his lust.

During her performance she spotted President Jefferson Davis seated in a wing-backed chair near the stage. Juliette's stage presence took over from the many years of entertaining the customers at Le Mouton Noir. During the next song she winked at him behind her fan, then danced down the stairs and tickled him under the chin with the ostrich plumes. He laughed.

She ran back to the stage and continued entertaining with song, dance, and mime. Her endurance was extraordinary. She continued for three hours straight. Time melted away. The audience was voracious. They clamored for more even after they had completed their medley. So, they improvised with other songs and finally ended in the Marseillaise.

Finally, Juliette improvised a little ditty and sang, "I am finished, I am done, tonight is ended, no more songs will be sung." Both Juliette and Mme. Bernard curtsied and bowed to thunderous applause and a standing ovation. People crowded around them. At the forefront was Jefferson Davis. He grabbed Juliette's hand and smothered it in hard kisses. He said, "I am overcome with great pleasure by your glittering performance. It has come at a much needed time."

"A million thanks," Juliette said effusively. "I must rest. Please excuse us both." The audience continued to applaud as they ascended the stairs. At the landing both ladies bowed one more time.

Before Juliette drifted off to sleep. She saw all the men and women in the audience in her mind's eye. The women had envy and awe on their faces and the men's jaws were slack with amazement and longing. In her fatigued state, she luxuriated like a drunkard in the sense of power it gave her. Then she asked herself, is it a tool for good or evil?

Part 3
Assault on Juliette

The happy sound of chirping birds woke Juliette from a refreshing sleep. Bouncing out of bed she danced around the room happy and rested. Mme. Bernard gently snored. She was not an early riser. Juliette let her sleep. She slipped out of the room in her robe and went quietly to the kitchen. Phinney was busy cutting ham into slices.

"Good morning, Phinney." Juliette said happily.

Phinney looked beaten down, but mustered, "Morning, Misstus Juliette."

Juliette sensed her sad mood. "How is everything going?"

"Like use'al, Misstus Juliette. I do count my blessings, clothes on my back, food in my belly." She paused as she touched her abdomen. "I can walk, talk, think, and see. I am sad cuz one of the young'uns, Callie, has been whipped bad and hast to lay in the dirt. So now her wounds are infected, bad. So bad infected, pus is oozing and now she has a fever. I knows cuz one of the field hands tol' me on the sly. I'm not allowed to see her. My going would be known by Mastah Armstrong. I trust in the Lord that somehow she'd get help, so I went ahead and made some poultices from tree bark." She lost her composure and her shoulders heaved silently as tears ran down her face. She squeaked, "It's so hard!"

Juliette laid a hand on her shoulder and said, "Please God, help us to know how to help Callie." A quiet interlude passed.

176

"I can't do anything right now, but could you bring me a bucket of hot water, the poultices, and portions of ham and cornbread. I will be trying to figure something out while you do that."

Phinney did as she was told, and brought the hot water, ham, cornbread, and poultices to Juliette's room. Juliette went behind the silk partition and used some of the hot water poured in a bowl and lavender soap to wash herself. She dressed in a dark wine-colored dress with a high collar and had a large hoop cage under it.

Juliette had rummaged through her trunk and found an oil cloth which had protected her packed clothing from moisture. Mme. Bernard woke up and groggily observed Juliette as she tied the poultices in the oil cloth with ribbon taken from Mme. Bernard's sewing basket. Using more ribbon, she attached the oil cloth encased poultices to the exposed grid of the hoop skirt. She tied dried lavender on the other side of her hoop skirt. When done, she dropped her skirt over the hoop cage. She then selected a tall hat with plumes. She carefully wrapped the cornbread and ham in a pillowcase taken from her bed pillow. She put that under her hat.

Not quite alert to the new day, Mme. Bernard said, "What are you doing?"

"I'm going for a morning constitutional to get some exercise. Oh, and Phinney has brought us some hot water to refresh with the lavender soap. There is half a bucket left for you behind the screen."

Juliette grabbed her parasol and quietly descended the stairs. She exited the back door. Walking past the overseer's cottages, she heard loud snoring. Continuing her walk, she made it all the way to the field hand's cottages. They were shacks with no doors. There were gaps in the boards from knotholes and poor construction.

She knocked on the first shack's door frame. "Hello?" she ventured. A skinny ragged, black boy peered out at her. His eyes large with wonder.

"Could you tell me where Callie is, little boy?"

Without a word, he pointed to a shack two door frames away. She went to it and knocked on the door frame. This time she peaked in and saw a young girl about fourteen in years laying on a dirty blanket. Her legs were bare, with scourges festering with pus. The wounds were from O'Leary's whip.

"Callie?" Juliette asked. The girl's eyes opened, and her dry cracked lips parted.

"Yes'm." Callie said weakly. Callie seemed disoriented, only staring at the ceiling, not seeking out the owner's voice.

"I'm going to try to help you." Juliette saw a water pitcher on a small table. Fortunately, there was some clean water in it. Juliette took a handkerchief from her sleeve, poured some of the water on it and gently wiped off the pus from Callie's wounds. She then untied the oil cloth from the cage of her hoop skirt, which held the poultices, unwrapped the oil cloth to gain access to them. The little boy was watching Juliette.

She asked him, "Could you get some more water?"

He answered, "Yes Misstus, ders a stream behind here." He grabbed the pitcher and left.

The oil cloth was big enough for Callie to lay on and much cleaner than the filthy blanket. Carefully, Juliette moved Callie onto the oil cloth and placed the five poultices on each thigh, belly, back, and buttocks. She gently secured the poultices with the ribbon from the hoop skirt.

The little boy came back with the pitcher of water.

"Thank you." Juliette gave him the filthy blanket and pus tainted handkerchief. "Could you wash these in the stream and hang them on a bush to dry, then give them to Callie when dry?"

"Yes'm." He runs to do it.

Juliette takes the ham and cornbread enclosed in the pillowcase and puts the food on a tin plate next to Callie. She shakes the crumbs from the pillowcase and rips it to make a large rectangle cloth, then drapes it over Callie's body. "This will have to do until your blanket is dry." Juliette takes the lavender and crushes the dry leaves around the perimeter of Callie's mat. It repels flies and other bugs. Callie seems to have gone fast asleep.

Silently Juliette prays that Callie will be alright. The little boy reappears. She instructs him, "Make sure Callie keeps the poultices on the rest of the day. Encourage her to eat and drink. Remove the poultices at bedtime and be sure to give her the clean dry blanket."

"Yes'm." He smiles at her.

Juliette heads back to the main house which is hidden by a row of trees. As she passes the first couple of trees, she begins to hear heavy footsteps gaining on her. Whirling around she sees that it is O'Leary.

"Why, good morning Mr. O'Leary." Juliette smiles nervously.

"I'll make it even better, you two-bit whore. Strutting around on stage like a shameless hussy last night!" O'Leary reeked of whiskey. Although he assumed a wide stance, his body weaved back and forth. He reached toward her as he added, "You nigger lover!" He tore her bodice and ripped off two buttons.

"How dare you!" Juliette poked him with her parasol. O'Leary slapped her face and she fell. Out of nowhere a small bull terrier appeared. He grabbed onto O'Leary's pant leg. It gave Juliette an opportunity to get up and run.

Juliette ran all the way to her room. Mme. Bernard opened the door.

Breathlessly Juliette gasped between words, "O'Leary attacked me and hit me in the face! He called me names!" She collapsed into a chair.

"Where is he?" Mme. Bernard was enraged that she had not been attentive to her chaperone duties.

Juliette cried out, "Just past the house servant's cabins!"

Mme. Bernard rushed out of the room and collided with Mr. Armstrong and Mr. Jefferson Davis on the landing.

She said, "Come with me! This is an emergency!"

Wordlessly they followed her out past the servant's cabins. Although O'Leary had lost his balance and was in a prone position, the dog had not let go of his pant leg. He continued to try to detach from the dog in a fruitless effort.

"There is the culprit! He tried to rape my dear Juliette! I demand justice!"

Jefferson Davis said, "There's my dog, Lozie. Looks like she doesn't like him much either! Here Lozie! Lozie come here!"

In the past, Clayton Armstrong had shared a dark comradery with Sean O'Leary, but now it was obvious he was in competition with Armstrong's own tarnished intentions for Juliette. O'Leary's presence could no longer be tolerated.

"O'Leary, you are fired. You are banished from Veil Wood. I don't want to see you on the premises again."

As he staggered to his feet O'Leary said, "You are protecting a nigger lover."

Mme. Bernard was incredulous. "That's all you are going to do? We now have witnessed his foul language! That man assaulted and injured Juliette!"

In Armstrong's unspoken view, he couldn't fault O'Leary for the same temptation he himself felt. He was in a quandary as to what to do next.

Jefferson Davis said, "I do agree with you Mme. Bernard. I can't tell a man what he is to do on his own property. After all, a man's home is his castle. But to even things up---" Davis, at this point, punched O'Leary in the stomach. O'Leary doubled up, then fell to the ground.

Armstrong sheepishly opened his wallet and tossed some money at O'Leary, then gruffly said, "Get out of here!"

They all walked back to Juliette's room. Juliette was in bed and Phinney had put a damp cloth on her forehead. Jefferson Davis was first, carrying Lozie. Mr. Armstrong and Mme. Bernard followed up the rear.

Davis said, "I hope you are feeling better, dear Juliette. It seems Lozie has taken an instant liking to you." At that point, the dog wriggled out of his arms, jumped on the bed and gently licked her bruised cheek.

Juliette was feeling better but mentally still anguished over how close to harm she had been. Feebly she pet Lozie, "I feel so drained of energy."

Armstrong said, "O'Leary has been fired and banished from Veil Wood."

Davis added, "And punished."

Observing the dog's devotion to Juliette, Davis said, "It looks like Lozie has chosen you as her new mistress. Juliette, do you accept her as your own?"

Juliette said, "That dog saved me from grave harm. I would love to have her as a pet. Is that alright with you Mr. Armstrong?"

"W-Why, certainly." It was a less than an enthusiastic response from Armstrong. Now there would be a constant impediment to any opportunity with Juliette.

Mme. Bernard took charge. "Thank you, gentlemen, for your help. As you can see Juliette needs to rest."

The men filed out of the room leaving Mme. Bernard, Phinney, and Juliette alone with Lozie. Juliette touched Phinney's hand as she turned the damp cloth to put the cooler side to her brow. "Don't worry, Phinney, I took care of Callie through God's grace".

Mme. Bernard said, "So that's why you went on a walk this morning with those things tied to your hoop skirt and food under your hat!"

Juliette smiled. "Yes, Mme. Bernard. My conscience wouldn't let me rest if I had not helped Callie. It would also be a sin of omission if I had failed to help her. As Father Clancy said, be of courage, prudence, and wise actions. My mind is at peace for Callie at this moment."

Mme. Bernard appeared introspective, "It seems that several good things came from that evil assault by O'Leary; he was fired and banished, you acquired a guard dog who will now keep Armstrong at bay, and the slaves will not be treated so cruelly."

All three said, "Thank God!"

Mme. Bernard kept vigil at Juliette's bedside. She mended the tear in Juliette's dress and replaced the buttons. Later, she went to the kitchen to prepare tea and a light lunch. Meanwhile, the news of O'Leary's banishment had spread throughout Veil Wood. There was a suppressed joy among the slaves.

In the afternoon Mrs. Armstrong and her brother, Terrell Bouldergreve, came to visit Juliette in her room. Juliette was feeling much better and was seated in a chair with Lozie in her lap. With time to meditate on the brief and pivotal attack by O'Leary on her person, she tried to make sense out of the senseless by numbering the sequence of events and emotions at each point:

1. Initial attack by O'Leary, fear, shock, anger.

2. Arrival of Lozie at the scene, coming to the rescue, relief, courage, escape.

3. Mme. Bernard demanding justice from Armstrong, comfort, vindication.

4. O'Leary fired and banished, peace and relief.

5. All should be peaceful and well with her, but Juliette would return time and again to how close she was to having been violated. If that violation had occurred, how utterly destroyed would any future be for her. Combined with a sense of complete desolation was the memory of O'Leary calling her a whore and a hussy. Juxtaposed with what she felt in her dream, which was an avarice for power over men as she performed on stage. It made her reassess her flamboyant entertainment.

She thought to herself, I need to blend in with the woodwork.

Bouldergreve and Mrs. Armstrong entered the room. Mrs. Armstrong was solicitous, "I do regret that O'Leary tried to sully your virtue. If you would allow me to make reparation for this horrid affair, I would like to give you Phinney as a peace offering. Clayton has agreed to it. Would our meager offering appease your injured person?"

Bouldergreve added, "If one of my daughters had been attacked like that, the attacker would have been shot on the spot." His statement was lending credence to his sister's offer and to Clayton's less than adequate punishment of O'Leary.

Juliette smiled, "Thank you. I do accept." She left it at that, cautious to not reveal how grateful she was to have Phinney free from Mr. Armstrong.

Bouldergreve and Mrs. Armstrong were visibly relieved. "Continue to rest. Thank you for graciously accepting our offer," Mrs. Armstrong smiled as they both left the room.

When alone, Mme. Bernard intently studied Juliette, "Now we have one more blessing to be grateful to God, Phinney is out of the control of Mr. Armstrong. Yet I detect that you aren't quite back to the bubbly Juliette. Can you tell me why?"

After hesitating a moment, Juliette said, "I am in a quandary. I love to entertain yet by what O'Leary said, it is I who invited the attack, by my behavior on stage. To add to that, just as I was drifting off to sleep after my performance last night, I almost felt drunk with the power I have over men. Now, I feel as if I should disappear into the woodwork because I almost ruined my future."

Mme. Bernard took a moment, then said, "Juliette, you have a wonderful gift to entertain. There will always be lustful men and envious women. That is part of life. By having someone assault you from an evil free will, does not make you at fault. I can learn from it. You can learn from it. I have learned to be a more vigilant chaperone. As for your dream of being drunk with power over men, that is a temptation you can resist with daily prayer and God's grace. I have to improve myself by becoming a morning person like you. Perhaps with the help of a strong cup of coffee."

They both laughed.

The next day Juliette was feeling much better. Phinney had moved into their chambers as a personal maid. Phinney enjoyed spoiling Lozie with tidbits of meat from the kitchen. With food as an enticement, she would coax Lozie to beg, play dead, and fetch, among other tricks.

During breakfast in the dining room, Juliette learned from President Jefferson Davis that he would be leaving for the South's capitol of Richmond, Virginia.

Solemnly Juliette said, "Thanks so much for Lozie."

"Why my dear lady, the dog seems to have a strong free will and chose you. I had little to do with it except bring her to Veil Wood." Davis said.

Clayton Armstrong was also at the dining room table eating breakfast. He looked on the scene with ambivalence. Honored to have President Davis as a house guest, yet he was still jealous of the attention given to Davis by Juliette. He was in emotional turmoil from the fallout of O'Leary's actions.

"Reluctantly, I must depart." He rose to his full height, which was well over six feet. He bent over Juliette's hand and kissed it, then waved farewell to all present in the room which also included Mrs. Armstrong, Terrell Bouldergreve, and Mme. Bernard.

They all rose and followed him to the portico where more than a dozen men in gray uniforms were mounted and waiting for him with an extra horse.

Easily, Davis straddled his horse. He nodded to them a final goodbye. The entourage departed with the sound of pounding hooves. All those on the portico watched in silence until they turned onto the main road.

Terrell said, "Sissy, I was going to stay a bit longer, but I received a letter from home, and I must get back. My wife isn't used to long absences. It is necessary that I leave tomorrow morning."

"Terrell! You've only been here three days. I'm so disappointed that you aren't staying longer."

"I shouldn't have told you that. All I have are women folk and my father-in-law. He is still grieving hard from the loss of his wife. They are overwhelmed running the plantation without me. I do have a couple of overseers. But as overseers goes, there's more O'Learys out there than you think."

A bit more subdued, Mrs. Armstrong said, "I do understand, especially after what happened here recently, my dear little brother." She patted him affectionately on the shoulder.

As they were conversing, Lozie came running from upstairs and then happily ran around Juliette. Armstrong sauntered to the side veranda and lit up a cigar. Terrell and Mrs. Armstrong sat in chairs nearby.

Juliette said, "Come Lozie, let's go for a walk to the main road." It was fun to watch the dog run, sniff, and explore. At the same time, Juliette had overheard of Terrell's early departure. It would mean that Mr. Armstrong would be less hindered except for Lozie. Maybe the dog would be enough. A pounding of hooves and the rattle of empty wagons made Juliette look to the main road. A sole driver was pulling two wagons as he turned onto Veil Wood's lane. It was Beamus Paxton!

"Bonjour, Monsieur Paxton!!" Juliette yelled and waved at the same time.

He halted the wagons. "Why, good morning Juliette!"

"You are back early! I thought it would be two weeks. It's only been five days. What happened?"

"You could say I was intercepted by our own Confederate troops. I was two days out and came across our soldiers and they were kind enough to take the goods directly to their destination in Montgomery. It saved these horses extra wear and tear." Paxton smiled.

"What good fortune!" Juliette exclaimed. "Are you very tired?"

"Not really. Though, last night I was. I was planning to arrive last night but was too tired. Not too far from here was a small inn run by a widow lady. I shared a delicious meal with fellow travelers and slept well in one of her rooms. So, I left there at dawn and have arrived here. I have no complaints."

By this time Clayton Armstrong had strolled down the lane to Paxton. "You're back early, Paxton."

"Mission accomplished." Paxton smiled happily.

"Come in! You deserve a drink after eating so much road dust. Let's gather in the library."

Paxton parked the wagons which were hitched together. They all went into the Library to hear the news. Of his journey. Everyone settled in comfortable chairs. Armstrong poured Paxton a shot of whiskey.

Paxton began, "As you might remember, I departed Saturday morning. The weather and road conditions were optimum for travel. I traveled for two days. Nighttime I would pull the wagons into the shrubs and trees so I wouldn't be easily seen, then slept till daylight. Monday afternoon, I came upon a Confederate convoy. I told them I had supplies to deliver to military headquarters in Montgomery. In talking, the commanding officer of the convoy told me his destination was also Montgomery and his superior's name. Once he had volunteered that name, I revealed that the supplies were for his troops. He suggested he could take the goods the rest of the way since he had two empty wagons. He was a very thorough young man. I gave him the list of goods. He copied it and asked for your name and address and wrote that down, too. He also said he would send a letter of receipt signed by that superior upon arrival in Montgomery and send it by courier to you. I hope all this meets with your approval, Clayton."

"While we are waiting for the courier, you can stay here at Veil Wood and rest. Once I get the signed receipt, then you might be on your way." Armstrong stated flatly, lacking warmth.

Paxton responded disappointedly, "Fine with me. Now that I had some whiskey and sat a spell, I'm getting tired."

Mrs. Armstrong said, "You are welcome to rest in your old guest room upstairs."

"Thanks. I'll take you up on that." He got up and wordlessly went to the door.

Juliette and Mme. Bernard were the next to excuse themselves. Lozie followed. The Armstrong's and Bouldergreve remained.

Once they were in their room, Juliette said, "It almost seems the next question is, what will Mr. Armstrong do if the courier doesn't show up?"

By dinner time the courier still hadn't shown himself. After dinner they all retired to the parlor. Mme. Bernard played some beautiful piano music. Juliette still didn't feel good enough to sing. During Mme. Bernard's performance they all heard an insistent pounding on the front door. It was the courier. He asked the butler to see Armstrong.

The butler led the courier into the parlor. After a brief greeting, the courier handed Mr. Armstrong a document. Armstrong studied it for a long time. Grudgingly, he said, "The goods have been delivered to the correct place. You can leave, soldier."

Paxton smiled, "Well, Clayton, I will be leaving in the morning since the mission is confirmed legitimate."

Armstrong responded testily, "Don't be in such an all fired hurry to leave, Beamus! I might need to send you somewhere else."

Paxton hesitated for a second, then ploughed in, patience by the wayside. "Confound it, Clayton! I have delayed going home to New Orleans long enough! I haven't been home in four months! I need to go home and check on my family."

"Well you just do that! Be selfish! Go home!" Armstrong yelled.

Juliette wanted to jump into the fray but knew nothing could be gained by arguing with Armstrong. Instead, she walked over to Mme. Bernard who was at the piano and whispered in her ear. Mme. Bernard began to play "Lenore" and Juliette began to sing the lyrics. Attention was deflected from the argument. Juliette sang several more calming ballads. Everyone found a seat and listened.

Afterward, she said, "It is late, and I think we all should get a good night's rest."

Beamus gratefully stood. Juliette linked arms with Beamus and whispered in his ear, "Don't forget, I am going with you tomorrow morning."

"How could I?" Beamus smiled wearily.

Armstrong glared at them. Seemingly thwarted at every turn. Many frustrations weighed on his self-absorbed mind; the loss of O'Leary, his right-hand man, Phinney, his sex slave, and Juliette, a potential conquest. A deadly reckoning of slights festered in his mind. He went to the library for a drink.

The next morning Juliette woke early. She woke up Phinney who was sleeping on the chaise lounge, then Mme. Bernard. "It is five in the morning. My plan is to load up the wagons with our trunks and valises before seven. Is that possible, Phinney?"

"Yes Ma'am! And Lozie too!" Phinney said gleefully.

After dressing for travel, Mme. Bernard and Juliette went downstairs for breakfast. A new cook had taken over Phinney's position. A plump woman slave in her mid-thirties hustled around the dining room table, efficiently setting the table with plates and silverware.

"Mistusses, yous up early, early!" She said as she finished arranging the table.

"Yes, we are! There is more daylight for travel." Juliette said.

Beamus entered the room appearing happy and refreshed. "Good morning, ladies!"

"Good morning, Monsieur Paxton! The ladies said in unison.

He added, "It IS a good morning! Finally, we are going home to New Orleans. My bags are packed and already loaded on the wagons and ready to go."

The door of the library opened. Out stumbled Clayton, bleary-eyed. "There you all are! Did I hear you all are leaving?"

All three nodded their heads in surprise. Armstrong heaped into a chair at the dining room table. He narrowed his eyes. "I cannot allow anyone to leave!" he pulled out a flask from his coat pocket, drained it, and slammed it on the table. It was obvious that he had been drinking throughout the night.

"By the way," Clayton sneered, aiming his gaze at Beamus. "If and when I allow you to leave, don't bother to pick up your French imports at the wharf warehouse, I donated them to Jefferson Davis for the war effort. Ha ha! You'll be traveling light with just your travel trunks!" He finished with a crooked evil smile.

Juliette felt her heart tumble. She glanced at Beamus who had turned red with anger, then set his jaw in forced restraint. Mrs. Armstrong had taken in the whole scene from the stairs. She descended and went into the library and returned to the table carrying a tall glass of whiskey. Silently, she sat down across the table from her husband placing the glass of whiskey in front of her. "Good morning folks. From what I overheard; it sounds like Clayton doesn't want you all to leave."

Mrs. Armstrong touched Juliette's hand in a purposeful way, as she was beside her. She turned her head toward Juliette and away from her husband. Winking at Juliette, she said, "You all just relax and enjoy breakfast and stay another day." All except Clayton noticed her wink.

Juliette understood the wink. "Why, certainment. One more day won't hurt a thing."

Clayton noticed the whiskey in front of his wife. Grabbing it, he said victoriously, "I'll drink to that!" and drained the whole glass.

In silence they ate breakfast. Soon Clayton's head lay on the table. He was unconscious. The cook brought out more bacon, cornbread, and coffee. In spite of Clayton, they all ate heartily.

Mrs. Armstrong spoke, "I apologize for my husband's heavy-handed ways. Now that he is in a very deep sleep, you folks can leave like you had planned. In fact, I am leaving too. Terrell will take me to our widowed sister for an extended visit for Christmas and most of January. Clayton was gone for four months to France while I was here at Veil Wood. It is now his turn to keep the home fires burning."

All were spellbound by Mrs. Armstrong's talking spree.

"Th-thank you, Mrs. Armstrong. You know your husband well." Juliette said.

"Too well." Mrs. Armstrong said disdainfully.

"Vera Lee, I will need to retrieve my trunks from your husband's warehouse in Mobile. For that, I will need an extra key and wagon."

"Certainly." She rose, went to her husband, reached in his vest pocket, retrieved the key, and gave it to Beamus.

"Thank you." He said.

"By the way," Mrs. Armstrong unhooked her diamond broach fastened at her throat and put it in his hand with a key. "I can't make up for all of Clayton's tomfoolery, plus your loss of goods, so this might help a bit. Your wife, I know, loves jewelry, especially broaches."

Beamus, unaccustomed to Mrs. Armstrong's candor and kindness said, "Vera Lee, that broach is a family heirloom. I would think that you'd want to hand it down to your children."

"I only have two sons whose wives don't like to visit here, for obvious reasons. I can't blame them. But I do know and am fond of your wife. You are both good people. Just keep it and hush."

Beamus knew that he had encountered a rare and beautiful gesture from Mrs. Armstrong. He was moved to bow deeply and kissed Mrs. Armstrong's hand. "I will be forever grateful for your generosity and kindness. And how well you know your husband and how to deal with him. This morning's events have been seared into my memory forever."

Mrs. Armstrong blushed, embarrassed by his gallant display of words and actions. She firmly grasped him by the shoulders and turned him toward the door and gave him a little push. "Oh, get on with you! You and your falderal."

"When you are done with the key, leave it with Tessie at the Black Eyed Pea. You can take your sweet time sending the wagon and driver back to Veil Wood, if not in this lifetime, the next!" Mrs. Armstrong smiled broadly still pink from Beamus's kiss on her hand.

All was finally ready for departure within the hour. There were two wagons. Mrs. Armstrong had lent one driver, Chitlin for one wagon. Beamus manned the other lead wagon with Juliette and Mme. Bernard as passengers. Chitlin and Phinney followed in their wagon.

As Beamus and company departed from Veil Wood's private lane, Terrell and Mrs. Armstrong waved to them from the portico. Rufus helped load up luggage into Mrs. Armstrong's carriage for her departure.

Juliette yelled, "Bonne Voyage! Merci! Thanks again!"

Terrell and Vera Lee waved and smiled.

The weather was crisp and cool as they made their way to Mobile Bay. By ten o'clock they had arrived at the wharf. While the wagons were being loaded with Beamus' trunks, Juliette and Mme. Bernard decided to walk the dog over to St. Mary's Parish.

Juliette knocked on the door. Irene opened it. "Good morning, ladies!" Nathaniel, Elizabeth, and Veronica chimed in a greeting also.

While they were talking, Lozie slipped through the door to greet the children. She especially liked Nathaniel, bathing his face in expansive licks. Nathaniel asked, "Can I go outside and play with the dog?"

"By all means. You'll discover Lozie knows a few tricks. Especially, if you reward her after each trick with a tidbit of meat scraps from your kitchen." Juliette informed them.

All three children were excited. With Irene's permission, they took some meat scraps from the kitchen and went out to play with Lozie.

Irene said, "I'm so glad you stopped by. Would you like a cup of mint tea?"

"That would be wonderful!" Mme. Bernard said.

While they were enjoying the tea in the cozy kitchen, Juliette said, "We are headed to New Orleans to visit Mr. Paxton's Plantation. Here is the address." Juliette handed a paper to Irene. "If you receive any mail for me, would you forward it to the New Orleans address?"

Irene said, "Of course!"

Father Clancy opened the kitchen door and saw the two ladies at the table with Irene. "Well look who's here, safe and sound and fit as a fiddle."

He gave both lady guests a hug. "I suspected we had visitors when I saw a small dog playing with the children."

Juliette laughed. "So good to see you Father Clancy. Prayers do open many graces and blessings. We left Veil Wood with an extra blessing, our little dog, Lozie." Juliette then explained what transpired when Father Clancy had left them on Monday; her performance, O'Leary's assault, Lozie's rescue of Juliette, Jefferson Davis giving Lozie to her, receiving Phinney as her own maid servant, and Mrs. Armstrong's many kind deeds.

I do see God's grace in your narrative." Father Clancy said after listening intently. "I was also praying for everyone at Veil Wood."

"Thank you for that, and everything. We are now on the way to New Orleans with Mr. Paxton. I have left that address with Irene to forward mail there. It is St. Andre's parish."

Father Clancy said, "St Andre' Parish! I know Father Gibbon who is the pastor there. He was a fellow seminarian back in Ireland. He is like a brother to me." Father Clancy smiled, and added, "He is my brother in Christ."

"That is good to know." Juliette responded. "Now we must get back to the wagons before Mr. Paxton counts us tardy and leaves without us."

They went outside to collect Lozie and say goodbye to the children. Unaware of the adults, the children were playing fetch the stick with the dog.

"Children! Mme. Bernard and I are leaving. Can we have a hug goodbye?" Juliette spoke loudly over the playful commotion.

Nathaniel was the first to hear Juliette. Reluctantly, he walked over with his sisters and Lozie.

"I see you have made friends with Lozie." Juliette smiled at Nathaniel.

"Yes Ma'am. That's the nicest smartest dog I've ever played with." Nathaniel pondered silently, then said, "I know orphans don't have much say over themselves but if Mistress Juliette and Father Clancy would agree, I could teach Lozie a whole bunch more tricks. Could we keep her for a while?"

All was silent then Juliette remembered how Lozie had rescued her. "Nathaniel, Lozie, has a strong will. Let's see who she chooses."

"Lozie, do you want to stay with Nathaniel or go with me?"

Lozie whined and laid down at Nathaniel's feet. She looked up expectantly.

"Father Clancy, it looks like Lozie wants to stay here. Is that alright?"

"Yes, because it will help teach the children responsibility for another creature."

The children jumped for joy while Lozie scampered around them.

"Nathaniel, you are the oldest of your siblings. Please be a good example of how to act responsibly with Lozie." Juliette hugged him in parting.

"I will, in everything I do." Nathaniel said solemnly.

She tousled his hair to lighten the mood. "Until we meet again."

Mme. Bernard and Juliette gave a few more hugs and said their goodbyes then headed back to the wharf. The wagons were loaded and ready to go. The two women climbed aboard with Beamus and they began their journey to New Orleans.

CHAPTER 10

Part 1
Loss of Second Lieutenants

It was a beautiful sunny morning in late September of 1862. Lieutenant Colonel Winslow, Major Lester, and Reverend Blake were sitting under an ancient, stodgy pine tree. Evidently, it had been full grown by Revolutionary War times, but that silent witness would not reveal its unique history. Presently, Winslow's men had camped for the last two months at the same wooded area not far from the Tennessee River. It was a convenient location for reception of army supplies that were floated down the river by boat then hauled overland by wagon to camp.

One such wagon had just arrived in camp. The wagon was being unloaded of supplies. Winslow watched the men receiving rations as he fanned a fly away with some paper documents. The soldiers waited patiently in line as standard rations were portioned out. As for now, they were fortunate to have their diet supplemented with foraged beef, pork, poultry, and vegetables, yet the mainstay was hardtack and coffee.

Hardtack was a plain flour and water biscuit. It was called hardtack because it was unleavened and baked till dry and crisp. A day's ration would be nine hardtack biscuits, but there was usually enough for those who wanted more. While hardtack was nutritious, a hungry man could eat his ration in short order and still be hungry. Coffee was very important to the men also. It usually was brought to camp in an oat sack. The quartermaster apportioned it among companies. It had to be fairly divided among the men. One method was to spread a rubber sheet on the ground and put as many equal piles of coffee as there were men. The coffee ration was appreciated by the soldier. It was an unspoken rule that when a soldier needed to drop out of the march, he could build a fire and cook a mess of coffee.

Winslow's thoughts were elsewhere as he had problems on his hands. "I'm losing too many second lieutenants." He stated flatly to Major Lester and Reverend Blake. He continued, I am not losing the majority of them in a charge or in combat. It seems like a few were killed in ordinary accidents like a misfired or malfunctioning rifle. It is very puzzling."

Winslow compressed his lips as he fixed his gaze on Major Lester, "I have noticed in retrospect, that some of those now dead, second lieutenants were shined up like stars. They were overbearing to the men down to the most picayune detail of protocol."

"Yes, I noticed that too," Blake mused. "Not too long ago, maybe a week, I saw a soldier carrying water to camp and was unable to salute a certain second lieutenant in a timely fashion. So, this certain second lieutenant had the poor fellow strapped to a spare wheel on the caisson. That soldier was in the sun for hours."

"Why didn't you tell me about that Reverend Blake?" Asked Winslow brusquely.

Blake averted his eyes. "I am not to interfere with orders of duly appointed officers. Higher authority told me this. Besides, you were at general headquarters." He finished weakly not satisfied by his explanation.

Major Lester appeared uncomfortable as he cleared his throat and shifted his glance to the line of soldiers collecting their rations. "I am parched. I need some water." He excused himself and headed for the water bucket.

Reverend Blake made full eye contact with Winslow. In a low voice he said, "Why do you think those second lieutenants got all shined up like stars? Because those second lieutenants knew how to play Major Lester by being his spit and polish disciples. So, Lester turned a blind eye to their shenanigans." Blake's gaze shifted back to Lester as he drank from the water dipper about thirty feet away.

Winslow enlightened by Reverend Blake said, "I have had enough of Napoleon's spit and shine falderal, wherever it comes from. Hmm, I think I will snare me a rabbit."

Winslow nudged Reverend Blake as Major Lester approached, "Continue Rev."

"Well, I can talk about the second lieutenant's mistakes now that he is dead. That was Private Von Kluge on the caisson wheel." Said Blake.

"Dad-burn it! That man on the wheel was in my command!" Exclaimed Winslow.

Did Von Kluge Kill that second lieutenant?" asked Winslow.

"No, he didn't. Von Kluge was in camp all day. He was extremely fatigued, had sore muscles, was sun burnt, and was suffering from sunstroke." Blake continued, "I remember this, on September nineteenth, same day, at the small battle of Iuka, the second lieutenant fell off his horse dead. The soldiers he was leading were witness to this. Since they hadn't yet come upon the battle scene, it could have been an enemy sniper. That is just a guess on my part."

"Too bad circumstances put me at General Headquarters when this was going on." Said Winslow regretfully.

To distance himself, Major Lester added, "When you are gone, Colonel, the second lieutenants will play. I mention that group because the more experienced officers don't have time or energy to persecute the soldiers."

"My second lieutenant losses have been disproportionate as I look at the casualty sheets: four second lieutenants and five soldiers have died this month. Three of those second lieutenants died under suspicious circumstances and the last was killed prior to engaging the enemy at Iuka. The five privates died on the battlefield from enemy fire, confirmed by fellow soldiers." Winslow mused as he reread the casualty list.

"That percentage is high for second lieutenants, I agree. I know that they were all from Topeka, Kansas, and had joined us right after Fort Donelson. The fact that they came from the same town cast doubt on their character." Concluded Lester.

"Interesting reasoning, Major," Said Winslow, "If, in fact, the deceased were truthful about their place of origin. By the way, how did you know they were all from Topeka?"

"Why, why," Stuttered Major Lester, "It was on the casualty list."

There was a long pause. Winslow handed Lester the casualty list and quietly asked, "Where?"

Major Lester's eyes darted frantically over the casualty list as he searched for city and state of the dead. Some of the deceased did have city and state listed. But none of the four second lieutenants did. "Oh, I forgot! I remember asking each of those four, there place of origin when they first arrived here after Fort Donelson. "Lester said weakly.

"Good memory in attaching names and hometowns. This adds to the mystery of their deaths, all second lieutenants, all allegedly from Topeka, Kansas, and now Major Lester's opinion that they were of dubious character." Reflected Winslow.

"Hmm…I'm going to ponder on the situation a spell, and I do better pondering when I walk. Blake and Lester, you are excused." Said Winslow.

Winslow walked throughout camp observing soldiers attending to various activities. He saw Von Kluge sitting on a stool oiling his pistol. "Hey Von Kluge!" Winslow addressed him and at the same time waved his hand for the private to remain at ease.

"Hi, to you Sir."

I heard not too long ago; a second lieutenant tied you to a caisson wheel in full sun for several hours."

Von Kluge's lips thinned from the distasteful memory, "That's right, Sir."

"I want to apologize to you on that action. That second lieutenant is now dead."

"Right sir. He's dead, Second Lieutenant Shelly. That day he was killed at Iuka, I was in camp."

"Acknowledged. Besides that, what information or impressions do you have in particular? Anything would be helpful."

"I recall it was early August and we had been on a foraging mission. The horses had been rode hard. Mine was in a lathered sweat, so as we neared camp, I dismounted and was brushing down my horse. I was out in the periphery of camp, in the brush. I must not have been noticed. From my location, I heard Second Lieutenant Shelly and the three other second lieutenants talk like they had known each other a long time. It was mentioned that they had come from Kansas as second lieutenants and joined our unit just after Fort Donelson. The gist of what I overheard was that they were members of the Knights of the Golden Circle. Before the war, one mentioned burning down parts of Lawrence, Kansas, to get rid of the Free Soilers. Also, one of them said that they were originally from Missouri.

"Border ruffians." Stated Winslow.

"There was no way I could have told anyone because they seemed to have gained the confidence of the higherups. My horse did whinny softly when there was a lull in the conversation. I suspect they knew I had heard them. I high-tailed it out of there on my horse. They saw me. After that Shelly made it tough on me." Von Klug hesitated. "He plain dogged me. He'd come upon me when I wasn't expecting him. Like he had nothing better to do than to make me salute or examine my boots."

Von Kluge sighed. "Finally, he caught me with the water buckets, and I couldn't put them down fast enough to suit him, so he had me fry in the sun.'

"Desperate actions from desperate men." Observed Winslow. "You being tied to a caisson wheel got everyone's hackles up."

"You called that right, Sir. Maybe when they went to the battlefront, it came down to just a good marksman spotting a Reb spy. Or even that marksman could have been a Reb sniper who shot one of his own unknowingly."

"Continue with your pistol cleaning." Winslow moved on. He remembered Von Kluge had come from Germantown, Ohio, with another young man. Winslow knew him by sight but couldn't recall his name.

That soldier was butchering meat with his buddies. The tall, blond well-muscled soldier was doing an expert job dressing the beef. He had skinned it and was cutting it up in portions with a highly sharpened saber.

"Come here soldier."

"Me, Sir?" Asked the soldier as he was unaccustomed to being addressed by the top man of the outfit.

"Yes, you." said Winslow.

The soldier walked toward Winslow, coatless, sleeves rolled up above his biceps, and His hands covered in blood. He saluted palm out to keep the blood from dripping on his face. Instead, the blood made a detour down his forearm and dripped off his elbow.

Winslow returned the salute and commanded, "At ease. What's your name and rank soldier?"

"I am Private Wilhelm Miechin, Sir."

"How long have you been with our outfit, Private Miechin?"

"Since Fort Donelson."

"Did you join up by your lonesome or with friends?"

"There was several of us that got patriotic fever. Five of us came from Germantown, Ohio, and joined up at Fort Donelson."

"Wilhelm, how do you like camp?"

"Fine...now, Sir"

"What do you mean by, 'fine now'?"

"Some officers had made life miserable around camp. They are no longer here, and things are much better, Sir." Said the soldier with a smile.

"Did you shoot Second Lieutenant Shelly at Iuka?"

"No Sir, I did not. I was under the command of Lieutenant Campbell in Company B. Ask him. He will verify it"

"Go fetch him for me Wilhelm." Winslow ordered.

Moments later Wilhelm brought Lieutenant Campbell, a small wiry man in his forties, to Winslow. "Lieutenant Campbell, did Private Wilhelm Miechin ride in Company B the day that Second Lieutenant Shelly was killed?" Asked Winslow.

"Yes, Sir. Private Miechin was about five feet in front of me with a pistol in hand. We were at some distance from Shelly who was in Company L. I'd gage the distance from my company about a quarter to half a mile, way out of pistol range." Added Campbell as he arched his eyebrow for emphasis.

"Lieutenant Campbell, you are excused. Miechin, stay with me."

Winslow's amber eyes pierced deep into Private Miechin's glassy blue eyes. Winslow said, "You seem to have uncommonly high spirits. Is everyone as happy as you?"

"Yes, Sir! We have the best commanding officer in the army!"

"Private Miechin, you are excused."

"Major Lester!" Winslow shouted.

Lester was at his side in seconds. Winslow commanded, "Find Ezra, send him here to blow assembly."

"Yes, Sir!"

Soon Ezra was by Winslow's side blowing assembly on the North end of camp. The men ran in all forms of dress and undress, buttoning coats on the run. Winslow noticed one soldier in particular. The cuffs of his trousers were frayed, his knees were bare, and his hair stuck out of the holes in his cap. Winslow made a mental note that the next spare pair of pants must go to that man. The woods were full of briers and thorns, so trousers didn't last long.

The men gathered around Winslow. He began to speak. "Men, I have reason to believe that a second lieutenant, now dead, overstepped his authority and strapped a man to the wheel of a caisson and left him three to four hours to suffer. Anymore company punishment will come from me. By my authority only will it be determined whether or not to execute punitive measures to any soldier under my jurisdiction. Is that clear? "Yes, Sir!" The soldiers shouted back.

"Another item that needs addressing, furloughs. I will be giving out furloughs to one company of men at a time. That's the usual procedure. Some of you men have sneaked home and back on various excuses. Now, we will have furloughs in a timely and orderly fashion. Company A will go first. Dismissed!"

As the men returned to their activities, Winslow walked back to his tent with Captain Tobias. Winslow said to him, "My men are all in good spirits and I don't want harsh orders from the top creating dissention. The army of the Potomac allows it with Bounty Jumpers. Why didn't you step in, Captain Tobias?"

Tobias said, "My hands were tied. Not only did Shelly, the ringleader of the other second lieutenants have Lester eating out of his hand by cottoning to his spit and polish ideas, Lester bamboozled the rest of us by saying he would go over heads to a General he knew to get his way."

"I think a reckoning is due." Winslow stated flatly.

"You bet." Tobias agreed.

"There is bird that needs a tether on his foot." Winslow said as they neared their tent.

Upon entering the tent, Major Lester was sitting on his bunk and polishing his boots. Winslow continued, "The damage is done. I can only try to avoid a repeat of the same." He glared at Lester. He motioned for Captain Tobias to have a seat on his bunk.

"Major Lester, a large portion of this fiasco rests on your shoulders concerning the second lieutenants. I have gathered information from several sources and gleaned the common thread of their witness. You blackmailed your fellow officers to not disclose the cruelties done to our soldiers by those second lieutenants. I am quite tempted to recommend a demotion for you, but that would involve the upper brass and a lot of lag time to get it done. Captain Tobias you are a witness to what I say. Major Lester, you will remain a major, but you will now be strictly limited to requisitions. You can shine up all you want but if there is a need for a dress parade that order will come from me."

Major Lester was seething with anger. He stood up and yelled, "You can't do that to me! I have influence. I will tell my General friend what you have done to me!"

"Go right ahead. I'd like to see how this plays out. I know the name of that general. Independent of how you contact him, I will send him a full report of the second lieutenant incident as well as your insubordination on many occasions as well as this present act of insubordination. Also, I will send a copy to General Grant."

Stymied, Lester stomped out of the tent then yelled back, "I'll ask for a transfer."

Winslow replied, "It's not happening under my watch. I know what you are capable of doing so you'll stay close to me where you can do little damage."

After Lester was at a distance, Tobias smiled and said, "A bird has been tethered."

Part 2
Discovery of a Stowaway

Chitlin was in fine fettle. Happy to leave Veil Wood and enter into an adventurous journey, his body language betrayed his joy with exaggerated flourishes as he finished loading the wagons with suitcases, trunks, and miscellaneous items.

Juliette and Madame Bernard walked into view. The wagons were loaded and ready for departure. Beamus would drive the lead wagon with Juliette and Mme. Bernard. Chitlin would follow with Phinney.

Juliette exclaimed to Mme. Bernard, "We will be like pioneers discovering America!"

Mme. Bernard was caught up in Juliette's excitement and added, "Mais oui! I can hardly wait to go!"

Beamus was standing between the two wagons, "I know where I am going, and I am as excited as you ladies to leave!" They all laughed, happy to escape the dark brooding Veil Wood.

Phinney had seated herself by Chitlin in the rear wagon, smiling from ear to ear. She was a bit nervous which was revealed by the rhythmic tic of her left eyelid.

It was eleven o'clock in the morning. All had climbed into their respective wagons and proceeded down the north road away from the wharf. Soon the wagons were on the outskirts of town headed in a westerly direction. The further the distance gained from Veil Wood, the lighter their moods became. Not too long after, Chitlin broke into song. He sang 'Camp Town Races' and Phinney joined in with the chorus. The sky was clear, the air crisp and fresh. Soon they were silent, enjoying the new scenery and pleasant weather. The lulling sound of the horses clopping hooves, was comforting as they made their way westward. Around mid-afternoon they pulled off the road to eat a late lunch of dried fruit, beef jerky, and bread. Phinney had packed water jugs and tin cups to accompany the meal. There seemed to be no distinction between master and slave for they all sat together in the grass as they ate their lunch. Phinney looked worried and barely ate a piece of bread.

Juliette noted her behavior, "What's troubling you, Phinney?"

"Nothing Mistus. Ah jus' never been on a trip away from Mastah Armstrong's place. Ma last trip was when I came there from ma home in Georgia. That was nine year ago."

"That is a long time between trips." Acknowledged Juliette as she assumed that was the reason for Phinney's nervousness.

When they resumed their journey, Beamus effused confidence as he recognized landmarks from previous trips, fences, houses, certain shaped trees, even a threadbare scarecrow.

Juliette was sitting next to Beamus in the wagon when he said to her, "Although we are in the Deep South, it is best to avoid towns which own sharp ears and keen eyes for other travelers. During war time there is more lawlessness. Also, Confederate soldiers might take our wagons for their own use."

They traveled along quietly, more alert to unusual sounds. An hour later, they noticed a lot of dust pluming up above the trees a quarter mile in front of them. Beamus pulled off the road behind some scrub brush and Chitlin followed suit. Soon, about forty Confederate soldiers hurtled past their hiding place. Through the screen of the brush, they saw the flash of sabers and heard the hooves beat the dry dirt road. It was a detachment hurrying to some destination. After a considerable wait to see if there were any more soldiers, they cautiously resumed their journey.

They traveled several more miles. When they reached the crest of a hill, Beamus signaled to Chitlin to halt. He took out a spy glass from the satchel by his feet. He stood up in the wagon and studied the terrain for a couple of minutes. He announced, "It looks safe to continue."

They traveled a couple of hours more. Dusk had come. They came upon a humble farmhouse with a small barn located behind the house away from the road. "It's late. It would be nice to sleep in a bed, so I will see if the proprietor is able to offer accommodations for the night. Otherwise, we'll just go down the road a piece, pull off the road out of view and snooze in the wagons." Beamus said.

Beamus got out of the wagon and knocked on the farmhouse door. A tall spare woman answered. They had a conversation. She then accompanied him to the wagons. She said, "You folks are welcome to spend the night here. I have two rooms to rent plus a barn. For supper, I have a fresh pot of chicken soup and some bread made today."

"It sounds very inviting. Thank you." Said Juliette.

"Then it's settled." The woman said. "Park your wagons behind the barn and come have some supper." Beamus and Chitlin followed her instructions and parked the wagons behind the barn.

Juliette, Mme. Bernard, and Beamus went inside. It was a neat and tidy home. Roughhewn chairs and benches were adorned with crocheted blankets which added softness. There was a framed colored print from a fashion magazine hung on the parlor wall for an added touch.

The woman of the house emerged from the kitchen and extended her hand to the ladies and Beamus. "I'm Millie Slocum. Children! Come out. It is safe." Millie waited as two children came out of a bedroom.

"These are my young'uns, Ned and Lily." Ned appeared to be about eight years old and Lily was about three. Ned continued to hold Lily's hand protectively.

My husband is off fighting so occasionally renting rooms helps us out while he is gone." She explained.

The delicious aroma of chicken soup wafted to their nostrils. "Supper is ready. Come have a sit in the kitchen." Millie added with a big smile. She motioned them to sit down at the table. The meal consisted of chicken soup with dumplings and bread with fresh churned butter. It was Spartan but delicious. Chitlin and Phinney were served on the porch. After they ate, they retired to the barn.

When all had finished their supper, Millie said to them. "I figure you all are tuckered out from traveling. Let me show you the bedrooms." They all rose from the table and followed Millie.

"Here is the room for the ladies." Millie said as she opened the door." It was lovely and simple, blue gingham curtains graced the window and a blue and yellow quilt covered the double bed. For Mr. Paxton she opened the door next to the ladies. It was the children's room.

"Oh, I think I will just sleep in the wagon. I still will be paying you the same." Beamus smiled reassuringly.

"Alright then." Millie acquiesced with dignity. Now she would be able to sleep in a private room with her children instead of the parlor.

After being shown their room, Juliette and Mme. Bernard walked to the wagons for their small valises. "I have been so long sitting in the wagon that I'd love to go for a stroll." Juliette looked askance to her friend.

"Certainment! It's good for the health." Answered Mme. Bernard. They strolled around the clearing surrounding the farm. Eventually, they ended up at the wagons to collect their things. Beamus was there getting blankets for himself. Phinney was there too, acting especially fidgety as the women approached.

"Mistus Juliette and eve'body, ah have somethin' to say." Faltering a bit, she continued. "I has to tell you that ah brought Callie wit us. She wuz so beaten and all, ah jus' could not leave her" looking bravely into Juliette's eyes she divulged, "Ah put her in your trunk, Mistus Juliette."

There was shocked silence for a moment. Then Juliette, alarmed said, "Phinney! Let her out so she can breathe!"

"Ah will!" As Phinney opened the trunk she added, "Callie had a hollow wood stick to breathe through a hole I had cut in your trunk for the stick to grab air. Sorry for the hole, Mistus Juliette."

"Phinney that was brilliant! With everything going on at Veil Wood before our departure, that was wonderful how you had the presence of mind to rescue Callie!" Juliette exclaimed as the others smiled at Phinney.

Phinney wasn't used to lavish compliments. She just looked at her feet and spoke softly. "It wuz the only thing I could think about. Poor Callie wuz on my heart. Iffin ah did nothin', ah knows ah'd be sad about it the rest of ma days."

"Poor Callie is right!" Mme. Bernard said as she regarded the emaciated frame of Callie as she tremulously emerged from the trunk, hastily opened by Juliette.

"How pale and wan she is! She needs to move around after being confined for so long." Observed Beamus.

Callie smiled weakly and stood up on thin scarred legs with the recent scourge marks of O'Leary's whip. She stepped out of the trunk, pausing to find her balance. She weaved in the air still weak from torture, infection, and a sparse nourishment.

Mme. Bernard supported her around the waist and held her hand. Callie walked tentatively; ten feet then sat on a tree stump exhausted.

"O'Leary is a cruel taskmaster." Beamus said to Juliette. "He never would be employed on my plantation."

"He is more than cruel. He is an evil man who finds pleasure in hurting the helpless. I find that despicable." Added Juliette.

Acceptance of the stowaway by all finally sunk in for Phinney as she smiled in relief. Hurriedly she went to Callie at the tree stump and gave her some chicken and bread and a cup of water. Phinney had packed plenty of blankets, so she went to the barn with an armload and made two beds in the soft hay for Callie and her. Beamus and Chitlin unharnessed the horses to let them graze and drink while they each laid down some blankets in their respective wagons for their beds. Mme. Bernard and Juliette went to sleep in the room in the house.

The next morning the aroma of coffee, ham, and eggs greeted their noses in pleasant welcome. Everyone had slept well and now ate well. There would be no hot meal until the end of the day. Millie packed them a lunch of dried apples, ham and bread. Beamus paid Millie well in gold coin for all she had done.

Even a journey falls into a routine. Up at dawn, travel, avoid people on the road, then find a place to sleep, composed the daily activities of their journey. The fresh air and scenery kept everyone's spirits up. Callie improved in health with good food and Phinney's motherly care. It took almost two weeks to arrive at Beamus Paxton's plantation.

Beamus had been in an apparent state of excited agitation in the three days prior to their arrival at his plantation so when they made the final approach on the private lane to his plantation, he barely had parked when he jumped from the wagon and made his way to the front portico shouting, "Apollonia, Apollonia! I have missed you so!" She had been sitting on a chair there. Beamus had then taken her hand and bent down on one knee and kissed her hand.

"Beamus, I have sorely missed you." She answered in a half fretful half passionate voice. She was a tiny birdlike woman, small featured with brown hair and eyes.

"How are you Apollonia? You look a bit pale." Beamus said studying his wife.

"I 'm doing better. Just after you left for France, maybe a week, I took a tumble down the stairs. Ever since then my hip hurts when I walk."

"You maybe fractured it." Beamus said worriedly.

"I did something to it but there's no doctor around, now that the war is on." Apollonia said resignedly.

Juliette, Mme. Bernard, Chitlin, Phinney, and Callie were at the base of the steps of the portico. Beamus looked from his wife to his traveling companions, "Apollonia, I'd like you to meet my fellow sojourners." He introduced them to her.

Juliette said, "Hello, Mrs. Paxton. I couldn't help but hear what happened to you. You might not have a doctor available, but Phinney here, can make healing poultices and give great massages.

"That is good to hear. Maybe after dinner Phinney could give me a massage." Mrs. Paxton studied Phinney.

"I'm happy to hep out." Phinney responded.

A plump black woman came out on the portico. Mrs. Paxton said, "You all, this is Mumsy. She has been in my family since before I was born."

"Mumsy, good to see you." Beamus smiled

"Bout time you come home!" Mumsy said reproachfully.

"You are so right. I am too old and too tired for all the risks and challenges of travel. Mmm. I smell fried chicken!" With that, they all went in for a fried chicken, cornbread, and greens.

Beamus said, "Good timing for dinner and Mumsy usually makes extra."

Chitlin, Phinney, and Callie helped Mumsy serve the food then retreated to the kitchen for their meal. Phinney asked Mumsy to save all the chicken bones for soup.

Later, Phinney gave Mrs. Paxton a massage. Lightly touching her hip bone, Phinney informed her, "You did crack your hip, but the pieces are still able to mend 'cause they are close together."

She made Mrs. Paxton comfortable then went to the cook house. She asked permission of Mumsy to make a broth of chicken bones, local herbs, and apple cider vinegar.

She observed to Mumsy, "Your Misstus is small boned. She's done having babies and her bones are weaker now. She needs greens and bone broth soup every day."

Somehow Mumsy didn't take offense at Phinney. The common objective of improving Mrs. Paxton's health aided in the peaceful mingling of their mutual knowledge. By now Phinney was showing which added to the excitement of a new life coming to fruition. Also, with Callie and Chitlin in the picture, a new dynamic had been created. For Mumsy the long loneliness had been dispelled and now she had a new family to share joys and sorrows.

Beamus Paxton's plantation was elegant with old world flavor. It was situated southeast of New Orleans in the environs of the small hamlet of Violet. Built in the early 1800's by Apollonia's grandfather,

Maurice Doucette, made it one of the older antebellum plantations. Mr. Doucette had named the plantation Cypress Lane.

Apollonia was the only surviving Doucette from her immediate family. An older sister and younger brother died of yellow fever as young children. Her parents, Claud and Isabelle, compensated for the loss of their two other children by spoiling the sole survivor, Apollonia. It was a very close bond between parents and child. When Beamus appeared on the scene, all three had to approve of him. He easily passed muster and was welcomed into the family. Beamus and Apollonia had been married only one year when the tragic news came to them that Apollonia's parents had died on their return voyage from France. They had died in a hurricane in the Gulf of Mexico on the last leg of their trip home. It was a sad time for Apollonia.

With the death of her parents, all contact with France had been severed. Although Beamus had made an effort to find his ancestral in-laws on his last trip to France, it proved fruitless. The language barrier and time limits made Beamus abandon it.

Apollonia had inherited the old plantation, Cypress Lane. Apollonia had a strong desire to remain there. Beamus was accepting of her wishes. Beamus and Apollonia had two children, both girls, Charlotte and Mavis. They grew up and married and moved considerable distances from their parents due to their husbands' family ties and work opportunities.

Apollonia had taken an immediate liking to Juliette and Mme. Bernard. Their French accents and conversation reminded Apollonia of happier days long before the war when her parents, in their prime, were the proprietors of Cypress Lane.

It was after supper the second day of their stay that Apollonia discovered some of Juliette's talents. They had entered the parlor which contained a piano. Both Mme. Bernard and Juliette gravitated toward it. Soon they were singing Christmas carols in French.

"What joy you stir in my heart when I hear those songs. My mother, Isabelle, would sing and play the piano often. And at Christmas, to hear those songs, it makes me nostalgic for that special time." Apollonia sighed deeply as she reveled in the memories. "Cypress Lane was in its glory then. We had many slaves caring for the plantation, flower gardens, cotton fields, livestock, and horse stables. It was in top condition." Her voice trailed off.

The plantation was in a steep decline. There were several factors. Beamus had been gone five months in his travels. Apollonia had poor management skills. Besides that, the country was in the middle of a civil war. Presently, the North had put a strategic priority in seeking the surrender of New Orleans. With the North breathing down the neck of the Deep South, it incited many slaves to run off to help the North. Cypress Lane was one among many plantations that lost slaves in this manner. Besides Mumsy and the new arrivals, there was perhaps ten other slaves that remained, those too old or too young to leave.

As small compensation for the underhanded way Clayton Armstrong had claimed Beamus' goods, the acquisition of two wagons and the slave Chitlin was modest recompense along with the diamond brooch from Mrs. Armstrong.

Actually, there was no way to return Chitlin. Chitlin sensed his predicament and was relieved to have escaped from Veil Wood. Sealed in silence by all, there was no mention of Chitlin's return to Clayton Armstrong, his rightful owner. Content, Chitlin fell into the job of chauffer for the Paxton's.

On the third day after their arrival Beamus, Apollonia, Juliette, and Mme. Bernard were talking after a good breakfast.

"Now that you've rested a while would you ladies like to go on tour of the area?" Beamus asked. Both Juliette and Mme. Bernard nodded excitedly.

Apollonia smiled. "Beamus is a wonderful tour guide. I'm not up to it yet. You all go and have fun. I'll stay here and let my hip mend some more."

Soon Juliette and Mme. Bernard had changed into appropriate clothing for the outing. While they were getting ready, Mumsy who oversaw the house and kitchen, directed Phinney in packing a picnic for the sightseers. They were out of the house by ten in the morning and in the carriage traveling down the lane to the main road.

"Since it is only three days to Christmas, I thought we could make it a dual-purpose trip, see the sights and pick up some greenery to decorate the house for Christmas. Are you ladies up for it?"

"Of course! We are on a small adventure. I love everything about Christmas." Mme. Bernard exclaimed.

"Me, also!" Juliette chimed in.

Wearing the widest of grins Chitlin silently affirmed the happy sentiments. Chitlin chauffeured them in a carriage, his head held high as he sported the new royal blue livery he had been outfitted with and took in all the new scenery as they traveled. Although Juliette and Mme. Bernard brought along their fans as a precaution, both felt relaxed in Beamus Paxton's company, right down to the twitch in his mustache.

As they passed an open field, Beamus pointed to it and said, "This is Chalmette where we fought part of the war of 1812. Those British were slow to learn that we had meant business in the Revolutionary War, so we had to rehash it."

"Perhaps not slow to learn, but quick for an opportunity to regain America. Conquering land is always popular," Mme. Bernard observed.

"It didn't start out as a land grab. The Napoleonic War was going on in Europe. At first, the British, being France's major adversary, put a blockade on trade on any port in Europe under French jurisdiction.

Then they forced or impressed some. U.S. sailors from our ships to theirs. That caused some ill will. Then a squabble ensued among the countries whose ports were affected. The coup de grace was that we had some war hawks in the U.S. Congress who wanted to duke it out with the British. So, we burned York in Canada, a staging area for the Brits. Then they burned Washington and the White House.

Beamus then motioned to Chalmette Field with his hand. "Here at Chalmette raged a huge battle. Andrew Jackson was undermanned and out gunned by British General Pakenham. Needless to say, our troops had low morale but still triumphed. The Brits lost two thousand men as well as their General Pakenham. The tragic irony was that peace had been declared two weeks earlier in Europe. The end result was that we were still standing as a nation after that war. It was our second war of independence.

A long, peaceful silence followed as the group reflected on the history lesson. There was still the comforting clippity-clop of the horse's hooves. They came upon some tall pyramid-shaped log constructions, some thirty to forty feet high on the bayou.

"These structures will be bonfires on Christmas Eve. Some will be burned on New Year's Eve to welcome the New Year. Notice the interiors are not solid wood but brush and dry tinder. It makes for a brilliant fire." Beamus said, adding, "The Cajun folk have been doing this as long as I can remember.

As they approached, they saw a group of men filling the hollow pyramid with smaller limbs and sugar cane stalks. "Hey Bijoux! How's it going?" Beamus shouted at a short, dark, spare man.

"Monsieur Paxton! Bienvenue! Vous etes encore au Luzianne!" the small man shouted back.

Both Juliette and Mme. Bernard perked up when they heard the French patois. Chitlin stopped the carriage. They all debarked and walked closer to get a better view of the structure.

Juliette said to the man, "Bonjour Monsieur! Comment allez-vous?"

The small man in his forties grinned ear to ear while his dark eyes darted to Juliette then Mme. Bernard. "Je vais bien. I am guessing you ladies parlez un peu d'Anglais."

"We do. I'm so happy to meet you Bijoux. It's been a while since we talked in French to someone besides ourselves. I am Juliette Bellechasse, and this is Mme. Simone Bernard. We come from Paris, France."

"So far from your peaceful country to a country at war with itself. That is a whole day's worth of discussion. For the present moment, I bet you'd enjoy celebrating Christmas in the best way. So, I invite you all to go to mass then come here for Revillon with lots of good food and a big bonfire." Bijoux smiled.

"It sounds so wonderful! I'd truly enjoy a good celebration of our Lord's birthday! Would that be possible Mr. Paxton?"

"By all means! Christmas is in three days. If Apollonia is up to it, we'll all go"

They all got back into the carriage and continued with the tour. The countryside thickened with cottages as they approached New Orleans. Soon they were in the heart of the city. Beamus proudly stated, "We are now in Vieux Carré or the French Quarter. Since New Orleans was damaged by two major fires in the late 1700's, the only building not burned was the Ursuline Convent built in 1751. The nuns have a boarding school for girls and do hospital work as their ongoing work."

Beamus continued, "The French settled Louisiana in 1699. Spanish influence crept in until 1768 when the Creoles expelled Spanish governor, Antonio De Ulloa. The revolt was crushed by Spain as they regained power over the area until 1803 when Louisiana was transferred to France. It was only in the hands of the French twenty days before it was transferred to the United States from Napoleon Bonaparte for fifteen million dollars. So, in one hundred years it changed ownership four times, a real hot potato for ownership!"

"Here is St. Louis Cathedral rebuilt in 1850. It has been the site of the Catholic Church since 1727," Continued Beamus.

"What a beautiful Church! May we stop and visit?" Juliette asked.

"Certainly." Beamus answered.

They entered the church quietly. It was beautiful as beams of light created a visible path to the crucifix over the altar as well as the tabernacle beneath it. Solemnly they went to the pews, knelt and prayed for their own intentions. The peaceful calm atmosphere seemed to increase.

As they were exiting the church a man in priestly garb opened the church door. "Bonjour." He greeted them and smiled. He was a medium sized man with brown hair and twinkling eyes.

Mme. Bernard and Juliette said at the same time, "Bonjour, Cure'."

The priest smiled, "Monsieur Paxton, I am happy to see that you are back from France, safe and sound." He looked intently at the ladies and continued, "It seems that you brought back some citoyens de France."

Beamus smiled.

"I am Father Marc-Andre' Gibbons. Welcome to St. Louis Cathedral and the beautiful city of New Orleans."

After introducing themselves and finding out the Christmas mass schedule, they climbed into the carriage for the return trip to Cypress Lane. Once outside the city, they found a beautiful clearing. They spread a blanket and enjoyed the cold chicken, bread, sweet potato pie, and cups of cool water.

Afterward, they strolled about and collected greenery for decorations. Later , as they made their way back home, Juliette ruminated on her long trek from France to Cypress Lane; first settling her affairs in France, making sure her parents were safely situated, the emotionally disturbing revelation of the South's reason for engaging in the Civil War, then the attack on the Tambeau by a Union gunboat, flight to Cuba, then being secreted by Captain Belmont in Mobile Bay, the horrendous stay at Veil Wood under Clayton Armstrong's oppressive hand, the torture of Callie by O'Leary, and the traumatic attack on Juliette also by O'Leary. All this, for James Lambert who is defending the South. Her initial enchantment with James was all but gone. She had little desire to see him. Cypress Lane and the company of the Paxton's was the first real peace she had felt since leaving her home in France. Out of obligation, she had written the letter to James and his family. She hoped they would not contact her.

As they entered the foyer, Juliette said to Beamus, "Thank you so much for the wonderful day. I haven't felt this peaceful in a long time."

Beamus smiled back at her knowingly, "I can say the same for myself."

Once they had put their cloaks and extra items in their rooms, both Juliette and Mme. Bernard came downstairs and put the greenery in place making the house festive for Christmas.

"Mme. Bernard, preparing for Christmas makes me recall that my last Christmas was spent in Paris with my parents," Juliette wistfully reminisced.

"And I would spend it with you and your family going to mass and celebrating Revillon at Le Mouton Noire," added Mme. Bernard less wistfully, recalling her early widowhood. "Juliette, this will be fun to celebrate Christmas in a new place and with new people."

"You are right. My parents will be enjoying their first Christmas in the country with all the farm animals, and with my father, Joseph Gastineau!" Juliette cheerfully added.

Mumsy entered the room and announced, "Supper is ready."

They all entered the dining room and sat at the table. The meal began with 'bone soup' which had greens in it. Shrimp gumbo on a bed of steamed rice was the main course. Black eyed peas and cornbread accompanied it. Mumsy had made a delicious shoofly pie for dessert.

They all moved to the parlor. Once settled in a chair Apollonia said, "I feel so much better since I've been eating bone soup. I have it twice a day, at dinner and supper. The ache in my hip has lessened considerably. Of course, Phinney's massages are a huge help. What also helps is having my home filled with my husband and good people. That has certainly lifted my spirits. God is good." With that, she smiled.

"You are so kind Apollonia. Thank you for having us. It is so peaceful here." Added Juliette. Soon, they all went out on the front porch to enjoy the evening twilight. Not too long after, Mme. Bernard and Apollonia excused themselves and retired for the evening. Juliette and Beamus lingered a while longer.

Juliette was thinking about the stark difference between Clayton Armstrong and Beamus Paxton. Armstrong ruled his plantation with a heavy hand with a sadistic overseer in the person of O'Leary. He gave license, and personally used and abused his slaves in a disgraceful manner. She then thought of sweet, kind Beamus and how incongruous he appeared to be as a slave owner and friend of Clayton Armstrong. Her puzzlement weighs on her.

Compelled by the conundrum, Juliette asked Beamus, "How did you and Clayton first meet?"

"I met Clayton five years ago through a mutual acquaintance."

"What were the circumstances of the meeting?"

"To be honest, we met at a slave auction in Mobile. I bet you are wondering how we could be friends that long. It is simple, first, it was business, second, I saw him only a few times the first two years, third, when he finally met my wife and I, we were on our best southern gentlemen behavior. Then because of the rumors of war, both of us sought new cotton markets in Europe. When trying to make a livelihood I can get along with a high degree of unpleasantness. It was our third trip to France when we met you. I'm a mellow fellow and can virtually get along with a rabid skunk at midnight. So, it was with Clayton. That is, until we ended up at Veil Wood. With you as a guest on his property it apparently unleashed some male chest beating. When a married man, past his prime acts in that manner, there are no excuses."

"Phinney is carrying his baby." Juliette stated flatly. Closely watching for his reaction.

Beamus' face fell and aged before her eyes. He was bereft of words.

Juliette had been thinking of the implications for a while. "What makes a man commit adultery with a slave, sire a child, and then let his own blood, own offspring, be a part of the institution of slavery? I cannot fathom it."

A long, deep sigh escaped from Beamus. "Welcome to my personal moral quandary. That is the most repugnant of behaviors. It is pure evil, plain and simple. There are good and evil slave owners. Clayton is evil. I have seen it rot other slave owner's brains. They start off seeking their furtive pleasures. Then they feel compelled to continue. At a certain point they can't stop. Then they lie to themselves. They seek the blinders of denial so they can wallow in darkness."

"It is like the Bible said, they become a slave to sin." Juliette added, "How ironic, the master of the slaves becomes the enslaved."

"I am a man with many failings. One of them being that I don't have much backbone. I am a native of Louisiana and raised here with the institution of slavery. I do treat my slaves the best I can without making waves with other slave owners. I love my wife, yet she would never leave this way of life, so I put a little water in my wine and abide."

"Is there any joy in that?"

"In fleeting moments, in the small details of the day. I do find solace or even little joys. As I go on in life, I simply try to appreciate little things, a good cup of coffee, a birdsong, new blooms of flowers, sunrises, sunsets, my wife, my children, and good friends."

"It sounds like you are a prisoner waiting for freedom." Observed Juliette.

"Aren't we all? We are born, we live for a while, then we die. Every day is one day closer to the end."

"Do you have faith in Christ? We will have life everlasting with Him."

"I certainly do, as much as I can fit Him in." A firm edge to his voice signaled Juliette to delve no deeper.

Someone sighed profoundly. Juliette wasn't sure if it was Beamus or her. Maybe neither of them nor both. A long sad silence ensued. Inertia weighed her deep into the wicker chair. Beamus too, seemed immobilized. A span of time elapsed. How long or short, neither gaged. Only a cold damp breeze ended it. Signaling a retreat from the elements, Beamus stood up.

"Juliette, it is getting cold and drafty and I don't want to leave you alone in the dark. Let us retire for the night."

"Alright, Beamus." Juliette responded. They said goodnight on the landing. The bedroom door was ajar, and Juliette could see Apollonia reading by the oil lamp. She headed for her room where Mme. Bernard was gently snoring.

As Juliette laid her head on the pillow, she felt a kind of sadness for Beamus. A thought floated into her mind, to take no stand was a stand. That would be an agony for her, knowing the truth and not acting on it. Yet on further thought, she was in the same predicament as Beamus. Presently, she could do nothing but play along, not making waves. How she wished to be up north fighting to end slavery. She concluded that it came down to patience, perseverance, and prayer. God knows her heart. He will open a door at the right time. She fell asleep.

On Christmas Eve day there was a bustling about the house as all pitched in to make the day special. Mumsy was busy in the cookhouse preparing vegetables to put around the pork roast she would serve at supper. Phinney went out in the woods with Callie to collect greens for a side dish. Chitlin was grooming the horses. Mme. Bernard was doing some last-minute sewing, capitalizing on the sewing machine she had found at Cypress Lane. Juliette had gone to the cook house earlier and had taken a bath and washed her hair and had braided it. She chose an outfit that would be appropriate throughout the day. It was a wine-red damask gown.

Mumsy had also prepared baskets as gifts. They contained pecans, dried peaches, paw paws, and jars of molasses. It was a tradition to give out baskets to the less fortunate on Christmas Eve day.

Right after dinner, about two o'clock in the afternoon Beamus announced, 'Would you, Juliette and Mme. Bernard care to accompany me on a round of visits to the local inhabitants?"

"That would be delightful!" Juliette exclaimed as Mme. Bernard smiled in agreement.

Within the hour they were in the carriage loaded with baskets. Beamus, Apollonia, Juliette, and Mme. Bernard were on board. Chitlin was at the reins. The first stop was at the slave quarters on Beamus' property. There were at least fifteen cabins. Only three were occupied. About ten slaves emerged from the last three cabins at the end of the row.

"Good afternoon, Tanner and Charles." Beamus waved to an elderly couple. They were surrounded by eight children ranging in age from three to twelve years of age.

"Good afternoon, Massah Paxton, Sir." Charles said.

"We've brought you a couple of Christmas baskets. Hope you enjoy them." Beamus said as he handed them to Charles.

"We will, Suh." Said Tanner, a weathered old woman with white frothy hair and gnarled hands. All of the ten were tidy, wearing clean mended clothing. Happy for the gifts, they waved to Beamus and the others as they continued on their way.

As the horses plodded along to the next destination, Juliette's thoughts centered on all the reasons she had risked so much to come to America. First, she had fallen in love with James Lambert or, had she fallen in love with the idea that she loved him? Before she had met him, she had felt trapped and disillusioned with the lack of a future by the example of the jaded people who had been customers at Le Mouton Noire. When she had laid eyes on him at the Hotel de Ville, she had felt an attraction. He was handsome with polished manners and honeyed words. Yet, when the waiter had spilled punch on his boots his face had hardened. His personality was an enigma. In a whirlwind of idealized romance and physical attraction, they had become engaged. He had purchased a new wardrobe for her and a beautiful diamond necklace when he had proposed. It had upset her that his courtly manners had disappeared after the proposal as he had tried to take more liberties with her. He wasn't quite the gentleman then. The last time she had seen him was at the Paris train station. He never said that he loved her at any point in their relationship, not even at the Paris train station.

He had ended his note concerning her voyage with 'fondly'. Now, half a year later, after a dangerous voyage that James had failed to impart to her the perils she could encounter, and now having been exposed to the raw evils of slavery at Veil Wood, which James had alluded to as preserving the southern culture, she had a sickening self–revelation. She felt physical revulsion at the thought of James. Why had he been to Paris? To sell cotton which had been raised and picked by slaves. He enjoyed the fancy balls, travels, and money which came from slave labor. She concluded that the only reason she would want to see James was to return the diamond necklace and wardrobe he had purchased for her.

Now here she was at Cypress Lane in Louisiana. Beamus Paxton was a much more magnanimous slave master than Clayton Armstrong. Yet even here at Cypress Lane, there were slaves, from Mumsy, the house slave to Charles, Tanner, and the youngsters. She had brought three slaves from Veil Wood, Chitlin, Phinney, and Callie. And now, in Phinney's womb, new life. Will the baby be able to live in freedom? The child had little hope for love, romance, travel, or an enduring family.

Uneasiness gripped her. She could not endure these circumstances much longer. Any tender feelings for James had died. Presently, she was happy to have contacted the Lamberts so that it was possible to return the wardrobe and diamond necklace that James had purchased for her. That would be the end of it. To quell her anxiety, she silently reasoned with herself, nothing can be done now, it's Christmas Eve day, I'll focus on Jesus. They stopped at several more homes. Warm Christmas wishes were exchanged. One Cajun gentleman gave Beamus a bucket of crawdads. Soon it was dusk, and they had returned to the plantation, and sat down to a late supper of pork roast with all the trimmings and a bonus of boiled crawdads.

Apollonia was spent from the earlier trip in the carriage, so she decided to stay home for the evening. After supper they packed up some more baskets and embarked on their next foray. This time they headed to St Louis Cathedral in New Orleans. Along the way, people had put lanterns on their doorsteps. At first the lights were sparse as there were few houses. Then as they neared the city, the houses were in closer proximity and the lanterns glowed a golden, welcoming ambience as they entered New Orleans.

Chitlin helped them out of the carriage at the entrance of St. Louis Cathedral. The pews were almost full, but luckily, they found a half empty pew midway to the altar, enough seating for all of them.

Father Gibbon offered the mass. For a few moments Juliette felt transported back in time to her church in Paris. She recalled Father Sevigny's homily, there is hope. Jesus Christ is born. Before Juliette knew it, mass had ended, and they were in the carriage headed to the bayou where Bijoux's bonfire was located. It wasn't hard to find in the dark. All the bonfires along the bayou had been lit and beckoned them with leaping flames of various hues, pale yellow, orange and blue. It was a feast for the eyes.

"Joyeux Noel!" Bijoux shouted to them over the crackling din of the fire.

"Joyeux Noel, aussi!" Shouted Juliette in return.

They all climbed down from the carriage. Chitlin parked the carriage at a good distance because fire spooked the horses. They collected the Christmas baskets from the carriage for Bijoux's family and friends.

Bijoux said, "I would like you all to meet ma famille." He motioned them to follow him.

As they came closer to the Bijoux's large bonfire, they noticed that there were several small campfires spread over a distance. Nearing the closest campfire, they discerned faces in the flickering light. Bijoux said, "Here we are! This is ma famille. I have four children that are still at home with me and here tonight. I would like you to meet ma femme,

Felicity, and my four boys, Jean-Baptiste, Jean-Marc, Jean-Louis, and Jean-Pierre. The children were between the ages of eight to fourteen.

"Enchantez!" Exclaimed Juliette and Mme. Bernard in unison and offering them a handshake to each one. At the same time Beamus, Juliette, and Mme. Bernard, handed them gift baskets. They all said thank you.

The Bijoux family was all of small stature with dark eyes and dark hair. Felicity was cooking a pot of ham hocks with black eyed peas and a pot of shrimp gumbo over the fire. As Juliette became accustomed to the dark, she began to make out other faces at other campfires, all happy. Soon all the Cajuns and their guests were standing around the big bonfire singing Christmas carols. Many had banjos and harmonicas. There had been chairs that had been placed at a respectable distance to the bonfire. In their group Bijoux supplied glasses for all and a bottle of anisette.

"Let us toast to the hope Jesus brought to the world, Notre Sauveur!" They all clinked glasses. At the same time, the bonfire sent out many noisy sparks into the air like fireworks.

"Des éclat de feu! God heard your toast to his Son." Juliette observed.

Bijoux added, "Those sparks sent skyward are prayers from us sent to our loved ones, wherever they are. God knows who."

Juliette felt comforted as she sensed her parents were celebrating Revillon in the new inn in the country. She sent a loving prayer their way when the next spark exploded heavenward.

CHAPTER 11

Lt. Col. Winslow and his men, in the latter part of September 1862, set out on a routine foraging party. The Union Army was influencing the southern economy. The tightening of the blockade created a shortage of clothing as well as many other items. Every able-bodied person not directly in the war was helping on the home front. Therefore, many a southern belle had to face the reality of actual work such as knitting, darning socks, mending, and making uniforms of homespun fabric.

Winslow and his men had selected another plantation to forage. Now being seasoned in the art of foraging, which is a kinder word for raid, all precautions had been taken. From previous raids, the soldiers had garnered much experience in being shot at: missing buttons, shredded hats, and creased ears by old flintlocks attested to the perils of the forager.

A big plantation was spotted on the crest of a hill near a small creek. A forlorn elegance emanated from its regal structure. Degraded by faded paint and neglect, it had lost its battle with time. The men advanced through the main avenue leading to the house. It was lined with great live oaks covered in shiny leaves muted with a dappling of Spanish moss. The men dismounted midway on the avenue and tethered their horses to the trees. Scattering into the adjacent field's tall grass, they formed a sparse circle of men that surrounded the house. Winslow had reduced the men to an effective few. Well camouflaged by the tall grass, they stealthily approached in an ever-tightening ring that narrowed, all paused where the tall grass met the lawn. They waited for Winslow's signal to advance which was his saber waved above the tall grass for the next in line to raise their saber, till it went full circle. When Winslow observed its completion, he stepped through the remaining brush but kept hidden as he surveyed two women sitting in rocking chairs with a table between them on the lawn. A blond woman dressed in a blue satin dress was knitting something very slowly. The other older woman who was dressed in homespun apparently, was teaching the blond how to knit. In between words of encouragement, the older woman chomped rapidly on a wad of tobacco to the rhythm of her own clicking needles.

"Abigail, mighty fittin' you askin' me over." The old lady cackled.

"No one can knit like you Minnie." Abigail responded.

As the old woman chewed the large cud of tobacco she would spit and hit a nearby oak tree with good aim. Suddenly a squirrel appeared on the lowest limb of the oak tree and studied Minnie for a moment. Minnie stared back at the creature then hit him squarely with brown, slimy spittle. The squirrel hightailed it to a more distant tree. Minnie belly-laughed at the squirrel revealing missing teeth and those remaining were brown with tobacco stains. There was nothing alluring about Minnie observed Winslow. Even her figure was as lumpy as a sack of potatoes. On the other hand, Abigail was clean, neat, and tidy in her blue satin gown. The blue satin went well with her eyes and faded blond hair. She had a sallow complexion and heavy but regular features. When she smiled a dimple appeared making her more appealing. Abigail kept an eye on Minnie's messy tobacco juice that was dripping down her chin. Abigail discreetly moved her chair a few inches further from Minnie. Minnie wiped her face with the back of her hand to remove the tobacco juice. "Do you reckon you got a hot brew for me to sip on? I git so durn thirsty when I knit. I could eat a crumb or two if you have any vitals?"

"Why sure thing, Minnie. I'll call Moses and he'll fix us up with some sorghum cake and good hot chicory coffee. Abigail's face brightened as she called for Moses. A slender black man appeared elegantly dressed in a white ruffled shirt, a maroon swallow-tailed coat, tapered black pants and shiny black shoes. He was the top slave of the house.

After listening to Abigail's request, Moses responded, "Yassam." His white hair glistened, and an easy smile revealed even white teeth. "Right away, Ma'am." he left for the house.

All of a sudden, Minnie blew out the tobacco cud and with a big pop it hit the oak tree. Abigail smiled with relief. Soon Moses reappeared bringing a silver pot of coffee and some sweet-smelling sorghum cake. He placed the tray on the small table between them. Minnie was smacking her lips in anticipation. Abigail straightened up and checked her surroundings. Her view narrowed to some bushes rustling by themselves as there was no breeze. Minnie continued smacking noisily as she gobbled up her portion of cake.

"Minnie, hush! Do you hear something odd?"

Minnie perked up and sat still like a hound dog. Both her cheeks bulged with cake. Out of the bushes emerged Winslow. He took his hat off and bowed extremely low. "Good afternoon, ladies. I am honored at the extreme pleasure to find such genteel ladies as you at home."

Dumbfounded and flustered, Abigail could hardly speak. Finally, she haltingly asked, "What do you want?"

"I want your livestock which includes cattle, pigs, and poultry. I won't harm you or your home. I'll try to make it as painless as possible." Said Winslow. Winslow adapted himself so readily to his surroundings that he squatted down between the two women to watch them enjoy their refreshments while his men were busy stealing, horses, cattle, pigs, and poultry, and keeping the slaves quiet. Although the chickens were squawking, the pigs were squealing, and the dogs were barking.

Abigail was flummoxed by Winslow's presence and the noisy raid that was going on in the background. She hadn't touched her coffee or cake. With presence of mind, she thoughtfully asked, "Sir, may I offer you a cup of coffee and a piece of cake?"

"Thank you kindly, Miss Abigail. I heard your name mentioned whilst in the shrubbery. My name is Frank Winslow." He was pleased to accept. The coffee tasted good and he was thirsty. Too bad the women folk couldn't have been prettier, he thought to himself. I sit here with a frightful hag and Abigail appears to be a spinster because there is no gold band on her left hand.

Between mouthfuls of cake Winslow asked, "Miss Abigail, where is your man?"

"Sir, I am not married, nor have I ever been. I guess you could rightly call me an old maid. Now you are taking my food from me. Won't you spare me a little for my servants and myself. I also try to help my only friend, Minnie who lives in the swamp at the end of the creek."

"A lovely woman like you, not married? Well look at me, I am in my early thirties and still a bachelor."

Frank looked at Minnie's stained and wrinkled mouth as she produced a corn cob pipe stuffed with tobacco and a piece of flint. With familiar expertise, Minnie placed the pipe stem in the gap in her sparse teeth. She then tapped the flint with a coffee spoon over the pipe which produced a spark. Simultaneously, she cupped her hand around the spark which fell into the bowl of the pipe. She sucked a powerful pull of air through the stem of the pipe and successfully ignited the tobacco. She then tossed a careless wink at Frank. He visibly cringed.

Minnie must have noticed the cringe. She said, "Funny thing, menfolk never took to me. Probably saved me a passel of trouble." With that, she picked up her knitting and Abigail's and went to the house.

After Minnie had left, Abigail shut her eyes and became introspective. She spoke slowly and emphasized each word. "You wouldn't even need to be a bachelor." Her eyes were wide and transfixed on Frank's eyes.

Frank became uneasy with the steady reverenced gaze that seemed locked on his eyes. Although an excellent flatterer of women, there was usually some coquettish resistance which he had come to expect of the male-female repartee. Abigail had succumbed to a powerful spell that he must have cast. She was in a trance. He had not intended it. It was just that the coffee had tasted so good.

"I will leave enough provisions for you womenfolk and the slaves. I am not cruel. We all need to get through this war. Your plantation looks so neglected that it was an easy guess that a man's care for it happened long ago."

"You are very kind and handsome." Said Abigail mesmerized. "Where did you get your lovely head of auburn hair?"

"From my mother." Frank thought 'the poor old maid was desperate for affection. I will string her along to please her.'

Frank reached for Abigail's hand and held it firmly. He looked into her eyes and asked, "Are you lonely?"

"More than I can say." She looked at him forlornly.

"Have you ever been in love?"

"Yes, once. It must have been fifteen years ago. It's a very sad story. The worst part is the one I loved married my best friend."

"You must have suffered a broken heart."

"That, indeed, I did."

Let's walk down the avenue of oaks."

Abigail's face lit up with happiness. Her dimple appeared, accenting her smile. Color had come into her once sallow face and her blue eyes sparkled in the speckled light. It was a miraculous transformation, observed Frank. He was drawn to put his arm around her waist as they slowly walked down the avenue of oaks.

They stopped and Frank caressed her now rosy cheek with his hand and said slowly, "May I kiss you, Abigail?"

"Oh Yes, do, please. I have been wanting you to do so."

Frank kissed her kindly, without passion. Passion seemed unknown to her for she said, "I haven't been kissed like that in years. Please don't go away! There will never be another one like you!"

Frank smiled thoughtfully and said, "Abigail, this is war, and we kiss as friends. Don't take me serious or be upset as I do think you are a true lady."

Abigail's hands dropped to her sides, then she pulled her head erect and bravely smiled. "I am not upset." A tear trailed from her eye.

"The best thing you can do is forget me as soon as you can." Frank said as he wiped the tear from her cheek.

"An old maid never forgets. There are too few things to remember." Their hands clasped as they slowly walked back to the plantation.

Foraging operations were completed. Frank gave his men orders to return to camp. He lingered as he wanted to give Abigail a gracious farewell. Abigail was standing at the front entrance blankly staring as the men left with most of the livestock, depressed and disappointed. Frank slipped up beside her and gave her a kiss on the cheek. She wheeled around and threw both arms around Frank's neck smothering him in kisses.

Frank pulled away gently. "Abigail, I have come to say good-by and thanks. You have been a wonderful hostess."

"Forgive me, Frank. I have not been a proper lady, but you have added so much to a lonely lady's life. I have so many lonely days, at least this one won't be one of them." Said Abigail.

Frank looked at the downcast face of Abigail and could not fault her for any folly for he was certainly part of the cause.

"Must you go now?" She asked discreetly.

"It is with deep personal regret that I do." Frank answered somberly. He hugged her, walked a few steps, turned and bowed, then walked toward the oaks where his horse was tied. She waved farewell.

CHAPTER 12

In the beginning of the Civil War, the Union soldier usually was self-sufficient. He would provide his own weapons and uniform. As the war progressed and as harsh conditions took a toll on clothing, weapons and other items, the soldier then became more dependent on the government for supplies. More dependent but not totally dependent. At first, the Government issued items in a more generous format such as the soldier's uniform. It was usually a double-breasted coat, heavily wadded, with two rows of big brass buttons on a long-tailed coat. Gloves were a necessity, especially in cold weather. They were usually buck gauntlets with long cuffs. As the conflict dragged on the government war chest dwindled and economic measures were taken. It was noted by the appearance of short-waisted, single breasted coats with one row of buttons and shorter cuffed gloves.

It was a mid-morning sunny day in October. Winslow was speaking to the quarter masters of each company. "I ordered new clothes for the men, pants especially. New pants are so necessary for my men since they get their pants torn and ripped going through the brush and timber. My own clothes consist of a fairly good coat, but my trousers are in want."

Winslow almost laughed as he added, "I'll soon lose my dignity if the clothing order doesn't come through. My knees are out, and the seat of my trousers is so threadbare that my underwear will soon be exposed."

The men had gathered in little clusters on the road into camp in anticipation of the ordered pants. Some of the men were hatless, many with big rips in their trousers. Others who had been scouting looked as if a skirt hung from their belts. A boisterous few were parading their shredded garments by dancing an Egyptian Shimmy Dance. All happily awaited the arrival of the wagon that carried the clothing order.

The wagon and two mules came into view as it breached the crest of a nearby hill. Slowly, the mules wended their way to the camp entrance. Excitedly, the men converged on the wagon and seized its contents, all the men in camp, five hundred fifty total. Fifty men were absent since they were on leave. Officers and soldiers were befuddled as they examined the items they had grabbed. Those items were solely bluecoats. There was not one pair of pants in the entire order.

Winslow's smile had transformed into a grim line. Anger had overcome him. He shouted, "Those sons-of-bitches at headquarters… to hell! Sergeant Dillon come here!"

Sergeant Dillon came over holding a coat by the collar dragging the rest in the dust.

"You were out scouting recently. Did you find anything promising?"

"Yes Sir, I did." said Sergeant Dillon who had been scouting the day before. "I came upon a plantation with two massive barns and other large barns. There was a sign at the entrance that said The Mearle Plantation."

"Ah yes. I have read about Jonathon Mearle in some outdated southern newspaper. He is a southern politician. Rumor has it that he hoards needed supplies from his own Confederate troops. More or less validated by the big barns you noticed, Dillon. "

"Bugler, blow assembly!" commanded Winslow. Ezra, who was close by, willingly blew assembly. The men gathered.

"Men, I am extremely vexed, in fact angrier than any of you could be about this whole deal today. I have been informed by the wagon driver who delivered the coats that there are no more pants. There are pants in Paducah, Kentucky, and if the driver goes that far to get us pants, we will be naked as jay birds and retired to the old folks home by the time he'd return. In the meantime, I have been informed that Sergeant Dillon has spotted a politician's plantation. Even the southern newspapers cut him no slack. He is a real scallywag. Bugler, sound mount for a full-numbered foraging party!"

A wild commotion ensued as saddles were hurriedly secured to the horses, pistols holstered, and carbines packed.

"Sergeant Dillon, lead the way!" Yelled Winslow. The men went into formation of four abreast following Winslow with Dillon in the lead.

Five hours into the expedition, Dillon motioned for the men to stop. He then pointed to a distant white building that sat high on a bluff above the Mississippi River. They resumed the journey and approached the plantation along a river path that was dense with trees. The horsemen were well-camouflaged from above by the thick canopy of leaves on the trees. The route was cool, and damp and the leaves had just begun to fall and rustled as the horses made their way as the Mississippi River roar muffled the sound of their approach. From above, the house came into full view. The men stopped to admire the beauty of the building in full sun with soaring columns glistening white like a majestic queen. Most of the men continued up the bluff on a path that was in the shelter of the trees and brush. Winslow signaled them to spread out. The men, old hands by now, were executing the order as by second nature.

One soldier noticed the grim countenance on Winslow's face. He whispered to his neighbor, "The old man seems real put out by the southern politician."

They deployed and then reined up waiting for charge to blow. Charge was blown. In one grand swoop they surrounded the entire plantation including all barns and outbuildings. The more experienced horsemen had clamored up the steep bluff as the other men on the bluff went the opposite way until the circle of soldiers had surrounded the entire plantation and all buildings.

Winslow made his way to the front of the plantation. A plump woman sat on the porch with a male servant standing by. The woman was the first to talk. "You damn Yankees show up when my man is gone to Richmond!" groaned the woman. She was a big-stomached woman with a chubby face, darting eyes and thin lips. Gray haired and unafraid, she was about fifty years of age. Some soldiers behind Winslow had drawn their pistols and held them at the ready.

"Do you have any guns in the house, Pansy Mearle?" asked Winslow adding her full name because he knew it from the southern newspapers.

"No, I don't!" hollered the woman.

"Lt. Glasser, Deerfield, and Captain Bell, search the house!"

"You don't have the right!"

"I have five hundred fifty rights and reasons." Said Winslow.

As the three men went to search the house, Pansy reached under her chair. Winslow immediately pulled a colt pistol from its holster and cocked it as he aimed at her head. She heard the click and put her hands in the air.

"Permit me, Madam, to receive the enemy's arms." Smiled Winslow as he grabbed the dueling pistol from under her chair.

While the three officers were in the house searching and Winslow waited on the veranda with Pansy, a horrific noise commenced. It sounded like rocks on metal.

"Your dumb soldiers have found the frying pans for the Confederate Army!" exclaimed Pansy.

By now the men were like six-year-olds with drums. There was clanging and banging with rocks and sticks and singing and shouting. It was a happy noise.

Winslow said, "A lot of good those pans are doing for the Rebs, collecting dust in your barns. Why weren't they given to your soldiers?"

"My man was going to play the hero and at the same time, make a good profit by selling them to the Confederate Army," said Pansy.

Pansy's aged body servant had been trembling with fear. He began to weave in the air in an unsteady motion. Winslow felt sorry for his extreme agitation. "Tell your servant to have the empty seat by you."

"I will not!"

"Alright then. Hey Dad, please sit in the empty chair there and relax. We are not here to hurt you." The black man collapsed into the empty chair and put his head in his hands with his elbows on his knees. A shuddered breath escaped his lips.

Sergeant Dillon, who had been searching the barns appeared next to the veranda. "Col., you were right. It is a very greedy politician's house. We have found everything in thousands; frying pans, pots, rifles, caps, cannon, and most importantly, pants!"

"Bring some pants here, sergeant. I'll put on a pair through the courtesy of the state of Mississippi, Madam." said Winslow eyeing Pansy. By now Pansy Mearle stared coldly with ice-blue eyes and a thin, purse-lipped frown."

"I never dreamed I would find such a jackpot. I could have raided many southern generals around here, but why bother honorable men, unnecessarily? The politicians are a sure thing when it comes to hoarding. How obtuse of me to not factor in the common denominator, GREED!"

Sergeant Dillon returned with four or five pairs of pants of various sizes slung over his arm. He had already donned a pair of trousers and was well pleased with them. He kept stroking the material of the trousers on his arm in continued enjoyment. "Col., you have a choice of sizes amongst these pants."

"I am on the large size so I will take the pair in the middle." said Winslow.

"Madam, may I use your hallway…perhaps your library to disrobe in?" Winslow winked an eye at the plump woman.

"You may not!" yelled the Rebel woman.

"Sergeant Dillon, cover that woman while I'm inside…. changing into my exquisite southern trousers of the finest weave. I beg take leave of you madam." He gave Dillon the dueling pistol, then with a flourish, he bowed low to Pansy. He then stepped inside the house with all the pants the sergeant had brought.

Sergeant Dillon was covering Pansy with her dueling pistol while inside Winslow shouted, "Glasser, Deerfield, Bell! Come here! We have some pants for you!" Winslow playfully added in a falsetto voice, "Dillon! Keep that woman out of here while we change clothes!"

In a low voice he asked the men, "Did you find anything?"

"Some old French dueling pistols." Sad Deerfield.

"I found another old dueling pistol on the woman of the house and Sgt. Dillon is using it now. Go out and ask Dillon where the pants are located then have your men dispense them to the soldiers."

"Right away Col.!" Bell said as Deerfield and Glasser followed him out to the veranda wearing their new pants. Dillon had overheard and pointed the men to the barn containing the pants.

Col. Winslow came out to the veranda and sat on the railing in his new pants. Dillon kept a steady bead on Pansy as she sat in her rosewood chair with legs crossed exposing a delicate pantaloon. As he sat there a general bedlam of noise broke out as some excited soldiers wheeled out a large cannon and aimed it at the river. A half charge of powder was put in and the fuse lit. It ignited and the roar of the cannon was heard for miles.

Corporal Angenlak appeared at the veranda. He had quickly been promoted from private to corporal for his expert horsemanship and decisiveness in the battlefield. His face was ashen as he spoke. "Col. Winslow, would you come with me? I need you to inspect something."

"Certainly, Angenlak."

Winslow followed him past the two large barns and most of the other buildings. They came upon the scene of a ragged black man shackled spread eagle to a square framework of beams, his wrists attached to the upper beam and his ankles to the lower beam. The man appeared lifeless as a bloodhound gnawed on his foot. Immediately Winslow shot the dog dead.

He went to the man and checked for a pulse in the man's neck. No pulse was found. The body was still warm and the scourges from a whip had cut so deep on his back that the rib bones were exposed. The fresh blood dripped into the dust of the earth and formed mud balls. At that moment both Angenlak and Winslow vomited. They recovered. They then took off their hats. Winslow said, "May he rest in peace."

They both heard a rustling in the nearest shed. Winslow gave a serious wink to Angenlak and said," Corporal lets burn this small shed down and these beams used for torturing this poor man and probably others to death. The fire will be in honor of his sad death."

"Yes Sir!" replied Angenlak

A small man with blood all over shirt and carrying a bloody whip ran out of the shed. "I surrender!" shouted the man as spittle shot out between his teeth.

"What's your name and purpose here?" Winslow demanded.

"My name is O'Leary, I-I'm the overseer Here."

"Did you scourge this man?" Winslow asked.

"Yes. He was a runaway! I needed to make an example of him!" O'Leary said defensively.

"An example of what? It's an example of your blind hate illustrated by the heinous torture, mayhem, and murder you have perpetrated on this poor individual." Winslow continued, "I couldn't treat an animal in such a vicious way."

Winslow was distracted by a little black girl coming out from behind a tree. She was about five years old with many tiny braids. Her small frame was heaving in anguish. She cried as she fell to her knees in front of the shackled man, "Daddy, daddy, my daddy!"

"Winslow could barely keep it together," Mr. O'Leary! Drop that whip, hands in the air! If you make any odd moves. I will shoot you square in the head! Corporal Angenlak check Mr. O'Leary for any other weapons."

Angenlak frisked O'Leary and found a knife and derringer in one boot and another derringer in the other boot. He also found a key to the shackles and showed it to Winslow. Winslow motioned for Angenlak to unshackle the dead man with the key. Angenlak did so. All this time the little girl had been crying. She continued crying as she followed the corporal as he carried her daddy to a grassy spot and laid him gently there. He took off his bluecoat and covered the dead man the best he could.

"Daddy, you are free now! Please come home wit me! You's all I gots! Wake up!" she touched her daddy's now cold hand and shrieked loudly, "Daddy!" An unearthly keening seemed to come from her very soul as she realized that her father was dead. Some other slaves emerged from hiding and came to comfort her.

Winslow was taking in the whole sad event. Something snapped. "Angenlak, shackle Mr. O'Leary then give me the key."

O'Leary tried to escape but Angenlak was quick and tackled him to the ground. There was a violent fight. A loud crack was heard. O'Leary had stopped struggling, He groaned and grabbed his upper right arm.

Lieutenant Colonel. Winslow, I broke the man's arm. It wouldn't be humane to shackle him now."

There was a long pause. "You are right, Angenlak. We will take him to camp and have Doc set his arm. A providence has taken place. Now he won't be able to whip anyone because he is out of commission for a long spell. So, throw the key into the woods." Angenlak did so.

There were many large bloodhounds in nearby kennels surrounded by a strong fence. They had been trained to be vicious hunters of run-away slaves. Their training had corrupted them for any other purpose. Winslow and Angenlak shot them all. They then set fire to the shed and bloody beams.

With O'Leary in tow, Winslow and Angenlak made their way back to Pansy on the veranda where Dillon was faithfully keeping a bead on her. As they approached the noise of the men grew into a roar.

"Men! This is enough celebrating. I do agree that this was a big deal, but let's calm down. My nerves are near shot!" Winslow shouted with a tired smile. "Hitch up the horses to the cannons, drive the cattle, and get the wagons ready with the foraged items. Lt. Campbell reported forty wagons with plenty of horses to pull them. The wagons will need drivers so some of you men can give your horses a break, hitch them to the back of the wagon you drive."

Lt. Campbell, who was nearby, said to Winslow, "This Mearle politician must really have some pull if he can get away hoarding thousands of items." Campbell thoughtfully added, "Politician Mearle has committed treason by withholding much needed items from the Confederate Army."

"It is sad for the Reb cause but good for the Yanks. By the seizure of these goods it will expedite the end of the rebellion. By the way, Campbell have you seen any young male field hands?

The old white-haired slave that Winslow had told to sit down earlier, overheard the question. He got up and said, "General, when you came here causin' da big commotion, all dem young field hands took off. Dey done dat dis very day of the jubilee you put into motion."

"I'm glad the field hands took off. I have never seen such grisly treatment of slaves. I kind of thought those Abolitionists had exaggerated a bit too much. They are so sadly right. Captain Bell, we will go through military procedure, order the barns burned!"

Pansy Mearle was aghast, "I beg you not to burn them!"

Winslow said, "Just burn the two big barns. Leave the smaller ones for the remaining slaves, the owner and his wife." Orders were executed.

The old colored fellow was soon surrounded by the remaining slaves, young children, old men, and women. One ragged woman was cuddling the poor little girl who lost her daddy to O'Leary's whip. The old man made a motion, and they all began to sing 'Swing Low Sweet Chariot' and several spirituals after that. It was beautiful. The vocal tones were rich, loud, and clear and rose higher as the flames intensified and seemed to reach the stars. It cast a beautiful glow over the slaves and soldiers. Pansy was covered in darkness except for part of her face. All that could be seen was a deep thin-lipped frown in the light of the flickering flames.

There was a solemn break in their singing as they watched the flames die down. Winslow said to the old man, "Old fellow, for your own good and your people's good, stay here on this plantation. We have no place for you around camp. We do have a lot of brush country people as refugees, poor people fleeing. They are the meanest, toughest group I have ever met. You will be safer here. Your mistress will treat you well… NOW."

Turning to Pansy, Winslow said, "I've been on other plantations where the owners have been kind to their slaves. Some of the slaves were given a small share out of the cotton crop or sale of furs trapped. I met one slave who had better clothes on than my Sunday best at home, plus he had three hundred dollars in gold. When President Lincoln officially sets them free, some arrangements must be made for them to make a living and their children to learn the three 'R's". By showing up at this plantation, I have already freed most of your slaves. Now Madam, most of your slaves are gone, your bloodhounds are dead, and the big barns are ashes. If you don't treat these remaining slaves better, your house will burn next. What do you have to say on this, Pansy Mearle?"

"I promise to faithfully abide by what you suggested," said Pansy meekly, wearily overcome by the quick succession of events.

Winslow mounted his horse and then yelled to his men, "We'll be off men!"

The forager's horses, wagons, and cattle took up three miles in length on the roadway hugging the Mississippi River. The men content with the day's adventure sang lustily:

Yankee Doodle went to town, a riding on a pony,
Stuck a feather in his cap and called it macaroni!
Yankee Doodle keep it up, Yankee Doodle dandy.
Mind the music and the step and with the Rebs be handy!

Their voices trailed off as they sought words to rhyme.

Evening twilight was rich with the scent of fall leaves, the sound of water lapping along the river shore, the horses trotting and the cattle mooing. Winslow was a mix of thoughts and feelings. Weary yet satisfied, yet sadly reaffirmed in why he needed to be in the war. The little girl's keening cries were forever stamped in his memory.

CHAPTER 13

Part 1
Kidnapped

Juliette was in high spirits as she scrubbed the kitchen floor of the Ursuline convent. Her happy mood was further elevated as her thoughts lingered over the most recent developments in her life. The pleasant aroma of chicken and rosemary bubbling noisily in a pot on the fire's grate synchronized with the morning warbling of the birds outside the kitchen window which created a comforting sensory background for her reflections. She was dressed in one of three gingham dresses that Mme. Bernard had recently made for her. All her other dresses were too fancy for workday chores. Her hair was sensibly braided and restrained under a white cotton kerchief tied at the nape of her neck.

Pausing from scrubbing, she sat back on her heels and ruminated on what had transpired since Christmas. She had begun to feel restless and bored during the prolonged stay at the Paxton's. Indeed, they were exceedingly kind and gracious but being a house guest had taken a toll on both guests and hosts. Juliette felt it was mutual imposition on everyone's privacy. She observed that Chitlin, Phinney, and Callie were content and thriving under Mumsy's maternal care all with the happy expectation of Phinney's coming baby. Plus, they all enjoyed the benevolent Paxton family. So, some loose ends had been tied up in a nice bow. She had talked to Mme. Bernard and it was mutually agreed that they move closer to the church in New Orleans and find a position helping the church there if possible. The Paxtons were sad for them to leave yet pleased also that the ladies were excited with their new goal.

It was two weeks into January of 1862 on a Sunday after mass. Father Gibbon was at the entrance of the church shaking hands with parishioners as they departed. It was Juliette and Mme. Bernard's turn to shake hands with the Father.

"Thank You for a wonderful homily and mass. I have wanted to mention that I have met your good friend, Father Clancy who is a priest at St. Mary's church in Mobile. He sends you greetings." Juliette said.

"Thank you for the kind words and the message from my good friend, Father Clancy."

"I was wondering, Father, if there was any work that Mme. Bernard and I could do for the church? We want to move to New Orleans proper, to find a position, and have the wonderful benefit of attending daily mass."

Father Gibbon paused then said, "Presently, I don't have any positions open for you ladies, but I do know the Ursulines often need help. Their many female students need private tutoring and personal attention. There might be areas in which both of you could help. Since you're already here in New Orleans, why don't you go to the convent and tell Mother Superior Margaret Joseph that I highly recommend you both."

That very morning, they both went to the convent entrance. Mme. Bernard knocked on the door. It was opened by a cheerful petite and plump nun of about age fifty. "Hello ladies! Do come in! I am delighted you have come for a visit. I am Mother Superior Margaret Joseph."

After introductions, Mother asked if they would like a tour and both women nodded yes.

Leading them to the school and dormitory section of the convent, she said "We enroll female students from the ages of eight to sixteen."

She led them past classrooms where a few students were studying or doing homework. They walked down a corridor which held the dorm rooms for both students and the nuns. The rooms were Spartan holding the bare essentials: a crucifix on the wall above a narrow bed, a nightstand with a candle and a bible, a washstand holding a water pitcher, bowl and towel, and three hooks on the wall for clothing. There was a small window in each room facing an inner courtyard which had plump contented chickens, an herb garden and a well with a bucket sitting on the rim attached to a rope. The rope was wound on a roller. They continued the tour visiting the large dining room, kitchen, and infirmary, then back to Mother's office.

After following Mother into her office, she motioned for Juliette and Mme. Bernard to be seated "so my dears, what brings you lovely ladies here today? I surmise it's not only for the tour you came."

Juliette smiled and looked at Mme. Bernard as she responded, "I think I speak for both of us. We would like to know if there are any positions open for us here. Some of my skills are cooking, cleaning, singing, dancing, and piano. If Mme. Bernard would permit me, she is talented at sewing, tailoring, mending, teaching piano and the arts of the theater. Obviously, we are both fluent in English and French."

"What a perfect answer to my prayers!" exclaimed Mother. "We are short-handed during this war. There are only ten nuns to help with teaching, tutoring, cooking and all that you have mentioned. You haven't seen any other nuns today because it's Sunday. On Sundays they all volunteer at the local hospital to give the overworked nurses extra help. You are both a Godsend. I hope you realize that I can't pay you ladies. What I can offer is food and shelter."

Juliette said, "It isn't a question of money. We just want to be of good use to the church in some way. Actually, Father Gibbon sent us here under his recommendations."

Mother Margaret Joseph beamed with joy. "When can you start?"

Within the week Juliette and Mme. Bernard moved into their humble quarters at the Ursuline Convent. Happily, they settled into a busy routine Juliette did everything from cooking, cleaning, dancing, and singing lessons. Mme. Bernard taught piano, mended clothes, and was creating costumes for a play so the students could hone their skills in acting. They both agreed to remove the gold sewn into the hems of many of Juliette's dresses from the Confederate money exchanged for gold coin back in Paris by Joseph Gastineau her friend and father. They gave it to Mother Superior for the good of the convent.

Mother Superior said," Thank you so much! You didn't have to do this. It will come in handy for the student's new books, school supplies, and fabric for making new school uniforms."

"Consider it job insurance. If there was no convent, we wouldn't have a job." Juliette smiled

Work settled into a pleasant routine of morning prayers, rosary, mass, breakfast, then helping wherever needed. Juliette gravitated toward the culinary duties. Frugal and skillful, she planned the first week's menu with some of the convent's chickens. The first dinner she made for the students and nuns was roast chicken, mashed potatoes, gravy and greens. It was a big hit.

To preserve the leftover meat and bones, she put it in a tall milk canister with a tight lid and a rope around its neck and sank it in the courtyard well where the cooler temperature preserved it. The next meal was chicken gumbo. She had kept the bones and put them in a big stock pot and simmered them for a couple of days. When it was ready, she gathered extra eggs from the chickens and made egg noodles to cook in the strained broth which was another meal. Several parishioners donated food items. One parishioner was a butcher and would regularly send over various cuts of meat, soup bones mostly and occasionally a ham. There was also another parishioner who would fish for a living and would bring the catch of the day on a Friday.

Juliette felt so content and peaceful in her present circumstances that she was inspired to write James her big decision:

Dear James,

January 29th, 1862

Hope all is well with you and your family during the hard times of war. The war has made things difficult at many levels. There is less choice of food at the market because many farmers have gone to war. There are more difficulties in travel because of railroads damaged by opposing factions. There are many other austerities too numerous to mention. Being in the thick of it, I am sure you have seen these conditions in abundance.

Our long separation under theses austerities, as well as time to reflect on our hasty engagement have given me pause, in an agonizing scrutiny of my conscience I have come to the firm conclusion that I can never marry you. To know that you support the evil institution of slavery has changed my mind about us. During my stay in the South, I have been witness to very grave matters spawned by slavery which I will not commit to writing. Be assured that you are rid of me and now free to marry another.

At your convenience you can pick up the trunk of clothes you purchased for me as well and the diamond necklace.

Sincerely,
Juliette Bellechasse

About three weeks later she received a letter. It was delivered by a Confederate soldier.

Dear Juliette,

February 9th, 1862

I have just received your letter. It was a serious blow. I won't parse words in another letter to you. We need to talk face to face and hash it out. I will try to get to New Orleans soon.

Yours,
James

It was now mid-March. Juliette had received the letter a few days earlier. She had all but forgotten about James whether by distraction, present duties, or willful suppression of his memory or all these combined. She pondered on the whole James episode from their meeting at the hotel De Ville, their mutual attraction, romance, the dangerous voyage, Armstrong's treachery at Veil Wood, Armstrong's impregnation of Phinney, O'Leary's attack and finally her escape with Beamus Paxton to Cypress lane. Above all, knowing that James wholeheartedly supported the institution of slavery. It reaffirmed that there was not one iota of fondness for James. He left her cold. She could hardly wait to be rid of the last connection she had with him, the trunk load of dresses he bought her in Paris as well as the diamond necklace.

Her mind's eye went to the convent entrance with the adjacent closet where she had placed her two trunks. The one black trunk held all of James purchases. The other green trunk held all the dresses Mme. Bernard had made for her. Also, the personal items her birth mother had given her posthumously; the daguerreotype of her mother, the letter and the native dress. She would keep the green trunk and store it for the future. In the meantime, the three gingham dresses Mme. Bernard had made for her were her work clothes. The other two hung in her cell.

It was late Friday morning. Juliette was cooking a large pot of shrimp gumbo for lunch. She was singing happily. The windows were open, and she could hear the cheery birdsong that seemed to answer the musical question, 'Where have you been Billy Boy?'

Suddenly, Mother Superior entered the kitchen, "Do you know a young soldier named James Lambert?"

Startled, Juliette said, "why, yes I do."

"He is waiting in the front garden at the entrance and wishes to talk to you. Do you wish to talk to him?"

"I do need to talk to him. I need to tie up some loose ends." Responded Juliette.

Reassured, the Mother said, "Alright then," and left.

Juliette quickly walked to the entrance and approached the side-front garden where James was seated on a bench. He stood up as soon as he saw her. He clutched a bouquet of flowers. His face was inscrutable.

"Hello, James. You have come a long way for the trunk of clothes you bought for me." She said somberly with arms folded." Anyway, it has been packed and ready for months."

He waved the bouquet in her face. "Is that any way to talk to your fiancé?"

"I know you have read my letter of January 29th. In it I clearly released you from our engagement."

"Whoa, whoa! Not so fast! We had a verbal contract of marriage. You don't just break an engagement with one sentence in a letter, like you cancel an order from the greengrocer! What has changed you so?" James exclaimed

"Many things. Things I have meditated on and things I have witnessed firsthand within the institution of slavery at the Armstrong's plantation. Plus, you purposely hid your view of being pro-slavery by talking to me of only the social aspects, parties, balls and dances. I am shocked, revolted, and nauseated when I deeply ponder owning another human being." Juliette paled as Phinney and Callie came to mind.

"Juliette, I've invested in you with money, clothing, jewelry, and my unconsummated hope in marriage to you." James deeply sighed and laid the bouquet on the bench. He turned his back on her seeming to be deep in thought.

After a pause, he turned to her face to face. His eyes had changed from clear gray to gun metal gray. He said resignedly, "Very well Juliette. It's not over, but for now, let's have a truce. Since I am here, I will go ahead and take the trunk. Since I know it's bulky, I will need your help carrying it to the carriage."

Without hesitation Juliette said, "I will be happy to help you. Let me show you where it is."

She led James just inside the front entrance vestibule where the trunks were stored in the nearby closet door.

James said, "There are two trunks here."

"Yes, the black one is your purchases and the green one is my possessions."

James acknowledged it by picking the handle at one end of the trunk. She picked up the other handle. James had a wider stride than Juliette, so she had to watch her step and hurry after his lead. They progressed through the front gate to an enclosed carriage mostly hidden by shrubbery that grew along the lane. Two soldiers emerged from the carriage.

James made an abrupt signal of extending his arm with his hand in a fist and his index finger pointing at Juliette. Before she knew it, one soldier was behind her back, bound her hands, gagged her, while the other had bound her feet. They quickly deposited her inside the carriage out of sight.

Again, James signaled one of the men to follow him back to the convent. Quickly they returned with the green trunk.

Soon they were all aboard the carriage, three inside and one outside in the driver's seat. James yelled out the carriage window to the driver, "Skedaddle, Corporal Connor."

The carriage bolted into motion and fled the scene. Juliette squirmed against her fetters for quite a while. Finally, exhausted, she fell asleep. Observing Juliette, James said to his tall lanky fellow soldier, "lieutenant Combs, I am mighty tired and need a nap. Watch Juliette for a while. In a day or two we'll turn in this carriage and horses at the Mississippi state line and pick up our fresh horses and wagon."

Combs nodded at his friend and peer, "Sure thing, James."

As they left the city far behind, Juliette awoke from her nap and squirmed even more. Combs took pity on her and removed the gag and blindfold. He silently offered her a canteen of water from a crate behind him which held a lot of food stuffs such as beef jerky and dried fruit. He brought the canteen to her lips and nodded encouragement to drink. She drank some water and as she did so, noticed James asleep next to her. She choked on the water. The noise roused James from his slumber. He stared at her.

"As I know you better, James, the less I approve of your choices. In My country of France, it is a capital offense to kidnap people!" Juliette sputtered.

"Juliette, Juliette, I'm not kidnapping you, I'm, going to marry you! It's as simple as that!" James cooed in an unctuous voice while smirking triumphantly.

"Against my will!" Juliette shrieked.

"Tut, tut, don't stress. I am protecting you this very minute from all the bad things that could happen out there." James nodded at the passing wild countryside.

Juliette kept silent. There was no point in arguing with James He was hell bent on his warped plan.

Lieutenant Combs was keenly studying her. Recognition lit up his face. "I know you! You are the Juliette who sang and danced for President Jefferson Davis at the Armstrong Plantation! I was part of the retinue of soldiers who accompanied him there. We were invited to watch the performance. Miss Juliette, you were spellbinding! My fellow soldiers and I still talk about you."

Juliette was surprised then warmed to the lieutenant. "Thank you, I am pleased you enjoyed the performance.

James was astonished by Combs comment. He looked at Juliette with new eyes. They narrowed with envy. Resentfully, he said, "Never once did you mention that you were a talented performer!"

"And you never told me you were pro-slavery or that you would lower yourself to kidnapping!"

All three were reduced to an uncomfortable silence for a long while.

Hours later Juliette broke the silence and said, "I need to get out and stretch my legs and answer the call of nature. Am I allowed?"

James looked out the window and noticed a thick stand of trees and just beyond that a turbulent river. It offered the perfect containment feature. He yelled out the window to Connor who was driving the carriage, "Pull over Connor! We are going to stretch our legs." He then untied all of Juliette's bindings.

Juliette rubbed her wrists and ankles. "Thank you for stopping."

Combs opened the carriage door, climbed out, then helped Juliette to the ground. The other two had exited the carriage also. She walked to the stand of trees. Her mind darted wildly at the frightening circumstances in which she presently found herself. The rushing river looked intimidating. She didn't know how to swim. The three men were intimidating because they had demonstrated the use of force. If she ran there was no place to go. She chose to cooperate and returned. She might find an opportunity to do something later. There was no Mme. Bernard to ask advice. She thought, 'I will just have to play along with the situation until I receive a better opportunity. God will help me, I pray. I know the whole convent is aware of my disappearance and they are now praying for my safety.' That thought gave her comfort as she returned to the carriage where the men were waiting.

The first night they let Juliette sleep in the carriage and furnished her a blanket. Each man took two-hour shifts guarding her. The next night all the men were too exhausted. Everyone slept. The next few days were blurred together by fast travel and short nights. At the outset, when her blindfold had been removed, she noticed that they had passed on the west side of a lake with a sign stating it was Lake Pontchartrain. After that, there near a town marked Ponchatoula, was a ferry that took them, the carriage and horses across a river. Right before the Mississippi state line. The carriage and horses were exchanged for three fresh horses and a wagon. The men put the black and green trunks in the wagon as well as the remaining foodstuffs. Connor hooked up two of the horses to the wagon and Combs rode the third horse.

Most of the time Lieutenant Combs would ride alongside the Wagon Connor was driving. Occasionally, Combs would scout ahead. On one such scouting Combs came back and said to Corporal Connor, "pull off the road behind the brush and wait for some soldiers to pass.

Corporal Connor did as he was told. A party of about sixty soldiers thundered by on their steeds. Juliette looked at James and asked, "Why do you hide from your own men?"

James winced, "because they are unaware of my trip to get you."

Juliette became introspective weighing the onslaught of events since her abduction. Meticulous planning was the key to the whole operation: Connor and Combs at the ready to bind her, the enclosed carriage to hide her as she passed through town, the foodstuffs so there was no need to interact with the local people, the exchange of fresh horses and a wagon for the rented carriage. And now Combs scouting ahead to avoid their own soldiers. What a painstaking plan. It was all to acquire herself and her trunks of clothing. She was a thing, a possession. James had never said he loved her. Even now as they rode in the wagon while Connor drove. James had a vice-like grip around her waist. It was not a loving embrace but a jealous claim of ownership.

Juliette thought James had acted differently while traveling in the carriage with Lieutenant Combs. James had kept a respectful distance. Perhaps It was because Combs kind gestures toward Juliette kept in check any primordial moves on James part. Now that Combs was scouting ahead. James true self was revealed. An idea popped into Juliette's head. On a short break to stretch their legs. She went to the green trunk and took out a bulky wool shawl and a linen cape. She put on the shawl and the cape for two practical reasons: she was cold in her thin cotton dress, and it was a barrier to James grasp. It was a prop that Mme. Bernard could appreciate.

On the evening of the sixth day of travel, the men decided to camp early in a brushy area. All were weary of the long, intense journey. Corporal Connor made a campfire and brewed some coffee for the small group. There was only beef jerky and dried apples to go with the hot brew. They all sat around the fire warming themselves when they heard the distinct sound of breaking branches. Four Confederate soldiers appeared. Of the four, the tallest and highest-ranking soldier spoke, "Good evening. I am Captain Haywood. I have been sent on a mission to gather Confederate forces at Corinth, Mississippi, by order of General Albert Johnston."

Pompously, James stood up and addressed Haywood, "Captain Haywood we are headed in that direction. In short order we men will arrive at Corinth."

"Duly noted Lieutenant------?" Haywood's eyes lingered questioningly on Juliette.

"I'll not stop you as you continue on your urgent mission."

The Captain and his men rode off.

They all settled back around the campfire. Combs said, "We are in a day's ride of Fair View." He looked encouragingly at Juliette. "Soon you can have a hot meal and a proper bed."

Juliette smiled at his kindness, saying nothing.

James lit into Combs, "Do not speak on personal issues with my fiancée!"

"Hey James! There is nothing personal in what I said. We are all looking forward to an end of this journey with a hot meal and a good night's sleep! You need to calm down."

James glared at him but kept silent.

Juliette stood up and announced, "I will retire for the evening." She climbed into the back of the wagon, spread her blanket and lay on top of it wrapped in her shawl and cape. There was only room for her between the trunks.

The next day was full of a vague anticipation for Juliette, now that the journey would end. Her mental faculties were dulled by fatigue and not eating much. She dozed off and on during the last leg of their journey. Anxiety wove itself into the anticipation. What happens then, a rushed wedding? Dread entered her thoughts.

By sunset they had arrived at Fair View Plantation. As its name implied there was a panoramic view that surrounded the plantation. As

Juliette was helped from the wagon she ached with fatigue and dread at the same time. Coupled with hunger and light headedness as she put her foot on the ground, she looked toward the plantation and saw two dark silhouettes with a glowing chandelier behind them. She became very dizzy and everything faded to black, she was soon unconscious.

Something damp was pressing on her forehead. Juliette opened her eyes. Sun light was streaming from a window onto the bed where she found herself. Again, she felt the damp cloth dab at her brow. With her eyes she followed the arm from her forehead to its owner, a young black girl. She was about age fourteen.

Juliette's head cleared. She asked the girl, "How long have I been here?"

The girl answered," two days Miss."

"Oh." Juliette said as she noticed that she was in a clean white night gown. Also, that another person was in the recesses of the room.

"Who's there?" Juliette asked.

That person came closer. It was a slender woman in her fifties with gray hair in a tight bun. Her face resembled James, even the gray eyes. "Good morning. I am the mistress of Fair View, Henrietta Lambert. Her expressionless face was only animated by the action of her jaw.

Juliette sat up. "Then you must be James mother!"

Mrs. Lambert nodded.

Mme. Lambert, I was kidnapped by your son and two other soldiers! I had written James that he was free of me except for the trunk of clothes and necklace he had purchased for me in France. He came to the convent where I was staying in New Orleans on the pretext of retrieving the trunk. He pretended to take the trunk as I assisted him in carrying it to the carriage. Suddenly I was bound by those men and kidnapped.

Mrs. Lambert said to the girl, "You can go now and help in the kitchen Letty." The young girl left.

"I demand to be returned to New Orleans!"

"I am sorry that he kidnapped you and relieved that you had broken the engagement because it had been an unspoken agreement between the Lamberts and Durands that their youngest daughter, Ophelia, was to marry James. As soon as you fainted two days ago a retinue of soldiers appeared on the heels of your arrival and whisked James, Connor and Combs to Corinth. There is something brewing in Corinth. So, James is elsewhere. That is a reprieve from his plan to marry you. Now I know for certain that you don't wish to marry James. I will try to help you with some plans. I do know I cannot help you go back to New Orleans. I will figure out some other location to hide you. I will let you rest.

Juliette was relieved that Mrs. Lambert was on her side and that she would think of a safe place for her to hide. She noticed that both her trunks were in the room. She arose from the bed and went to the green trunk then dressed in a plaid wool dress for the day. Once dressed, she proceeded down the stairs. She noticed it was a lovely house as she descended the stairs, sparse in furniture, yet cozy in its simplicity. Letty emerged from the kitchen with a steaming bowl of broth and fresh bread.

"Letty is that for me?" the girl nodded at Juliette. "If Its permissible, I'll eat it in the dining room."

The girl led her to the dining room and motioned for Juliette to be seated. She then unloaded the tray of hot broth, warm bread, a napkin, and a spoon. Juliette ate with gusto. When she had finished, her fatigue had come back so she went up to her room to rest. She slept many hours and when she awoke it was dusk. There was a knock on the door.

"May I come in?" asked Mrs. Lambert.

Juliette said, "Please do."

Mrs. Lambert spoke. "Juliette, I want you to hear out my plan. I have sent word through a trusted friend to my sister, Pansy and her husband, my brother-in law, Jonathon Mearle to come to an important gathering here. If all goes well, they should arrive here in two or three weeks. In the meantime, I want you to meet, make friends with, and assist James true intended, Ophelia Durand. Both of you young ladies could plan a lovely party at my house. Invite my friends and the Durands friends. James told me before he left that you could sing and dance. Hopefully, you could include Ophelia in the actual entertainment. She is such a shrinking violet. Make her sparkle and shine. Then you can slip away with the Mearles to their plantation which is over a hundred miles from here. Near the shores of the Mississippi River.

"Thank you for the plan of escape."

"An added plus is that when the war is over, you can take the riverboat back to New Orleans." They both smiled.

Part 2

The next morning Juliette was feeling much better. So much so, that she managed to take a bath and wash her hair in the cook house. She felt alert and rested. After returning to her room, she changed into a navy-blue satin dress for the day and put her hair up in a bun. She went downstairs for breakfast and found Mrs. Lambert seated at the dining room table.

"Good morning, Mrs. Lambert," Said Juliette cheerfully.

"Good morning." Said Mrs. Lambert.

There was cornbread, ham, coffee and molasses that had been placed on the table.

"I have had the privilege of meeting you, Mrs. Lambert. When will I meet your husband?"

Mrs. Lambert said, "That's up to him. I will be frank with you. Several years ago, he was kicked in the head by a mule. It took a long time for him to heal. He hasn't been quite right ever since. He has seizures occasionally, but not as often as a few years back. So, as you may surmise, I am the one who runs the plantation. So there, that's out of the way."

"Well, thank you for explaining it so well. Now I won't pepper you with more questions." Juliette responded.

Mrs. Lambert cleared her throat. "Now onto our plan of mutual benefit. I need to clarify some things. First, time is of the essence because James' could be relocated at any time while in the army, so I have invited Ophelia Durand for lunch today so you both can get acquainted and off on the right foot. Next, of course, is that the planned party is really for James to switch his attention and affections to Ophelia. Before he went to France and met you, those two were sweet on each other. Hopefully you can draw out some talents in her to help win James over."

"I am anxious to start!" Juliette smiled.

Ophelia arrived in the late morning in an open carriage driven by a slave. From the front window Mrs. Lambert and Juliette saw the carriage approach. Both went out on the front veranda to greet her.

"Ophelia! I am so happy you could make it!" Mrs. Lambert exclaimed.

Ophelia descended from the carriage and mounted the three steps to the veranda. Mrs. Lambert gave Ophelia a brief hug, then said, "Ophelia, I want you to meet my house guest, Juliette Bellechasse."

Both young ladies politely shook hands. Ophelia was small, barely five feet tall.

"Come inside girls, I want to have a little chat with you." Mrs. Lambert said.

They entered the main parlor where a welcoming fire blazed in the hearth. They all settled in chairs near the comforting glow.

"As is plain as the nose on my face, the war has dragged on and dragged down the spirits of the people. People seem so glum and beaten down. So, my plan, with both of you young ladies being on the creative end, will be to put together a musical performance for many guests in a few weeks."

Ophelia looked in wonderment at Mrs. Lambert but said nothing.

Mrs. Lambert continued, "So if we are going to lift the spirits of our guests the performance must be cheerful and happy. I will of course, try to invite James and his fellow officers and soldiers as well as neighbors and friends. So now, before I go to attend to the needs of the plantation, do you have any questions?"

"Yes, do you have a piano?" Asked Juliette.

"Yes, it's in the ballroom." Mrs. Lambert.

"Wonderful! That's all I need to know." Juliette responded.

Mrs. Lambert left. Juliette studied Ophelia. She was barely five feet tall, slender, regular features, dark brown hair, and brown eyes with very pale skin.

Juliette inquired, "Tell me about yourself, things like, do you sing, dance, play a musical instrument? Do you have hobbies, interests, things like that? How old are you?"

Ophelia smiled shyly. "I'm eighteen. I really don't sing, dance, or play a musical instrument. My four older sisters, when they were home, did all that. I like to do hand work, mostly tatting. In fact, I would like to give you this handkerchief. I just finished doing the lace on it this morning before I came here." Ophelia opened her purse and gave her a beautiful white, lace-edged handkerchief.

"Well, thank you, Ophelia! It's truly kind of you." Juliette smiled. "My gift to you will be honing undiscovered talents. At eighteen you have many that even you are unaware of. So, let's move to the piano in the ballroom and find out!"

Juliette settled onto the piano bench. "I'm going to sing part of a familiar song, 'Where Have You Been Billy Boy?', and I want you to sing the same chorus."

Juliette sang the chorus then nodded to Ophelia as a cue to follow suite. Ophelia sang slightly off key and didn't hold her notes long enough at certain points. They practiced and practiced some more. Then Juliette had her practice the music scale so that she could find the right note and register. Her singing quickly improved.

"Now let's animate the song with facial expressions and movement. I'll show you what I mean. Acapella, Juliette sang the song as she stood up and added facial expressions and action to the song. She put a puzzled expression on her face with a finger on her lower lip as she sang, 'where have you been Billy Boy? facing an imaginary Billy. Then when the imaginary Billy responded, she stepped into his spot and became Billy and sang with thumbs in pretend suspenders, 'I have been to seek a wife, she's the joy of my life, she's a young thing and cannot leave her mother!"

Ophelia was delighted, "Let me try!"

Juliette saw the excitement on Ophelia's face and was heartened by it. "Oh, please do!" Their practicing went into the late afternoon.

Time melted away. Each morning, at nine, Ophelia would arrive at Fair View and practice a variety of happy songs with Juliette, discovering an aptitude for dancing, singing, and mime. She would reluctantly leave late in the day sometimes missing an evening meal at home. Letty would bring them fruit and nuts to snack on so that they could continue practicing the performance and therefore would not lose inspirational momentum. The days fled in an invigorating blur.

Three days into meeting Ophelia, Juliette was at breakfast with Mrs. Lambert, when a slender stooped man in his fifties appeared at the table. His clothes were shabby, frayed but clean. He said, "Henrietta, who is this young lady at table with you?"

"This is Juliette, a house guest and a friend of our good neighbor, Ophelia Durand." Henrietta responded, then added. "Juliette, I would like you to meet Chauncey Lambert, my husband." Juliette smiled.

"He said, "Pleased to meet you, Juliette." Then he sat down across the table from her. He filled his plate with bacon and flapjacks.

After a short while, he looked up in puzzlement and his eyes met Juliette's. "Where is your home Juliette?"

She said, "I'm originally from Paris, France. Presently, I call New Orleans my home."

"So, what is our connection with you?

Juliette had to think quickly to avoid explaining her prior engagement to James and the treacherous kidnapping he perpetrated on her person. "I'm an entertainer. Word had spread about me. My last important performance was in Alabama. The guest of honor at that performance was President Jefferson Davis and many soldiers along with civilians from that area. I was brought here by some soldiers that had witnessed my Alabama performance. I have been asked to help lift the morale of the soldiers and civilians located in this area with a cheerful performance showcasing the local talent of Ophelia Durand." She needed to placate Mrs. Lambert in the matter if she were to escape Fair View and James. Her heart was in Mrs. Lambert's plan to make Ophelia appealing to James. There was great potential in Ophelia's emerging talents. A striking dress, hairdo, make-up, and of course, an ostrich feather fan would be perfect props to nudge Ophelia to a coup de theatre performance and win over James.

Several days later, Mrs. Lambert received an answer to the invitation she had sent to Pansy and Jonathon Mearle. It was during breakfast when a military courier arrived. Mr. and Mrs. Lambert were at the breakfast table as well as Juliette. Letty, who had answered the door, brought the soldier to the dining room table.

The soldier said, "I have a message from the Mearles for you." Mrs. Lambert stood up and took the sealed envelope from the soldier, opened it and read the contents. She smiled.

After reading the letter, Mrs. Lambert said, "Wait a moment Corporal. I will send a note with you, back to them. She went to her writing desk and wrote a note, sealed it, and handed it back to the soldier. "Please give this to the Mearles. Before you go, you are welcome to eat some breakfast in the kitchen."

"Thank you, Ma'am. Will do." Said the soldier as he exited through the kitchen door.

After he left, Mrs. Lambert announced, "I have some good news. The Mearles are two days distance from here. They should arrive mid-morning of the second day of travel. So now we get the word out that the party will be in two days."

Everything went well in the planning of the event. That evening some older men came to Fair View who had heard of the performance and offered their skills as musicians. The Lamberts and Juliette had just sat down in the parlor after supper when they knocked on the door. Letty brought them to the parlor. There were three of them. The tall balding lanky gentleman was the spokesman for the group.

"The reason we're here is word got out mighty fast about this performance and we all play musical instruments and want to help. My name is Cooper and I play the banjo." He then pointed to a slender man with sharp features and a chubby man with curly salt and pepper hair. "Noah and Josh both play really good on fiddles. Noah also plays the piano. If this performance needs to be taken to other places to cheer the soldiers, we have a four-seater wagon to help bring it to them."

Juliette exclaimed, "Wonderful! I will take you up on your kind offer. Please show up a couple of hours early tomorrow so I can go over the medley of songs that have been chosen."

The Mearles arrived two days later at noon. The Lamberts, Juliette, and Ophelia greeted them as they climbed the steps onto the veranda.

The carriage they had debarked from was quickly driven away to the rear of the house by a small stocky figure in a dark coat.

Mrs. Lambert gave Pansy a hug. "So good to see you sister. It's been a long spell."

Pansy was all decked out in a crimson damask gown that clung to her ample waist as the skirt billowed in the breeze. "Good to see you too, Henrietta. Time just shoots by and so much has happened since last I saw you." Pansy said.

Pansy's husband, Jonathon, was a portly man with an expansive belly clothed in a perfectly fitted silk vest and twill suit. On his right hand he wore three gold rings with diamonds. "So good to see you, Henrietta and Chauncey."

"Do come in and tell us all the news." Mrs. Lambert encouraged.

Moments later they were seated by the cheery, crackling fireside. Letty brought a tray of glasses filled with sherry. Jonathon's wavy, snow white hair encroached on his cheeks partially covering well-tended lamb chop sideburns which framed a cherubic countenance with a perpetual smile. He said, "Pardon me in my rudeness in not asking who these young ladies are."

Mrs. Lambert said, as she pointed to Juliette, and then Ophelia, "This is Juliette Bellechasse from New Orleans and Ophelia Durand, my neighbor's youngest daughter."

"Delighted to meet you young ladies. I understand you both have worked hard on the upcoming performance." Jonathon said as his eyes dwelt on Juliette. Both girls smiled and nodded to him.

"Yes." Said Pansy loudly as her eyes narrowed and darted between Juliette and Jonathon. "Nice to meet you girls." Her thin lips disappeared into a narrow line.

Mrs. Lambert said, "These girls have been practicing hard for the performance. I have caught snippets of it. Of course, the mastermind behind it is Juliette. Word has traveled about her wonderful performance for President Jefferson Davis. Ophelia is her ingénue who has really blossomed under Juliette's tutelage. My hope is that the performance tomorrow will cheer our soldiers and neighbors and build morale. As I wrote you in the note, I cannot be selfish with Juliette's talents, so that after the performance, she has agreed to return with you folks to perform in your area to cheer the troops stationed there."

"What a kind gesture!" Jonathon said

Pansy interjected, "The Mearles certainly need some cheer since we were raided by the damn Yankees in late fall! They burned our two biggest barns, shot all of our bloodhounds, stole our goods, and to top it all, fifty of our prime male slaves ran off during the ruckus! If I ever get my hands on that Frank Winslow, I will ring his neck!"

Chauncey Lambert had been silent until now. "Pansy Mearle, your plantation is a perfect target with all your barns on a high bluff overlooking the Mississippi River, just expect more raids till the war ends, if it ever does."

An awkward silence ensued during which Juliette pondered Pansy's revelation of the raid. All the people in the room were related to, or actual slave owners. She was required to indirectly maintain the slave system by cheering the Confederate troops so that they would be energized to fight. She felt ashamed and asked God to forgive her and allow her to escape soon somehow. She felt like a bird in a gilded cage. She would have to play along a while longer.

Mrs. Lambert regained her composure." Why yes, Chauncey, all the plantations, us included, could be raided. It's one more reason for our troops to be cheered by Juliette's and Ophelia's happy performance.

The morning of the performance the musicians showed up with their instruments. Juliette gave them the music that they were going to perform. They stayed in the ballroom and practiced until the performance with a break for lunch. Meanwhile, Juliette went through her trunk and found a black crepe dress with a high collar and long sleeves. She found an old pair of glasses in the nightstand drawer missing both lenses. It would be a perfect prop.

She went to the fireplace grate in her bedroom and collected some ashes in her palm then applied them under her eyes creating dark circles. Then she went to the wash basin and washed her hands. Dusting some talcum powder on her cheeks, lips, and face, dramatically contrasted with the dark circles under her eyes. She put on the glass frames and looked in the mirror. Pausing for a moment, she didn't' recognize herself. She tested a few facial expressions and was impressed by her transformation into a haggard, wan schoolmarm.

Days before she had completed a dress rehearsal with Ophelia. Juliette had shortened one of her own dresses, a red satin one, for Ophelia's performance. With full make-up, hairdo, fan, and dress, Ophelia was breathtaking and confident as she sang through the rehearsal without mistakes.

Ophelia arrived about three o'clock to prepare for the performance. She knocked on Juliette's door. Juliette said, "Come in."

Ophelia whisked in the door then looked at Juliette. "Juliette! You look sick! Since when do you need glasses?"

"Ophelia, you are the star, and I am the dark sky so all can enjoy your sparkle."

Ophelia giggled. Juliette gave her a hug.

Because of the prior dress rehearsal, it was easy to prepare Ophelia and even improve on hairdo and makeup.

When they were done, Juliette said, "Now, I am going down to the musicians in the ballroom. When you hear the melody of 'I Dream of Jeannie With the Light Brown Hair' that will be the cue for your entrance which will start at the upstairs landing, then down the stairs and into the foyer. Of course, do this in dramatic fanfare using the fan to hide and reveal your face and swirl the gold cape. We have practiced so you know the rest from that point on."

"I do, but I'm a little nervous." Ophelia said.

"You'll do fine. The music will prompt you for each song in the order we rehearsed them."

At that moment, they heard a thunder of horses arrive near the house.

"Alright, that's my cue to go down and get situated at the piano." Juliette said.

Juliette hurried down to the ballroom and sat at the piano with Cooper, the banjo player, and Noah and Josh, the fiddlers. There were about fifty civilians. Then about a hundred officers and soldiers entered the ballroom. Some more soldiers were in the entry way where the stairs were located. When the audience had settled down, Juliette began to play 'I Dream of Jeanie With the Light Brown Hair'. The musicians joined in.

Ophelia had made her way with flash and pomp and was encouraged by the soldier's shrill whistles and shouts.

Ophelia entered the ballroom and made her way onto the stage platform. The chandelier glowed above her head. She threw off the cape and revealed her red satin dress and unfurled the red plumed fan. Then Juliette played 'Where Have You Been Billy Boy?' Ophelia had been advised at this point to go into the audience and find James, bring him on stage, as if she were singing only to him. Ophelia did just that. After a few choruses she had James singing Billy's response. The audience loved it. She gave James a kiss on the cheek and sent him back into the audience. The crowd roared with pleasure and gave a standing ovation. From Juliette's camouflaged vantage point, she observed that Ophelia had James' full attention as well as the whole audience. She performed several more songs to the appreciative audience.

There was a short intermission. Ophelia went into a nearby room. During the intermission, the musicians played a cheerful tune. Juliette, from her vantage point, saw that James was talking to his mother and that she had pointed in Juliette's direction. He walked toward her.

James strained to see her better since she and the other musicians were in a shadowy corner of the ballroom beside the stage. "Is that you Juliette?"

"Yes, James." Juliette said solemnly, then coughed into her handkerchief.

"Since when do you wear glasses?" He asked.

"You see, James, as I've told you before, you don't know me." She nodded sadly and continued, "I don't feel too well. I hope I haven't contracted anything contagious."

He stopped short.

"I think it wise that you keep your distance, to be on the safe side."

He immediately backed away, then turned and rejoined his mother, and the Mearles as the second half of the performance began. Ophelia was back on stage in one of her own party dresses. It was a diaphanous emerald green dress with a flouncy skirt. She gave a charming performance. It was faultless. When the entire performance was finished, she received a thunderous, standing ovation. People in the audience lingered to compliment her as James put a protective arm around her shoulders.

Juliette observed James actions and breathed a sigh of relief, she thanked her fellow musicians, then quietly left for her room. No one seemed to notice because all eyes were on Ophelia. Once in her room, she washed her face. She packed her green trunk. She put a note on top of the black trunk that held James' purchases. It simply said, 'James, here is the trunk with the items you purchased for me in France, along with the diamond necklace. You can give the necklace to Ophelia, just never say that you bought it for another woman. For the clothes, have all the dresses hemmed three inches for Ophelia. Again, don't mention me. Destroy this note after reading it. Yours, Juliette'. She sealed the letter in an envelope, put James name on it and put melted candle wax to seal it again.

Juliette put on her nightgown, climbed in bed, and immediately fell asleep and slept soundly. She was awakened around five in the morning as the soldiers prepared to depart. There was a loud clatter of hooves as the soldiers left. She arose from her bed and dressed for travel.

As she exited her room, she observed Letty was collecting chamber pots that had been placed in the hall for cleaning. "Letty, please have my green trunk loaded on the carriage. I am leaving the black trunk here."

"I'll have the green trunk put on the carriage, Misstus Juliette." Letty said.

"Thank you."

Juliette continued to the dining room. The Mearles and Lamberts were there.

"Good morning, Juliette!" Mrs. Lambert exclaimed. "Last night was a great success! James proposed to Ophelia!"

Juliette smiled in relief. "How wonderful!"

"They plan to marry on James' next furlough, probably the end of June. They don't want to wait out the war because who knows when it will end." Mrs. Lambert said.

"That's a wise judgement for the engaged couple." Juliette responded.

Pansy said, "We'll be leaving right after breakfast with Juliette. She can work her magic in our neck of the woods." Juliette smiled weakly in agreement.

Not long after, the Mearles carriage had been loaded with all the suitcases, the green trunk, and some cold lunches for the journey. As they boarded the carriage she was helped by the coachman. Glancing at his face she recognized him. It was Sean O'Leary from Veil Wood! He leered back at her savoring her shocked expression. Her heart filled with dread.

Once all the passengers were settled in the carriage, Jonathon announced, "We should make it home in two days, three at the most. Hopefully, we will make it to Batesville this evening to spend the night with friends."

Juliette was in such inner turmoil by the knowledge that "O'Leary was the coachman that what Jonathon said barely registered with her. They stopped at Oxford for a late lunch. O'Leary ate his lunch at a distance under a lone tree while they dined near the carriage on a blanket. Juliette thought maybe I have the upper hand in this situation because O'Leary left Veil Wood in disgrace. Even President Jefferson Davis punched O'Leary. Now, somehow, I have become a popular entertainer. Maybe we can peacefully coexist. With that thought she was much comforted.

They stopped for the night at Batesville at a private home, friends of the Mearles through political connections. The trip continued without incident. On the morning of the third day, they arrived at the plantation. Juliette observed the burnt debris of what remained of the two large barns. The plantation was in top condition.

"Finally, we are home!" Jonathon exclaimed.

Pansy said, "It's always the best part of a trip to get back to our home sweet home."

Juliette smiled sadly as she remembered the New Orleans convent and Le Mouton Noir. Both had been happy homes for her. Soon she was unpacking her trunk in the guest room. It comforted her to know that the Mississippi River was close by. She thought hard and came up with a wild idea, 'I could float on a log down river back to New Orleans and back to the convent and my dear friend Madame Bernard. They must be so worried. Juliette feared water, so she sadly dismissed her impractical plan.

Meanwhile O'Leary was thinking also, 'if Juliette doesn't mention that I assaulted her, then I can keep my new job as coach driver for Mr. Mearle.' Since the raid on the Mearle plantation the past autumn, when O'Leary broke his upper arm in a struggle with a Yankee, he hadn't healed sufficiently to wield his whip to discipline the slaves. He had been offered the coach driver job by Mr. Mearle and thoroughly enjoyed it because he was often taking Mr. Mearle to and from Richmond, the South's capitol. He enjoyed the sights and people he would come across. He decided in his mind, 'I will try to be quiet and keep a low profile. It will be easier since I am mostly in Richmond now.'

Travel had exhausted the Mearles and Juliette. The evening of the first day back, they all had gone to bed early. The next day Juliette awoke early to the happy sound of birds twittering near the open window in her room. She got up and sat in a chair by the open window. It overlooked the Mississippi River from a high vantage point as the plantation was on a steep bluff. Quietly, she studied the beautiful view and discerned the sound of the rushing river. The sound lulled her into deep thought. 'Less than month ago, I was so happy at the Ursuline Convent helping with the cooking, teaching, and cleaning. Then I was kidnapped by James who was hell-bent to marry me, never mind that I had released him from the engagement. I had become an object to possess. Thank God for Mrs. Lambert's plan, Ophelia's talent, and Madame Bernard's lessons of theater and props. Ophelia had shown like a sparkling star and I had used make-up and props to appear as a sickly schoolmarm. It had been James change of mind to let go of me and to propose to Ophelia. I can see that God's hand was in it throughout the ordeal. A greater good had come of it, James let go of me and made Ophelia happy with their engagement to be married. Now I am trapped as a bird in a gilded cage to sing songs of cheer to the Confederate Army. God allowed it. God's plans continue to weigh heavy in my life so I will continue to trust in Him. Increase my trust dear Lord even more through your grace.' She then dressed for the day.

Both Pansy and Jonathon were at the breakfast table. Once Jonathon noticed that Juliette had entered the room, he stood up and said, "Good morning, Miss Juliette. I hope you had a restful night."

"I did, thank you. Good morning to both of you."

No words came from Pansy's lips, but a quick stretch of her lips meant as a smile. There was no warmth behind it.

Juliette sat at the table and quietly said grace then crossed herself. She poured a cup of coffee and had some corn bread.

Jonathon said, "Mercy me, I just got home and have to leave for Richmond right after breakfast. With the war on, the South must be ever vigilant. My carriage is packed and waiting with my trusted coachman, O'Leary.

Juliette said, "I'm sorry that you must leave so soon."

Jonathon said, "I am sorry too. But early this morning a courier brought a message that I was much needed in Richmond. I am content to know that you will be cheering our troops with happy songs while I am gone. I want to thank you in advance by helping our soldiers in this manner."

Juliette said, "What else can I do? If my humble performance lifts spirits, then I thank God. For it might be that soldier's or that person's last day on earth. If he or she has joy in their heart, it gives me peace in mine, Mr. Mearle."

"Well said. Please be at ease in this house. You are welcome to call me Jonathon and my wife Pansy."

"Thank you then, Jonathon and Pansy."

Breakfast was over. Jonathon said, "Regretfully, I must now depart for Richmond." He stood up and gave a peck on the cheek to Pansy. Then bowed to Juliette. He hurried out the front door to his carriage. It left right away.

Pansy turned to Juliette. "I enjoyed Ophelia's performance at Henrietta's home. I never really saw you sing or dance."

"I was beside the stage playing piano with the other musicians. Ophelia was an attentive student to my instructions. Her talent bloomed. I am happy you enjoyed her performance." Juliette said.

"I'm thinking that in three to four weeks we could have you perform here. What do you think?"

I am ready now, except that I would have to get word to Cooper and the other musicians to come here. They all live around Fair View."

"I could send for them. One of my overseers can do it. There are a lot less slaves to oversee since the raid. They have a little time on their hands."

"Wonderful! Those gentlemen have already played with me and know many songs. Once they get here, I will be ready to perform. I think I can do two performances a week. It wouldn't always be here at your house because Cooper has a wagon and can go to where the soldiers are." Juliette wanted to keep busy.

Pansy said, "Let's not wait. I'll have those musicians fetched right away. Once they're here, we'll get the word out. Maybe in a week or less you'll have your debut performance here!"

Cooper, Noah, and Josh were summoned. They arrived at the plantation within five days. They were delighted to be useful for the performance. The first performance went well. Juliette tapped into the established repertoire of music and songs. No longer a musician in back of the stage, but a singer. At the first performance at the Mearle Plantation, many soldiers, neighbors and civilians had gathered. Her notoriety seemed to have increased.

The twice weekly performances were rapidly gaining in popularity gauged by the increasing size of the crowds. Not every performance was the same. Juliette enjoyed mixing many different songs in her performances. She chose some from her native France, some she had learned on the bayou in Louisiana, and some she had learned from Cooper and the other musicians. She was busy which made the time pass quickly. Most of the time Juliette would perform at the Mearle Plantation, but soon she was traveling to hospitals to cheer the wounded. It was hard to see the horrible injuries that the soldiers endured: amputations, gaping wounds, missing eyes, head wounds, shell shock, and simply those waiting to die. At those hospital performances she would pray not to break down in front of those wounded, but instead power through them. Keeping one thought in mind, 'I am here by God's will and these men might not be here tomorrow.' It was at the hospitals that she began to end her performances with Amazing Grace. She held up until the end and then would find a secluded place and weep into the gift of Ophelia's handkerchief.

So again, her life transitioned into a new routine of performances. The wounded soldiers were not routine. At the field hospitals she would linger after the performance and try to talk to each soldier before leaving. Many languished there with no chance of recovery. At one of the hospitals after she had performed, she saw a young boy with a wide, blood-stained bandage around his chest. He might have been barely sixteen.

Juliette knelt by his side. "Hello soldier, what's your name?"

"Luke, Ma'am. You must be an angel that God sent because I just prayed for someone to help write a letter to my Ma." His voice was raspy as he tried to breath. "I have a piece of paper under my pillow. There is ink and pen on the table next to me.

Juliette took the paper and picked up the pen. "I'm ready Luke."

Luke began, "Dear Ma, I am sorry I can't make it home to see you. Tell Nellie and Susan that I love them. Love you too Ma. I am wounded bad and will die soon. I will see you again in heaven, Love, Luke. Please send the letter to Mattie Benson in Tupelo, Mississippi. Thank you."

Juliette said in a choked voice, "I'll make certain your mother gets the letter."

Luke's voice became a whisper. "That was the last thing I needed to do. Bless you." His eyes closed. He had a slight smile on his lips. He was gone.

Juliette wept.

Part 3

Juliette awoke to a strong morning breeze that ruffled a strand of hair across her face. It also noisily flapped the curtains on the window near her bed. Still half asleep, she got out of bed and went to the window. The invisible effects of the wind rustled the leaves of the trees below and roiled the waters of the Mississippi River.

She mulled over her present situation. More than a full year had passed since she had moved to the Mearle Plantation. It was now the end of May 1863. Pansy, who had been barely polite to her at their first meeting at Fair View, was now outright hostile. They mutually avoided each other unless Pansy needed her for entertainment purposes. Another thought entered her mind, James Lambert, her former beau, who had kidnapped her from the convent in New Orleans and spirited her to Fair view for the purpose of marrying her. Neither his mother, Henrietta Lambert, nor Juliette wanted them to marry. So, they both planned to distract James from that marriage by having James pay attention to his former sweetheart, Ophelia Durand. Juliette had helped Ophelia turn into an excellent entertainer, singer and dancer. At Ophelia's premier performance she captivated James. They were married within the month of June. Sadly, for them, on September 19, 1862, he was killed at the battle of Iuka, just three months later. Word had come from Henrietta that Ophelia was inconsolable. Although Juliette had bad memories of her kidnapping, she had forgiven James. She had been happy for Ophelia who genuinely loved James and now felt empathy for Ophelia's sorrow.

Whenever Jonathon, Pansy's husband, would return to the Mearle Plantation for a brief visit, Pansy's jealousy would flare into malicious mischief. Her favorite means was molasses. At first it was only smeared on Juliette's outside bedroom doorknob. When Juliette encountered the molasses as she was leaving her room, she reentered, washed her hands of the molasses. She thought the situation out and concluded that she could never acknowledge this prank because she knew the nearest slave would be punished which would be old Micah, the house servant. So, she began to wear a housecoat with large pockets and long sleeves. In one pocket she carried some folded sheet music and a pencil. In the other was a small oilcloth bag which held a damp rag. The oilcloth was wide open for quick access. So, the molasses smears on the doorknobs continued wherever it was likely for Juliette to touch. She would wipe them up promptly.

Pansy noticed the housecoat and asked, "Why are you wearing a housecoat, Juliette? You didn't wear one before?"

"I've found that I can store my sheet music in my pocket and work on it when I have an inspired moment, so I don't have to run all the way up to my room and lose my thought."

The molasses pranks escalated into new locations. Fortunately, Juliette caught a glimpse of Pansy as she smeared molasses on Juliette's designated chair at the breakfast table one morning. She was just about to enter the room when she saw Pansy smear her seat with molasses. She slipped away undiscovered and went back to her room.

An idea popped into Juliette's head. She put on a pearl earring her mother, Michelle, had given her back in Paris. Then she put the other pearl earring in the music sheet pocket. As she entered the dining room where breakfast was being served, she said to Pansy, "I have misplaced my earring or dropped it here yesterday during dinner. Could you look around your chair to see if it rolled that way? I will look on the floor over here."

As she knelt on the floor, she quickly wiped her chair seat and at the same time babbled about how her earrings had been a gift from her mother which added to the distraction.

"Voila! I have found my other earring!" She put it on.

Juliette than sat down on her chair and poured some coffee and sipped it slowly savoring it.

Pansy glared at her and then her eyes narrowed as she continued staring belligerently at Juliette. Pretended ignorance of this, and all previous molasses pranks was the only avenue of choice. Otherwise, to mention it to Juliette was to admit guilt.

Pansy snidely ventured in a sarcastic tone, "Well, how's Miss Juliette doing today?"

"I am very happily enjoying a good cup of coffee." She looked as blank faced as possible and smiled graciously.

Privately, Pansy seethed because of Juliette's lack of reaction to the pranks. The pranks faded away. What didn't fade was Pansy's anger. There was no vindictive triumph for Pansy, only smoldering frustration which refined itself into pure hate.

Juliette chose to be absent from the Mearle Plantation as much as possible. She would entertain with her trio of musicians anywhere else, mostly hospitals and other gatherings. Her trunk full of costumes was always kept in Cooper's wagon ready to go.

Juliette was so homesick for the convent and Mme. Bernard that it made her heartsick. She continued to linger on the comforting thought of the friendly and loving people at the Ursuline Convent in New Orleans and her guardian and chaperone, Mme. Bernard.

She thought to herself, 'I am so disappointed by most men I have met by their lecherous behaviors. I know that there are good men also, like Beamus Paxton, Joseph Gastineau, and my dear father, Antoine!' She thought further, 'Of course all the priests I have met have been wonderful, Father Sevigny, Father Clancy, and Father Gibbon. Those are either father figures or priests! Oh Lord, my heart yearns for an honorable man, a gentleman. Where is at least one? Please give me hope!"

Pansy had told her yesterday that she was to entertain a small gathering of neighbors and friends at the Mearle Plantation the next evening which was today.

Juliette dreaded being in the same room with Pansy. At least Jonathon would be absent. Perhaps Pansy's jealousy wouldn't be so intense. She prepared for the day donning her housecoat and steeled herself for the day.

At the present moment, Pansy was at the dining room table eating breakfast. She smirked to herself, 'Juliette knows about the molasses and pretends nothing happened! I'll fix her wagon tonight at the performance! I know that she often uses the burgundy winged backed chair in the ballroom in many of her songs as a prop. I have already stuck some needles in the seat cushion so that when she plops down in that chair, she'll hurt her keister! Ha, ha!' She laughed to herself as she took a second helping of flapjacks and molasses.

Aloud Pansy said, "Let's see her ignore that, and in front of a whole audience!" she spoke to an empty room.

A few minutes later Juliette came downstairs and into the dining room where Pansy was eating.

"Good morning, Pansy." Juliette politely said. "About this evening's performance, are there any songs you'd like to hear?"

"Why yes! The Old Armchair by Henry Russell. It's a touching song with beautiful lyrics."

"I know the song and the lyrics. It's very sad. It will make people morose."

"There won't be any soldiers here, so they won't get sad. Indulge me, won't you?

"Certainly." Juliette answered.

"And by all means, use the burgundy winged back chair as a prop"

"Thank you, Pansy." Juliette answered, puzzled over Pansy's emphasis on the use of the chair.

After breakfast, Pansy went on her errand of informing her neighbors about Juliette's performance that evening. Of course, Pansy took her fanciest carriage and finest horses to accomplish the task.

Back at the plantation, Juliette continued to ponder over Pansy's strange song request and her emphasis on using the burgundy wing backed chair as a prop. She went to the ballroom to check out the chair. She grabbed the armrests and wiggled them. She noted as she did so that the chair was sturdy from the armrests, to the legs, and including the back. Then she lightly put her hand on the seat cushion and was grazed by several needles imbedded in the cushion. So that was the malevolent prank that Pansy had planned! Quickly, she removed the needles, then brought them to her room and deposited them in a nightstand drawer.

Resignedly, she thought, 'I must always be on my guard! It is so tiresome.' She plopped on the bed, sitting hunched over her lap as she thought about Pansy's seemingly endless treachery. It overwhelmed her. She laid down and surrendered to her fatigue.

As she yielded to sleep, her thoughts puzzled over the question, 'how could anyone in good conscience fight for the preservation of slavery?' Then many who championed slavery appeared before her in her mind's eye. Juliette was able to read the faces of them all: Clayton, Henrietta, Pansy, Johnathon, O'Leary, even Beamus! She saw in their faces desire for power, greed, lust, sadism, compliance, and fear. Then maggots emerged from their mouths, eyes, and ears consuming their flesh until all that was left were empty skulls.

It jolted Juliette from her sleep. She thought, 'I am in the pit of hell! It's all a huge masquerade. They all dress up in fancy clothes and act respectable, yet they do unspeakable, dastardly deeds against the poor, helpless slaves.

In revulsion, Juliette quickly left the house, walked down the winding path to the Mississippi River. She walked in a southerly direction distancing herself from the plantation and what it represented.

She shouted to the trees and river, "If I could jump on a log right now in the river, I would do it! I could float down river to New Orleans and then go to the convent from which I was kidnapped! If you wanted me to see the evil here, God, I see it! I no longer fear the river! It's my friend! It will take me back to New Orleans, Mme. Bernard, and the convent. It's my only happy home in this far away land!"

She sat on a rock by the shore, buried her head in her hands and cried a long time. Her tears diminished as she heard a soft scraping. She looked up and saw what appeared to be a wooden door caught among the rocks near her in the shallow water. Upon closer examination, it was a large, thick coffin lid made of solid oak.

A wry smile came to Juliette's lips. "Thanks for hearing me Lord. You certainly have a sense of humor in answering my prayer. I wonder if it was to get me over my fear of water and drowning. Well, I think I will stash my customized raft right here under some brush. I now can form a plan because of Your gift."

She looked upward. "Of course, on my part, it is human nature to make plans. On your part, you might or might not allow them. But I must go forward in my plan because it feeds my hope."

Now Micah, the old slave had been in earshot of Juliette's rant of floating down the river to New Orleans. He was picking cherries for the cook's pies. He was hidden among the trees. He couldn't blame Juliette for wanting to skedaddle. Pansy was a cruel master in his experience with her. More power to Juliette. He would miss her for the entertainment and protection he had witnessed as she wiped the molasses from the doorknobs. Juliette was a rare woman in his mind.

The breeze picked up as she climbed the steep path back to the plantation. She prolonged her stay out in the fresh air by thinking of paying a visit to the musicians who were now lodging in the previously abandoned overseer's cabin. Her plan was taking shape. She saw Cooper's wagon with her trunk in the back. She knocked on the door. Cooper opened the door.

"Hello, Cooper, Noah and Josh." She said as she saw the other two past Cooper's shoulder. "I thought I would just check up on all of you to see how you all were doing."

Cooper hesitated, "I can only speak for myself, Miss Juliette. I'm doing fair for my age."

Noah, who was the pianist appeared to have lost some weight as his once chubby cheeks were now deflated and limp. He said, "Traveling so much has taken a toll on my digestion because of odd schedules and eating unhealthy."

Josh, who was the fiddler said, "It's a tough life entertaining." He had dark circles around his eyes.

"You know even though I am younger than you, I feel pretty drained. So, I was thinking that we all take a break and letting you gentlemen go back to your homes around Fair View."

They all looked relieved and broke into smiles.

Juliette continued. "I don't know if you heard that Ophelia Durand, who married James Lambert, became a widow after James was killed at the battle of Iuka, September 19, of last year. Word has it that Ophelia is still deeply aggrieved by her loss. So, my thinking is that I don't really want to entertain at all, at least for a long time. So, I will send my trunk full of costumes to her via your wagon. But first I will take out my personal items. Once you get back and rested, maybe you could persuade Ophelia to entertain with you locally, around Fair View. That might help her with her grieving."

She continued, "Now you don't have to follow any of my suggestions except let's take a long break from this hectic lifestyle."

The men laughed again.

"Cooper is there any pen and paper here?"

"Yes," Cooper said as he went to a small desk, opened the drawer and produced an ink pot, quill, and paper.

Juliette went to the desk and wrote rapidly. She looked it over and blew on it to dry, then spied some white sand in a jar in a cubby hole of the desk. She sprinkled it on the remaining wet ink then shook it free of sand which dropped to the dirt floor. She then folded it to create an overlap, then lit a candle on the desk and dripped wax on the flap to seal it closed.

"I will put this letter in the trunk. It's for Ophelia whenever you have the chance to give it to her."

"What I say next is important if we are to get our much-needed break. Please do not mention to anyone of our plans for a break during or after tonight's performance. Then no one can change our minds."

The men nodded their heads in agreement.

Juliette went to the trunk and gathered up her personal items, among them, her birth mother's letter, picture, and African dress. She put everything in a large oil cloth bag that was also contained in the trunk. She then placed the sealed letter on top of the dresses and closed the trunk.

She returned to the cabin, "Now I will give you all a hug good-by and my thanks for all the sacrifices you have made to cheer our troops at all these past events. Of course, most heart wrenching were the dying at all the makeshift hospitals." She hugged each man with genuine affection.

Solemnly, she said, "Adieu." As she closed the cabin door.

She glared at the plantation and still couldn't put a foot in it yet. She thought, 'I might as well be as ready for departure as I possibly can so I will take another stroll to the river and deposit my oil cloth bag on my raft.' She made it to the raft and put her bag on top of the raft and added more brush for camouflage.

Now she could endure returning to the plantation because hopefully, this would be her last evening there. Peace entered her heart. She went up to her room and happily prepared for her last performance when she heard the creaking wheels of the carriage and clopping horse hooves approach then stop. The door below opened and slammed shut.

Pansy's high-pitched voice shouted orders to the slave. "Lolly, go make the punch! Micah, put out the cookies, pies, and everything else on the reception table. Hop to it! It's almost seven o'clock!"

After the commotion of Pansy's return, Juliette returned to the task of preparing herself for the performance. She had put on her cream-colored satin dress with the leg of mutton sleeves which had laces at the wrists to tighten the sleeves and matching satin slippers. She slipped her freshly washed lace handkerchief, a gift from Ophelia, up her sleeve and tightened the laces on both wrists. Her hair was down around her shoulders in waves that ended in curls.

All preparations for her escape had been made. It calmed her to think of it.

Music floated up to her room. It was 'I Dream of Jeanie with the Light Brown Hair'. It was her cue.

Part 4

The siege of Vicksburg had begun, and the time in effecting the siege was forty-six days. It began May 18, 1863.

General Vale and Lieutenant Colonel Winslow were discussing the situation in Vale's tent in his camp.

"The main army has to be fed, and your outfit, hands down, is the best foraging operation I have ever come across. Thanks for bringing the cattle earlier today. Dinner will be beef stew." Said Vale.

Vale continued, "I know I would have been butchered by now If I had taken all the chances you take. You know those fifty slaves that you freed from the Mearle Plantation? They came to this camp. One of the slaves I talked to, told me that on the plantation the owners would tell them frightening stories of the Yankee Devils to keep them from running away. So, when you and your men showed up as vilified agents of the devil, there was no way in their minds that they would contend with the blue devils, so they escaped certain death by leaving. The fifty stumbled into my camp and found out the true evil was slavery and that they were now free with no harm coming from us. They were relieved. I had Colonel Melton take those who wanted to fight for us outfitted and put in the regular army. The others who felt like cooking or sewing, I kept here. I gave four hundred pair of trousers that you had confiscated to Colonel Melton's men, but I will have them use the surplus fabric cut from the trousers, as they are tailored to fit, to be used as patches on the best of what is left of the union trousers. According to the rules of warfare, the men shouldn't have a piece of enemy garb on. But those Reb pants have a blueish gray cast to them, and no one knows the difference unless he looks closely. In a few days of wear, it won't matter because those pants will be covered in mud and dust.

Winslow smiled in appreciation of possession Vale's good news, then changed the subject. "General Vale where are you from and what is your background?"

"I am from St. Louis, Missouri. I am a surveyor and farmer. I was a West Pointer and graduated. At the time there was no openings in the army, so I took up surveying since I had learned the rudiments at the Point. It was hammered into us that never were we to pillage. My eyes are open now. Ulysses Grant was way ahead of that point of view," Vale laughed at his own joke. "He's the one who initiated foraging in the Western Campaign. We couldn't keep supplied without pillage and forage. If we had no food for the brave and willing fighters, I would be afraid of the consequences. I feel better with you around, Winslow, you don't bother with personal property."

"Some of my men took a razor from that politician's house," admitted Winslow.

"Well, that's not silverware or furniture." Vale said reassuringly.

"I understand that you are a good lawyer, Winslow. In fact, Reverend Blake shared that with me. I will keep it in mind. You never know when you'll need a lawyer." Vale said.

"As a lawyer, and General Grant commanding you to forage for food, you have to follow orders and so it was acceptable. But clothes, pans, and what all…" Vale ended with a mischievous wink.

"I stand on the old saying, possession is nine-tenths of the law, especially when encountering e-greed-ious hoarding by a politician," Winslow smiled and added, "The articles captured could be useful for the Rebel Army as well as the Union Army, so the Union acquired the goods."

Vale smiled back, "There are some great bonuses in foraging besides acquisition of goods. I have heard tell of your romantic dalliances."

Winslow blushed and floundered for words. Then to relieve his awkwardness, he pulled a comb from his pocket and ran it through his unruly locks. More composed, He said, "I have been unusually fortunate in meeting so many kissable women on my foraging duties, and a kiss can't cause much harm. In fact, it seems to lift the women's spirits."

"No, Winslow, a kiss can't cause much harm and can be mighty helpful. Say, have you ever considered growing a beard, or is it by being clean shaven, you succeed so well in your romantic endeavors?"

"Could be it helps." Winslow responded.

There was a sudden mood change in General Vale as he pulled an unopened letter from his vest. Tenderly he held it against his chest. He was about to put it back.

Winslow interrupted his intentions as he politely inquired, General, how's everything at home for you?"

"Alright so far. I have an unread letter from my wife, Ruth, so don't know the present status quo. My sister Helen sometimes writes me. Helen is twenty-six and not married yet," said Vale as he eyed Winslow as a possible prospect.

"She probably won't be till the war is over. I won't. It's impossible to make plans. Why don't you read the letter aloud if it is not too personal?"

Vale opened the letter with his pocketknife and carefully unfolded a neatly written page.

Dear Ira,

I take pen in hand and will devote some time to write you. The children are well. I am in good health. Paul is nine today. I baked him a cake and Louise is helping with the frosting. Every waking hour they talk of their daddy. Paul can ride a horse like a trooper. I didn't want him to at first, but old Bess is gentle. Paul now rides to town by himself and brings back sugar, flour or whatever I need or can get. Louise is much company. She talks all the time, mostly asking when is daddy coming home? I have some hens sitting on some eggs for spring hatching. The raspberries have been picked and still are coming in. Those copperhead snakes sometimes lurk in the berry patch though, so we throw rocks in before picking.

Your salary is enough so Paul wouldn't have to work so hard in the field, but he insisted on planting ten acres of corn for the animals and I helped him seed it. It was hard work as you may remember. Every spare minute I knit socks and mittens for our boys at the front. I know it is springtime but I'm looking ahead. It's better to be prepared than not.

I remain your loving wife,
Ruth

"It seems your boy, Paul is a good helper to his mother," said Winslow.

"Indeed, he is!" responded Vale proudly.

"When Vicksburg falls, why don't you have the family come down on a riverboat." Winslow said haltingly as he pondered his words.

Vale was attractive in a beat-up way. His thick Sandy hair matched his thick drooping eyebrows which rested over sky blue eyes, a craggy face and full beard. When he smiled and flashed perfect teeth, he transformed into a handsome man, virility personified. He reached for some extra fine cigars that had found their way into Winslow's vest pocket which was exposed by his open coat.

"Nice cigars you have here." Said Vale

"Yes. My men keep me in cigars and tobacco." Said Winslow as he lit Vale a cigar.

"Today is May 30th, and the siege has been going on for twelve days," said Vale. "The people of Vicksburg are a stiff-necked lot! Who knows how long it will last? We already have a slew of wounded men. We have got to have more sheets, comforters, bedding, and mattresses. Anything helpful for their recovery!"

Vale continued, "So many have severe wounds. If they get a wound in the head or the stomach it is almost always fatal. I happened to see one fellow along the road waiting for an ambulance. His leg had been amputated nearly to the hip. Everything had been done that medical science and human compassion could accomplish, circumstances permitting. Still, I doubt that there can be much hope for him."

A somber Winslow said, "I know…I have seen so much blood spilled and so many lying along the roads. Many are just made comfortable in so many cases."

Winslow winced. "Saw one soldier with his windpipe severed by a bullet, another with a bullet in his stomach and he still walked to the ambulance. Vale we are fortunate."

Vale said, "For the one much is given, much is expected."

Winslow hesitated as though putting his thoughts in order. "May I ask you this General, does mattresses, bedding and the like, constitute legal demands of warfare."

"Yes, since we have none and none is available to us. It would come under foraging. Upon acquisition of goods, you can leave receipts for the goods. After hostilities, those affected can claim the receipts for goods used." Answered Vale. "Where in the Sam Hill can you get bedding and such. You've already raided the Mearle politician and took everything."

"True, we cleared out the big barns and burned them down. And at that time, I told Mrs. Mearle I would not touch the house. Times have changed. It is a bigger than normal plantation. I'm banking on that politicians hoarding tendencies. I want to revisit that plantation. It is a foragers dream. Besides the images of our maimed and suffering soldiers haunts me. I won't be able to sleep until I have done my duty. My men and I will go tonight while we still have the Mearle wagons. On the last raid Captain Bell searched the house for weapons and came upon a locked attic door. It is a sure thing there are more hoarded items in the attic. Especially, since it is locked. It needs investigating." Winslow pulled out a pocket watch, a gift from his men.

"It's four o'clock now." Winslow said.

Vale said, "An army can't travel on an empty stomach. There is plenty of hot beef stew in the mess tent. You all eat before you go. Call me Ira and I'll call you Frank. It has been good to get to know you better, Frank."

"Thank you, Ira. The same for me. You are right. A good meal should always precede action."

Winslow poked his head out of Ira's tent and yelled to Sgt. Morrison. The sergeant who was at a nearby campfire came to Winslow and said, "Yes Sir."

"Pass the word around sorta low, that after supper, we got to go out and roundup bedding for the wounded. Don't shout it around as there are many Rebel scouts within earshot. We will all eat before leaving." Ordered Winslow. He came back into the tent banging his saber on the tent pole.

"Wise decision to stay for a good meal, we have excellent cooks from the Mearle Plantation. You are in for a treat."

Winslow peered out of the tent door and saw his men line up for dinner. They had all kinds of shapes and sizes for mess containers. They held them in hand at the mess tent to receive the delicious smelling beef stew. One of the cooks appeared at General Vale's tent bringing two meals on fine china.

Where did you get these dishes?" asked Winslow to the recently liberated slave.

"Ise brought dem wid me from massah's house. You sho preciates dem ah sees."

"Why, yes…we do!" Smiled Winslow.

The two men finished their meal of beef stew and hardtack. They wiped their mouths in satisfaction. Vale brushed crumbs from his whiskers.

Vale leaned back on his cot and patted his belly affectionately. "Let me know in the morning how you come out."

Winslow's horse was saddled and waiting for him. The rows of horses looked like a big wall in the gloaming of the day. Winslow scaled his horse as Ezra sounded mount. Nightfall arrived with the waning of the moon which gave sufficient light for their journey. When they arrived at the Mearle plantation, the soldiers stealthily surrounded it. The big house was in festive mode with many outside lanterns lit and many cheerful candles glowed and flickered in all ground level windows. Lively piano and fiddle music could be heard accompanied by the singing of 'Where Have You Been Billy Boy?' by a beautiful female voice.

The whole scene lifted Winslow's spirits. He smiled as he observed to Major Lester who was beside him. "Looks like a party!"

"And so?" Major Lester sarcastically questioned.

Winslow ignored his response. He motions to his men to dismount and tether their horses to the trees along the perimeter of the expansive lawn. "Major Lester, stay with the horses."

Winslow motioned to his men to approach the house on foot. Once at the house they dimmed all the outside lanterns.

Winslow quietly said to Sgt. Morrison as he peered in a window from the shadows. "From here I only see a few old men and lots of beautiful women, Sgt. Morrison you and your men disarm the old men and Mrs. Mearle. Tie her up and join me in whatever I am doing. Whisper the word around." His eyes twinkled with devilish mischief.

"Yes Sir." Morrison smiled.

Winslow came closer to the window as Morrison and his men went in to disarm and secure the building. His heart stopped as his eyes fell on the beautiful songstress. It was the girl of his dreams! Her long loose black hair reflected cobalt blue in the candlelight. She was in the midst of winking at one of the old men in an exaggerated manner. Her eyes were the color of peridot green and her complexion glowed from the efforts of entertaining. She swirled in a cloud of cream-colored satin as Winslow's men blew through the front door with the damp spring air. Then her eyes became big with surprise and her heart shaped mouth was partly opened as she forgot the next lyric to sing. Winslow's mouth salivated as he rushed in the door and embraced her. The rest of the men followed suit, and each grabbed a pretty girl in one fell swoop. The piano and fiddle music had trailed off into silence. The women screamed.

Winslow spoke loudly, 'Do not be alarmed we are not here to harm you. We are merely here for provisions. But first, may we have the pleasure of dancing with you lovely ladies? I see that there are no men represented here your age. Musicians, some dance music please!" A lanky tall man on the banjo was first to start. The pianist and fiddler joined in.

Winslow, who had not let go of the green-eyed beauty, now gave his full attention. They began to dance. Winslow's eyes consumed every detail of her features as he asked, "What part of heaven are you from? May I ask your name?"

Spellbound by the handsome soldier, she answered, "I come from Paris, France. Juliette, my name is Juliette Bellechasse."

Equally mesmerized Winslow said, "My name is Lt. Col. Frank Winslow. You don't know how happy I am to finally meet you."

Both entranced, they continued to dance. The waltz ended. Winslow came back to reality, then yelled, "Keep playing!"

He turned to Juliette, "May we go for a stroll on the veranda?" She nodded in agreement.

As they stepped outside, he took both her hands and faced her squarely. "Juliette, as I have experienced life, it can change all circumstances in an instant. War especially can have that power on the grand scale. I won't mince words for that very reason. For a long time, I have dreamed of a woman like you. Now providence has given me the opportunity to finally meet you. There are only so many moments of opportunity in life to lay your soul bare, to be embraced or trampled. So here goes, my soul has yearned for you in my dreams, long before this encounter. Time is all we have in life, measured by crude instruments, sundials, hour glasses, clocks, and watches."

At that moment Frank reached into his vest and hands Juliette his pocket watch. "I love you Juliette. Now that I have met you, all my dream filled yearnings for you have been realized this vey night. My watch is a token of love for you because my time is now in your hands."

Juliette was deeply moved as she raptly listened to Frank. Tears welled up in her eyes as she pulled from her sleeve, a lace handkerchief scented with lavender. "Here is a token of my love for you, Frank, my handkerchief. Many tears have been shed in this handkerchief in grief and sorrow. It is only a piece of cloth, but I give it to you as a souvenir of this very moment. It is a moment in which I feel that I've known you forever. I was on the edge of despair before you arrived. God has sent you to me to give me renewed hope."

A tear rolled down Juliette's cheek. Frank took the handkerchief and wiped the tear away. Then he covered his nose and mouth with it and deeply inhaled the damp lavender scent. He put it in his vest pocket.

With the unabashed mutual avowals of love, Frank said, "Dear Juliette, you are heaven sent. I have been praying for you to come into my life." As he took her open right hand and placed it on his cheek, pressing it deeply into his skin as if etching every physical sense of Juliette into his soul and memory.

As they stood in the moonlight, they found themselves in an ardent embrace which led to a long kiss into blissful oblivion. It seemed like eternity, yet not long enough. When they released each other, they then both ached to be close again.

Frank looked to the stars for strength. Never in his life had love disarmed him so completely. "I am very much pained to leave you Juliette. God has answered my prayer by the fact that I have finally found you, so now I will hope and pray to find you again and marry you after this war. If God allows it, I will see you again. Until then I will have a small part of you, in the tears held by your handkerchief. It will be kept next to my heart." He tenderly touched his vest pocket.

"This moment in time shall be suspended at 9:41 Post Meridian on your watch until we are together again. It will be kept next to my heart also." She took a lacing from her sleeve and slipped the watch link onto the lacing, tied the lacing ends together and put the watch around her neck and slipped the watch into the front of her dress.

"Now dear Juliette, I must obey my superior's command and collect much needed bedding for injured and dying soldiers.

His long, lingering gaze on beautiful Juliette was cut short by self-willed determination. "Duty calls."

Juliette understood. They walked back into the ballroom as the last dance concluded. Winslow noticed that Pansy Mearle had been tied to a comfortable wing-back chair near the musicians. He motioned to Sgt. Morrison to untie her. She indignantly rubbed her rope-imprinted wrists and glared at Frank.

Winslow addressed the soldiers, "Men, go upstairs and get some bedding. We're running over time."

The raiding party made quick work collecting bedding from the open rooms. Lt Deerfield showed some cleverness. He sent some soldiers to fetch several wagons that they had left on the edge of the property and simply had the remaining soldiers throw the bedding out the upstairs windows to the waiting wagons while a subdued roar of siege guns could be heard.

Pansy Mearle smirked at Winslow, that's our guns trained on you Yankees. You must have a lot of wounded to come in on us like this."

"Here are the receipts for goods taken," Winslow said as he handed it to her, scornfully observing the plump repulsive woman.

A tremendous commotion was going on upstairs, feet pounding, castor wheels screeching, glass shattering. Corporal Malland stomped down the stairs to Winslow. He said that the attic was locked, and Lt. Deerfield needed the key.

"The keys, Madam." Commanded Winslow to Pansy

"I won't give them to you!" sneered Pansy.

You better, or I'll have the soldiers kick down the door." Said Winslow firmly.

"Here is the key." As she lifted her skirt and dug in the pocket of her pantaloons and produced the key. The Corporal grabbed the key and ran up the black marble staircase and then to the attic.

Upstairs, the Corporal said, "Here's the key, Lt. Deerfield!"

"Good," the lieutenant said and opened the door to the attic. The soldiers' eyes were met with a myriad stash of brand-new blankets, comforters, mattresses and sheets. Since the goods were all brand new, the men carried the precious loot downstairs and out to the wagons.

Pansy Mearle, outraged screamed, "You dam Yankees won't win this war even if you steal my possessions!"

"That's your opinion. My opinion is we steal from rich politicians and give to the poor and injured like Robin Hood. And if word gets out that you kept these items from your own Confederate Army, someone might want to tar and feather you!" Proclaimed Winslow.

The last of the men brushed past Pansy Mearle out into the night to carefully pack their loot for transport to camp. The men were full of pep having had a wonderful evening of dancing and gathering much needed supplies for the wounded.

Winslow spotted Juliette on the far side of the ballroom, approached her again and kissed her hand tenderly, "Until we meet again dear Juliette," then bowed. She smiled and nodded slightly.

He left her and walked back toward the entrance where Pansy Mearle smoldered in anger. In passing her to leave, he said, "If any harm comes to Juliette while she remains here, accidental or intentional, I will hold you responsible, I personally will tar and feather you. His eyes locked onto her eyes with grim earnest.

Pansy lowered her eyes and turned away weak with fear.

Winslow Whisked past her and disappeared into the night. He mounted his horse and joined the men on the journey back to General Vale's camp. His heart was filled with joy and hope with the thrill of finding the girl of his dreams. He felt for her handkerchief to reassure himself that Juliette was real.

CHAPTER 14

Frank Winslow's encounter with Juliette, the girl of his dreams, had been a life changing event. Before he had met her that fateful evening at the Mearle Plantation, his pleasant dreams of a dark-haired beauty would dissipate like morning mist. Then, it was much easier to concentrate, plan and execute the tasks of the day. But now, he had met Juliette, held her, kissed her, and smelled the lavender scent of her handkerchief. His dream girl had become a flesh and blood reality essential to his purpose and will-being.

In a new way, Frank agonized over the already two and a half years the war had gone on. He felt melancholy over how much longer the war could go on because it was keeping him from Juliette.

Grim pragmatism would then enter his reasoning as he was brought back to reality by the boom of the siege guns at Vicksburg. Frank prayed that he would be able to focus on the war and its demands. He thought, 'maybe there's a way to end the war sooner. If I notice any opportunities, God, let me know that those opportunities, if taken, will speed the end of this war.' In his deep thoughts cold comfort came to him in a simple equation, 'the end of war equals Juliette.' That equation kept him more focused in the present moment. If he became distracted by his daydreams, strong self-will put him back in the moment by repeating, "The end of war equals Juliette."

The siege guns of Vicksburg roared incessantly. When there was a momentary lull the men would look at each other and wonder why they had quit.

Confederate men and women in the entrenchments were growing short of food within their confines. Rats and other hopeless rodents were boiled and eaten by the inhabitants of the fort. The bluecoats on the outside, had chicken, geese, and ducks in great abundance.

On the morning of June 10, 1863, Winslow was in his tent busily writing Widow Hardy back in Topeka. Suddenly, General Vale appeared inside the tent and affectionately put a big paw on Winslow's back. "Frank, I was with Colonel Melton the other day and came across a deserted plantation. I am asking you to move in there because we need your tents near the battle at Vicksburg. You can house most of your men inside the barns, out buildings, and main house. I'll leave you a few extra tents for any surplus of men without shelter."

"Will do, Ira," replied Frank as he folded the letter and placed it in the envelope.

"Too bad about Colonel Melton and his foraging troop. Here lately, he gets into all kinds of unexpected predicaments. He has lost a few men and officers. It seems the Rebels know his every move," said Genera Vale glumly.

"Smells like spies in the outfit," replied Frank.

"No…Seems more like plain old bad luck."

"A person can make their own luck to a high degree," Frank said.

"I don't think he does enough scouting. Lots of rivers around these parts, you know."

Ira continued, "Recently, he led his command away from the Rebels who were following them. He came to a deep river. Colonel Melton told his men to follow him as he was going to swim across the river.

They were mostly on foot except for a few wagons with scavenged items. Melton is an excellent swimmer, but he didn't ask if the rest were. The men followed him. This was about a week ago. The men are still trickling back into camp. Some nonswimmers were captured along with the horses and the wagons full of booty."

"Ira, I was in a fix like that once. I was out in similar terrain as Colonel Melton. The Rebs were a mile or more behind me in pursuit. We had come upon a deep river which blocked our escape. I spied a boy on a horse with a rifle. I yelled, draw sabers and charge. We came bearing down on him. Mind you, I was charging a ten or eleven-year-old boy. He was a Rebel boy who I surmised, was familiar with the area. I reasoned this in a split second. The charge was sounded far enough away so that he could make a dash for it while the trees and brush hid the oncoming Rebel soldiers from view.

Frank continued, "The boy high-tailed it to the nearest shallow part of the river and quickly crossed ahead of us. Lickety-split, my company of men followed and soon were hidden in the thick of the trees on the other side of the river. The Rebel Cavalry showed up too late to see where we had crossed the river. I think Melton did the best he could in the heat of the moment."

"I think you are more cunning than Melton. You seem to reason things out," said Ira.

"I have had enough close calls in the past two and a half years of war; buttons shot off, bullets cutting through the shoulder pad under my epaulet. Recently, a Reb shot a hole through my hat; didn't knock it off my head, though."

Ira smiled. "I'm going to keep Colonel Melton in camp for a rest up. Like I said, his men are still straggling into camp even after a week's time.

Outside the tent, the sound of voices and a hubbub arose. Captain Bell yelled outside the tent flap, "Colonel Winslow, sir, asking permission to see you!"

Winslow opened the tent flap and saw that a tall dark stranger was bracketed by Captain Bell and Sergeant Morrison.

"We found this guy, says he is from California, Sir," Morrison volunteered.

"I will do the interrogating, gentlemen," said Winslow sternly. The austerity of his countenance made him appear more handsome than usual. It was raining. The moisture made Winslow's hair tighten into ringlets.

"What's your name?" Winslow asked.

"Angelo Topero."

"What brings you this far east?"

"I want to join up with a horse bunch," replied Angelo, his dark eyes shining.

General Vale's curiosity had been whetted. He stepped forward and asked, "Topero, how did you get here from California?"

"I rode a mule part way, floated on a river a ways, I sneaked a ride on a Confederate wagon in Texas. The driver never asked which side I was on," said Angelo.

"Well...I half-way believe you, Angelo. If you came all that way from California, you must have some gumption and persistence. You must have some proud parents." Vale observed.

"I don't have parents that I know of. I am an orphan. I was raised in a Spanish mission in Santa Barbara. I did have some good people that taught me right from wrong, the priests and nuns who raised me. So, I came here to help free the slaves. Slavery is plain wrong."

"It heartens me to know that there are good people in California that raised you well. Now I completely believe you. I will have you report to Colonel Melton. He needs a good scout for his outfit. You are him."

"How old are you, Angelo?"

"Nineteen, sir." His smile flashed brilliant white teeth which contrasted with his dark bronzed skin and dusty brown civilian clothes.

"As I have mentioned, I am going to put you in Colonel Melton's cavalry, but first you are going to scout, as a spy over near Grenada, Mississippi, and find out what's going on there." Said Vale.

"You'll be back in three or four days. Try to find out how much supplies of every sort the Graybacks have, mix with the people, listen much, speak little. Be sure to have the exact location in your mind so that you can find it again. If you can make it from California to Mississippi, you are a natural tracker. Plus, as for spying, you'll fit in with your dark complexion. Sergeant Morrison will accompany you to the outskirts of Grenada and wait for you while you infiltrate camp."

"You men can go now." Vale concluded as he addressed, Topero, Morrison, and Bell.

They left.

General Vale shifted his weight from one leg to the other. The rain glistened like glass beads on his well-oiled boots. "I must get back to headquarters. You can move up to the abandoned plantation today since its still morning, Frank. I have a barge waiting for those tents. It's docked on the Mississippi, less than five miles straight west of here." He nodded his head as he left the tent.

The men had been loafing in their tents most of the morning avoiding the rain.

Captain Bell was instructed by Winslow to get the word out on the quiet that the men were to move to the abandoned plantation minus most tents.

After learning the news, Ezra came into the tent and asked, "What's up Colonel?"

"We are to give these tents to the infantry because they need them worse than we do," he said as he hastily scribbled an address on the envelope to be mailed.

"Oh, and where do we sleep?" Questioned Ezra.

"We are going to an abandoned plantation so we need to pack up these tents and haul them to the barge on the river which will take them to the soldiers in need. We've got a bad day to move but move we must. The rain is incessant."

Ezra smiled resembling a contented squirrel. "Rainy days back home, Ma would bake bread. I can almost smell it. Right out of the oven she would give me a warm slice with fresh churned butter melting on top. Mmm Mmm, sooo good! Speaking of Ma, she just wrote me a worried letter. She had read in the newspaper how awful the southern prisons are. Have you heard how awful the men suffer in the prisons there?"

Winslow's expression became grim as he said, "Ezra, the suffering of the soldiers is unbelievable. I hear tell the men are lying, weltering in their own blood, suffering beyond description. There is a huge shortage of food, clothing and medical supplies. I reckon it's getting worse. Pray for them and for us so we don't get captured. Then perhaps we can hasten the end of this war." His thoughts instantly flashed to Juliette.

More than a week later Lieutenant Colonel Frank Winslow was sitting in his new quarters at the abandoned plantation. It was toward three in the afternoon. He was seated at a desk in the corner of the dining room with his elbows propped on the desk and his fingers tightly clutching his hair. He was in mental anguish. He thought, 'I cannot just sit around doing nothing for even a short stretch of time. I want this war to end soon! It is torture to be idle. At least we have scouted a wide perimeter of land around the plantation. Thankfully, we have discovered a 'Y' shaped rail connection some distance from here. The trains seem to run a bit haphazard. At least, as reported to me by a Yankee spy, there is at least one train per week which usually runs in the evening on a Thursday or Friday. Well, It's Thursday afternoon. Once there, we can wait it out through Friday, if needs be.'

Winslow changed position. He put his booted feet on the desk, crossed at the ankles, tilted back on the two rear legs of the chair, fingers locked at the base of his neck, and continued in his thoughts. 'I am uneasy. My men are too. Inactivity for the past few days is wearing on all our nerves. My plan will alleviate that problem soon. At least for a while. General Vale is at headquarters so sneaking out of camp is an easy matter. Of course, I get to thinking of Juliette, get restless, no outlet. So, I make an outlet. End of war equals Juliette. Even if I am a forager, I have a train raid in mind. It might end the war sooner.'

Winslow called Ezra who was in a nearby room. "Ezra, call assembly."

"Yes sir!" He slightly muffled his bugle as he stepped outside to blow assembly. Spies were a problem.

The men came in groups. Winslow had donned a rain slicker and cap and high boots when he appeared on the plantation veranda. It was raining steady.

He addressed his men from the steps of the plantation. "Men, we are going out to stop some rolling stock from rolling on the Confederate Railroad."

The men were all young and wearing eager grins that seemed a mile wide.

"I just knew the old man would come up with this!" A fellow in the back of the group exclaimed.

Winslow continued, "Men, this will be brief. We will all be out in the rain so be sure to wear slickers. Our nighttime guide will be a former slave from this plantation. His name is Tom. He says he is knowledgeable about the terrain in these parts, otherwise, I wouldn't risk the raid. You all take some grease and towels. From reconnaissance done earlier, there has been found a hill where the train must pass on the upgrade. It is the perfect place to grease the tracks and derail the train. Of course, the grease has to stick to the rails so use the towels to dry the tracks then grease a section at a time. Some of you will go into the train, some will surround the train. "A" Company through "I" Company will be on the opposite side of the tracks to "G" Company through "L" Company's position. Once the train is derailed, volunteers will get on top of the train, if needed. It will give some of you boys a thrill." Winslow's eyes crinkled at the corners and sparkled playfully.

"Be ready in ten minutes. Dismissed!" He finished.

"Saddler Chester, get my horse! I will saddle Ben to expedite our departure." Commanded Winslow.

The men were ready in less than ten minutes. They started out in a northeasterly direction in double file. No word was spoken. Anyone seeing the troops would assume it for another Confederate cavalry troop in the dark of the night.

The freed slave was an excellent guide and knew the country well.

Winslow broke the silence. "Tom, why are you so familiar with the terrain?

"Ah was a carriage driver fo de owner wha you is stayin', Gen'al."

"Tom, I am not a General, I am a Lieutenant Colonel."

"Yo hab de bearins ob a gen'al and yo is brave to be leadin' all dem men, Kun'el.'

Tom pointed out the twists and turns of the road. Ten minutes beforehand, he anticipated some oncoming night riders by asking Winslow and his men to wait under a bridge while those men passed. The country was now definitely the enemy's. A few lights in scattered cabins twinkled in the distance as the rain beat down in heavy drops. Dogs barked as they passed. None of the cabins occupants came out to check as to why. It was too rainy, too late, too dark.

All were depending on the guide to get them to the railroad. No talking was the order of the hour. From a bird's eye view, the caravan of men on horseback appeared like a silent snake on the prowl. The party rode for three hours at a jogtrot. Soon after, they came upon the train tracks.

Winslow commanded. "Get the towels out and the grease!Since it's still raining, quickly dry a small stretch of track at a time then quickly grease it. Repeat the same action until you have run out of grease and dry towels."

The men were quick to comply. Two men on each rail wiped it dry with a towel while two men speedily greased the dry section. The example of the four men caught on. Many groups of four men claimed a stretch of rail and copied the first group. Within minutes, several hundred yards of rail were well greased and ready. Nearby the tracks there were many bushes and trees, so the horses were well concealed.

The companies of men were properly divided on each side of the tracks. The men furthest from the upgraded slope had loose tree limbs and surplus rails to pen the train in after it had passed by. It seemed that there was no way that the engineer could escape the trap. If he went up the incline, grease and gravity would stop him. If he was able to back up, he would be blocked by the wood rails and limbs that the men had put on the tracks.

Time was passing quickly as the men talked amongst themselves in excited whispers. They had been there about an hour. At last, they heard an oncoming train. All hid themselves in nearby bushes as the light from the engine's lanterns shone toward them, although the light was feeble. Winslow could tell that the train was heavily loaded according to the extra labored huffing and puffing of the engine. Winslow had his men evenly posted on each side of the tracks.

Sgt. Morrison, Captain Bell, and Lt. Col. Winslow were with the men detailed to throw logs and debris on the tracks after the train had passed.

"Pass the word along that if a battle ensues, all men fall to the ground and shoot up at the enemy," ordered Winslow curtly. On down the line, Winslow could hear the perfect repetition of his order. The rain had lightened to a gentle and steady pace. It was ten P.M. The engineer was unmindful of the coming event.

Lt. Col. Winslow, Sgt. Morrison, and Capt. Bell peered down the track to check the length of the train in anticipation of blocking its rear with debris, when they noticed a second train. Its dim lantern lights indicated it was closely following the passenger train. It was a military freight train.

"Bell," whispered Winslow, "You and twenty men jump in the passenger train."

Winslow gave a riveting glance down the track, then back to the men and continued, "Myself and twenty of you men will jump the engine crew in the freight...Any volunteers?"

"Private Wells, reporting." A young cavalry man said.

"Private Laker, Sir!" the other husky lad said.

"Good!" Said Winslow emphatically.

The trains were drawing close and the rain was easing into a steady drizzle. Both trains were going at a pretty fast clip. Perhaps the engineers were anticipating the upgrade.

Winslow said absently, "Maybe they'll get past the hill."

Private Laker said, "Sir, I think the boys up front know that if anything misses on the greasing, they have spikes to spare to put on the rails that will throw the engine."

"Train wreckers all! Private Laker you smack of prior experience." Winslow smiled at Laker as he sheepish grinned back at his superior.

"In civilian life we'd get twenty years for committing a crime against the railroad.

They all laughed even though everyone was soaked to the bone. Spirits were high.

"Load pistols." The order was given and passed down the line.

The men had forgotten this chore in all the excitement. Those who had dueling pistols had their fellow soldiers shield their weapons and powder from the rain by huddling over each other. The men with the colt revolvers simply put cartridges in the pistol chambers.

The passenger train was now abreast of them and moving swiftly. It ran over the tallow on the tracks and encountered the upgrade slope of the hill. The wheels spun madly without traction. The engine derailed itself gently as the passenger cars screeched to a halt. The engine landed just past the gravel border surrounding the tracks onto an even span of grass. Quickly the engineer and fireman got out to see what the matter was.

"Hands up, both of you!" barked Lt. Campbell.

The engineer and fireman quickly complied and were frisked.

The passengers in the train were thoroughly shaken up and tossed off their seats. Those standing had been thrown to the floor. None of the passengers knew what had hit them until several details of men simultaneously charged into the three passenger cars, patted all down, and confiscated weapons. While this was happening, another detail of men added logs and debris to the caboose end of the passenger train. The conductor wielded a pistol that was slashed from his hand by a soldier's saber.

Next, the military freight train slipped on the rails, lost traction, and lowered its speed. The freight nudged the logs at the caboose end of the passenger train. The men at the rear of the freight train added logs to the end of its last car which kept it from drifting backward.

Winslow, Laker, and Wells were at the rear so when the freight hit the logs on the track, they swiftly ran up to the engineer's cab.

The engineer was still in his cab with the fireman when they got there. They were busily trying to get forward motion out of the engine to no avail.

The privates stepped into the cab; their dark slickers shimmered with raindrops with the reflection of light from the firebox. The engineer was elderly. His assistant was not much younger.

"Hands up!" Ordered the young soldiers in unison.

The engineer quickly threw up his hands. The fireman chose to fight the two Yankees with his coal shovel. As he raised the shovel to strike Private Wells, Private Laker shot his colt aimed at the man's heart. He missed and hit the shovel handle. It knocked the fireman down giving the appearance that he'd been shot. He hit his head on the floor and was unconscious. Winslow checked his neck. There was a pulse.

Captain Campbell appeared after hearing the shot. He took over the capture of the freight train.

Winslow, Laker, and Wells ran up to the passenger train. The conductor who had his pistol slashed from his grasp by a saber moments earlier, surrendered meekly. The passengers were mostly officers of the Confederate States Army and their wives. Some womenfolk were traveling alone to see their menfolk around Vicksburg. A few officers were ready to fight but the conductor pleaded, "Think of the women! They will get hurt! Don't fight here!"

Winslow entered the first passenger car and herded the passengers back into the rear cars assisted by vigorous shoves from the soldiers. A more resistant Rebel Colonel, who had tried to escape from a window in the first car, was tossed back into the rear car through a window where the passengers had been herded.

The men who had tossed him into the car shouted, "Lt. Colonel, meet a man who was too bashful to look you in the eye and say, "howdy!" The soldiers laughed in merriment.

With the many loud voices of the soldiers and the quick capture of the errant colonel, the passengers became stone silent.

Lieutenant Colonel Winslow announced, "I propose to parole every officer on this train here tonight."

He continued with a calculated piercing scan of his captives. "Do you object, or would you men rather go to prison and be away from your families, for who knows how long? Mississippi has a lot of forest country where you could hide whenever the conscription officer comes around. If any of you takes up arms again, and are captured, you will be promptly shot."

The wives of the officers who had been fearful and alarmed, now, upon hearing Winslow's proposition, looked thankful and relieved. Prior to departing for the train raid, Winslow had sat at his desk and prepared thirty documents of parole and prayed that his plan would bear fruit.

The women without escorts were not imposed upon. The wives of the officers took them under their care. All the officers except for the bashful colonel signed the parole papers.

Winslow eyed the colonel sternly and said, "Colonel, you are a prisoner of war!"

The Colonel was a large blond fellow. Everything about him was big, even his facial features. He was in his early forties and effused arrogance.

The paroles covered twenty-three officers in the Mississippi Division of C.S.A.

Winslow held the twenty-three pieces of paper. The officers seemed relieved to have signed the papers which read:

"I forever renounce allegiance to the Confederate States of America and hereby parole myself to Lt. Col. Winslow, of the 26th Kansas Cavalry, Commanding. Signed this day, officers name."

This was not the regular parole form. Winslow didn't have the exact wording, but it did the job.

The Reb Colonel said, "You Yankee dogs don't even know how to piss on a tree!"

Winslow turned to Laker, "Bind and gag this guy."

Laker had some rope and, in a heartbeat, had hog-tied the colonel. Then he stuffed his bandana in the man's mouth and grabbed a long silk scarf from a lady passenger. He tightly wound the scarf around the man's head and through his mouth and tied it securely at the back of his neck. The Reb Colonel continued to squawk in muffled tones.

The conductor, a man in his middle age, who had some basic wisdom, saw that fighting the Yankee Army was a vain effort. He calmly watched on throughout the paroling of officers and the restraining of the Reb Colonel.

Winslow had the whole situation under control. The Secessionists were collectively mesmerized by his decisive actions and strong words. The paroled officers seemed to have an appearance of relief in their faces upon seeing the Yankees had such a firm commander. Subdued and observant, they listened to him with a keen ear. Occasionally, they would glance with disdain at the hog-tied colonel when he squawked through his gag.

"All you people will be given fifteen minutes to get out of here. I have to fire the trains. You all are free to go."

No one moved.

"You are dismissed. Go!"

Just then Captain Bell came into the car. "We found some caps and black powder in the freight train! Lots!"

"Aha!" Chortled Winslow. Then he let out a loud whistle

"Now we are making headway! Get all the black powder you can. Distribute it equally in each car in their original containers for a more concentrated and powerful explosion. Make fuses long enough so the arsonists have time to escape. Be cautious with the powder. Make certain there are no persons in the cars. I believe that someone was knocked cold in one of the trains." Winslow said, thinking the men would do a more thorough check if he didn't reveal the exact location of the unconscious man.

"Yes Sir!" said Bell and disappeared.

The passengers put their heart into running away as they sensed the Yankee Colonel would be on time for blowing up the trains.

The soldiers stationed on the outside of the railroad cars had their eyes on Winslow and kept him covered.

Winslow addressed these and all soldiers once the powder and fuses were ready. "Men get out of here and take the prisoner and the unconscious man with you. Captain Bell and I will fire the trains."

Fifteen minutes elapsed after the main body of cavalry was out of danger. The two train engines and cars had been rigged with fuses that hung from the windows. All on the same side of the trains. The fuses were connected to barrels of black powder by soldiers savvy in demolitions. Bell and Winslow double checked the set-up of the fuses and powder of each train car and both engine cabs. It passed muster. During the inspection they came upon a container of kerosene in one of the freight cars. They made two torches out of tree limbs and rags, then each dipped their torch in the kerosene. They agreed on a plan on how to ignite the fuses and then escape in the same time frame. Both would have the same starting point, where caboose end of the passenger train meets the freight train engine. Both trains were roughly the same length. Winslow and Bell would take off in opposite directions. Once each reached the end of the trains, they would head into the woods and rendezvous later. So, they lit their torches and jogtrotted away from each other, speedily lighting each fuse. When every cab and train car was ignited, they galloped into the woods at right angles away from the trains.

Bell and Winslow met at the same path they had followed earlier to get to the trains. They rejoined the men and the former servant, Tom.

They were cued to look back by the boom of explosions which lit up the night sky in yellow flames.

Winslow said to Tom, "Do you want to go back to your people?"

"Tha's no people to go back to. All have gone. I's goin to stay wid you all in camp, suh."

"Suit yourself." Winslow said with a smile.

Their eyes returned to the blaze when a delayed explosion thundered and flared. Winslow's gaze lingered as his thoughts went to Juliette, 'the end of war equals Juliette. Dear Lord, how close am I?'

CHAPTER 15

Juliette was moonstruck by the whole encounter with Frank Winslow. He had come out of the night from nowhere and claimed her as his dream girl with candid eloquence. They had exchanged tokens of love, her handkerchief was now his, and his pocket watch was now hers. She reached for his watch which was hidden under the neckline of her bodice secured around her neck with the lacing from her sleeve.

Feeling the reassuring comfort of the round heft of the watch confirmed that Frank was real. Time stood still as she relived the astonishing event as he bared his heart sharing his unabashed love for her. It evoked her heartfelt pledge of love for him. Lovingly, she lingered on his phrases, 'I have dreamed of a woman like you. Providence has given me an opportunity to finally meet you,' and, 'my watch is a token of my love for you, because my time is now in your hands.' A euphoric sigh escaped her lips.

Frank was still in the ballroom talking to Pansy. After he had finished talking to her, he came back to Juliette and tenderly kissed her hand saying, "Until we meet again, Dear Juliette." He wavered for a moment, steeled himself. Then he was gone.

Pansy was intimidated for a while by Frank's threat to tar and feather her if she harmed Juliette. It was only for a moment, because all the jealousy, resentment, and stymied acts of treachery were building into an explosion.

All of Pansy's evil mischief had been foiled by Juliette. All the molasses pranks came to nothing. In addition, her hated enemy, Lieutenant Colonel Frank Winslow, who now seemed sweet on Juliette, who she hated even more, those two people were two huge obstacles to her inner peace. Frank had done enormous damage to her plantation, TWICE! On top of that, Juliette had steered her husband's attentions away from Pansy. Whenever he was home all he would say is,' Juliette this, and Juliette that.' It was nauseating! It dawned on her, now that Winslow had left, she had been tied in the exact chair where she had put all those needles in the seat cushion. She hadn't felt one prick! Even though she deduced that Juliette somehow figured out that the needles were there in the cushion and had removed them, it angered her that she had been foiled again. Pansy couldn't reason that by so doing, it had saved her some sore buttocks. So volatile was her unreasoning anger, it erupted into rage.

Since Frank's departure, Juliette was coming back to reality. It began to hit hard as Pansy approached her with an angry red face. Pansy screamed, "I have had enough of you Miss Hoity-Toity! I'm going to tear you apart limb by limb!"

Juliette had never faced such an enraged woman or heard such a horrible threat. It slapped her back into the moment. She backed away from Pansy then turned and ran. Cooper, Josh, and Jonah, the musicians, quickly got up and tried to restrain Pansy. They slowed her up with their mutual grasp, but she broke loose. It gave Juliette enough time to run out the door. She was so thankful that she had a plan of escape. She paused to take off her shoes and hike up her skirt. It freed her and like an agile gazelle she bounded down the path that led to the river.

Pansy had a delayed start because of the musician's brief hold on her. When she broke loose, she grabbed a knife from the buffet table. By the time Juliette arrived at the riverbank, Pansy was yelling at the top of the bluff, "I have a knife, now! When I get a hold of you, I'll cut off the hand that scoundrel, Frank Winslow kissed!"

Chilled by Pansy's deranged threat, Juliette cleared the brush that hid her coffin-lid raft and bag. In the moonlight, she saw that now there was a paddle. She put her torso on the raft and with all her might, using her feet as a contact with the shore and gave a mighty springboard shove. It was enough of a push to enter the river current. She wiggled until her entire body was out of the water. Swiftly, the current moved the raft in a southerly direction.

"I'm going to get you!" Pansy shouted.

As Juliette's raft gained distance, Pansy's voice became faint when the last she heard Pansy yell, "Oh, oh!" accompanied with the sound of breaking branches. These were the last words and sounds Juliette heard as she quickly floated away from the Mearle Plantation, out of earshot, out of danger.

She felt so exhausted from so many pivotal events of the day. It was all she could do to simply scrunch her soft bag into a pillow and place it under her head. She watched the moon, and some faint stars weave through wispy clouds. Although she had a healthy fear of water, the gentle rocking motion of the raft lulled her into a light sleep.

The siege guns started up. She awoke and looked for the moon. The moon had disappeared behind thick clouds. The siege guns were so loud Juliette thought she was near Vicksburg. She felt relieved that she had put some distance between her and the Mearle Plantation. She sat up and looked around as the moon momentarily emerged from the cloud cover. She could make out both opposing shorelines. They were at equal distance from her raft. The current was doing a good job of moving her craft downriver. There was no need to use the paddle. It brought to mind that some kind person must have overheard her yell her intentions to go to New Orleans. God wouldn't have simply plopped a paddle on her raft. She thought, He loves to use people as instruments of His will.

The black water and fast current reminded her that she couldn't swim, and she became fearful. She was thinking, 'How foolish of me to do this! I can't even swim! What was I thinking! Then again, if I had stayed back there, Pansy would have harmed me. Sorry God! I forgot you furnished the raft then the paddle. So, like dear Frank said, it's providential. So now I will try to embrace the whole predicament as a gift from you. There are three parts to your gift thus far, I desperately prayed for a log, you gave me a raft, of sorts. Which inspired me to prepare my luggage and tie up loose ends with the musicians. I also had prayed for a gentleman, voila, Frank Winslow. Finally, I was able to successfully escape! Formidable! My goodness, this trip has just begun! It's an adventure with many more parts, and all gifts. Thank you, God! Since Frank believes in providence it strengthens my belief too. I will pray to see him again."

The sound of siege guns became faint as she floated further south. Still dark, she laid back down and fell into a peaceful sleep.

The next time she awoke, it was dawn. She changed from her cream satin dress to the gingham dress that she was wearing when James Lambert and friends had kidnapped her. She did all this while sitting so as not to lose her balance and fall off the raft. She rolled up her satin dress and put it in the oilcloth bag.

The dawn's dim light became brilliant as the sun shone in full on a cloudless morning. She could see the details of the passing shores in the intense light. Upon further scrutiny, the shoreline was hidden by tree limbs which extended their burgeoning foliage over the actual shoreline obscuring it from view.

Juliette said out loud to the river, "Miss Slippy, please take me to the convent as fast as you can." She laughed at herself for giving the river a female name and talking to her like a person.

By noon, she realized that she was very hungry. It made her tired, so she slept on her stomach and draped the satin dress over her head to block the sun's burning rays. She woke when the sun was setting and realized that she was thirsty. As she was putting the satin dress back in her bag, she spotted a small bundle wrapped in newspaper, a bundle she had not packed. She took it out of the bag and opened it. There was a jug of water, some dried fruit, nuts, and cornbread. She thanked God and ate ravenously. After eating she felt much better. She sat up in the gloaming finish of the day and the beginning twilight of the evening.

Even with rationing of the remaining food, it was all eaten by the third day. There remained some water. For two more days she continued to float southward. Lack of food made her tired and listless. Then her craft ran afoul when the current slowed, and she drifted toward the west shore. Her raft became entangled in the reeds of a small inlet. Juliette could see no one around.

She cried out, "Help! Help! Please help me, someone, help!'

A blond boy, about the age of seven, emerged from the tall grass on the shore. "What's the matter Ma'am?"

"I'm stuck here and cannot swim!"

"Why Ma'am, you don't have to swim. That water is pro'ly knee deep for you. You can walk to shore. Try it! You can hang on to your raft as you do that."

"Thank you. I will now try." Hesitantly, she put her feet into the water in a sitting position, then she turned on her belly and slid into the water. The water was mid-thigh deep. She clung to her raft and pushed it through the reeds and anchored it to the muddy shore. Her legs had become weak from lack of exercise. She felt wobbly.

"Thank you, little boy for your help. What is your name please?" Juliette asked.

"Louie, Ma'am. How long have you been on that raft?"

"Maybe five days." Juliette said. Louie said, "That's a piece of time."

"Where am I now, or what's the nearest town?" asked Juliette.

"We are pretty near Francisville."

"Is that in the state of Mississippi?"

"No, Louisiana."

"Merveilleuse! "She was happy to hear that she had made it to Louisiana.

"Louie, I am so hungry! Where can I find some food?"

"Follow me!"

"I will, thanks." Juliette grabbed her bag off the raft and climbed up the riverbank.

Louie led Juliette through the woods to a cabin. There were many children playing in the distance away from the house. Some Louie's age, others older, and younger.

"My, how nice! You have so many brothers and sisters."

"No, they ain't my brothers and sisters, they are orphans like me and my friends."

"I am so sorry you lost your parents."

Louie looked sad and said, "Me too."

"So, who takes care of all of you?"

"That's too much to talk about. I'll just show you."

Louie opened the door of the cabin and said loudly, "It's me, Louie! A lady has floated on a raft for five days down river! She is here with me now, Ma'am."

A woman came to the door. She was in the shadow of the entrance which made it difficult to make out her features."

"Sweet heaven! Please, do come in, Ma'am."

"Thank you."

Juliette was surprised at how large the interior of the cabin appeared. Louie had followed them in.

"Please sit down and make yourself at home."

I would be content to sit but I am still wet from the river."

"Louie, go get the lady a dry towel."

"Yes, Ma'am!"

The lady of the house said, "I am Gladys, what's your name?"

"Juliette."

Juliette's eyes had become accustomed to the dim light. The parlor had several benches on the perimeter of the room with blankets spread over them. Her eyes returned to Gladys. She appeared to be a light skinned black woman.

"As you might surmise, those benches are beds for the orphans that come here. We didn't start off as an orphan home, it just happened. Of course, we went along with the plan of the Man upstairs. Life is more peaceful and joyful when you cooperate. The boys sleep here on the main floor and the girls sleep on the top floor." Gladys smiled and showed lovely white teeth.

"I also had my own children, two boys and a girl. They're all grown up and must have families of their own. As soon as they were old enough, they headed north to a better life." She smiled sadly.

Juliette asked, "Why didn't you go with them?"

"In marriage my husband, Murray, comes first and he wanted to stay. If you want to have inner peace your priorities are God first, then your spouse, your children, family members, and then the world."

Juliette felt confused. "So does your slave owner allow you to run an orphanage?"

"I am a freed slave. My prior master gave me and my husband this property years ago before the war. It was acceptable to the rest of his family also. We have a written agreement from him plus the deed to this property."

Louie came back and gave Juliette a towel, then went outside. She wrapped it around her waist and sat down in a chair across from Gladys.

"Gladys, I didn't mean to pry, but you are the first freed slave I've ever met. I've only heard about the freed slaves up north. I find it wonderful! Compared to the many bad situations which I experienced with troublesome slave owners in Alabama and Mississippi, it is so hopeful to find a freed slave in the Deep South."

Gladys warmed to Juliette's kind words. "To be honest, I am the fruit of my master's loins. I came to be because my father had lost his wife in childbirth. The baby, a boy, survived. As my mother told it, may she rest in peace, my master, also my father, sought comfort with my mother, a house slave. I was born soon after. My resemblance to my father was unmistakable. He tutored me in the three 'R's'. He had a wonderful library where, after daily chores I could read. Since we lived a more isolated life and being young and naïve, it was obvious to all on the plantation, my resemblance to him. I didn't officially know he was my father until I was sixteen. I had fallen in love with the carriage driver, Murray. Both of us were going to quietly 'jump the broom', get married, same thing. Anyway, the master heard about it and he helped plan the wedding in the mansion proper. His son had been sent to military school about two years before so wasn't present."

Gladys continued, "As a wedding gift, he gave us a parcel of land. This cabin was built on that piece of land which includes forty acres. Its forty acres of bountiful wilderness. We don't work the land with a plow, we reap what the wilderness produces. So, something really changed in my father's mind. He told me that he was my father right after my wedding and at that time gave Murray and myself the deed to the land and the agreement. Within a few months afterward, he had freed the slaves and sold his plantation. He then relocated somewhere up north. I can only think that after I was born, the truth of slavery must have hit him hard in the face, my face. I feel it was my resemblance to him that was the key that changed his heart. "

"That is quite a narrative!" Juliette exclaimed.

"How I do rattle on! You must be famished! Excuse me for a moment while I get you something to eat." Gladys said. She got up and went to the kitchen and brought back some cooked cold chicken, fresh sliced cucumbers and a tall glass of water.

"Thank you, Gladys." Juliette ate with gusto. After eating the meal, she yawned.

"The fatigue of your journey is catching up on you. Follow me. I'll take you upstairs to our guest room where you can sleep undisturbed."

"Thanks again."

Gladys led Juliette to a small bedroom with a small cot and a desk beside it.

"Please take a good nap as long as you need." Gladys said as she gently shut the door.

After five days on the raft, it felt good to stretch out on the cot without fear of falling into the water and drowning. As she surrendered to sleep, she still felt the familiar undulation of the river current. She fell into a deep sleep. When she awoke it was a new day. She looked out the window of the small room and saw the sun in full, just above the trees to the east.

She went downstairs and observed fifteen children of various ages, girls and boys, some black most white. They all sat at a big, long table in the dining area eating hot corn meal mush with cups of milk. Their hair was combed or braided and faces and hands clean as the silently ate. When they saw Juliette, they all chimed in, "Good morning, Miss Juliette!"

Juliette was pleasantly surprised and answered, "Good morning children!"

Gladys had been cooking a big pot of mush on the wood burning stove and had her back to Juliette. When she heard the children greet her, she turned and said, "Good morning Juliette. Hope you had a good rest."

"I certainly did. My nap lasted all night!" Juliette smiled enjoying the cheerful scene.

The children had finished their meal and in various voices asked to be excused. Gladys smiled and nodded to the children as they all went outside.

"Corn meal mush is on the breakfast menu this morning."

"It sounds delicious. I haven't had a hot meal or a cup of coffee for at least a week!"

"Well then, let's enjoy breakfast together and have a good visit. It's rare that I have adult company."

Juliette ate her breakfast with relish and savored two cups of hot coffee.

When they had finished Gladys said, "Let's move to the parlor where it's more comfortable and we can chat."

Juliette said, "Let me at least wash the dishes to help out."

"Don't bother. It's one of the chores the children do after the outside chores. It would mess them up with their schedule, besides, they love to help." Gladys smiled.

Juliette smiled and remembered loving to help her parents in the restaurant in Paris.

They both settled into large wooden chairs with handmade seat cushions, opposite one another.

Gladys said, "So now I'll ask the big question; you can defer to answer if you need to keep it private, or answer if you wish to share. My question is, what would bring you down the Mississippi River on a raft, which is actually a coffin lid, I checked it out last night, in the middle of a raging war?"

Juliette paused for a moment in self-reflection, then proceeded to answer. "There is no reason for me to defer from answering. I will tell you my story as best as I can recall starting with where it all began in Paris, France."

Juliette shared her meeting James Lambert at the Hotel De Ville in Paris, becoming engaged, her ignorance of slavery in America, her naivety in romance, crossing the ocean in a blockade runner schooner, being attacked by a Yankee gunboat, the schooner's sail being damaged by a cannon ball, learning of the reason for the war which was slavery, told to her on the schooner by the slave owner, landing in Mobile, the stay at Veil Wood, incidents leading up to O'Leary's assault, escape to Louisiana with a benevolent slave owner and three slaves, Mme. Bernard and Juliette finding a happy home at the Ursuline Convent, then being kidnapped by James after trying to break their engagement, being spirited to James' parent's home in Mississippi, Mrs. Lambert and Juliette's plan for making his former sweetheart appealing to James, James reclaimed his old love and letting Juliette go, she went with the Mearle's a good distance from James who soon married the other woman, Juliette entertaining the troops for morale, the jealousy, treachery, and rage of Pansy Mearle, and finally escape on the coffin-lid raft and ending up with Gladys in Louisiana.

"Well, don't that beat all! What a wild story! I believe every word. For one thing, I have read about the Mearle's greediness by them hording many useful items the southern army could have used."

Juliette said, "It is a crazy story. To add a footnote, I don't know how to swim. My poor guardian angel must be exhausted!"

Both women laughed in unison. At that moment, three men entered the kitchen door. The oldest of the three walked toward the women smiling. "It's so nice to come home to a pair of laughing women."

Gladys got up and gave the man a kiss. She turned to Juliette and said, "Juliette, I'd like to introduce you to my husband, Murray."

"I officially welcome you to the Vincent home. We enjoy visitors. You are a lucky guest because we caught enough catfish for a feast of a dinner tonight. Let me introduce you to my fellow fishermen. Pete and Clark come here."

Shyly the two youths came closer.

The tall, slim, dark-haired boy said, "Nice to meet you Ma'am. I am Pete."

The other youth was short, stocky with light brown hair. "Greetings Ma'am. I'm Clark."

Murray said to the boys, "Since we have a lot of fish to clean and fillet, get cracking. Also prepare the fire pit for grilling the fish."

"Yes sir!" Both boys said and left with purpose.

After they left Murray inquired, "At some level my mind is frantically trying to figure out how in the world, did our guest arrive at our backwater abode? Hmm, I'll just throw it out there, did you wash up on shore?"

Both Gladys and Juliette laughed till tears appeared.

Juliette regained her composure. "Formidable! You are a prophet! I did wash up on your shore."

Murray cocked his head sideways. He was made handsome by his quizzical smile and crow's feet around his deep brown eyes. "Now that answer is a Pandora's box of queries, I am too fearful to ask lest I offend, so are you able to simply tell your story?"

Both ladies laughed again. After the laughter subsided, Juliette said, "I will tell you my story as I have already told Gladys. But first, is there anymore coffee? I'd love one more cup, please."

Gladys poured coffee for all.

Murray sat down and listened to Juliette's story. She finished with the trip down the Mississippi River on a coffin lid for a raft and didn't know how to swim yet trusted in God's providence which allowed her to arrive at the present location unharmed. She ended the tale with, "I have made it all the way to Louisiana, so far so good."

Murray shook his head in wonderment. "Unbelievable! Truth is stranger than fiction, so I do believe every word. I want to be part of the story. The part where you go on from here to your destination, the convent in New Orleans! So, let's now concentrate on enjoying the rest of the day and a festive fish fry for dinner. I will peruse some possibilities to advance your goal during the rest of the day. After dinner and the children have gone to bed, I will share my thoughts."

The day flew by as Juliette enjoyed watching the children amiably completing their chores, washing dishes, feeding the livestock, milking the cows, gathering vegetables from the garden as well as other chores. Gladys had divided the children into three groups of five. The oldest of the group would lead them in their chores. Pete and Clark had finished filleting all the catfish. They also had prepared the fire for the grill. The fire was banked to give off steady low heat at one side of the grill where a big pot of gumbo simmered. There was a big stack of firewood nearby to feed the fire as needed.

When it was time for dinner, Murray announced to the children and all, "Children, I have a hot griddle on the fire pit grate. Be sure each of you have a plate and spoon because the gumbo is ready, and the fish will cook up fast."

Everyone was prepared.

Murray had a can of bacon grease and spatula as well as a pile of raw catfish fillets at the ready in another pan beside him. He dolloped some bacon grease on the griddle. It sizzled as he spread out the grease, then quickly he cooked off twenty fillets at a time. In less than ten minutes each batch was done. He fried up four more batches of catfish. The children's plates were pie tins. Pete and Clark would put some cooked fish in each child's pie tin as they filed by. Then Gladys would put a mound of rice and top it with the gumbo. Some of the gumbo ingredients were okra, tomatoes, onions, and other garden vegetables. The older boys would come back for seconds and thirds, typical of growing boys.

Gladys announced, "If you children have room in your stomachs, I have a treat, warm cornbread with wild honey!Murray brought back the honey on this recent fishing trip. Pete, the cornbread is cut so everyone can have a piece with honey. Go inside and dole it out fairly."

Pete smiled and nodded his head as he did as she asked.

After everyone had finished dinner, some children cleaned the outside grill, and some children went inside to do dishes.

When the chores were done, Gladys announced, "Children, get in your night clothes and Murray, Pete, Clark, and I will tuck you in with evening prayer time.

"May I help with evening prayers?" Juliette asked loudly to everyone.

Pete quickly responded, "Miss Juliette can help me!"

"Thank you, Pete." Juliette smile.

Pete was in charge of four young boys, Louie among them. They went to the parlor where their beds were located.

Pete tucked in the youngest boy first. He was about four years old. His black fluffy, crinkled hair framed his cherubic dark-skinned face and brown eyes. The little boy crawled into bed and pulled the covers up to his chin.

Pete said, "Asa, if you are ready, let me hear your prayers, and Jesus would like to hear them too."

"I'm ready." Asa said. "Sweet Jesus, Thanks that I gots a place to stay with food and a house and nice people to care for us. I do pray for one extra thing; may I have my own parents back to take me home. Thanks. Amen"

Juliette was touched by Asa's simple, prayer. The next two boys' prayers were as endearing, with the same grateful hearts and the same request for their parents to come and take them home. Finally, it was Louie's turn.

He settled into his blanket and began. "Thank you, Lord, for all that you've done for me today. I am sorry that I was losing hope of ever finding my parents. I was going to do something bad to myself yesterday but when Miss Juliette showed up out of nowhere and needed my help, that changed the picture. I was needed and had a reason to be here. Thank you. If Miss Juliette could come out of nowhere, maybe you could send my Ma and Pa to me in the same way. Thanks again. Amen.

Juliette held back her tears. It echoed how sad she had been before the coffin lid-raft appeared to help her plan to escape, just at the right time. Juliette kissed the four boys on the cheek good night.

Pete was a little flustered by Juliette's presence. He blushed from the demonstrative kisses Juliette gave to the four other boys.

To put him at ease, Juliette asked, "May I hear your bedtime prayers, or would you prefer more privacy, Pete?"

He hesitated then said, "Alright, if you want to." He kneeled at his bed near the other four boys. Those four had quickly fallen asleep.

"Dear God in heaven, thanks for all You have done for us here today. I do have one prayer request, that I can join the Yankees and help free the slaves. Amen."

Juliette then kissed him on the cheek and said, "Good night dear Pete. Sweet dreams."

He smiled at her as she left him and went outside where Murray and Gladys were enjoying the last embers of the fire. Gladys and Murray were sitting in wood chairs enjoying the warmth. Murray motioned for Juliette to a chair near them.

She sat down and enjoyed the heat emanating from the embers. Quietly, she thought about the boys' prayers. Juliette asked, "When I first arrived here, Louie said that all the children were orphans, yet when they prayed, they asked God for their parents. My question is, are these parents alive?"

Murray and Gladys looked at each other, then Murray answered, "Some could be. We don't want to take their hope away. It is necessary to hope."

"The only one who didn't mention wanting his parents was Pete. He wants to go fight for the Yankees and free the slaves."

"He is aware that his father died fighting for the South. His mother couldn't get over the loss of her husband and died just a year later. Pete was an only child. He ended up here. That was two years ago. Pete will be seventeen this September. This was the topic I was going to talk to you about. Pete really wants to join the Yankees to free the slaves. It is on his heart. So, the plan I came up with is, Pete will take you to New Orleans to the convent. Since New Orleans has been captured by the Yankees and is under Union occupation, Pete can simply join up there. Of course, he'll drop you off at the convent first."

"Will we be taking the raft?"

Murray laughed, "No way! Pete has worked hard during his stay here, so I have given him Fritz, a colt that he raised and trained to maturity. Fritz is a gentle horse. You both can ride him to New Orleans to attain your goals."

Murray continued, "Miss Juliette, not to be insulting, but you appear very thin and downright puny. Please stay with us a few more days eating regular meals and getting regular sleep so that your stamina will increase for the journey. Would you do that?"

"Thank you for your gracious offer. If it is not an imposition for you, I will happily take you up on it." With youth, good food, and ample sleep Juliette quickly regained her health.

The children were enamored by Juliette's presence as was Juliette with the children. The children's routine of chores had a long break after the lunch dishes were washed and put away. At that time Juliette would entertain the children with some songs from the many she had learned since coming to America. Clark would play the banjo by ear. He was a gifted musician.

In a week's time the day of departure came. Pete was more than ready. Fritz had his mahogany coat shined to a brilliant gloss by Pete. The saddle bags were packed as well as Juliette's bag. It was a large saddle that both Juliette and Pete shared.

The sad faces of the children looked up.

"Children, I'm so sorry I have to leave you, but by now you know the most important part of my own story, that I was taken away from my home, the convent, against my will, very suddenly, before I could serve those folks lunch. I am certain they prayed hard which has helped me get this far."

Juliette continued, "It's called providence when prayers seem to be answered quickly like my raft to escape danger. It might have been providential for Louie when I washed up on the shore. I'm so happy that you all say daily prayers. Keep praying children."

Louie said, "After the war, please come back to see us, Pete and Juliette!"

The children became peaceful and silent.

"Please remember us in your prayers. I'll be praying for you all." Juliette said.

"I will too." Pete said.

With those last words Pete and Juliette rode off on Fritz.

CHAPTER 16

It was a quiet July evening for Winslow and his men. When idle from scavenging, they would all sink into the doldrums. The listless mood was catching. Even Lieutenant Colonel Winslow was not immune. He paced back and forth in the ballroom of the old plantation where he and his men were now located. The confining walls seemed too oppressive, so he went out on the veranda and felt better as a gentle breeze caressed his face in the twilight. Calmer, he settled into a rosewood chair of which there were several clustered near him. He put his feet up on a nearby stool and fell into deep thought.

His thoughts led to the pervasive spy problem. The memory of the first spy encounter was when the green recruit, Lloyd Malland, who had been recruited the same day, was riding a new horse outside camp. He intercepted a man on horseback galloping at full throttle. Malland accomplished the capture by sidling up to the speeding horse and steering him into camp. Soon it was known that man was a spy because after a thorough search of his person, it was found, hidden in his hat band, a piece of paper written with the Yankees strength of numbers. Not revealing his name, nor succumbing to an offer of mercy, the military court found him guilty. He was shot at daybreak the next day.

The next experience with spies was the three so-called Second Lieutenants who infiltrated his company right after Fort Donelson.

At the time, Winslow had been distracted by many needs of his men; bolstering the morale of the wounded at a hospital a daytrip away, writing letters to families that lost a soldier in battle, riding to headquarters to bring back much needed horses, and many other tasks. When he came back and read the statistics on deaths in his company, his suspicions went into high alert when he noticed the three Second Lieutenants were dead. He recalled how spit and polished those deceased Second Lieutenants had been. He then questioned some officers and soldiers. A soldier who had been subjected to a cruel punishment, told Winslow that he believed that he was punished by those men because he had overheard the three Second Lieutenants mention to their fellow spies that they were members of the Knights of the Golden Circle. In that same conversation they gloated about illegally coming to Kansas to stuff the ballot boxes for a pro-slavery Kansas before the Rebellion. It led his thoughts to Lester. Of course, Lester was the unwitting pawn of these three Second Lieutenants because they zeroed in on his weakness for spit and polish by shining up to him with impeccable attire and the praising of the dress parade. Therefore, Lester turned a blind eye.

Now Colonel Melton and his men were being chewed up with strange happenings that smacked of spies. Winslow considered it more of an obdurate problem when they infiltrate and lower the morale by so-called officer spies harassing the common soldier. It causes a lack of loyalty to the real commanding officers. It is a perilous rift in battle. Winslow also acknowledged in his musing that the Reb scouts were thick about Yankee camps, so most orders were given in a quiet manner. Still, they were easier to work around than infiltrators. Colonel Melton must have been infiltrated. Especially evidenced by the snafu at the river crossing. He would never demand all to swim the river if many could not. He bet Melton was hauling a rope across the river to secure a safety lead-line for those who couldn't swim to follow. That would mean someone would have been told to tie the rear lead-line to a tree where the men were to wait as he swam with the other end of the rope to the other side. Most likely a Reb infiltrator didn't allow that rope to be tied to the tree. Then all hell broke loose. Wonder how General Vale obtained his information on this?

Winslow's thoughts drifted back to Lester. Where was he?

Ezra Peabody was walking nearby.

Wanting to talk to someone, Winslow said loudly, "Ezra, how's everything with you?"

"Fine, Colonel."

"How's your mother?"

"She's jest fine. I did send some money to her. She's doing tolerable well." Ezra said noticing he repeated himself which made him feel a bit awkward not knowing what else to say. Intimidated by Winslow's rank coupled with idolizing Winslow for real or imagined attributes, Ezra was dumbfounded into silence.

Winslow didn't notice. He said, "You haven't been getting any pay," as he filled his pipe with sweet smelling tobacco.

"Well, Colonel, I'm referring to the money I got awhile back." Ezra replied as he sat down in a chair nearby.

"I gather you still have some Confederate money from the train raid," mentioned Winslow in low tones as he inhaled his pipe and let the smoke drift lazily from his lips, then winked playfully at Ezra.

"Yes Sir, I have sent mom five dollars in CSA money. When she got it, she wrote back and tole me it was mighty purty but twarn't worth a whoop in Kansas," replied Ezra as he pulled in his neck and licked his protruding teeth, then shrugged his shoulders.

Taking his pipe from the firm grasp of his teeth, Winslow moistened his lips and half whispered, "I don't know that you have any CSA money. Rules of war. You understand?"

"I get you, Sir. It's a hush-hush sorta thing." Ezra grinned his buck-tooth grin, so pleased with the close intimacy of his hero.

Winslow stretched then massaged his arms as though trying to loosen his muscles while his feet remained on the footstool. "What's new around camp?"

"I hear when Vicksburg falls, we are to have a powerful lot of visitors." Replied Ezra, very straight-faced as though he were reciting a lesson to his teacher.

"I have heard that too."

Suddenly Winslow jumped to his feet, then faced Ezra as he placed his elbows behind him on the railing of the veranda, as he continued, "On the quiet, Ezra, I bet you ten dollars in CSA money that when visitors come, you know, parents, brothers, sisters, cousins, wives, and whoever, they will bring us lots of good things to eat."

Ezra smiled hopefully, "My taste buds are jest watering in anticipation for smoked ham and bacon. Those items have been sparse for a spell."

"We must never refuse gifts when intended with true giving behind them," remarked Winslow while patiently observing Ezra in a fatherly manner.

A messenger rode up. Winslow leaped down the front steps. The messenger gave Winslow the news in low hurried words, then rode away.

"Ezra, go inform the company commanders to gather in the ballroom!"

Ezra left the Colonel and ran to the various rooms in the plantation house and shouted, "The Colonel wants to see you in the ballroom now!"

Soon the officers had assembled in the ballroom looking very curious.

Winslow announced, "Men, the commander at Vicksburg has asked for a truce and terms of surrender!" Winslow smiled widely and wildly.

The joy was contagious. Soon the men were doing jigs, slapping their knees, and whooping and hollering.

Lieutenant Deerfield exclaimed, "We are finally making a dent in the Secesh territory!"

Winslow studied Deerfield as the lieutenant wriggled and squirmed as if dredging up long repressed joy. At the same time, he was trying to be nonchalant with weak enthusiasm. The enthusiasm became genuine joy when he yelled, "This means I get to see my wife!"

The metamorphosis was complete. Deerfield was a slight man with light brown hair who had been the epitome of plainness. Before Winslow's eyes, Deerfield's broken nose that had healed to the right and the crow's feet wrinkles around his eyes that now crinkled deeply as he smiled with deep joy, changed him into a very handsome man.

Winslow felt his joy and said, "Yes, Deerfield you will see your wife. This is a turning point in the war!"

Winslow continued, "The messenger also informed me that there had been a great battle fought and won up in Pennsylvania, not sixty miles from historic Bedford, in a town called Gettysburg."

Captain O'Cassidy of company "L" overheard Winslow and said, "Now life is worth living!"

O'Cassidy was a big man whose bright red beard was eye-catching as he continued, "These Rebels have been the toughest damn people to get the hint, yet!"

"Reckon they are getting the telegraph signal loud and clear!" Cracked Captain Bell, Provost Marshall.

"Hey men, do you realize today is Independence Day? It's the 87th anniversary of our independence!" Winslow exclaimed excitedly."

Winslow continued, "Since we have the time, we will properly observe and celebrate July 4th, the eighty-seventh anniversary of our independence!"

"Deerfield, go out on the veranda and shout the good news and for all the soldiers to gather for our celebration!"

Deerfield reflected out loud as he headed for the veranda, "Last year in Tennessee we were all down in the mouth on July 4th. Now we can make up for it!"

Deerfield announced the reason for the celebration to all those within earshot. Soon word spread and all the soldiers appeared.

The grandfather clock in the hallway ticked off time a few minutes ahead of Winslow's newest gift from his men, another pocket watch. As Winslow glanced at it, it brought back memories of Juliette. He then closed his pocket watch and put it in his pocket. He reached into his vest for Juliette's handkerchief and clutched it upon its discovery. It comforted him and increased his hope as he thought to himself, 'Vicksburg has surrendered. That battle is won. So is Gettysburg. We're making progress! The end of the war equals Juliette! How much longer sweet Jesus?'

Aloud he shouted, "Let's celebrate with much merry making!"

A while back on a raid, some of the scouts in the 26th Kansas Cavalry had found a barrel of homemade whiskey and brought it back to camp and stored it for a special occasion. They knew that Winslow would have it portioned out equally to each man. That was to be expected as he was fair to everyone. Even the boys who didn't drink, for they knew that was the rule. If those boys saw fit to pour the whiskey on the ground or save it for another day, that was their business.

The commanders had remained in the ballroom. Deerfield returned from the veranda making all company commanders present and accounted.

"Deerfield, get some black powder and a sack of dry corn!" Winslow exclaimed with child-like mischief.

"I always carry black powder in my saddle bag, and I know where there is a sack of corn." Deerfield quickly left on the errand.

Then turning to Captain Bell, Winslow said, "Get a gallon size stone jug or small barrel."

Bell dashed out to the cook house and returned with a stone jug. Bell showed the jug to Winslow. "Will this do?"

"It'll do just fine, Bell."

Winslow had a crooked smile on his face as he stood with legs spread apart and both hands shoved in his pockets. The only movements he made were shifting his weight from leg to leg and occasionally bending his knees slightly as though he was getting ready for a foot race.

Winslow said, "Let me explain what this is all about. My idea is to pour the black powder into the stone jug, then put a cotton fuse smeared with grease into it with six inches extended out of the jug. Then I will wedge the jug in the chimney of one of the many abandoned slave cabins. At this point I will lay the bag of corn on one side of the jug, then light the fuse. Hopefully it will explode, and the corn will shoot over a large area and then rain down like hail."

Enthralled with purpose, Winslow went out on the veranda where the soldiers were expectantly waiting.

"On this day, July 4th, 1776, eighty-seven years ago, this nation claimed its freedom from England. The American colonies officially separated from British rule in a document authored by Thomas Jefferson, appropriately called The Declaration of Independence. To honor those in the Revolutionary War who fought, and many died for our freedom, we will now honor them with as fine a celebration as we can muster in our present circumstances. To add to the joy, and perhaps a sign from God, both Vicksburg and Gettysburg have surrendered this very day. May this country be united and preserved forever!"

The soldiers whooped and whistled and yelled with approval.

"So, let's go blow our stack, out back, on a shack!" Winslow thundered waxing poetic.

The soldiers all followed him as well as all the commanders. Deerfield and Bell were close by. Winslow signaled for all the men to stop at a tree stump near an abandoned slave cabin. He motioned for Bell to put the jug on the tree stump.

Then in a falsetto voice with a theatrical lilt to his voice, he said, "Here is the receptacle that will hold the black powder. My assistants will help me funnel it into the jug."

Deerfield and Bell cupped their hands around the narrow neck of the jug while Winslow poured the black powder. Winslow announced in a loud voice, "I now need a cotton fuse dabbed with grease." Bell and Deerfield had forgotten that item.

One of the soldiers yelled, "I have a cotton bandana that's kind of greasy from cleaning my rifle!"

Winslow grinned. "My good man, that is perfect! Bring it here!"

The young soldier handed the greasy bandana to Winslow who in turn, twisted it into a cord and put half its length into the jug, leaving the other half hanging outside the jug as a fuse. Winslow thought, if anyone were handing out diplomas to people schooled in explosives, and their many uses, the 26th Kansas Cavalry would be in the upper third of the class.

The three men sauntered from the tree stump to the closest abandoned slave cabin. Winslow had taken the rope that had been tied around the neck of the sack of corn and threaded it through the jug handle then tied the ends together of the two-foot length of rope. He draped the loop of rope that held the jug over his shoulder. The jug dangled on his left hip. It freed up his right hand as he held the sack of corn in his left hand. He motioned to Deerfield and Bell to make human stair steps. Deerfield got on all fours with his back braced flat as the first step close to the cabin wall. Bell slithered between Deerfield and the cabin wall so that his back was flush to the wall. He squatted with his fingers interwoven in front of his chest. Winslow gamboled with light steps from Deerfield's back to Bell's spring-loaded, woven fingers. Bell boosted him to the cabin roof. Winslow landed easily like a cat on all fours. Winslow then scrambled to the chimney.

Winslow wedged the jug into the chimney making sure the fuse was clear of impediments. Then he put the sack of corn to the side of the jug. Meanwhile, Ezra had lit a pine torch which he tossed up to Winslow. Quickly, Winslow lit the fuse and threw the torch to the ground. He leaped from the roof and yelled to all as he ran. "Get out of the way of the blast!"

They all ran a good distance, then looked back expectantly. BOOM! It exploded and the dry corn peppered out in a wide radius. Some parts of the stone jug were hurled into the air. A few bricks from the chimney were dislodged and fell to the ground.

The men came back to the scene whooping and shouting with glee. "Hooray! Hooray!"

"Men," grinned Winslow as the perspiration ran off his head and matted his curls. "That is your commanding officer's Independence Day celebration! We have bonus triumphs on this special day with the surrender of Vicksburg and Gettysburg!"

The men joyously began to sing 'Rally Round the Flag Boys', all 550 men. The rich musical drone of their many timbered voices was a pleasant sound.

Night had fallen. Winslow strolled back to the plantation. Deerfield accompanied him.

Winslow said, "Go break out the whiskey, portion it out equally to all. Don't forget my portion. It's a good night cap to a happy fourth.

As Deerfield left, Winslow sat down on the steps of the veranda. He took out Juliette's handkerchief and smelled the faint lavender scent. He recalled her beautiful face and the tears he had captured from her cheek, the same handkerchief he now pressed to his cheek.

Winslow said in a whisper, "If it wasn't for this handkerchief, I would think that you didn't exist."

CHAPTER 17

Now that Vicksburg had fallen, the news had quickly spread to many northern cities through word of mouth and newspaper. Sergeant Morrison's mother saw it in the paper, wondered about the wellbeing of her boy, and then bought a ticket for five dollars on a riverboat steamer, and traveled to Vicksburg. Along with her, were many like-minded passengers on the same boat. Thousands came to see their loved ones on subsequent voyages from the north, some joyous, some sorrowful.

Mrs. Morrison brought a dozen chickens and half as many geese for her boy and for his friends. Mrs. Ruth Vale brought chickens. Mrs. Blake brought two dozen chickens. Mrs. Deerfield brought some ducks for her man so that he could have a good meal. Many, many others sent poultry to the Vicksburg area during the month of July and well into August.

Mrs. Morrison, the sergeant's mother, was met by him, and a joyous meeting ensued. In fact, all the 26th Kansas Cavalry were at the river to meet their loved ones. Mrs. Morrison firmly held Sergeant Morrison's calloused hands in a tight grip. She stared at him with eyes aglow and with her mouth seamed with smile lines. Her grip revealed that the backs of his hands were like rough leather from exposure and much use even though those hands had been protected somewhat by gloves.

Mrs. Morrison said, "Ted, I know you boys are hungry, so I brought you some chickens to share."

Sergeant Ted Morrison gave one look at the caged chickens sitting on the landing next to where Mrs. Morrison sat on her trunk. He turned pale green, his forehead beaded with sweat, then he managed a shaky smile.

He half whispered, "Er…Excuse me, Mother, I have to do a quick errand! Be right back!"

Morrison ran off the landing into some shrubbery leaving his mother with a bewildered look on her face. He was hidden from his mother's sight by the barrier of greenery. At the shoreline of the Mississippi, as he vomited long and hard into the muddy water, some soldiers were passing by on foot and they snickered at him, as they thought he'd had too much to drink.

Morrison thought to himself, "That chicken I ate at noon had turned. It darn near poisoned me. Chicken has no appeal. Now my mother wants me to eat more. Ugh!" He wiped his forehead and mouth with his bandana then returned to his mother.

Mrs. Morrison knew right away her boy had been sick. "What's the matter, Ted? You are pale as a ghost."

Morrison wagged his tousled black hair and responded, "I ate some poorly cooked chicken for lunch." At that point they heard other men retching in the shrubbery.

"Tsk, tsk!" said Mrs. Morrison under her breath as her brow furrowed and her eyes carried a worried look. "What will these men's stomachs be like when the war is over? I reckon stomach powder will be in high demand because of chronic stomach problems."

Sergeant Morrison rested on his mother's trunk where his mother sat also. Affectionately, she put her arm about her son's shoulders. Mrs. Morrison was a stately woman with dark eyes and dark hair parted in the middle and swept back into tight coils perched over each ear. She wore a black dress buttoned to the neck with no adornment. She had been a widow for less than half a year. Ted was the eldest of three sons. The other two were at home tending to all the daily farm chores. Ted was her favorite. The main reason was that Ted resembled her late husband. Her husband had died at Shiloh. Her eyes teared up as she hugged him hard.

Winslow was on the landing flashing his smile to all who passed by. He looked robust and happy despite the caged poultry and the pale somber faces of his men. Lemuel had sent him two dozen chickens also. Always resourceful, Winslow said to himself, "I will trade these chickens for a hog or something." The hurly-burly of the new arrivals mixing with the soldiers was fun to watch as he tried to guess which new arrival belonged to which soldier. A blond lady descended to the landing.

Mrs. Ruth Vale was met at the landing by her husband, General Ira Vale. She was petite, svelte, and stunning. Her blonde hair was as yellow as a sunflower petal and her eyes were the color of spring grass. Her facial features were chiseled yet softened by a fair complexion splashed with a few freckles. By the well fitted pale green dress she wore, she knew what enhanced her beauty.

General Vale forgot all dignity and smothered his wife in hungry kisses and embraces. Both had eyes full of tears as they pulled away and held each other at arm's length to drink in each other's countenances.

"How are Paul and Louise, my dearest?"

"My sister, Molly is taking care of them at our home while I visit you. That way Paul can keep up with the chores. Louise is happy to have Molly's company. I will come back with the children later."

"God bless Molly! What would we do without her?" Praised General Vale. General Vale's eyes were consumed with admiration for his attractive wife. "You don't know how good you look to me." His comment ended in a hardly audible horse whisper that only Mrs. Vale heard.

Quickly, General Vale led his wife to a waiting wagon. Some soldiers followed him carrying Mrs. Vale's luggage. Private Jones said to Private Smith, while both helped load the General's wagon, "Well, don't that beat all! I heard General Vale tell one of the captains how much he missed his wife's cooking. Looks like there was a sight more to miss!" The wagon was loaded and hurried away.

To speed things up, the soldiers helped unload the boat and piled up luggage on the landing. It created a barrier for many of the passengers and jammed up those trying to leave the landing. Winslow sent some of his men to the pile of luggage to carry the bags to the road where some wagons waited for families ready to leave. Guests could now easily make it to the road and claim their luggage. Now there weren't enough wagons to haul folks to their destination, so Winslow sent his men to bring extra buggies and wagons.

Lieutenant Colonel Boyd Melton appeared on the landing and observed the happy activity of the new arrivals of family and friends. His badly scarred outfit was close by him with the same idea. Melton spotted Winslow and casually walked over to him.

In an easy-going manner and a soft-spoken voice, he said, "Hey Winslow, haven't seen you in a while." As he extended his hand.

"It has been a spell!" said Winslow with a friendly grin and gave a firm handshake to the proffered hand.

"Melton, you are just the man I wanted to see! I have been thinking about you. That thinking has formulated into a question which I will now ask. It concerns the snafu you had at the river a while back. Here goes. Did you give orders for one of your officers to tie a lead-line on a tree behind you for those who couldn't swim, to follow across the river once you had initially swum over to the other side of the river and secured your end of the line to another tree?"

"Yes! You are on the money! It didn't work out, because my order was not given. I had entrusted that order to a Second Lieutenant who had joined my company right after Fort Donelson. Thank God, things have changed since I have Angelo Topero as a scout!"

Winslow asked, "Has General Vale been brought up to speed on those facts?"

Melton smiled, "Yes, thanks again to Topero for giving new information to Vale about the snafu. That Second Lieutenant that didn't give the order was a spy! He was a member of the Knights of the Golden Circle. Topero also weeded out other spies who were in my outfit also. It's so much better now."

"Winslow, changing the subject, I haven't seen you since right after Memphis had fallen. My men and I were on our way to a new location. It was getting late and we stopped at your location to camp for the night. You had just returned from scavenging and brought a prisoner of war. The prisoner of war was Captain Terrell Bouldergreve."

"Incidentally," continued Melton, "I have heard a lot about your amazing exploits, like the Bouldergreve deal, the train raid, and scavenging the Mearle plantation, twice! You sure hauled stuff from there like it was a Federal Store!" Melton chuckled good naturedly.

Winslow smiled. "Where there's a greedy politician, there is much to be had."

Melton's tone became more serious. "Captain Bouldergreve escaped from his guards at Paducah and is presently in our rear. He has made General, quite an advancement from Captain to General in one fell swoop."

Melton was enjoying his chat with Winslow. He shoved his hands deep into his pockets and stretched his shoulders back without removing his hands. "Topero has informed me that Bouldergreve is out to get you because you stole his horses and he doesn't go in for that type of proper stealing, as you refer to it. Bouldergreve will be a Bearcat on your heels from now on."

Winslow raised his voice as more passengers descended to the landing and were greeted by a noisy throng of soldiers. Both groups babbled in loud voices. "I don't fear Bouldergreve. Now that the river is mostly open, and our supplies will come steady, I won't have to scavenge as much so there is less likelihood of me encountering him. Since he is a General, he must be leading his men into battle. If vengeance is all that he has on his mind, it will suck up his mind, energy, and doom his men. If he is after me, I am ready."

Melton said, "Winslow, I'll do my part. If my men come across Bouldergreve or his whereabouts, I will keep you abreast of the matter as much as possible. In the meantime, keep an eye peeled." Melton gave a friendly slap on Winslow's shoulder.

Something caught Melton's attention. He moved quickly away from Winslow toward a beautiful brunette woman in a pink flouncy dress. She ran to Melton. They embraced. Winslow watched them both as they embraced. He noticed the woman had a gold wedding band on her left ring finger as she put that hand around the nape of Melton's neck.

Winslow thought, 'Melton, you lucky dog!'

Suddenly Winslow's attention was diverted to a young girl who had approached him and now stood in front of him with her head drooping. She appeared timid and nervous as she fumbled with the tie of her bonnet beneath her chin and blinked her eyes intermittently.

"Are you in the 26th Kansas Cavalry?" She asked.

"I am the officer in command," replied Winslow. "Lieutenant Colonel Winslow at your service."

"Pleased to meet you. My name is Susan Walker." Susan hung her head lower and deeply sighed. She started to talk to Winslow in an inaudible whisper directed at her feet.

Winslow said, "Susan, look at me when you speak, and talk louder," as he bent sideways enabling him to see her face.

Susan jerked her head up and stared into space avoiding eye contact. "I came from Topeka. I am pregnant and Pa says he won't have a harlot live on his place."

Winslow gave a low whistle and shook his head. "Tell me," Winslow spoke carefully, "What is your purpose here?"

"I married Martin Sims. I even showed Pa the license, and he tole me a soldier is no good a'tol cause Martin ain't taking care of me with money. But I said, them boys ain't been paid so Martin cain't send me any money. That said, made Pa madder yet so he burnt our marriage license into ashes." Susan's head drooped again.

"Susan, you are right about the pay. I will see if Martin is near."

Winslow looked around until he saw Ezra, then shouted, "Bugler, blow assembly!"

Ezra ran to an open space and blew away 'Boots and Saddles' for assembly. The men left their sweethearts, sisters, mothers, cousins, family and friends and rushed to the open space. They lined up and stood at attention.

"Martin Sims front and center!" Yelled Lt. Colonel Winslow.

Pvt. Sims came forward and saluted Winslow. He wobbled while standing at attention when he spotted Susan.

"Dismissed!" Shouted Winslow. The men ran back to their visitors.

Casually, Winslow eyed Pvt. Sims up and down with no expression in his face. The young private appeared very timid. He was small framed, brown hair askew, rounded shoulders, bow legged, and wearing a rumpled uniform. He was twenty-two years old.

Finally, Winslow said, "Susan Walker, here, tells me you and she are married. Is this so?"

"Yes Sir, we are married." Replied Sims from the corner of his mouth>"

"Did you send Susan money?"

Pvt. Sims eyes widened with surprise. "No money to send her, Sir"

"That is correct, Pvt. Sims, if you are counting army pay. There is none to be had now. I am assuming you had no other funds from family?"

"No money to be got, Sir."

"I will see if I can nudge the government to be more forthcoming."

An idea sprang into Winslow's head. "In the meantime, I will give you a chicken as a little compensation. My brother, Lemuel, sent me lots of these pesky birds."

Winslow's face broke into a good-natured smile. "For God's sake, Martin, kiss your wife! I know I'd be kissing mine if I had one!"

Prompted, Martin and Susan embraced each other shyly under the watchful eye of Winslow

Susan looked haggard being four months pregnant. "Colonel, Sir, would you be able to get us another marriage license? I feel so sad my Pa burnt ours."

"I will do my best in our present circumstances, Susan."

No marriage forms were available in Vicksburg due to the scale of destruction. Some of his men found some sheets of blank paper and pen and ink.

Winslow was momentarily stumped as to what to write. An empty chicken crate with a board on top was his desk. His soldiers had set it up on the side of the road not far from the landing.

Pondering the pregnancy, Winslow asked, "Susan, what was the date of your marriage?"

"March 20th."

Inspired, Winslow wrote Susan and Martin's marriage license four months back. Satisfied with the wording, he had Susan and Martin sign the document. To make it more legal, he signaled Reverend Blake and his wife, who were nearby, to sign as witnesses.

Word got out that marriage licenses were available. So many soldiers and their sweethearts lined up in front of Winslow's desk.

Ezra, who had been watching nearby, said to Winslow, "Colonel, you sure have started something!"

Winslow surveyed the large group of lovebirds. Reverend Blake and his wife were still close. "Reverend Blake, I know this is old hat to you, the marriage business, so with my greatest respect for your past experience, would you please take over for me?"

Reverend Blake was pleased. "I'd be happy to take over, Colonel. It is much more cheerful than praying with the condemned. I'll need you to stick around as a witness though, my wife will be the second witness."

Winslow shrugged his massive shoulders in agreement, turning his palms outward to complete the friendly gesture.

When all licenses were completed and signed by Winslow and Mrs. Blake, Reverend Blake announced, "All of you newly licensed couples gather under the tree over yonder and I will perform the marriage ceremony for all of you at one time. This includes you, Martin and Susan."

Reverend Blake performed a beautiful ceremony for all the couples. Winslow, Widow Morrison, and others with too many birds, gave each couple a chicken for a wedding gift. All the honeymooners found seclusion with no worries for the moment with enough poultry for some meals ahead.

Later that evening, Winslow entered the big plantation where he was headquartered. Once inside the ballroom he walked over to his desk. The jingle of his spurs echoed off the walls in empty tones. Winslow thought, 'Now I have ten of my officers reunited with their wives and a slew of my soldiers are all gone on their honeymoon! It's good timing for them, with a lull in the war.'

It had just begun to rain. Winslow walked to a nearby window, then peered out into the misty darkness. "I envy those honeymooners tonight. Blast it all!"

Ezra came into the ballroom. His smile was so expansive that his upper molars could be seen. "Colonel Winslow! I now have a purty girl who likes me enough that she asked if she could write to me!"

Winslow smiled. "That's great, Ezra! Tell me more."

"Well, her name is Miranda, Lieutenant Deerfield's sister-in-law. Amy is the Lieutenant's wife. Anyway, Amy brought Miranda and two other younger sisters on the river steamer."

"My word, Amy brought the whole clan!" Winslow laughed.

"Where can those three girls lodge for a spell? I was thinking since Lt. Deerfield and his wife want private time somewhere else, but didn't mention Deerfield's quarters, I was hoping that I could have the girls sleep there. Would that be alright?"

Winslow looked at the grandfather clock, it read 9:41 P.M. He remembered that moment in time spent with Juliette at the Mearle plantation. An idea came to him. He said. "Ezra, we don't know if those officers will show up in the middle of the night and want their rooms back so I will lend my private quarters to the three girls."

"Where will you sleep, Colonel?"

"This is on the quiet. I have just decided with Vicksburg defeated, The Rebs might take a week or two to get back to battle again. Along with that, my presently reunited officers and wives, and newlywed soldiers, will be spooning away for a long spell! So, I am quietly furloughing myself for a day or two of fishing. I need a change of scene. I ask that you don't volunteer my whereabouts. But if a superior officer enquires about me, you can say I went fishing. I have a strong inclination questions won't be asked with all the spooning going on. Ezra, I expect you to be tight lipped about it. While I am gone be respectful of the young ladies in your charge."

Ezra smiled. "Yes Sir! When are you leaving?"

"After I pack a small satchel and a razor, I should be out of here in fifteen minutes."

"Okay, Colonel. I will be mum on the matter unless asked by a superior officer."

"Carry on, soldier!"

Soon Winslow was packed and mounted on his horse, Ben. The rain had quit, and the clouds had disappeared revealing a sliver of moon to light the way. He jogtrotted Ben along the Mississippi River headed north. He needed to see Juliette. As he trotted along, he thought of Major Lester. That man was less likely to focus on polishing the troops since his wife arrived. It was the perfect distraction. The couple hadn't been together in over a year. That thought reaffirmed his decision to furlough himself.

It was near dawn when he came upon a landmark, it was a small crystal-clear creek that was about two miles from the Mearle Plantation.

He stopped at the creek and made a small fire. Easily, he spotted a plump catfish in the pristine water. From a nearby scrub tree, he broke a branch and made a sharp lance with the aid of his pocketknife. Patiently, he waited by the creek until the plump catfish was within striking distance. He stabbed it with his lance. The fish was completely impaled. Quickly he took the fish to a flat rock and gutted and butterflied it with his pocketknife. Again, he used his lance to weave the fish splayed open in a fixed position. He cooked it on both sides, turning it often over the fire. After breakfast, he noticed some daisies growing nearby. He picked a bouquet. Before he left, he buried the fire in the damp soil as well as the fish remains. He hopped on Ben with the daisies and headed toward the plantation.

As he approached the perimeter of the plantation's lawn, he cautiously hunkered down in the tall grass that surrounded the lawn, to assess the situation. He saw the old man he had called Dad on the first raid sweeping the veranda and whistling happily.

An old woman opened the door to the plantation and said loudly, "Micah! I made a good breakfast for you. Come and eat! You can take your time and enjoy the food since both the Mearles are gone to Richmond."

That information peaked Winslow's interest so he crawled closer to the big house. He moved without notice through the lawn to the side of the house which blocked the view of his approach.

"Lolly, thank you! I don't know if can get used to eatin' at a slower pace. It's strange not havin' Mistus Pansy yellin', 'Hurry Up!'"

"Well, we'll have time to practice cuz since Mistus Pansy broke her ankle and her wrist, and no doctor 'round here to tend to her, Master Jonathon jes' had to take her to Richmond where der is some good doctors for all of dem politicians. It will take a couple of months or more to heal. Knowing Mistus Pansy, once there, she won't want to leave. She likes to keep an eye on her man. The Mearles also hast to trust us to be the only caretakers of dis place. There was nobody left for that job. I'll go set the table for you." Lolly went back inside.

As Lolly was talking, Winslow had inched his way closer to the veranda where Micah was sweeping.

Winslow stepped onto the veranda. "Hello, Micah. Happy to know your name and that the Mearles aren't here. Is Juliette here?"

Overcome by the surprise of Winslow's appearance, Micah collapsed into a chair to catch his breath.

"Kernal, you surprised the starch outta me!" Micah continued, "Miss Juliette ain't here!"

Deeply disappointed, Winslow said, "Then, where is she?"

Micah had recollected his composure, noticed the daisies in Winslow's hands, and crestfallen face.

"Well, it's kind of a long story. Please come in for a cup of coffee and I will try to 'splain what happened since when you wuz last here."

Winslow was numb from the severe let down of the revelation that Juliette was not there.

Micah got up from the chair and motioned for Winslow to follow him into the dining room. Micah shouted ahead to Lolly, "Lolly, pour an extra cup of coffee! We have a friend come to visit! It's the Yankee Kernel!"

Mechanically, Winslow gave Lolly the flowers and sat down at the table with Micah.

Micah said to Lolly, "Lolly, I needs to 'splain what happened since the Kernel was here last."

"By all means, Micah. You go ahead." Lolly said as she sat down at the table also.

"Here Kernal, have a hot cup of coffee." Lolly said as she poured a steaming cup of the brew from the coffee pot on the table and gave it to Winslow.

Winslow absently took the cup and held it in his hand not drinking it.

Micah began. "Fust, I wants to thank you for coming by so that we can visit. I never will forget when I fust laid eyes on you! You gave us slaves hope that some people, the Yankees, were tryin' to set us free. But it was you, Kernal, who personally expressed this honor of freedom in such a big way with all your soldiers. You showed that you cared for us slaves. You all gave us dignity. Thank you so much!"

Micah paused for an introspective moment. "Miss Juliette is cut from the same cloth as you, Kernal. Miss Juliette honored us also. We house slaves really 'preciated all the small kindnesses she did. Miss Juliette protected us in small ways that were big to us. Mistus Pansy was so jealous of Miss Juliette it was plain awful. Especially when her husband came to visit. Master Jonathon had his eye on Miss Juliette. Mistus Pansy would flare up in jealousy so bad that she would do dirty stuff. She would put molasses on Miss Juliette's doorknob to her room, or molasses on the seat of her chair in the dining room. Miss Juliette figured it out early that if she complained, Mistus Pansy would punish us house slaves for it!"

Micah continued. "So, Miss Juliette began wearing a housecoat with pockets. She kept an oil cloth bag in one pocket which held a wet rag in it. She'd jus' wipe up the molasses on the sly and pretend nothing was wrong. I knows this cuz I watched her do it. I think this made Misstus Pansy even more mad. Cuz if Miss Juliette acted as if the molasses never happened, then how could she punish us slaves? It mus' have ate at Misstus Pansy's guts. So, the morning of the day you came for the bedding, I saw, Mistus Pansy putting needles in the cushion of a chair in the ballroom,

it's the only padded chair there. After serving Mistus Pansy and Miss Juliette breakfast, I overheard her say to Miss Juliette that she really wanted her to sing a song about a chair and to use the padded chair in the ballroom for that reason. When Mistus Pansy left to invite guests for the evening, Miss Juliette checked out the chair, found the needles and removed 'em.'"

Micah sighed. "Anyway, Lolly and me wuz hustlin' to get food ready for the party that evenin'. I'z out on the bluff pickin' cherries for pies that Lolly was goin' to make for that party. As I was pickin' cherries ah heard Miss Juliette a cryin' and talkin' to God down below at the riverside. She yelled real loud that she would jump on a log, if one showed up and go back to the convent in New Orleans where she had been kidnapped, even if she couldn't swim! Then she sat on a rock by the shore and cried her eyes out. Course, with all the yellin' and cryin' I wuz keepin' a close watch on her."

Micah took a big swallow of coffee and wriggled in his chair, finding a new position. "While she wuz deep into cryin', something wood like had washed up on shore near her. It wuz like a raft. Later, when I got close to it, I found that it wuz a fancy oak coffin lid! That's when I understood what she had said before when she fust looked at it, and tol' God that He had a good sense of humor. She pulled the coffin lid up on shore and put some brush and weeds over it to hide it. Later, after she talked to the musicians, she put a small bag with her belongings on the raft. In between my chores, I found and old oar and put it on the raft. I also put food and water in her bag."

Micah looked intently at Winslow's dazed expression and continued. "That evenin', durin' the party, you showed up Kernal. My, my, you and Miss Juliette shor' hit it off real good with all the dancin' and sweet talk! After your men were all done takin' the bedding, I heard you warn

Mistus Pansy 'bout not hurtin' Miss Juliette. It looked like Mistus Pansy wuz goin' to abide by you all rules. But as soon as you and your men left something must have snapped. That's when Mistus Pansy grabbed a knife off the buffet table and came after Miss Juliette. The three musicians slowed her down some, but she broke loose and ran down the bluff after Miss Juliette. Miss Juliette was so light on her feet! She had already made it to shore. She put the front part of her body on the raft and pushed off into the current with her feet."

Winslow, incredulous, said in a low voice, "My God, she can't swim!"

In response to Winslow, Micah said, "Kernal, I wants you to ponder some things 'bout this whole thing. Fustly, we all never knew you was comin' that particlur night. Secondly, a raft shows up and Miss Juliette puts her belongings on it. Thirdly, Mistus Pansy chased her with rage enough to do bodily harm to Miss Juliette but she escapes. All of it put together was a big surprise to me. But when you put God in the picture, it makes sense. Remember Miss Juliette had talked to God. She had sensed somehow that she had to leave the plantation. It was all so timely, or God's timing. After talkin' to God, a raft shows up, she has time to put her belongings on it, I had a chance to witness her prayer and I had time to add an oar and food to the raft. Another big thing, God must have really wanted you, Kernal and Miss Juliette to meet."

Micah rubbed his jaw. "Anyway, it was all meant to be. Miss Juliette escaped on the raft while Mistus Pansy threatened her with all the bad stuff she'd do to her. Instead, bad stuff happened to Mistus Pansy when she fell and broke her ankle and wrist. Vengeance is mine, says the Lord."

Micah poured himself more coffee. "So far as I know, Miss Juliette went back to New Orleans. Lolly and me keep prayin' that she made it fine. Now you knows what happened until she escaped."

Winslow was overwhelmed by Micah's account. Finally, he said, "Juliette couldn't swim yet she jumped on a coffin lid to float down the Mississippi during the siege of Vicksburg! She would have to float by the blasting guns if she even made it that far! Right there, are some insurmountable odds! That's scary as hell!"

Micah said, "Kernal, that is scary, but like the Bible says, sometimes you have to pick betwixt the lesser of the two evils. Miss Juliette chose the river over Mistus Pansy. So now I'm gonna ask for you to pray for Miss Juliette, for her protection. She mus' be a Chosen Chil' of God cuz all these things worked together: she asked for a log and got a raft, she had time to pack a bag, I heard her prayer request to God, I had time to add an oar and food, then you showed up and set it all into motion for her escape. You can help Miss Juliette by praying for her, every day, anytime of day, and be comforted that Lolly and me will be prayin' too."

Winslow appeared heartsick with a despairing countenance. "Then it's all my fault that she put herself at risk in that river. You just said I put it all in motion by showing up."

Micah exclaimed, "No, no! There is no fault! You were a tool of God. Iffin you hadn't showed up Mistus Pansy would have Miss Juliette trapped. God only knows the evil that woman can do to her fellow creatures." Micah shuddered.

Micah said, "Look on the bright side, we knows her destination, a convent in New Orleans. You can go there when the war cools down."

"That's true Micah." Said Winslow with a glimmer of hope.

Micah added comfortingly, "Wit Lolly, you Kernal, and me prayin' all the time for Miss Juliette, ah jus' knows she made it there. Let's claim the victory!"

Winslow stood up and gave Lolly and Micah a solemn handshake, then left for camp.

He took the same route along the Mississippi River. With new eyes he surveyed the river imagining Juliette on a coffin lid, not able to swim, floating by the blasting siege guns, in the dark of night. He shuddered, then desperately began to pray for Juliette for her safe arrival to the convent in New Orleans. Suddenly a double rainbow appeared over the river.

God had given him a sign. He said, "I claim the victory."

CHAPTER 18

It was the middle of June 1863, on a pleasant sunny afternoon. Pete and Juliette were mounted on Pete's horse, Fritz. It was the last day of their two-day trip from the orphanage to the convent in New Orleans.

Fritz had made good time as he jog-trotted both passengers on the last leg of their journey down the lane that led to the Ursuline convent. Pete pulled the horse to a halt at the front entrance. Both passengers dismounted. Pete tethered the horse to the fence.

"Pete, I am so happy that you are coming with me!" Juliette exclaimed.

"My pleasure, Miss Juliette." Pete smiled. Together they walked to the front entrance. Juliette knocked.

Mother Superior opened the door. Instantly, she recognized Juliette. Shocked and surprised, the nun hung onto the doorknob for support while she gasped for air. Then she put her other hand over her heart. A rosary dangled from that hand. "Juliette you have returned! We all feared the worst but prayed for the best! Only a few moments ago we finished praying a rosary on your behalf! Praise the Lord! Come in! Come in! I must fetch Mme. Bernard! She is not far!"

In less than a minute Mother Superior returned with Mme. Bernard.

Mme. Bernard tearfully embraced Juliette and clung tightly to her as she shuddered with emotion. Then she released her and found Juliette's hands and clutched them tightly. She diligently searched Juliette's face. "Juliette, Juliette, my dearest child! Oh, how I've missed your sweet face! Praise and Glory be to God! God has answered our prayers! Since that dark day in March 1862, to this very day, we have prayed a rosary for your safe return. Can you ever forgive me for any negligence on my part for your abduction?"

Juliette intently studied Mme. Bernard's care worn face. "Mme. Bernard, there is nothing to forgive! In my wildest dreams, I never thought James would do such a thing. God must have allowed it, because I have grown in my understanding of the complexities in human nature, love and hate, life and death."

Mme. Bernard hugged Juliette again, and said, "God is so merciful and kind! Welcome home, Juliette!"

Now that Mother Superior had calmed down, she gave Juliette an affectionate hug.

Juliette said, "I fervently prayed to God that I'd be able to return to all my friends here at the convent. With all our constant prayers joined together, God must have gotten fed up and sent me a coffin lid for a raft, and a deranged woman threatening me bodily harm as she wielded a knife, to get me over the fear of water, so I would float down the river without drowning, and landed at an orphanage for safety. After I rested there a while, my good fortune continued with Pete, here, bringing me the rest of the way home."

They all laughed.

Mother Superior said, "Come into the kitchen and have a cup of coffee and expand on the intriguing details of your perilous journey from the moment of your kidnapping until now."

The four entered the kitchen and smelled the inviting aroma of a simmering coffee pot on the nearby stove. Mme. Bernard poured four mugs of coffee and placed them on the table at which they all had seated themselves.

Juliette said, "I would like to formally introduce you to one of the heroes of my tale. This young man is Pete Larue who safeguarded my arrival here." Pete blushed with pleasure and stared into his coffee.

Mme. Bernard reached for Pete's hand across the table and said, "I am so happy to meet you and will always be indebted to you for keeping dear Juliette safe."

After Mme. Bernard released Pete's hand, Juliette affectionately put her right hand on Mme. Bernard's shoulder. "Pete, I would like to formally introduce you to Mme. Bernard who has been like another mother to me, as well as a teacher and mentor."

"Glad to meet you, Mme. Bernard."

"Pete, I would also like you to meet Mother Superior Margaret Joseph who runs this fine convent." Juliette said as she placed her left hand on the nun's shoulder.

Mother Margaret Joseph shook Pete's hand and said, "It's such a pleasure to meet such a brave young man! You are always welcomed here!"

"Thanks." He was mortified by all the attention.

Momentarily, the room was still as they all sipped their coffee. Juliette broke the silence. "Alright, I've mentally reviewed the events since my unplanned departure from the convent more than a year ago. Ready?" They all nodded their heads. Everyone listened raptly as Juliette told them of her abduction from the convent by James and his two soldier friends. One of the friends, recognized her as an entertainer for Jefferson Davis when he had been part of a detail accompanying the southern President to Veil Wood. James' plans for a quick marriage to Juliette were thwarted by her state of exhaustion upon arrival at Fair View and in addition, a company of soldiers whisked James away on a military mission. The mother of James, Henrietta Lambert never wanted James to marry Juliette, and no longer did Juliette. James' mother wanted him to marry Ophelia, his childhood sweetheart. Her reputation as an entertainer had reached Mrs. Lambert's ears. So, Juliette and Mrs. Lambert hatched a plan to switch James' attention back to Ophelia. Juliette was to teach Ophelia all the musical talents to the former sweetheart and regain James' attention.

Juliette continued her narrative, "After a week at Fair View, I fully regained my health and began to train Ophelia to be an entertainer. She was a quick learner and talented student. By the next furlough James appeared for Ophelia's debut as an entertainer. The audience loved her. At the same time, and as part of the plan, Pansy and Johnathon Mearle arrived as a means of escape for me, from James. Anyway, I kept a low profile as part of the performing musicians in the background. I had applied some soot and chalk to my face to appear sickly so when James sought me out, he seemed shocked. I also coughed into a handkerchief and warned James that I might be contagious. I was successful at switching his attentions to Ophelia. The next morning, I left with the Mearles to their plantation which is situated near the Mississippi River, a hundred miles distance from Fair View."

"After a short while it became apparent that Mrs. Mearle didn't like me. I had the musicians from Fair View join me at the Mearle Plantation and we entertained the Confederate troops around me, mostly at field hospitals. My purpose was to be absent as much as possible. Things were getting tense back at the Mearles. Pansy began to do evil mischief directed at me which flared up even more when her husband came home for a visit from his job in the Richmond Congress. That's when I went down to the river and prayed and cried to God that I couldn't take it anymore. I asked for a log so that I could jump on it and float down the river back to you all. God certainly heard me. He sent me a beautiful oak coffin lid at that very moment. I think God has a dry sense of humor." Juliette smiled.

"That very evening Pansy had planned a party at the plantation where I would entertain the local people. While she was out and about, inviting people, I said goodbye to my musicians and packed a small bag and put it on the raft. The night of entertainment arrived. I was singing to an old gentleman when suddenly the Yankees showed up on a raid. A Yankee Colonel began to dance with me and asked me what part of heaven I was from," Juliette sighed. "He was the answer to another part of my prayer I said at the river."

"His name is Lieutenant Colonel Frank Winslow. It was the most magical moment in my life. Words were said that touched us both. We exchanged souvenirs to remember that moment. Anyway, he had to bring the bedding he had taken from Pansy to the wounded Yankee soldiers. I was in a euphoric daze when suddenly, Pansy came at me with a knife. I ran down to the river and pushed off on the raft into the Mississippi River. The current caught the raft and I headed south." Juliette said excitedly "I was so happy to have an escape plan!"

"Some kind person had added food and an oar to the raft. A few days passed and I washed up at an orphanage. That's where I met Pete who took me the rest of the way here. Pete wants to join the Yankees because he wants to free the slaves. The couple who ran the orphanage are both freed slaves. That's another story." Juliette smiled at Pete.

Mme. Bernard poured more coffee for all, as she commented, "It was very inspired thinking to use ashes and chalk to make your face look sickly. You know how to use props to the highest degree!"

"I learned from a master, you, Mme. Bernard!'

Mother Superior said, "So you met a wonderful gentleman named Lieutenant Colonel Frank Winslow on the very night you had to escape! I imagine, that with his keen interest in you, he would probably check on you at that plantation very soon. You must let him know you are safe."

"You are right, Mother. I also worry about him because anything could happen to a soldier in battle." Juliette said.

All were silent for a moment.

Pete broke the silence. "Well Miss Juliette, if you'd write a note to Lieutenant Colonel Frank Winslow, I'd be happy to get it to him somehow since I'll be reporting to the Yankees at Occupational Headquarters here in New Orleans."

Oh, Pete, thank you! What a good idea!" Juliette exclaimed.

"I'll go get pen and ink." Said Mother Superior.

Everyone waited in patient silence as Juliette wrote the letter. It took some time as she gathered her thoughts and wrote in spurts of inspiration. Finally, it was done. Mme. Bernard gave her a lighted candle to wax seal the letter shut. Juliette then gave the letter to Pete.

"Thanks, Miss Juliette. I won't stay any longer. I noticed as we rode through New Orleans, a building with a sign saying, Union Occupational Headquarters. I'll head back there now and join up. Please pray for me that I can get this letter to Lieutenant Colonel Winslow."

"Pete, you and Lieutenant Frank Winslow will be in our daily prayers." Said Juliette.

The three ladies walked Pete to the door. Each of the three gave him a sound hug. He waved goodbye as he mounted Fritz and rode off.

Mother Superior said, "Now we must inform the others of your safe return for they have been so prayerfully concerned about you. It will strengthen their faith even more and increase their desire to pray often."

The students and nuns had assembled in the main dining room, for it was time for the evening meal. No supper had been prepared because

Mme. Bernard was the cook and had been completely distracted by the miraculous arrival of Juliette.

Mother Superior Margaret Joseph said, "Wait in the kitchen, Juliette so that I can announce your return."

"Certainly." Said Juliette.

Mother Superior went into the dining room full of students and nuns. "I have two announcements to make. The first announcement is that supper will be delayed a bit. The second announcement is that our prayers have been answered! Juliette has returned to us in good health!"

Juliette appeared at the kitchen entrance. All present flocked around her giving her hugs and kisses. Questions came at her in an overlapping avalanche of high-pitched voices.

Juliette smiled and put a finger to her lips sweetly, to silence them. She said, "My dear friends, thanks for all your prayers for my return! God heard you and me! I will now prepare a mystery meal for you. I have so longed to cook again. After that mystery meal and clean-up, I will tell you what has happened to me since I've been absent. So, no questions, please until all is done. That way I won't need to repeat myself. Thank you in advance."

Exuberantly, the students yelled, "Hooray! Hooray! Juliette is back! Our cook is back!"

Mme. Bernard ruefully smiled and mumbled, "Cooking was never my strong suit."

Mother Superior said to all, "Remember, let us all wait in patient anticipation for our mystery supper. I will see if Juliette needs help!"

Mother Superior entered the kitchen. She overheard Juliette ask Mme. Bernard, "What were you planning for supper, Mme. Bernard?"

I was planning on making egg noodles and cooking them in chicken broth for Chicken noodle soup."

"So, there must be plenty of eggs?" Inquired Juliette.

"Lots of eggs." Mme. Bernard smiled.

"Lots of flour too?"

"Oh yes."

"Wonderful! I will make crepes!"

Once the menu was decided Juliette went to work. She stoked up the stove with extra wood, then put a heavy rectangular griddle on top to let it heat. While it was getting sizzling hot, she whipped up three large bowls of batter, then greased the griddle with rendered lard and began cooking off twenty crepes at a time. Mother Superior and Mme. Bernard relayed them to the warming drawer beside the stove until all the crepes had been cooked. As soon as Juliette had finished, she asked the ladies to put out several pitchers of molasses and the platters of crepes on the dining room tables. All was ready within the hour.

Mother Superior said grace. "Bless us oh Lord for these Thy gifts which we are about to receive from Thy bounty and heartfelt thanksgiving for the return of our dear Juliette. In Jesus name, Amen."

After supper, the designated students for the evening, cleared and cleaned the tables, and washed the dishes. When they returned to the dining room, Juliette retold of the perilous saga of the past year from the kidnapping, to the float down the river, to the orphanage, and arrival at the convent.

At the end of her story, Juliette asked, "Are there any questions?"

Giselle, a girl of about twelve raised her hand. Juliette pointed to her in recognition. "Miss Juliette, why did Mrs. Mearle do such bad things to you, especially with a knife?"

"Giselle that is a good question that should be asked directly to Mrs. Mearle. I can only guess at the answer."

Mother Superior said, "It could be several things: insecurity, jealousy, or envy. Even if we have the knowledge of exactly what motivated her, she had free will to choose to do good or evil. She chose evil. The more we repeat certain actions, the more it becomes a habit. Repeated often enough, a person becomes enslaved by that habit, imprisoned by it. If that person wants to free himself from that prison, then with much prayer, and personal determination will he or she be able to do it."

Many students and nuns asked questions until bedtime.

Juliette announced, "Well everyone, I am very tired, and it is bedtime. Let us retire for the evening, alright?"

All were compliant with her request. Each gave Juliette a hug and a kiss good night. Soon all were in their beds and fast asleep. Juliette was the last to go to sleep in the comfort of her cozy cell.

Earlier, the same day, as it neared four o'clock in the afternoon, Captain Tobias, formerly under the command of Lieutenant Colonel Frank Winslow, sat at his desk and pondered his duties at Union Occupational Headquarters in New Orleans. He had been there less than a month.

He noticed during his stay thus far, that the citizens of New Orleans were an easy-going group of people. He thought, maybe they are such a mellow group due to so many turn overs of governance, first the French, then the Spanish, then French again, briefly, and now the Yankees. Whatever the reason his duties were not demanding.

Captain Tobias' office was an abandoned mercantile building. Abandoned because all goods were blockaded from entry into the port of New Orleans, so surmised Tobias. No goods, no sellers, no buyers, all were absent.

New Orleans had been under Union occupation since April 24, 1862, when a bold yet elderly Union naval officer, David Glasgow Farragut, along with Captain David Dixon Porter, through pure audacity, passed through the black smoke of cannon hellfire from two Rebel forts. Camouflaged by the black smoke screen, their ships received only moderate damage. Thus, the Yankees established an early foothold in New Orleans, a highly strategic location.

Faintly Tobias heard the jingle of the bell attached to the front door. A young man stepped inside. The young man had duffed his hat, held it in front of his chest with both hands, and cleared his throat. "Good afternoon, Sir. I am Pete Larue and would like to join the Yankees so I could help to end slavery and this rebellion."

Mildly surprised, Tobias said, "Well, Pete Larue, I am Captain Tobias. It is good to make your acquaintance. So, what kind of soldier do you want to be?"

"Well, I have my own horse. Can I be a horse soldier?"

"If you have a horse, you can certainly be a horse soldier."

"Great! By the way, I have an important letter for Lieutenant Colonel Frank Winslow."

"You do! Well, well! I know him personally. What is the letter about? Military business? Personal business?"

Pete said, "It is a personal letter from Juliette Bellechasse telling of her safe return to the Ursuline Convent in New Orleans. I heard her story how she met Lt. Col. Winslow. Basically, it's also telling she still cares for the Colonel."

Captain Tobias laughed. "Finally, Cupid's arrow has struck Frank's heart! Well, young Pete, I know where to send you as soon as Vicksburg is defeated, and the river completely opens. I will send you and your horse to Vicksburg.

CHAPTER 19

Since the defeat of Vicksburg, Winslow was made full colonel, Major Lester was made lieutenant colonel, Captain Bell was made major, and Private Ezra Peabody was made corporal. Emboldened by his advancement in rank, Lieutenant Colonel Lester pushed for more spit and polish among the soldiers. Since Colonel Winslow still outranked Lester, he squelched his plans for a fancy dress parade at every turn. Of course, that didn't stop Lt. Col. Lester to spit and polish himself to the highest degree possible. From a distance, with heavy gold braid epaulets, impeccably shined boots, and a dust-free uniform, he could easily have been mistaken for a general.

It was late in the morning toward the end of July as Lester entered the ballroom in his newly acquired uniform. Groups of officers had gathered in the ballroom sharing a cup of coffee and talking amongst themselves. Lester began to swagger about the room in his perfect attire in an attempt to garner favorable attention.

Winslow was seated at his desk with legs sprawled wide apart. He clapped slowly and loudly as Lester walked by him for the third time. "I do see you Lester. That's enough! The parade is over!"

Lester stopped in front of Winslow. Winslow was wearing dusty boots with spurs, and sleeves rolled up past his elbows. "Speaking of parades, I think it would be an excellent time, since the recent defeat of Vicksburg, to have a parade celebrating the victory."

Winslow said, "We already celebrated. I couldn't find you that night which was Independence Day. The men watched as I executed some pyrotechnics with black powder and a sack of corn. The lighted fuse to the jug of powder blew the corn everywhere from a slave cabin chimney. All the men whooped and hollered with delight. Then all of us received a portion of whiskey. You missed out on an opportunity to know the men better. It strengthens the bonds of trust which plays out on the battlefield."

Lester's face flushed into an angry red. "Winslow, you are missing out on the power to command esteem and the prestige of a dress parade!"

Winslow said, "If my men respond to my commands in the heat of battle, that is prestige enough for me." The groups of officers had been mildly amused by Lester's comment, and now were studying him to see if he would step beyond his rank. They all grinned expectantly.

Lester reined in his anger and left the building as he mumbled to himself, "My wife will be disappointed. She had prolonged her visit in expectation of a grand parade." He fumed with anger as he walked back to his horse and quickly galloped away.

After Lester departed, Winslow's focus returned to present concerns of the moment. 'I need a scouting expedition to find more food and supplies.' He thought. 'All the poultry that family and friends had brought had been consumed. I am disappointed that just like army pay for the soldiers is long overdue, so are the river steamers with food and supplies.' The responsibility of feeding not only his men, but many other outfits weighed heavily on his mind. He sighed long and deep. To add to the situation, many family members lingered with their soldiers and would be part of the demand for food.

He ordered that Sergeant Dillon and Major Bell appear before him in scouting garb. He chose these men because they had not received any company via the riverboat steamer, so they were free to scout.

Both men presented themselves to Winslow dressed in suits of butternut hue. To achieve that color the uniforms had been died with boiled walnut hull liquid. In an earlier raid, the scouts had found a bag of walnuts in one of the Secessionists cabins. The walnuts had two benefits; the nuts were food, and the hulls provided dye for uniforms for the scouts.

Winslow said to Ezra, "Gather all those who are on guard duty for the next two days into the ballroom. Do it quietly." Ezra nodded and left on his errand.

Colonel Winslow, from prior experience, had made certain that men on daily guard duty, and those to be on duty until the scouts returned, knew the counter signs of the scouts and had also been personally introduced to them.

"Since all you guards are here in full daylight, I want you to observe the current scouts who will be going on a scouting mission. Meet Sergeant Dillon. Please note that the Sergeant has a mole on the left side of his forehead near the end of his left eyebrow. Major Bell's distinguishing characteristic is a raised scar on the right side of his neck. Before you shoot anyone, I want you to bring every butternut to me, is that understood?"

"Yes, Colonel!" Responded all sixty soldiers in unison.

"If anyone shoots at you, you may return the favor." Winslow said with both hands resting on his hips.

He added, "I assure you that Bell and Dillon will not shoot at you."

Winslow ordered, "Guard detail report to your stations. Bell and Dillon, report to me in two days. Dismissed!"

The day had melted away till late afternoon. Winslow had dressed in full uniform, and hopped on his horse, to meet some returning furloughed officers at the Vicksburg landing. It felt good for him to get away from the confines of the plantation. The ballroom was empty upon his return. All windows were open as the gentle sound of rain plopped on the leaves and flowers surrounding the big house. Winslow stood and stared out the window and studied the scene. The setting sun peaked from a cloud and infused the other clouds with a pink glow that seemed to enhance the brilliant colors of the roses and made the leaves a verdant green. Even the aroma of the roses was more pronounced.

He went to the mahogany desk. He was in uniform. His sword clanked against the wooden armrest of the chair. Winslow unfastened his sword and let it clank to the floor. He sat in his chair and propped his spurred boots on the desk. He was all set to enjoy the sound of rain and the scent of the roses and thoughts of Juliette. It was humid so he unbuttoned his shirt to mid-chest.

Ezra and Lester entered the ballroom together. They paused at Winslow's desk. Lester sneered at Ezra, then said, "May I have a private word with you, Colonel Winslow?"

"Certainly Lester." Winslow smiled.

Winslow turned to address Ezra. "What's up Corporal?"

"I need something to do. I'm at loose ends."

"Well, go help the mess cook set up for supper."

"Ezra grinned. "Yes Sir!" He left for the mess hall.

Lester and Winslow were alone in the ballroom.

Lester appeared smug. "Winslow, on the last raid at the Mearle Plantation, as we were seizing bedding for the injured men, we filled up a lot of wagons. We still needed more wagons to hall all the bedding we found in the attic. There were no more wagons to be found, but there were a couple of gold gilt coaches which we used to get the last of the bedding removed to the field hospitals as well as the main hospitals."

"Yep. It was a good haul and helped many of the injured and gave comfort to the dying."

"Well, Winslow, since we now have a couple of these gilt coaches without purpose, I was wondering if I could have one for my own personal use."

"Now that you brought it up, I'll get you up to speed on that idea. That coach business has been stopped by orders from the top brass to put an end to that tomfoolery. General Vale told me if he caught any pompous ass in his command riding around in a coach, he would demote him and send him back east."

Winslow continued, "I know it's hard, Lester, to let this golden opportunity go by, to lord it over your fellow man. But, by heck, this military dictatorship is temporary. While I have a certain authority by rank, that of Colonel, I will exercise that authority aligned with truth and justice in dealing with malefactors and the enemy, and surprisingly, helping fledgling families get a decent start."

Slowly, Winslow got to his feet and walked over to the open window, his spurs jingled as he moved. The muggy weather caused the slightest effort to bring forth beads of sweat.

"When we had visitors via the steamboats after the defeat of Vicksburg, I was able to do good with the stroke of a pen. It was the case of Susan Walker. She was pregnant and her original marriage license had been destroyed. It was within my power to predate the certificate of marriage for Susan and her husband, Private Sims. Reverend Blake and Mrs. Blake were witnesses.

Winslow smiled. "It started a trend. Many of the young couples wanted to get hitched. The Reverend Blake took over writing the marriage licenses; then married them all under a tree. It was a beautiful sight to see all these newlyweds and imagine the wonderful families they would become. That is how authority should be exercised."

Lester was stony silent. He glared at Winslow as his face flushed red.

"I can tell you what you could do with the coach as long as it is stationary and not attached to a horse. You and your wife could spoon away there as long as you wanted!" Winslow winked at Lester.

"Bah! That is pointless! A coach is to be on the move!"

"Unfortunately, you'll be demoted if I see you riding around in the coach. As a fellow officer and friend, I will keep you from the temptation. We will make a bonfire of the two coaches real soon!"

That's the stupidest idea I've ever heard yet!" Lester said angrily and made his way to the front door.

"I'm trying to be kind and keep you at your present rank, Lt. Col. Lester!" Winslow shouted as Lester exited.

Winslow couldn't help himself, he shook his head and chuckled saying, "Lordy, Lordy, if his head was any bigger, he wouldn't make it through the door!"

CHAPTER 20

After two discouraging encounters with Colonel Winslow on the same day; the first one in the morning when Winslow told him there would be no dress parade, and the next, that same evening when Lester asked permission to use the gilt coach for his personal use, Winslow responded with a resounding rejection, replete with the threat of demotion.

Lester seethed with anger as he rode his horse back to the deluxe carriage house on the edge of the plantation property where his wife was waiting. It was a deluxe carriage house because it had a two-room apartment above the carriage house itself. The apartment was well appointed with thick carpeting and mahogany furniture.

He tethered his horse and walked up the outside stairs and entered the apartment.

"Hello, Tom." Florence greeted her husband. She was similar in appearance to her husband; thin, with birdlike features which included a prominent nose and a receding chin. Her modest suitcase had been placed at the entrance.

"Tom, I am all packed since you told me earlier today that there would be no dress parade. I do need to get home. The children have been with my sister a long time. I know it's a burden for her."

Lieutenant Colonel, still fuming from the last encounter with Winslow, said through his teeth, "Florence, do not worry! I will take you to Vicksburg in the gilt coach so that we can have a pleasant trip. I will book you into the hotel near the landing so that you will be at the ready for boarding the north bound steamer first thing in the morning!"

"I'm ready if you are!" Florence smiled excitedly.

It was a half-moon that illuminated the road to Vicksburg. They arrived in the wee hours of the morning. Lt Col. Lester helped his wife from the coach and grabbed her suitcase. Unnoticed by the couple were two men loitering in the shadows near the entrance of the hotel. There was another man observing the scene across the street also in the shadow of a building.

The Lesters entered the lobby and walked to the front desk. Lt. Col. Lester hit the bell and a man appeared from the back room.

Lester said authoritatively, "I need a room for the night."

The man said, "Lucky you! You get the last of the rooms. Every room is occupied! Most occupants here will be passengers on the north bound steamer to Moline."

Lester didn't volunteer any information. He signed the guest ledger, paid the man, and received the keys to the room. Once in the room, he turned to his wife. "Well, Florence, I guess this is goodbye for a while. Tell the children, Francis, Melvin and Sylvia, that I love them and hope to see them when I can get back to Pittsburgh. Keep this door locked at all times for your safety."

He gave his wife a brief hug and added, "I love you Florence.'

She returned the hug and said, "Love you too, Tom." He left.

Lester walked through the lobby of the hotel, out the entrance, and to the waiting coach. The two men who had been loitering near the entrance were no longer there. Lurking in the darker shadows of the side of the building they were now mounted on horses, expectantly waiting.

Quickly, Lester got in the coach and shook the reins putting the horses into motion for the trip back to camp and his private quarters.

One of the two men said to the other, "It's our lucky day! That's Lt. Col. Winslow! We are on mission! Let's make Gen'l Bouldergreve proud!" They followed the coach at a distance.

Later that morning, the same day found Winslow at loose ends waiting for Bell and Dillon's return. Those men had been gone less than a day. He was at his familiar desk in the ballroom tilted on the back two legs of his chair, feet crossed on top of his desk, hands entwined at the nape of his neck, with bent elbows framing his head.

A soldier walked in the front entrance and approached him. Winslow recognized him as one of General Vale's couriers.

The young soldier stopped at Winslow's desk. "Colonel Winslow, I have a message for you. Port Hudson, Louisiana, has surrendered about a week ago. Now the Mississippi River is free and clear at all points." The soldier added, "It is free for travel all the way to New Orleans!"

"Thank you, soldier, you are free to go.'

The soldier grinned, "Yes Sir!" and disappeared.

Winslow tilted forward so all legs of the chair were flat to the ground. Then he stood up and walked out to the veranda. He filled his pipe, lit it, and sat down in a rose wood chair as he pondered the good news, the Mississippi River is free and clear for travel all the way to New Orleans…

That brought to mind all that Micah had said of Juliette and many unanswered questions that information had created. Most startling was that she had been kidnapped! Why? By whom? For what purpose?

What did Pansy Mearle or her husband have to do with her? Why did she want to be at a convent in New Orleans of all places? Was she a nun?

Then his mind tackled the puzzle from a different angle. He remembered the thrill of the first time he saw the beautiful Juliette. When he had spied her from the front window of the Mearle Plantation. Juliette had been in the mode of extremely exaggerated flirtation with an old man. That would not be what a nun would do. Frank recalled what she had said to him after he had bared his soul to her. He treasured every word in symphony with every gesture. She had said to him, "I was on the edge of despair before you arrived. God has sent you to me, to give me renewed hope." And after he had given her his pocket watch, she had pulled a satin lacing from her sleeve and threaded it through the loop on top of the watch, tied the ends together and hung the watch around her neck. Then she said, "This moment in time shall be suspended at 9:41 Post Meridian until we are together again. He lingered over her powerful vow.

Faith was fluid. It seemingly ebbed away as he remembered what Micah related about what happened next. After he had warned Pansy that he would come back to tar and feather her if she harmed Juliette, he then, regretfully, had to leave and take the bedding to the wounded soldiers. Something made Pansy snap to make her come at Juliette with a knife. So, Juliette ran down the bluff, jumped on a raft not knowing how to swim, and pushed off into the Mississippi current. She floated south in the dark of night with siege guns blazing as she passed by Vicksburg, if she made it that far. From Micah's conversation with Lolly, justice was served for both the Mearles. Pansy broke an ankle and a wrist and is with her husband under a doctor's care at Richmond, watching Mr. Mearle like a hawk.

So many factors would have had to be excellent, even if she made it past Vicksburg; good weather, being unobserved, and a safe landing somewhere. His head buzzed with a swirl of new questions. Every essence of his being longed to go down river and personally verify that Juliette was safe and sound.

He took Juliette's handkerchief from his vest and smelled the faint lavender scent. Closing his eyes tightly, he relived their passionate kisses.

He mumbled a prayer. "Dear Lord, I can hardly think straight!Please help me!"

With eyes closed, he leaned forward and cradled his head in his left-hand seeking relief from the heavy weight of his thoughts.

Suddenly, he heard a familiar voice. "Colonel Winslow, it's me Captain Tobias and a new enlistee, Private Pete Larue."

Winslow opened his eyes and beheld the smiling face of his old friend and the young private. He got up from the chair and left his pipe on the armrest.

"Tobias! You are a sight for sore eyes!" He vigorously shook the Captain's hand and affectionately gripped Tobias' opposing shoulder with his left hand. He then shook Pvt. Larue's hand.

"I have missed our conversations and your good advice. I know you have had to move around a lot, wherever you were needed. Where are you now? Please sit down, the both of you."

Both men sat down. Winslow ladled some water from a nearby bucket into some tin cups kept nearby for the soldiers. He gave each visitor a cup of water.

"Okay Tobias, I am all ears. Get me up to speed on yourself."

"Presently, I am stationed at Occupation Headquarters in New Orleans. I am the second in charge. Pete, here, is a native of Louisiana and joined up recently. He wants to help end slavery."

"My word, Tobias! I was just puzzling on someone dear to me that was headed on a raft down the Mississippi river, couldn't swim, and went by blazing siege guns. I don't know if she even got that far." Winslow frowned.

"That's why we are here Frank. So, Pete, without further ado, hand Colonel Winslow the letter from Miss Juliette Bellechasse."

Winslow's face froze for a second.

"Yes Sir!" Pete handed the letter to Winslow.

Winslow eagerly took the letter and held it to his chest smiling.

Tobias said, "I know this is from your sweetheart. You'll need some private time to mull the letter over. Pete and me will sniff out where the mess hall is and check out the plantation. When you need us, just holler."

"Thanks!" Winslow ripped open the letter as the two men left. He began to read:

My Dearest Frank,

June 20th, 1863

First of all, I have made it safely to the Ursuline Convent in New Orleans. On the day I met you, I had already planned to leave the Mearle Plantation. Things were getting hard to deal with as Pansy was acting in a hateful manner. In desperation I had gone to the Mississippi shore and prayed for a means of escape. Suddenly, a type of raft floated up to me. God had quickly answered my prayer! I had also prayed to meet a good man. That prayer was answered later the same day!

So, with firm resolve that came from the first answered prayer, I went back up the bluff to the cabin where the musicians were staying. I told the musicians, who also had been away from home for a long time, that I was done entertaining. They were tired and wanted to return to their homes also. Privately, I said my goodbyes and told them not to share our plans. I went back to the plantation, packed a bag, and put it on my raft.

I did this while Pansy was out for the day informing neighbors and friends that they were invited for entertainment at her home that evening. I was to sing and entertain. That was the evening my life turned around when I encountered you, dear Frank. You were the good man I had prayed for! God had answered two huge prayers the same day!

I was in a happy bubble until an enraged Pansy came after me with a knife. I was prepared to escape and I did! I ran to my raft and caught the river current. I made it all the way past the battle guns at Vicksburg to an orphanage in Louisiana run by freed slaves. I was a bit weak after my journey but after more than two weeks of rest and regular meals, I was ready to go to the convent. Pete, the oldest orphan, wanted to join the Yankees and free the slaves. So, Pete was my escort to the Ursuline Convent in New Orleans. I am now safe at the convent with the nuns and students. They had prayed a rosary for me since I had been kidnapped. So, through their persistent daily prayers and God's mercy, I am home. Now we all are praying for your safety. My heart aches until I see your sweet face again.

Love and prayers always,
Juliette

Frank read and reread the letter. Satisfied he put it in his vest next to her handkerchief. Suddenly there was a loud ruckus coming from behind the plantation house. The veranda was a one level, open porch that bordered the entire perimeter of the house. Following the noise, Winslow jogged on the veranda to the back of the house. The back end overlooked the cook house, slave cabins and two barns. At a distance, on the corner of the property, still within eyeshot, was the carriage house. A group of men were shouting excitedly around a gilt coach attached to two horses.

Winslow spotted them, beckoned them with a wave, and shouted, "Come here men!"

Quickly the men approached Winslow. Some men from guard duty accompanied the coach while Major Bell and Sergeant Dillon led the horses.

Winslow yelled, "What in tarnation is this hubbub about?"

All the men shouted, "Lester has been killed!"

Winslow, shocked, regained his composure. "Major Bell please tell us your observations concerning Lt. Col. Lester's death."

"Sergeant Dillon and I were returning from scouting and approached our encampment from the back of the plantation when we noticed a gilt coach hidden in the thick brush and trees near the carriage house. The movement of the horses caught our attention. We went over to investigate and found Lt. Col. Lester with a rope around his neck, dead. We yelled for those soldiers nearby who were on guard duty to help us get the horses and coach out of the weeds."

"Apparently, he had been sitting in the gilt coach hitched to the horses returning from somewhere. I determined this because there was dried salt on the horses' backs from a lather. Those horses had been driven hard. I'm thinking there was more than one culprit for the murder of Lt. Col. Lester. Lester would have struggled and that would have excited the horses. So, someone took the reins to calm the horses while the other person or persons strangled Lester."

"You can witness the deceased for yourself, Sir." Major Bell finished.

Bell led the coach parallel to the veranda for Winslow's inspection. Winslow noticed that Lt. Col Lester was in full regalia, gold epaulets, his new uniform, and the emblem of his rank, the shining silver leaves. Lester lay face up with eyes open, glassy and bloodshot. His tongue was out, and his face was blue. The rope still coiled around his neck resembled a vengeful serpent.

Winslow yelled, "Corporal Malland, go get Dr. Fox and Reverend Blake!"

Dr. Fox and Reverend Blake were soon on the scene.

Winslow asked, "Dr. Fox can you determine approximately when Lester died?"

Dr. Fox climbed into the coach and began to examine the body. He unbuttoned the jacket and vest to gage the body temperature. "He could have died forty-five minutes to two hours ago."

A piece of paper fell out of Lester's open coat as Dr. Fox was speaking. Fox picked it up, read it and handed it to Winslow.

Winslow read it. Then read it to his men. "The note says: JUSTICE HAS BEEN SERVED TO WINSLOW. BOULDERGREVE'S MEN." It's a case of mistaken identity. I was the intended victim."

A man on horseback rode up to the group.

"Hello Colonel Winslow. I see that you have found Lt. Col. Lester's body. I was tracking the two devils who killed Lester. I was at a distance so as not to be detected by them. That worked against me. It gave these two evil doers time to do their dirty work. They had already eluded me when I came upon Lester and saw him dead. I had followed those same men starting at the hotel by the landing on the Mississippi River. Lester had pulled up in the gilt coach and brought his wife to check in for the scheduled steamer that would leave in the morning. Halfway back to your encampment Lester must have gotten wind that he was being followed by those men. He then rode his horses hard. He must have thought they had quit chase, so he slowed up. I slowed up and thought the same. Instead, those wily devils knew a shortcut. They arrived in advance of Lester, hid themselves until he was close to home and conditions were perfect, then murdered him in cold blood." Topero stated.

"They were long gone when I approached Lester and found him dead. I didn't alert you since that would take precious time away from tracking those men. It seemed to be well planned. Those men were wearing Yankee uniforms. They were headed back to the river. Before I could get there, they had boarded a steamer going south. It was too late for me to catch them. I do know those two men were Bouldergreve's soldiers from an earlier scouting trip south of here." Topero finished.

Winslow said, "Topero, you did the right thing to continue to track those two culprits instead of losing time, you found out where they were headed."

Topero was more at ease and added, "I do know that one of the stops that steamer makes is Natchez. I have recently done some scouting there and found that Bouldergreve and his men have an encampment there, for how long, that I don't know."

Winslow said, "As we now know from the note left on Lester's body, that he was a victim of mistaken identity. He was dressed up and polished to the hilt and easily mistaken for me of similar or higher rank. Of course, your commanding officer, Colonel Melton, informed me after the Vicksburg defeat, that Bouldergreve was out to get me, and you Topero, was going to keep an eye on the situation."

"I have done so, Colonel Winslow, to the best of my ability."

"You have done well, Corporal Topero."

Winslow focused on the group of soldiers and addressed Major Bell and Sergeant Dillon. "I know that this is an extra burden, but from what Topero said, Mrs. Lester is headed to Moline to catch a train. That steamer will make stops at Memphis and St. Louis in that order. Bell and Dillon, you are my most seasoned scouts."

Winslow continued, "You men have a wealth of knowledge about the terrain in these parts, especially along the Mississippi River. I want you both to get in your Union uniforms and head north to try to intercept Mrs. Lester at one of those stops. Please bring her back here to accompany her husband's body back to Pittsburgh. Once you have intercepted Mrs. Lester, take the next southbound steamer to Vicksburg. At least both you men and your horses can rest up on the way back."

Drawn to the commotion, Ezra, Captain Tobias, Private Larue, and many soldiers began gathering around Colonel Winslow and the initial group that had discovered the body.

Winslow commanded, "Dr. Fox, please prepare the body of the deceased for a long journey. You other soldiers who have carpentry skills build a presentable coffin and pour melted lead in the bottom. It helps slow decomposition."

Winslow continued, "Reverend Blake, Ezra, Topero, Captain Tobias, Lieutenant Deerfield, and Pvt. Larue, come with me to my office in the ballroom."

The men Winslow requested followed him into the ballroom. He motioned them to be seated in chairs near his desk. He began to pace. Turbulent emotions played across his face. He paced for a full five minutes. Finally, he said, "Here is my dilemma; it is of the utmost importance to treat a deceased officer with military protocol. To top that off, this was an assassination."

Winslow paused a moment. "It then becomes imperative that due homage is given Lieutenant Colonel Lester. Once Dillon and Bell intercept Mrs. Lester and bring her back here, I would like a three-man detail to accompany Mrs. Lester and the body of Lieutenant Colonel Lester home to Pittsburgh for a military funeral."

"I am gravely conflicted because my heart isn't in this sorrowful event. My heart is in New Orleans." Winslow sighed deeply. "Captain Tobias, I sense that you have been by-passed in advancement of rank by oversight. I will correct that presently. Captain Tobias your rank will be Lieutenant Colonel."

Tobias smiled with Winslow's pronouncement.

"My conflicted heart feels I should be one of the detail of men to accompany Lt. Col. Lester and his widow back east to Pittsburgh. Lt. Col Tobias, I am going to send you, Reverend Blake, and Corporal Ezra Peabody to accompany the Lesters back to Pittsburgh. I am confident that Corporal Peabody will play his most heartfelt taps at the burial. Tobias will be a worthy second for me. I cannot think clearly beyond that until I see Juliette."

Winslow sighed again. "While I still have a grip, Ezra, go to my quarters and bring back the silver leaves so I can make Captain Tobias an official Lieutenant Colonel."

"Yes, Sir!" Ezra exclaimed and went to retrieve the silver leaves. Soon they were in Winslow's hands.

"Stand up Captain Tobias."

Tobias stood up and Winslow walked over to him.

Winslow solemnly pronounced, "As God is my witness, and all these men present, you, Captain Tobias have duly and deservedly advanced to the present rank of Lieutenant Colonel."

Winslow pinned on the silver leaves on each side of his collar.

"We all salute Lieutenant Colonel Tobias!"

All present solemnly saluted him.

"It is now official!" Winslow said. "The clouds have begun to clear from my brain. Lieutenant Deerfield, you'll oversee our encampment until Major Bell returns."

"Corporal Topero, could you get permission from Colonel Melton to accompany me to New Orleans with a stop at Natchez?"

Topero answered, "I will ask Colonel Melton permission to go with you. His camp isn't but a half days ride from here! I should be back in the morning."

"Okay, proceed, Topero."

"Of course, Private Pete Larue, you'll be my guide to the convent in New Orleans."

"All you men are free to go and prepare for your travels and other duties."

"Yes Sir!" They said in unison and left.

With purpose, Winslow went to his desk and wrote up several papers. He took them to his quarters and packed them in his satchel along with other items for his journey.

CHAPTER 21

Winslow slept very little throughout the night. He had many decisions to make. His mind was a beehive of activity. Topero arrived early in the morning with permission to accompany Winslow on the trip to New Orleans with a side trip to Natchez.

Before Topero arrived, Winslow had roused Pvt. Laker, Pvt. Wells, and Corporal Malland to inform them that they would also be going to New Orleans with a side trip to Natchez. Winslow then went to the munitions shed and collected many bags of black powder, tin cups, fuses, and containers of kerosene.

Thus, Winslow had selected a competent detail of men with outstanding talents: Topero, an excellent scout, Wells and Laker, two highly experienced arsonists, and Larue, Malland, and himself, excellent horsemen. Winslow had the extra talent of being a smooth-talking lawyer.

Soon they were all packed to go. They left at seven in the morning and dogtrotted to the Vicksburg landing. By eleven they had boarded the southbound steamer. They remained on the main deck with their horses.

Winslow signaled them into a huddle to explain his plans. "Men, Corporal Topero most likely knows the whereabouts of Bouldergreve's camp. When we stop at Natchez, he will guide us there. Of course, we will keep a low profile. Now my plan is to parole the Rebs to myself which means they will have agreed to no longer fight and will hide from the conscription officers or be shot on sight if caught by us Yanks. This will include Bouldergreve. Even though two of his men came to kill me and failed because of mistaken identity, I will not enter into a never-ending grudge match. The less Reb soldiers fighting means the sooner the war ends."

"Anyway, let's all take a snooze and rest up for our mission at Natchez." The men smiled in agreement and each found a place near the horses.

It was late afternoon when they landed in Natchez. As soon as the men were on the outskirts, they stopped in a wooded area and dismounted.

Winslow asked, "Topero, do you have any good ideas on how to approach Bouldergreve's camp?"

"I have sort of a plan depending on if Bouldergreve's camp didn't move. If it's still in the same location near the Homochitto River, it will be less difficult to surprise them. When I scouted there a month ago, they were building a make-shift bridge to cross the river. The river is to the southern rear of the camp. If that bridge is completed, there will be four possible escape routes."

"Well, if they have completed the bridge, it needs to be blown up to cut off that point of escape. What are the three other points of escape like, north, east and west?" Winslow asked.

Pvt. Wells smiled. "Colonel, as soon as you asked Laker and me to join you on this trip, we knew to prepare for some fireworks."

"You both are as sharp as tacks." Winslow smiled. He then redirected his attention to Topero.

"Continue Topero."

"The north, east, and west areas are thickly forested which gradually slopes down to the river. The camp's center is where most all the tents and soldiers are located, on the clearing near the bridge. There are usually 15-20 soldiers guarding the perimeter of the camp at a radius of three hundred yards from the camp's center. The last time I counted the population, there were two hundred soldiers. So, the north, east, and west points would be more difficult escape routes because of thick forest and higher elevation. It would be sniper heaven for us Yanks."

Wells said, "Colonel Winslow, I am pretty good at sneaking past people, especially at dark. Once we know the camp is in the same location, and the bridge is near completion or completed, I can head to their camp a mile in advance, going eastward along the river shore. I would bring my horse with supplies to the starting point at the river shoreline, then advance eastward on foot. That way I wouldn't be so tuckered out when I haul the black powder on the last leg toward the bridge and camp. My horse would be far enough distant not to get spooked when I fire the bridge."

"That's a good plan, Wells. We better get closer to camp to see if it's still occupied."

They all mounted their horses. Winslow said, "Topero, lead the way."

"Yes Sir." Said Topero. The men followed him at a steady clip as the moonlight lit the way. After an hour's travel, Topero signaled the men to dismount.

"I detect the faint smell of campfire smoke. We are close to camp. I will climb a tree for a better view to reassess the layout, census, and status of the bridge. Also, Bouldergreve's whereabouts."

"Proceed." Winslow said to Topero.

Topero put a leather strap tethered to a spyglass around his neck, then walked to a very tall tree near the group. He scrambled to the top with ease. With the spyglass he surveyed the area for about ten minutes. He climbed down and reported back to the men.

"They are still in the same location and the bridge has been completed. There are about 140 men in camp. There were fifteen men on guard duty that I could see. I couldn't spot Bouldergreve so I will slip in closer to camp to find out his whereabouts."

"Okay, Topero." Winslow said.

Topero returned. "Bouldergreve is in camp! I only had to eavesdrop. Two Reb soldiers were on the perimeter of camp talking and mentioned that Bouldergreve was on a long call to nature. Then I spotted him coming out of the trees."

"Alright men, we now know that we may proceed with my basic plan which I will fine tune now. So, here's how we will go forward. Pvt. Wells, you go ahead with your aforementioned plan. I will give you ample time to get to your objective and prepare the bridge for firing. As a signal that you are ready, loudly whistle like a whip-poor-will when ready. Wells, after you signal us, you then will wait for us to signal you. That signal will be many little noisy bursts of ignited gun powder coming from the outside radius of the three other points around camp. As soon as you hear two to three of these small blasts, fire the bridge."

Winslow continued, "Topero, Larue, Malland and I will assist Laker in setting up the small explosions. Wells that reminds me to give you a couple of fuses. Do you need matches?"

Wells answered, "I pack my own matches. I also made my own surefire fuses." His eyes twinkled mischievously."

"Pvt. Wells, you are an exacting devotee of arson!"

They all laughed.

Wells mounted his horse and departed for the river shore.

The remaining five men rode closer to the enemy camp yet were still far enough distant to set up the explosions without detection.

Laker said, "Firstly, I need a couple of you men to crimp the edges of the tin cups inward, so they won't spill any black powder. Next, I need someone to poke two holes near the rims on opposite sides of the cups. After that, I need all these cups threaded with one long, thin rope, that I soaked in kerosene, through those holes in the cups. Next, we fill those cups with black powder. After that's done, we will string those cups up at least twelve feet above the ground in the tree branches in a rounded shape toward the camp. Be mindful that the rope, now a fuse, is thirty feet long, but once it is woven into those cups, will lose some length to about twenty feet."

When all was completed, Winslow said to Malland, "Take all our horses away from the impending blast. When the blasts are over, quickly bring the horses back. As soon as you return, we'll all ride into camp a whooping and hollering."

Topero said, "I will make sure Bouldergreve has remained in camp." He climbed up a nearby tree and nodded affirmatively to Winslow.

Winslow said, "Everything is set, Malland take the horses from the blasts!"

Malland had all the horse's reins and left in a dogtrot.

They all heard the whip-poor-will signal from Pvt. Wells.

Winslow looked at the rest of the men. "Ready men?" They nodded.

"Let's roll!"

Laker had positioned himself twelve feet up in the tree with the tin cup explosives. He struck a match and lit the fuse. He jumped to the ground into a soft pile of pine needles and ran for cover. Soon all the blasts were heard in a faultless sequence. By the fifth blast they heard a loud boom from the bridge. Malland returned with the horses. They hastily mounted the horses and rode into camp, whooping and hollering all the way to the center of camp.

"Drop your guns! Hands up! You are surrounded!" Winslow shouted.

Stunned, the Rebs dropped their weapons. Malland, Topero, Larue, and Laker collected the guns and stacked them in the center of camp. Laker poured black powder in a circular border around the weapons. Malland and Topero frisked anyone with suspicious bulges. The four men herded the Rebs into a circle. They each positioned themselves at four opposing points on the outside perimeter and aimed their weapons at the circle of Rebs.

Bouldergreve was standing in the circle of men. Winslow spotted Bouldergreve, dismounted, and walked over to him. Bouldergreve's mouth dropped in astonishment.

Winslow motioned to Bouldergreve to come forward out of the circle of men to stand beside him. Winslow announced in a loud voice, "I have not come to harm you Rebs, but to parole you. What I mean by parole is after you sign the paperwork, you men then make yourselves scarce and no longer fight in this war. If the conscription officer comes, you hide in the woods. If you return to fight, and if us Yankees see you, you'll be shot on sight. Of course, if you don't sign, we will take you prisoner."

There was a look of suppressed relief on the Reb faces.

Winslow studied Bouldergreve. "That parole includes you, General."

Winslow was prepared. He took the parole papers from his vest and a pot of ink with quill pen from his pocket. He placed them on a nearby tree stump. The soldiers lined up at the tree stump and in orderly fashion, they all signed the papers.

In line, one Reb said to the other, "I never wanted to fight for the greedy slave owners or the politicians who started this dang war, in the first place!"

Winslow said to Bouldergreve. "So, is it free man or prisoner for you?'

Bouldergreve had a lot going on in his head. First, he thought that Winslow had been killed by his men, now a noisy surprise attack. He also thought that Winslow would kill him outright as retribution for the death of the mistaken officer. Now a decision to sign parole papers or be a prisoner once again. The thought of being a prisoner twice was enough to prod Bouldergreve to cut into line and sign the parole papers.

"A wise decision, Bouldergreve, now perhaps there won't be as many widows and orphans, especially not for your wife or daughters. Many families might remain intact."

Floundering in conflicted thinking, Bouldergreve asked, "Why didn't you kill me Winslow?"

"Because no good can come from that. It makes for angry widows and orphans and breaks up the basic building block of civilization. You will have to live with yourself having had killed an officer by a dastardly and cowardly action. For your information, the man mistaken for me, Lt. Col. Thomas Lester was murdered by strangulation. When the fog clears from your mind, and this war is won by us, you need to make amends to his widow and three fatherless children. Otherwise, you will never have inner peace. You have free will, you choose. I can only advise."

When all had finished, Winslow collected the parole papers from the stump. He mounted his horse and his men followed suit. He glanced at where the bridge had been. It had disappeared. He had only expected a rift in the bridge near the shore. Wells must have found some weak points of construction. It would have needed multiple blasts strategically placed to totally demolish the bridge. Winslow had heard only one. Winslow thought to himself, 'I wonder how Wells did it?'

As a momentary barrier to the Rebs confiscated guns, Laker threw a lighted match onto the thick black powder that encircled the guns. While the ignited powder flared into a wall of flames, Winslow's men galloped up the slope and disappeared into the night, hollering and shooting their guns.

After riding hard for an hour, they stopped to see if any Rebs had followed them. Topero climbed a tree, checked their rear, and climbed down again. Topero said to Colonel Winslow. "Nary a Reb has followed us. I should add, that while I was in camp, I untethered all the horses I could see, while you were collecting signatures. I figured Larue, Malland, and Laker were just fine guarding the agreeable group of Rebs. When we left shooting and hollering, those Reb horses spooked and scattered even further from camp. I think that will help our lead time and distance us even farther from them."

Winslow smiled. "Good work Topero!"

Winslow's detail of men made it back to the safe environs of Natchez by daybreak where they found the Occupation Headquarters. Similar to the train raid, the surprise attack on Bouldergreve's camp was not to be mentioned since it was not ordered by Winslow's commanding officer, General Vale. They enjoyed a hearty meal of fried catfish and corn fritters, then boarded the next southbound steamer to New Orleans.

Once on the southbound steamer, there was a mellow mood of accomplishment as they leaned over the ship railing and watched the lush green shore pass by their view.

Winslow spoke quietly since all five men were near him. "Wells, how did you fire the bridge? I heard only one blast, yet you would have needed several blasts to demolish the bridge."

Wells smiled. "Well Sir, there were simultaneous blasts. I decided, once I studied the bridge, that I needed to rig the bridge for blasts at three of its weakest points. I was well prepared for all contingencies. Anyway, I had put all the black powder, fuses, and matches in an oilcloth bag sealed with a tightly knotted rope. So, when I tied my horse to a tree, I found a driftwood log nearby and a makeshift paddle. Rather than crawl on my belly to camp, where I could more easily be spotted. I pushed off on the log and paddled to the middle of the bridge."

Pvt. Wells continued. "Long story short, I found three weak areas in the supports of the bridge. I make special fuses that are different lengths but can burn in the same span of time. I used three fuses that had wide ranges in lengths. I lit the three fuses which starting point was the same. When each fuse met the black powder at the three different locations, it all ignited at the same moment. That's why you heard only one explosion. Of course, I was running like hell on the bridge toward camp. Everyone was distracted by the whooping and hollering so no one saw me. I ran back to my horse and rode up the slope where the small blasts had happened and waited for you. I checked the bridge from that viewpoint, and it was gone, floating piece meal down river."

"I should call you the Architect of Destruction.

Wells smiled.

That was fast thinking and good judgement, Wells. Also, Laker, Malland, Larue, and Topero you each played an important part to the success of this mission.

All the men said, "Thanks."

For the rest of the trip to New Orleans, the men slept soundly.

As Winslow dozed off, he cradled his saddle blanket under his head and thought to himself, 'The end of war equals Juliette.'

CHAPTER 22

Juliette was in the convent garden in late morning gathering okra, peppers, and tomatoes for the shrimp gumbo which she had planned to make for the mid-day meal. As she tended to the mundane task of picking produce from the garden, she recalled how social pressures as a guest, entertainer, or even a hostage, had forbade her performing any kitchen or household tasks. That thought made her heart burst with gratitude to be back at the convent to be free to do what she loved, cooking, cleaning, and teaching. She still liked to entertain but at a much slower and fun pace. What made it even better was the fact that she was with people who loved her, and she loved them, especially Mme. Bernard and Mother Superior Margaret Joseph. After she had been kidnapped from the convent, she had felt so alone, stressed, and homesick.

Now she treasured her deep sense of belonging, security, and being loved and appreciated. Here it was, the beginning of September, more than two months from her harrowing return, yet her memories of her journey to America and all the disturbing events up to now, only deepened her gratitude for her convent home.

Her mind boggled as she reviewed the crush of the stressful memories. She willed herself to return to the present moment. Back in the kitchen she placed her burgeoning basket of produce on the table. She rinsed the vegetables and put them on the cutting board. A sweet birdsong cued her from the window to hum a happy tune as she chopped the peppers.

Mme. Bernard entered the kitchen. "I heard you humming, 'Oh Susannah!', and it lured me to the kitchen, so I might as well help you since I am here."

"Oh, thank you, Mme. Bernard!"

Mother Superior entered the kitchen. She looked rattled. "Juliette! There is a man with a bouquet of flowers who just knocked at the front door! I spied him from the window. It was just like the last time when you were kidnapped! Déjà vu! Only this time the man is wearing a Yankee uniform!"

Juliette's hands flew to her mouth. They dropped as she realized aloud, "It might be Colonel Frank Winslow! Mme. Bernard, Mother, let's all go to greet him, just in case!"

The three ladies went to the front door. Mme. Bernard opened it. "Hello sir." Mme. Bernard said to the tall, broad shouldered man dressed in a clean pressed uniform with polished boots.

Winslow's eyes instantly locked onto Juliette's eyes. He doffed his hat and said, "I am beyond pleased to lay eyes upon you again, Miss Juliette!" Winslow continued, "What brought me to your door today is your timely, compassionate letter which defused my worry about your welfare, and that you were safe and sound. It is thanks to Private Pete Larue that I received that letter. Also, thanks to him, I received excellent directions to this convent." He handed the bouquet to Juliette.

For a moment, Juliette marveled at Winslow's eloquent greeting and the shock of his appearance at her door. Regaining her composure, she said, "I am so happy to see you again!"

Juliette added, "Colonel Winslow, all the nuns and students pray a daily rosary for your safety and welfare. It is an answered prayer that you are here, with us now, in good health. Praise the Lord!"

She became practical. "Thanks for the flowers. Oh, do come in and have a cup of coffee while I prepare lunch for the residents. Then if you have time, we could have lunch together. I do hope you like shrimp gumbo."

"Why Miss Juliette, any meal I'd share with you is pure ambrosia." Frank displayed a dimpled smile.

Juliette blushed and smiled. "I would like to introduce you to Mme. Bernard and Mother Superior Margaret Joseph."

"Enchanted, my ladies." Winslow said as he shook each woman's hand.

The two ladies warmed to him. Mme. Bernard ventured as she took the flowers from Juliette, "Why Juliette and Colonel Winslow, I think Mother and I can complete the gumbo ourselves. Both of you can enjoy a cup of coffee in our walled garden and really get to know each other. Our garden offers more privacy for a good conversation."

"Thank you, Mme. Bernard and Mother."

Moments later, Juliette and Frank were sitting together on a bench in the garden sipping coffee. Frank noted how reserved Juliette had become. Her quiet behavior was a huge contrast to the first time he had laid eyes on her. In that first encounter, she was bold and wildly flirtatious with an old man in the audience at the Mearle Plantation. His first impression was seared into his memory as it came to his mind and senses, he reviewed it again. Juliette had been dressed in a cream colored satin dress that dramatically contrasted with her cascading black hair which reflected a cobalt sheen in the candlelight with the fragrance of lavender and her beautiful face and sweet singing, it had held a mesmerizing invitation for Frank.

Now Juliette's head was covered by a white cotton kerchief with only a glimpse of her hair in a braided loop that slightly peaked out at the nape of her neck. She was dressed in a simple yellow gingham dress with a white apron and her sleeves were rolled up above her elbows.

Frank broke the silence by pulling the gift of her handkerchief from his vest pocket. "Juliette, we seem to be meeting as strangers now. If it wasn't for this lavender scented handkerchief and all the beautiful words we shared, and that mutual passionate kiss, it seems almost a dream. Do you still have the watch I gave you?"

"Why yes, Colonel." She pulled the watch into view from her bodice. "I also feel as if it was a dream. We only have shared one wonderful night."

"Somehow God put us together. You said I was an answer to prayer. So, let's not throw the gift of 'us' away. Let us really get to know each other. And please call me Frank."

"Well Juliette," Frank began. "I could ask you a thousand questions to understand who you are. Rather, now I simply ask you to tell me everything about you that you think is noteworthy starting with your background in France, why you came to this country, and how you ended up in this convent."

"Formidable! That's a long story! I will be very frank, Frank." She smiled at her joke. "It's because I have learned a lesson in truth the hard way."

"I am all ears!" Frank smiled.

Juliette looked pensive as she collected her thoughts. Absently she sipped her coffee. "I was born April 20th, 1840, in Paris, France. My ancestry is this, as far back as I know, from my birth mother's letter, my great grandmother was pure Abyssinian from near the Sudan region of Africa. Her name was Kitha. She was sold by her own parents as tribute to another tribe. They in turn, sold her to Arab traders. She worked in an Arab home as a slave. Eventually, a French man bought her. I don't know his name. Kitha gave birth from that relationship, to my grandmother, Daheera. Later, another French man became interested in my grandmother and Daheera gave birth to my mother, in 1822. This man, my grandfather, must have been working for the French settlers in Algeria. So, when the French embassy opened in 1830, Daheera, her daughter, who was my natural mother, Teresa, must have moved there when she was eight. Anyway, my mother matured and became the concubine of a minor French official while at the embassy. The minor official retired and took my mother to Marseilles, France. Soon after my mother was brought to France, that minor official died."

"My mother had little money. She left for Paris where she did the only thing she knew, prostitute her body."

"Are you shocked and disgusted? Would you like to leave?" Juliette asked as she intensely scrutinized Frank's placid face.

"Not in the least." Frank said calmly. Please continue."

"Eventually, my mother was in an exclusive relationship and became pregnant with me. This changed her outlook. She cut off the relationship with her birth father without telling him that she was pregnant. Anyway, I think she was deeply sorry that her child would be a bastard." Juliette checked Frank's expression which was as placid as before.

"In desperation, she went to a nearby Catholic church to confess to a priest. He immediately placed her with the local nuns who taught her basic sewing skills. So, after I was born, she had a respectable job and tried to care for me. Sadly, it was short lived. She died of consumption when I was two years old."

"Fortunately, the same priest was present when my mother died in our dingy apartment. He told me this later. He gave my mother the last rites, then immediately brought me to my adoptive parents, Michelle and Antoine Bellechasse, who welcomed me into their home."

"The Bellechasse's were a childless couple who ran a restaurant. When I was six years old, they enrolled me in the local parish school. With such loving parents who encouraged me, I became a quick learner. After completing my daily lessons, I would have time on my hands and became bored. There was a kind nun there who was bilingual. She was from England, fluent in both French and English. She took pity on me. After I completed my daily lessons, she would teach me English. I discovered that I had a passion to learn English. I would make my parents and others practice with me; Mme. Bernard included. I was a nuisance on that subject." Juliette laughed.

"By and by, my parents were getting older and I could tell they needed help running the restaurant, so at age fourteen I quit school to help them fulltime. I thoroughly enjoyed being useful to my parents. Our restaurant was called Le Mouton Noir."

Juliette became introspective. "In English it translates to The Black Sheep. Funny thing, that's a fitting name for me."

She cleared her throat. "I embraced all the duties that a restaurant offers, cooking cleaning, and shopping for supplies. I also enjoyed singing, dancing, and entertaining the patrons."

"Six years passed. Anyway, I was becoming disillusioned with Napoleon the third. He increased the tax burden on small shops, restaurants, and other businesses. Also, all the prospective men of my age who frequented our restaurant seemed to be perpetual students or absinthe drinkers without goals. Not much improved were the shopkeepers and government employees. They had arrived at their goals which were dead end jobs. Anyway, that's how it appeared to me."

"It was so blah! I was so downhearted that I shared this with Monsieur Joseph Gastineau, a longtime patron of our restaurant, who worked for the government. To cheer me up from my dark mood, he told me he had received an invitation to a general reception at the Hotel de Ville. It was a gathering for government employees and other interesting people.

He had no desire to attend. In a kind gesture, he gave the invitation to me so that I could attend. This invitation put me in a euphoric mood full of high hopes and expectations. This joyful anticipation lasted for several weeks until the day of the reception. I used the time to have a dress altered to my size and styled to the current fashion. On the day of the reception, I was prepared. I arrived at the Hotel de Ville in my newly altered and updated dress and nicely coiffed hairstyle. Soon I met a handsome man, James Lambert, from the state of Mississippi. He described an ideal life of parties and picnics. I was so naïve!"

"Just as he had intentionally failed to tell me that slavery was deeply entrenched in the southern culture, I too failed to tell him that I was born to a former slave, a bastard, an orphan, and then adopted. At some level I recognized that he was an arrogant man. I stuffed that into my sub-conscience." She added, "Not once did he say he loved me."

"I thought I had fallen in love with him. Rather, in retrospect, I had fallen in love with the idea that I loved him."

"I wanted him to love me, so I omitted telling him my history. At this point you can see both of us were duplicitous in our actions. I would never have left France if I had known!" Juliette's eyes widened. "Since he kidnapped me later in our relationship, maybe if he had known that I was the illegitimate daughter of a former slave, I would have been kidnapped much earlier, in France!"

"He seemed to be smitten with the physical Juliette, not the real Juliette. He did meet with my parents and asked them permission to marry me. He gave me a lot of money and directions on which ship I was to take to America. I had to tie up loose ends with my parent's situation. I had only two months to resolve many things. As I mentioned, I was concerned about my parent's wellbeing since they were older, to continue to run the restaurant In Paris, with or without help, would be too burdensome. Anyway, Msr. Joseph Gastineau came to the rescue.

"One evening at the restaurant, I shared my dilemma about my parents with Msr. Gastineau. He also had a dilemma. His was that he had inherited his father's inn but had no one to help him run it. Otherwise, he would have to sell it and remain in the city when he would have preferred a life in the country. I suggested that my parents could help him in the slower pace of a pastoral setting. So, we asked my parents if they would like to move to the country to help him. They were delighted with the idea. Our two dilemmas were solved!"

"Also, Msr. Gastineau, being knowledgeable in the matter of Confederate paper money, exchanged it for gold coin. I divided it between my parents and myself."

"Next, I needed a chaperone. Who better than Mme. Simone Bernard? She was a widow without children. She had been my piano teacher, my seamstress, my mentor, and a good friend. Really, my only female friend. I had been so busy helping with the restaurant, there was no leisure time for me to develop friendships. Msr. Gastineau was a friend also, but not as intimate as my friendship with Mme. Bernard."

"So, two months later in October of 1861, Mme. Bernard and I boarded a schooner called the Tambeau in the port town of Le Havre destined for America! On the first day aboard the Tambeau, I learned some shocking news from the only two other passengers on the ship. I learned that the Tambeau was a blockade runner, a renegade ship carrying contraband that would try to elude Yankee ships, whose sole purpose was to capture or destroy blockade runners. One of these passengers asked, why would my fiancé put me in harm's way? It was a good question."

"Next, at suppertime, I learned that slavery was an institution in the South! It was another horrible revelation! I was so revolted by this, I excused myself from the table, letting them assume I was seasick. Naivety popped up its simple head again!"

"Once in my cabin, I tried to calm down by distracting myself by opening a package that my mother had wrapped for me before her death. My parish priest had kept it for me and gave it to me before I embarked on the voyage to America."

"I opened the carefully wrapped package, a posthumous gift from my birth mother. It contained a native dress from the Sudan area of Africa, a daguerreotype of my lovely mother, and a letter written by her. I read the letter which contained a description of my ancestry. I also learned that my longtime patron from Le Mouton Noire, and good friend, Monsieur Joseph Gastineau, was my birth father! By then I was reeling from all that I had learned that day: slavery was an institution in the South, the Tambeau was a Yankee target, and Joseph Gastineau was my birth father! My father was Joseph Gastineau, a man I knew and loved! I was so exhausted, I passed out in my clothing and slept 16 hours until late afternoon of the next day."

Frank looked at her with a tender gaze. "That was a lot! You fell asleep so that you could digest all of that!"

Juliette felt more at ease. Frank was a good and empathetic listener.

"Yes, indeed, it was a lot! I had to hide my ignorance of slavery from everyone except Mme. Bernard. Mme. Bernard had a rich background from the theater and life itself. She gave me such good advice on how to disguise my facial expressions and moods. With the aid of props, as she called them, I was mostly successful. It was items like parasols, hats, even make-up to impress or dissuade. Along with these various props, I would employ broad, open questions to draw an individual out into a long answer which gave clues to that person's truer character. What a brilliant woman!"

At that moment, Mme. Bernard appeared. Both Juliette and Frank laughed.

"Mme. Bernard, are your ears burning? I was just talking about you to Frank!"

"All good, I hope." Mme. Bernard smiled.

"Of course!" Juliette exclaimed.

"Back on track to my purpose, I had let you two prattle away so that all the students and nuns have eaten, and now are back at their lessons. It's your turn to eat. Come into the kitchen where all is ready for you, a decent table, warm food, and privacy."

Soon Juliette and Frank were seated at the kitchen table with steaming bowls of gumbo and Frank's bouquet decorated the table. Juliette said a prayer of thanks.

"Frank, I haven't revealed that much about myself, ever! It amazes me that I still have more to tell! Of course, right now let's enjoy the gumbo."

They began to eat. It was delicious. Both Juliette and Frank would look up and smile at each other in between bites. It was a comfortable silence. After lunch, they went back into the garden. Each had a steaming cup of coffee and sat again on the bench.

"Juliette, please take all the time that you need to tell your story. I have furloughed myself for a couple of weeks. Right now, you are on a roll and your memory is primed. So please continue if you'd like."

"Alright, Frank. As I mentioned, Mme. Bernard is a wise mentor. She emphasized being a good listener and drawing people out with broad questions such as you have asked of me. Your beginning question was, tell me anything you consider noteworthy of yourself." She smiled.

"After all the revelations I had received in one day, my mind sorted through it to make it more manageable, more mundane. It was hard. I relied heavily on props like fans and hats to hide my face. I also practiced keeping a blank expression on my face.

"Back to the voyage. Eventually the Yankees spotted our ship and got a direct shot on the Tambeau at the beginning of a rainstorm. The cannon ball went straight through the main sail, missing the mast. It was quickly repaired by one of the crew. The Yankees were in a steamer, fighting tall waves. They could only follow at a slow, measured pace. We had the advantage of the increased wind velocity which was propelling us further from them. Also, the high waves would intermittently hide our schooner from the Yankees view. We escaped our attackers. We ended up in Cuba for proper repairs and supplies."

"After a brief respite of a few days on solid ground with fresh food, we headed to Mobile Bay. The Captain of the ship was very careful. He timed our arrival for the dark of night. The two male passenger's goods were unloaded directly into a private warehouse. As quickly as the ship was unloaded, it disappeared into the night heading back to France."

"I should mention the two other male passenger's names; Clayton Armstrong was the man who had informed me of the institution of slavery in the South and to whose home was close to Mobile; Beamus Paxton was the quieter, gentler man whose home was near New Orleans."

Juliette yawned, covering her mouth with her hand. "I'm sorry, Frank. I feel so drained from telling you my long story. If it's agreeable with you, may I continue tomorrow morning?"

Frank said, "Why sure. I will look forward to seeing your lovely face again. What's the best time we can resume your fascinating narrative?"

"How about 9 o'clock in the morning? By that time breakfast is over and the students are at lessons. Tonight, I will prepare the midday meal for tomorrow so that Mme. Bernard and Mother will have an easier time of cooking it for the students."

Juliette walked with Frank to the front gate. Frank took her right hand and kissed it as he bowed. Their eyes locked and he said, "Dear Juliette, I will count the hours until I see you again."

Juliette blushed. "You are so sweet, Frank! Thanks for being such a good listener. I look forward to your visit tomorrow." Now mounted on his horse, Ben, Frank tipped his hat to Juliette and rode away.

The next morning Frank arrived at the convent promptly at nine in the morning. He knocked on the door. No sooner had he knocked; the door opened.

"Good morning, Frank. You are right on time! Please come in!" Welcomed Juliette.

Frank smiled and kissed her hand again like yesterday. "Good morning, Juliette."

Frank followed her into the kitchen where a fresh pot of coffee was simmering. Juliette poured two cups of coffee and offered him one. They went into the garden and settled on the bench now covered in a thick knit blanket which added more comfort.

"Thanks for the extra padding."

"It will make my long story less painful for our derrieres and I will be more focused on my story." She laughed.

They both paused upon hearing the happy trill of a birdsong. Frank had wrestled with his thoughts as he rode Ben to the convent. Restraint should be the main objective of the day, but he just wanted to kiss and hug her a thousand times, propose marriage, and set a wedding date. Patience won out as he remembered her story from yesterday and the rapid barrage of life changing events she had experienced up to that point. He mused, she was so brutally honest about being born to a former slave and that she was a bastard, it was almost as if she wanted to get rid of him. These thoughts reinforced his resolve of being patient. He became philosophical in thinking, at least I can enjoy her presence for another day.

They both studied each other in contented silence.

"Sorry, Frank, for staring at you." Juliette said. "It's just that you have such a likeable face."

"Why Juliette," Frank smiled, "you flatter me!"

Juliette smiled widely. "It's the truth!"

She took a deep breath. "Alright, I am now ready to continue my story. As I recall from yesterday, we had landed at Mobile Bay, unloaded goods in a warehouse, and the Tambeau departed for France. We then spent the night in a hotel. Clayton Armstrong, one of the two passengers, was the one who lived nearby. He sent a messenger from the restaurant where we had breakfast, to his plantation, to send some slaves to bring us back to his residence."

"Mme. Bernard and I had assumed our stay at the Armstrong's would be brief. We then would leave with Beamus Paxton for New Orleans. We were proved wrong in short order."

"Before our eyes Clayton Armstrong seemed to make a dramatic change. He talked abusively to the slaves, he openly lusted after me, even in front of his wife. Mme. Bernard and I were dumfounded then crestfallen."

"Once in our chambers at Armstrong's plantation, Mme. Bernard and I discussed our predicament. Theatrically, as if in a play, Mme. posed the choice that I could either portray a meek woman or a bold woman in our current situation. She advised me to be a bold woman and display my entertainment talents. So, I followed her advice. For the evening meal we dressed in our finest evening gowns and made a grand entrance. It caught the Armstrong's and Beamus by surprise by the slack-jawed expressions on their faces. After our meal was finished, we went into the parlor where there was a piano. We placed ourselves by the piano where Mm. Bernard played the keys, and I sang many songs. Our small audience seemed to enjoy it immensely."

"The only problem was that performance further enflamed Clayton Armstrong rather than subduing him. We excused ourselves to Beamus and the Armstrong's and retreated to our chambers. That night, we locked our door and put a chair up against it. My trepidation increased. Alone with Beamus at breakfast the next morning, I asked him how soon could we leave? I hoped we could leave that very morning. It was not to be! After we had retired to our chambers after our performance, Clayton had asked Beamus to deliver goods to the Confederate soldiers in Montgomery. It would take two weeks for the round trip. We couldn't leave until Beamus returned. We were trapped!

"Beamus left quickly for Montgomery. Both Mme. Bernard and I were crushed by this cruel turn of events. Supposedly, to get us back into a better mood, Clayton sent us Phinney, the cook slave, to give each of us a backrub. We were surprised to learn from her that she had purposely cut off her left pinky finger when a child. She explained that she thought by amputating her finger she was damaged goods, and no one would buy her. At eleven years old she felt that way, she would be returned to her parents. It didn't happen. She was sold for a lesser price to Clayton Armstrong. Nine years later she had become a cook at the main house. Soon after, she was forced to have sex with Clayton Armstrong which seemed agreeable to Mrs. Armstrong. Phinney was now several months pregnant with Armstrong's child. It was a deepening nightmare! The three of us prayed for Divine intervention."

"The same day, that afternoon, Clayton insisted we take a tour of the plantation. There was no choice, so we complied. On the tour we observed that the field hands were dressed in rags that barely covered them, exposing old scars and fresh wounds. The overseer was introduced to us as Sean O'Leary. That man smeared fresh blood from the tail of his whip onto his trousers and sadistically gloated over whipping a defenseless slave girl. Both Armstrong and O'Leary laughed in common glee about this abuse. It was too much!"

Frank asked, "Did this O'Leary have wide spaced teeth, and was short and muscular?"

Juliette said, "Why, yes!"

"O'Leary must have left the Armstrong Plantation and ended up at the Mearle Plantation."

Frank continued. "On the first raid, prior to your move there, us Yankees had come upon an awful scene. O'Leary had shackled the father of a little girl and whipped him to death. It was heinous! I will forever be haunted by his daughter's surreal keening cries over the loss of her father. I snapped and immediately commanded a soldier to shackle O'Leary and mete out the same punishment to him. O'Leary resisted my soldier's efforts. I heard a loud snap. O'Leary's upper right arm broke. The soldier pleaded with me that God's justice had been served. I knew that by the way O'Leary's arm broke, he would never wield a whip again. After the raid, we took him to camp and had Doc set his arm. He recuperated a spell then disappeared."

"Sorry I interrupted you, Juliette. I just wanted to tell you his whipping days are over. Please continue."

"That is a comfort that God's justice was served. So, getting back to the tour of Armstrong's plantation, it became unbearable to witness O'Leary and Armstrong's mutual enjoyment of the torture of a helpless slave. Mme. Bernard pretended to swoon which abruptly ended the tour. Thank goodness!"

"We were quickly brought back to the plantation. Mme. Bernard was carried by a slave to our chambers. We both felt so helpless and afraid, so we prayed. Mme. Bernard came up with the inspiration, or realization that we needed to go to mass. More than that, we needed to go to confession. The nearest Catholic Church was in Mobile.

"Somehow, all the doors opened for this to happen. Mrs. Armstrong offered us a carriage to town. Although Mr. Armstrong tried to stop our carriage, Mme. Bernard, who had been a woman of few words up to that time, surprised him with a forceful explanation that we were Catholics and were obliged to go to mass and that we would return on Monday. He was stunned and relented. We went to confession at St. Mary's Catholic Church in Mobile. Father Clancy was the priest and our confessor. We stayed for the weekend at the rectory with his aunt and three orphans. We explained in detail to the priest and aunt our situation. We dreaded our return."

"To comfort us, Fr. Clancy accompanied us on our return, all the while we prayed a rosary. Lo and behold, when we arrived, there seemed to be signs of answered prayer! First, the outside of the plantation was decorated with colorful bunting, secondly, Mrs. Armstrong had transformed from a plain dour woman into a smiling elegant and gracious woman, and thirdly, there were many guests, Terrell Bouldergreve, her brother, as well as the guest of honor, Jefferson Davis, and a large retinue of soldiers."

Frank didn't interrupt about his acquaintance with Bouldergreve

"Mrs. Armstrong was happy to see me because I was the entertainment for all these people, especially for the guest of honor, Jefferson Davis."

"I was feeling confident that there was safety with many guests around the plantation, so I told Fr. Clancy he needn't stay so he could return to his duties at St. Mary's."

"Mme. Bernard and I pulled out all the stops for our performance that evening. Frank, as we first met at the Mearle Plantation, I do pretend to flirt. That's part of the act. So, this particular night, I flirted with Jefferson Davis. I danced and sang almost every song I knew. At the end of my performance, the crowd roared with approval. Mr. Davis complimented Mme. Bernard and me. All were happy so we retired to our chambers exhausted and slept soundly."

"The next morning, I woke up before Mme. Bernard and went to the kitchen. I came upon Phinney who was upset because she was prohibited to leave the big house to go help Callie, the slave girl who had been brutally whipped by O'Leary. Phinney had food and healing poultices prepared for her. She wanted to know how to get them to her. I came up with the idea that I could hide these supplies on my person. Once in my chambers, I hid items in my hat, I tied some to the framework of my hoop skirt, and other places." Juliette blushed at realizing how intimate was this disclosure to a man she had met only one other time.

"I then strolled as nonchalantly to where I thought Callie would be. A little slave boy directed me to her cabin. I worked as quickly as I could, cleaning her infected wounds, applying poultices, and putting food and water near her. The little boy helped too."

"Anyway, on my return to the main house, out of nowhere, a drunken O'Leary assaulted me! He tore the front of my dress and would have continued the attack if it wasn't for a ferocious dog who also appeared out of nowhere and defended me. I was able to escape while the dog clamped onto O'Leary's pant leg and kept him there."

"I ran all the way to my bed chambers where Mme. Bernard was resting. Once she had heard what happened, she went into action! She ran out of the room and ran into Jefferson Davis and Mr. Armstrong. She demanded justice from Mr. Armstrong with Mr. Davis as a witness."

"The end results were O'Leary was fired and banished, Jefferson Davis, whose dog saved me, gifted me his dog, Mrs. Armstrong gave me, Phinney as my own personal maid, all wonderful blessings. The same morning Jefferson Davis left, Beamus Paxton returned! It was much earlier than expected. It was because some Confederate soldiers had met Beamus by chance and were headed to Montgomery. Since they had empty supply wagons, they transferred Beamus's load to their wagons. The officer in charge would send a courier with a receipt to the

Armstrongs. Mr. Armstrong was visibly angry as I surmise his evil plans had been thwarted at every instance."

"When a Confederate messenger showed up with a receipt that the supplies had been received by the correct officer, Mr. Armstrong began to insult and demean Beamus. Beamus excused himself and went to his chambers. I can only surmise that Beamus' early return had thwarted Clayton's plans again. So, seething with anger, he went into the library and shut the door. With Beamus back we packed our trunks during that night so we could leave in the morning with Beamus.

"Clayton must have continued to drink throughout the night in the library. The next morning Beamus, Mme. Bernard, and I sat down to breakfast in the dining room. Happily, we talked about our impending journey. Suddenly a drunken Clayton emerged from the library. Adamantly, he insisted that we could not leave and sat down at the table with us. Mrs. Armstrong must have overheard as she descended the stairs. She poured a tall glass of whiskey and placed it by her husband, then seated herself between me and him. Everyone but Clayton saw her wink as she said, they can all stay a while longer. Clayton saw the tall glass of whiskey and said, I'll drink to that, and downed the whole glass at once. Soon, he passed out."

"Mrs. Armstrong said, you are free to go, and walked us to our waiting wagons. She apologized for her husband's behavior and gave Beamus a beautiful brooch for compensation for goods seized from him by Clayton. Ever since the party, Mrs. Clayton had transformed into a much kinder person. She sent us off with a friendly wave."

"We made it safely to Beamus' plantation near New Orleans. There were two wagons. Chitlin, a slave, was driving one wagon and Beamus, the other. So, Mme. Bernard, Phinney, and I were passengers. Later we discovered that Callie had been a stowaway in my trunk with a reed for an air pipeline poked through the trunk to breathe air, thanks to Phinney's ingenuity. I want you to understand that I do not own these people. I was only too happy for them to escape the cruelty of Clayton. Fortunately, Beamus is a kind slave owner. All of us fit in at that plantation."

Juliette's thoughts turned introspective, "My goodness! Phinney must have had her baby a while ago! That baby must be a year and a half or more. It would be so fun to see them again."

"I digress. Anyway, after a while, both Mme. Bernard and I were tired of being house guests and living out of our suitcases, so we sought employment in New Orleans. We asked the priest in the New Orleans area, Fr. Gibbons, for work. He immediately suggested we visit this convent for employment. We were quickly hired by Mother Margaret Joseph.

"Of course, by witnessing how truly despicable the institution of slavery was, I soon wrote my fiancé, James Lambert, that I no longer wished to marry him. I sent the letter to his parent's address. I also mentioned in the letter that he could have the trunk of clothes and diamond necklace that he had purchased for me, if he wished to come and get them."

"Anyway, a short time later, I received a letter from him stating that he couldn't address my concerns in a letter and needed to talk. Not long after that, he showed up at the convent door with a bouquet of flowers as you did the other day. After a short argument that we should remain engaged, he pretended to agree with me about our breakup. He said he would take the trunk of clothes he had purchased for me as well as the necklace which was contained in the trunk but needed help in carrying it to his carriage."

"As I helped him carry the trunk to his carriage, there were two soldiers waiting for me. They gagged and bound me. I was being kidnapped! They brought my other trunk from the same closet, so all my clothing was loaded onto the carriage."

"As you might conclude, my abduction was well planned. James had two soldiers at the ready with ropes and gags. So, I was spirited away over several days of travel. There was no way for me to escape out in the wilderness with three men watching my every move. One of these men who had been part of the retinue of Jefferson Davis at the Armstrong Plantation, recognized me as the entertainer for the audience there. When James heard that I was an entertainer, he was surprised and jealous. He became angry and possessive that he hadn't known this about me. I said that I didn't know he was a slave owner either."

"Anyway, we finally arrived at the Fair View plantation. Upon arrival, I was so exhausted that I passed out. When I awoke, I found out I had been put to bed to recover. James was absent because he immediately had to report to his superiors. I met James' mother while recuperating. As soon as I was better, I found out that we both didn't want James' plan to marry me. So, we hatched a plan to divert James' attention to his former sweetheart, Ophelia."

"The basic plan was to train Ophelia as an entertainer which would take the focus off me and put it on Ophelia. The other part of the plan was that Mrs. Lambert was to invite her sister, Pansy Mearle and husband Jonathon Mearle to the entertainment and party. I was to leave with the Mearles and thus, there would be at least one hundred miles west of James, an inconvenient distance."

"Ophelia was easy to like and an apt pupil. She had hidden talent and quickly learned many songs and pantomimes by heart. The night of entertainment arrived. I was purposely in the background as a musician. With a little makeup I appeared pale and sickly. I acquired a cough for a nice touch and would cough into my handkerchief."

"Ophelia had made the handkerchief that I eventually gave you. With loving care, she had tatted the lace edging. Don't worry, I often wash it." Juliette smiled.

"Ophelia was the star of the show. The audience gave her a standing ovation. When James sought me out, he was shocked by my appearance and fearful of my cough. It worked! He now was truly focused on Ophelia."

"Anyway, I left the next morning with the Mearles. I was happy to be so near the Mississippi River, even though I couldn't swim, it comforted me knowing New Orleans was straight south by boat."

"Pansy was a jealous and unpleasant woman. She would do malicious mischief to me. It would increase in frequency if her politician husband came for a visit. My only escape from her was to go elsewhere and entertain the southern troops as often as possible."

"It was so heartbreaking to see the young boys dying before my eyes. I would try not to cry in front of them. Ophelia's handkerchief was well employed."

Frank pulled Juliette's handkerchief from his vest again, studying it with new eyes. "I have held this dearest souvenir of yours close to my heart. No wonder I cherish it so. It must hold a true part of your most pure heart since you poured so many compassionate tears into its cloth." Then he held it to his cheek and tenderly gazed at her.

Juliette's eyes filled with tears. "Oh Frank, I have kept your watch close to my heart because you gave me hope in my darkest hour." She pulled it out her bodice and the time was stopped at 9:41.

"Dear Juliette, I love you so! You mean all that there is in this life that has meaning for me."

Juliette hugged him. "Frank, I love you too, so very deeply. To know that such a good man exists cheers my heart and feeds my hopes!"

They paused in silence and studied each other in tender silence.

"You know the rest of the story from my letter. So, my story is finished."

"Juliette, your story is finished, but our story has only just begun." Frank said with a dimpled grin."

CHAPTER 23

It was now the third day of Frank's visits to see Juliette at the convent. He had listened intently as she filled him in on her life in Paris, her ancestry, birth mother, her adoption, the many revelations revealed to her aboard the Tambeau on her journey to America, her first love turned sour, kidnapping, escape, and return to the convent. As Frank approached the convent door, he thought, 'Juliette has run the gauntlet of mental jolts that could break a weaker person.'

He was musing on Juliette's remarkable endurance and mental strength as he knocked on the door of the convent.

Almost simultaneously the door was swept open by Juliette whose appearance had changed. Her facial expressions were more candid, fluid, and easier to read. Her eyes were dilated and full of affection. She was dressed in a beautiful periwinkle blue satin dress and wore pearl earrings, and her hair was not covered. It was skeined back into a bun. "Good morning, Frank."

Frank was momentarily astonished by her metamorphosis. Juliette noticed his hesitation and pulled him into the convent. Once inside, gave him a loving hug. Frank answered it with a stronger embrace and a passionate kiss.

She unlocked herself from his grip, gasping for her breath, she said, "Frank, we both need a strong cup of coffee! I want to hear your story."

Soon they were seated at the familiar bench in the convent garden. After sipping the cloud-emitting brew, he regained control of his emotions. "Here goes! I was born September 29, 1828, on a small farm outside of Covington, Indiana. My parents were Martha and Jack Winslow. I have a brother, Lemuel, who is eleven years older than me. I also have two younger sisters, Eliza and Sara. Mom had it tough. The reason that there was eleven years difference between Lemuel and me, was because Mom miscarried three little girls. She named them for the month each arrived: April, May, and June. Also, she had a full term, stillborn boy she named Jack, after my Dad."

"It always touched my heart how mom honored my dead brother and sisters with a small family funeral. The four of them were buried in a cemetery plot on the knoll of a hill near the edge of our land. When the season permitted, she would place bouquets of wildflowers on their graves."

"By age four I had a new sister, Eliza. My parents worked hard to support the family. Mom had more pluck than good health. When I was eight, she delivered my sister, Sara. Mom's health quickly deteriorated after Sara's birth. So, on the same bed where life had arrived in Sara, death also came two weeks later for my Mom. Mom was so brave on her death bed. She said her tender goodbyes to each of us. Her focus then turned to the welfare of Sara. She told us that the neighbor lady, Abigail Hartman had recently given birth to a little boy, and Sara needed a wet nurse. Mom soon died just minutes after this last request."

"Lemuel and I brought Sara to the Hartman's on the same night Mom died. Both Lemuel and I were broken and sad. Mrs. Hartman answered the door. Events took on their own momentum. Her new baby boy was asleep in a crib by the glowing fireplace. Somehow Sara's crying let down Mrs. Hartman's milk. The front of her dress became drenched and some dripped on the floor."

"Mrs. Hartman said she had ample milk and immediately took Sara and began to nurse. At first, Sara choked on the gushing milk from Mrs. Hartman's breast. Soon, Sara mastered the flow, her little face beaded as she hungrily took her fill. We were mesmerized by the whole procedure."

"I asked Mrs. Hartman, is that the milk of human kindness? I had heard it somewhere." Frank chuckled a little.

"Lemuel had a logical yet pat answer, telling me, yes, Frank, Mrs. Hartman is human, has milk, and is kind!" Both Juliette and Frank laughed.

Frank continued. "Many years later, I was reading Shakespeare's, Macbeth. I came upon the phrase, "milk of human kindness". It was in the context of those who lack it. I pondered that he might have witnessed a similar event of a breastfeeding mother nursing an orphan whose mother might have died or was abandoned. That might have inspired him to come up with that phrase."

"Frank your thoughts are deep and logical yet so touching." Juliette said.

"That was the beginning of the scattering of my family. It was not in a bad way; it was just one of those changes that come with life. Anyway, Sara was being raised by the Hartman's. The Hartman's were kind and always included us for Sunday dinners. Eliza yearned for her mother and soon transferred her affections to Mrs. Hartman. After Mrs. Hartman noticed Eliza's behavior, she asked Dad privately if Eliza could stay to help with the younger children since she was with child again and would appreciate the extra help. Dad gave permission. So, Eliza happily moved to the Hartman's. In the meantime, Lemuel had married a lady he had met in church. Dad asked Lemuel to take over the farm. Dad and I moved to a cabin he had built years earlier that was situated near the family cemetery plot where Mom and her other children were buried. Dad and I were Lemuel's farm hands."

"My Dad pined away for Mom. He had lost the will to live. Soon, Dad was dead and buried next to Mom. May they rest in peace." Frank was silent for a moment. "That was an example for me, of true love. I'll never forget."

"I felt I no longer belonged on the farm. My brother Lemuel and his wife had started a family by that time. I became wild and got into a lot of mischief. I got tired of frittering my time away, so at the age of fourteen, I decided to go out on my own, in search of a new life."

"My brother didn't stop me. With his approval, he gave me Jubal, my first horse, Mom's Bible, and stationary, to keep in touch."

"I headed west until I neared Quincy, Illinois. I met up with an older couple, the Smythes, good people. I worked as an extra hand on their farm. We weren't too far from the Mississippi River, about a half day's ride. I stayed with them for almost five years. During that time, I became acquainted with their daughter, Ruby, and her husband Herb. And their children. Herb was a preacher and a lawyer. A routine developed that at the end of the workweek the Smythes and I would go to church where Herb preached, then end up at Ruby and Herb's house for Sunday dinner. I sure enjoyed it. It was fun spinning yarns for the four children. I also did horse tricks and showed off my physical prowess chinning myself, climbing, etc."

"Herb took an interest in me. He encouraged me to read his law books. I would practice defending imaginary clients in debates with Herb. It honed my skills for later. Herb was an excellent tutor. After a while, I gained Herb's trust. One Sunday he took me to his barn where I had my first encounter with an escaped slave. It was earth moving to see the whip scars on this poor man's back, and the gut-wrenching story of his wife and children being sold like so much cord wood."

"Herb told me, 'this man needs to get to Canada because the slavers want to catch him and return him to the plantation. Frank, I need you to take him to the next point north on his journey. My absence would be noticed. No one would pay heed to your doings.' "

"Herb was right. I was just a farm hand. I took on the happy task of bringing that slave and many others closer to freedom, which I am proud to say."

"By the age of nineteen, I felt it was time to move on. Herb had given me the gift of lawyering. I didn't feel too bad leaving because Ruby and Herb's children had begun to help out on their grandparents, the Smythe's farm."

Eventually, I ended up in Topeka, Kansas. With the money I had saved from being a farm hand, I bought a storefront office and hung up a shingle above my door stating, Lawyer.

"My business boomed, not so much in the courtroom, but in helping settlers have their land surveyed per each land claim. I had hired Rodney Black, an experience surveyor whose previous job was with the Federal Government. The Federal Government was slow in providing section maps. So, by the time Rodney had completed surveying each land claim by each settler, those settlers felt confident enough to build their farms and plant crops. So, when we did get a section map, and most of it had been surveyed by Rodney, and it totally agreed with the government maps, our reputation grew as a reliable law office for surveying. I was so swamped by requests from settlers for that purpose, I hired a competent assistant. I will never regret hiring Widow Hardy."

"Widow Hardy did a terrific job by creating an easily accessible filing system for all documents. I have entrusted her with running the office until this war is done and won."

"I recently sent her a letter about the land that I myself, had claimed and asked her to have a house built for me. My heart had stirred to have a home of my own, to welcome me after the war. I look forward to a cozy home waiting for me." Frank's tender gaze lingered on Juliette's face.

He cleared his throat and continued. "As my business became profitable, Kansas earned the title of 'Bloody Kansas'. Outside factions were fighting over whether Kansas should be a slave state or a free state. Then Senator Stephen Douglas helped introduce the Kansas-Nebraska Act which passed through Congress. That bill allowed Free Soilers and Slavers to do as they please. Both factions rushed to these territories in large groups. That Act created chaos, murder and mayhem. I had little time for social life. So, when the whole country entered into the Civil War, I was personally ready to settle the question of slavery once and for all. Before the war, as a lawyer, I had become active defending Free Soilers in various capacities. So, by my high profile in this matter, I ended up a Lt. Col. by popular vote. I yearn for this war to end. My hope is fed by the fact the Yanks control the full length of the Mississippi River. That's my story."

"Juliette smiled. "That was fascinating. May I remark on some similarities that I noticed about us?"

"By all means! What are your thoughts?"

"I noticed that since both your parents had died, you were an orphan like me. Of course, you were an older orphan. Then a kindly couple took you in on your journey west."

"That's true, Juliette. The Smythes were like another set of parents, kind and honorable folk. If they are still alive, I would enjoy seeing them and Ruby, Herb, and their kids."

Juliette continued, "Since we were both adopted by good people, how would you feel about adopting an orphan or two? There are so many from this war."

Frank lit up. He immediately surmised that the question implied marriage. He was ready. He knelt at her feet and took her hands in his.

"Juliette, I love children. Adoption is a wonderful idea! Ideally, it takes a married man and woman to raise them. Of course, we would welcome our natural children too. Dear Juliette, will you marry me as soon as this war is won?"

"Oh Frank, I joyfully accept your proposal because I love you!"

"And I love you Juliette with the very essence of my being!"

They embraced and kissed what seemed the longest yet shortest time, for love is timeless. It lives on forever.

EPILOGUE

Frank and Juliette told Mme. Bernard of their plans for marriage once the war was finished.

Mme. Bernard was delighted by their plans. Mme. Bernard shared her decision that she would remain at the convent as a teacher. She felt completely fulfilled for her desire for children, by mentoring and educating the convent students. After the war she became a permanent fixture at the convent. She had found her niche.

Before the war ended, Juliette and Mme. Bernard made two visits to the Paxton's. On their first visit, they discovered that Mrs. Paxton's health had dramatically improved thanks to the tender care of Phinney. The improvement in Mrs. Paxton very much pleased her husband.

Chitlin and Phinney had jumped the broom. Her firstborn was a little girl she named Freedom. After that Chitlin and Phinney had a little boy, his name was George. Callie had regained her health and enjoyed helping Mumsy in the kitchen.

A few months later, Juliette and Mme. Bernard returned with clothes for the children, and a wedding gift for Chitlin and Phinney, a gold coin from the exchanged Confederate paper money for gold coins.

On that visit Beamus told Juliette that he was sure the north would win, and he would be happy and relieved that he could officially set his slaves free. He wouldn't leave them in the lurch. After the war, the freed slaves eventually lived in the improved housing he had. They worked for wages, put their children in school, and now could openly attend church.

Frank furloughed himself several times to visit Juliette. On these visits he studied to be Catholic. With the help of Father Gibbon, he entered the church in the spring of 1864. Frank and Juliette visited Murray and Glady's orphanage by the Mississippi River where Juliette had landed on the coffin lid raft. Frank met Louie. After the war, they brought Louie with them on their honeymoon to France. The newlyweds shared the joy of their marriage and newly adopted son, Louie, with Juliette's adoptive parents, Michelle and Antoine Bellechasse, and birth father, Joseph Gastineau. The country inn had prospered and was a popular vacation spot for many.

The happy couple and Louie, moved to Topeka, Kansas, and met Widow Hardy. From a letter Frank had sent her explaining a house plan, she had a beautiful, large yet cozy home built, ready and waiting. Widow Hardy became a contented Grandma Hardy to all the Winslow children.

They were an incredibly happy couple. Louie was Frank's hunting buddy. The Winslow's had ten natural children and many bonus children that needed food, shelter, and clothing, a kind word or a job with dignity from time to time. There was much celebrating at the Winslow home; Thanksgivings, Christmases, Easters, baptisms, first communions, confirmations, and many other events.

Juliette and Frank both lived a long and joy filled life. They left a trail of happiness in their example to others, in their children, grandchildren, great grandchildren, down to this present day.

Biography of George Richardson

George Richardson was born in 1920 on a farm in Indiana to William and Ruby Richardson. Growing up he worked hard on his fathers farm with his three younger brothers, and became close to his grandfather, Homer Richardson. Homer would share stories he'd witnessed as a drummer boy in the Western Campaign under General Ulysses S. Grant in the Civil War.

Homer's father, uncles, and grandfather all served during the Civil War. His father James Bailey Richardson served in the Cavalry, and his grandfather Alexander, and one of his uncles, Ed, were stationed at Fort Donelson.

George was inspired by his grandfather's stories and served in the U.S. Army during WWII. While he was stationed in North Africa, his company was in pursuit of German General Rommel, "The Desert Fox". After he was promoted to Staff Sergeant he was a crew chief over airplane maintenance and he had the distinction of working on President Roosevelt's plane at the Yalta Conference and saw Stalin, Churchill and Roosevelt all together.

After the war he married Eleanor Morgensen. Together they had three children. Eleanor knew how much George treasured Homer's stories, so she encouraged him to write a book about them. It would have fictional characters with true events using Homers' stories, and George did research on the Civil War to fill any gaps.

In 1976 George became ill with two acute types of Leukemia. On his deathbed he asked his daughter Ramona to rewrite it. He died at age 56.

Biography of Ramona L. Vallee

Ramona L. Richardson (Vallee) was born in December of 1948 in Cedar Falls, Iowa to George and Eleanor Richardson. She had a wonderful childhood in small town America. In her teens she enjoyed reading, writing, and learning French in school. Later discouraged by a college counselor who told her that writing was an overcrowded field, she decided to quit college. After working as a waitress, she saved enough money to go to beauty school and became a hairdresser. She met her husband Fred of 42 years, on a blind date. He was French Canadian which intrigued her. They had three children.

Long ago she made a promise to her dad on his deathbed to finish the Civil War novel he started. Many years later, she's finally able to fulfill her promise after writing Expression of Honor, and feels at peace now.